Microsoft® Office

Access 2003

VOLUME I

ROBERT T.
GRAUER
UNIVERSITY OF MIAMI

MARYANN
BARBER
UNIVERSITY OF MIAMI

PEARSON
Prentice
Hall

**Upper Saddle River,
New Jersey 07458**

To Marion —
my wife, my lover, and my best friend

Robert Grauer

To Frank —
I love you

To Holly —
for being my friend

Maryann Barber

The Library of Congress has catalogued the
comprehensive edition as follows:

Grauer, Robert T.
   Microsoft Office Access 2003 / Robert T. Grauer, Maryann Barber.
      p. cm. -- (The exploring Office series)
   Includes index.
   ISBN 0-13-143478-0
   1. Database management. 2. Microsoft Access.   I. Barber, Maryann M. II. Title. III. Series.
QA76.9.D3G71959 2004
005.75'65--dc22   2003064810

Executive Acquisitions Editor: Jodi McPherson
VP/ Publisher: Natalie E. Anderson
Associate Director of IT Product Development: Melonie Salvati
Senior Project Manager, Editorial: Eileen Clark
Project Manager: Melissa Edwards
Editorial Assistants: Jodi Bolognese and Jasmine Slowik
Media Project Manager: Cathleen Profitko
Marketing Manager: Emily Williams Knight
Marketing Assistant: Nicole Beaudry
Production Manager: Gail Steier de Acevedo
Project Manager, Production: Lynne Breitfeller
Production Editor: Greg Hubit
Associate Director, Manufacturing: Vincent Scelta
Manufacturing Buyer: Lynne Breitfeller
Design Manager: Maria Lange
Interior Design: Michael J. Fruhbeis
Cover Design: Michael J. Fruhbeis
Cover Printer: Phoenix Color
Composition and Project Management: The GTS Companies
Printer/ Binder: Banta Menasha

10 9 8 7 6 5 4 3 2 1
ISBN 0-13-143440-3 spiral
ISBN 0-13-145179-0 adhesive

Contents

three

Information from the Database: Reports and Queries   103

four

Proficiency: Relational Databases, Pivot Charts, and the Switchboard   161

Getting Started with Microsoft® Windows® XP

What does this logo mean?

It means this courseware has been approved by the Microsoft® Office Specialist Program to be among the finest available for learning **Microsoft Access 2003**. It also means that upon completion of this courseware, you may be prepared to take an exam for Microsoft Office Specialist qualification.

What is a Microsoft Office Specialist?

A Microsoft Office Specialist is an individual who has passed exams for certifying his or her skills in one or more of the Microsoft Office desktop applications such as Microsoft Word, Microsoft Excel, Microsoft PowerPoint, Microsoft Outlook, Microsoft Access, or Microsoft Project. The Microsoft Office Specialist Program typically offers certification exams at the "Specialist" and "Expert" skill levels.* The Microsoft Office Specialist Program is the only program approved by Microsoft for testing proficiency in Microsoft Office desktop applications and Microsoft Project. This testing program can be a valuable asset in any job search or career advancement.

More Information:

To learn more about becoming a Microsoft Office Specialist, visit www.microsoft.com/officespecialist

To learn about other Microsoft Office Specialist approved courseware from Pearson Education visit www.prenhall.com

---

*The availability of Microsoft Office Specialist certification exams varies by application, application version, and language. Visit www.microsoft.com/officespecialist for exam availability.

Preface

Continuing a tradition of excellence, Prentice Hall is proud to announce the new *Exploring Microsoft Office 2003* series by Robert T. Grauer and Maryann Barber. The hands-on approach and conceptual framework of this comprehensive series helps students master all aspects of the Microsoft Office 2003 software, while providing the background necessary to transfer and use these skills in their personal and professional lives.

The entire series has been revised to include the new features found in the Office 2003 Suite, which contains Word 2003, Excel 2003, Access 2003, PowerPoint 2003, Publisher 2003, FrontPage 2003, and Outlook 2003.

In addition, this edition includes fully revised end-of-chapter material that provides an extensive review of concepts and techniques discussed in the chapter. Each chapter now begins with an *introductory case study* to provide an effective overview of what the reader will be able to accomplish, with additional *mini cases* at the end of each chapter for practice and review. The conceptual content within each chapter has been modified as appropriate and numerous end-of-chapter exercises have been added.

The new *visual design* introduces the concept of *perfect pages*, whereby every step in every hands-on exercise, as well as every end-of-chapter exercise, begins at the top of its own page and has its own screen shot. This clean design allows for easy navigation throughout the text.

Continuing the success of the website provided for previous editions of this series, Exploring Office 2003 offers expanded resources that include online, interactive study guides, data file downloads, technology updates, additional case studies and exercises, and other helpful information. Start out at www.prenhall.com/grauer to explore these resources!

Organization of the Exploring Office 2003 Series

The new Exploring Microsoft Office 2003 series includes four combined Office 2003 texts from which to choose:

- **Volume I** is Microsoft Office Specialist certified in each of the core applications in the Office suite (Word, Excel, Access, and PowerPoint). Five additional modules (*Essential Computing Concepts, Getting Started with Windows XP, The Internet and the World Wide Web, Getting Started with Outlook,* and *Integrated Case Studies*) are also included.

- **Volume II** picks up where Volume I leaves off, covering the advanced topics for the individual applications. A *Getting Started with VBA* module has been added.

- The **Brief Microsoft Office 2003** edition provides less coverage of the core applications than Volume I (a total of 10 chapters as opposed to 18). It also includes the *Getting Started with Windows XP* and *Getting Started with Outlook* modules.

- **Getting Started with Office 2003** contains the first chapter from each application (Word, Excel, Access, and PowerPoint), plus three additional modules: *Getting Started with Windows XP, The Internet and the World Wide Web,* and *Essential Computing Concepts.*

Individual texts for Word 2003, Excel 2003, Access 2003, and PowerPoint 2003 provide complete coverage of the application and are Microsoft Office Specialist certified. For shorter courses, we have created brief versions of the Exploring texts that give students a four-chapter introduction to each application. Each of these volumes is Microsoft Office Specialist certified at the Specialist level.

This series has been approved by Microsoft to be used in preparation for Microsoft Office Specialist exams.

The Microsoft Office Specialist program is globally recognized as the standard for demonstrating desktop skills with the Microsoft Office suite of business productivity applications (Microsoft Word, Microsoft Excel, Microsoft PowerPoint, Microsoft Access, and Microsoft Outlook). With a Microsoft Office Specialist certification, thousands of people have demonstrated increased productivity and have proved their ability to utilize the advanced functionality of these Microsoft applications.

By encouraging individuals to develop advanced skills with Microsoft's leading business desktop software, the Microsoft Office Specialist program helps fill the demand for qualified, knowledgeable people in the modern workplace. At the same time, Microsoft Office Specialist helps satisfy an organization's need for a qualitative assessment of employee skills.

Instructor and Student Resources

The **Instructor's CD** that accompanies the Exploring Office series contains:

- Student data files
- Solutions to all exercises and problems
- PowerPoint lectures
- Instructor's manuals in Word format that enable the instructor to annotate portions of the instructor manuals for distribution to the class

■ Instructors may also use our ***test creation software***, TestGen and QuizMaster.

TestGen is a test generator program that lets you view and easily edit testbank questions, transfer them to tests, and print in a variety of formats suitable to your teaching situation. The program also offers many options for organizing and displaying testbanks and tests. A random number test generator enables you to create multiple versions of an exam.

QuizMaster, also included in this package, allows students to take tests created with TestGen on a local area network. The QuizMaster Utility built into TestGen lets instructors view student records and print a variety of reports. Building tests is easy with TestGen, and exams can be easily uploaded into WebCT, BlackBoard, and CourseCompass.

Prentice Hall's Companion Website at www.prenhall.com/grauer offers expanded IT resources and downloadable supplements. This site also includes an online study guide for students containing true/false and multiple choice questions and practice projects.

WebCT www.prenhall.com/webct

Gold level customer support available exclusively to adopters of Prentice Hall courses is provided free-of-charge upon adoption and provides you with priority assistance, training discounts, and dedicated technical support.

Blackboard www.prenhall.com/blackboard

Prentice Hall's abundant online content, combined with Blackboard's popular tools and interface, result in robust Web-based courses that are easy to implement, manage, and use—taking your courses to new heights in student interaction and learning.

CourseCompass www.coursecompass.com

CourseCompass is a dynamic, interactive online course management tool powered by Blackboard. This exciting product allows you to teach with marketing-leading Pearson Education content in an easy-to-use, customizable format.

Training and Assessment www2.phgenit.com/support

Prentice Hall offers Performance Based Training and Assessment in one product, Train&Assess IT. The Training component offers computer-based training that a student can use to preview, learn, and review Microsoft Office application skills. Web or CD-ROM delivered, Train IT offers interactive multimedia, computer-based training to augment classroom learning. Built-in prescriptive testing suggests a study path based not only on student test results but also on the specific textbook chosen for the course.

The Assessment component offers computer-based testing that shares the same user interface as Train IT and is used to evaluate a student's knowledge about specific topics in Word, Excel, Access, PowerPoint, Windows, Outlook, and the Internet. It does this in a task-oriented, performance-based environment to demonstrate proficiency as well as comprehension on the topics by the students. More extensive than the testing in Train IT, Assess IT offers more administrative features for the instructor and additional questions for the student.

Assess IT also allows professors to test students out of a course, place students in appropriate courses, and evaluate skill sets.

New! Each chapter now begins with an introductory case study to provide an effective overview of what students will accomplish by completing the chapter.

CHAPTER

1

Getting Started with Microsoft® Windows® XP

OBJECTIVES

After reading this chapter you will:

1. Describe the Windows desktop.
2. Use the Help and Support Center to obtain information.
3. Describe the My Computer and My Documents folders.
4. Differentiate between a program file and a data file.
5. Download a file from the Exploring Office Web site.
6. Copy and/or move a file from one folder to another.
7. Delete a file, and then recover it from the Recycle Bin.
8. Create and arrange shortcuts on the desktop.
9. Use the Search Companion.
10. Use the My Pictures and My Music folders.
11. Use Windows Messenger for instant messaging.

hands-on exercises

1. WELCOME TO WINDOWS XP
   Input: None
   Output: None

2. DOWNLOAD PRACTICE FILES
   Input: Data files from the Web
   Output: Welcome to Windows XP (a Word document)

3. WINDOWS EXPLORER
   Input: Data files from exercise 2
   Output: Screen Capture within a Word document

4. INCREASING PRODUCTIVITY
   Input: Data files from exercise 3
   Output: None

5. FUN WITH WINDOWS XP
   Input: None
   Output: None

CASE STUDY
UNFORESEEN CIRCUMSTANCES

Steve and his wife Shelly have poured their life savings into the dream of owning their own business, a "nanny" service agency. They have spent the last two years building their business and have created a sophisticated database with numerous entries for both families and nannies. The database is the key to their operation. Now that it is up and running, Steve and Shelly are finally at a point where they could hire someone to manage the operation on a part-time basis so that they could take some time off together.

Unfortunately, their process for selecting a person they could trust with their business was not as thorough as it should have been. Nancy, their new employee, assured them that all was well, and the couple left for an extended weekend. The place was in shambles on their return. Nancy could not handle the responsibility, and when Steve gave her two weeks' notice, neither he nor his wife thought that the unimaginable would happen. On her last day in the office Nancy "lost" all of the names in the database—the data was completely gone!

Nancy claimed that a "virus" knocked out the database, but after spending nearly $1,500 with a computer consultant, Steve was told that it had been cleverly deleted from the hard drive and could not be recovered. Of course, the consultant asked Steve and Shelly about their backup strategy, which they sheepishly admitted did not exist. They had never experienced any problems in the past, and simply assumed that their data was safe. Fortunately, they do have hard copy of the data in the form of various reports that were printed throughout the time they were in business. They have no choice but to manually reenter the data. ▓

Your assignment is to read the chapter, paying special attention to the information on file management. Think about how Steve and Shelly could have avoided the disaster if a backup strategy had been in place, then summarize your thoughts in a brief note to your instructor. Describe the elements of a basic backup strategy. Give several other examples of unforeseen circumstances that can cause data to be lost.

1

New! A listing of the input and output files for each hands-on exercise within the chapter. Students will stay on track with what is to be accomplished.

PERFECT PAGES

hands-on exercise

1 Welcome to Windows XP

Objective To log on to Windows XP and customize the desktop; to open the My Computer folder; to move and size a window; to format a floppy disk and access the Help and Support Center. Use Figure 7 as a guide.

Step 1: **Log On to Windows XP**

■ Turn on the computer and all of the peripheral devices. The floppy drive should be empty prior to starting your machine.

■ Windows XP will load automatically, and you should see a login screen similar to Figure 7a. (It does not matter which version of Windows XP you are using.) The number and names of the potential users and their associated icons will be different on your system.

■ Click the icon for the user account you want to access. You may be prompted for a password, depending on the security options in effect.

Click icon for user account to be accessed

(a) Log On to Windows XP (step 1)

FIGURE 7 Hands-on Exercise 1

USER ACCOUNTS

The available user names are cr
Windows XP, but you can add or d
click Control Panel, switch to the Ca
the desired task, such as creating
then supply the necessary informati
user accounts in a school setting.

10   GETTING STARTED WITH MICROSOFT WINDOWS XP

Each step in the hands-on exercises begins at the top of the page to ensure that students can easily navigate through the text.

Step 2: **Choose the Theme and Start Menu**

■ Check with your instructor to see if you are able to modify the desktop and other settings at your school or university. If your network administrator has disabled these commands, skip this step and go to step 3.

■ Point to a blank area on the desktop, click the **right mouse button** to display a context-sensitive menu, then click the **Properties command** to open the Display Properties dialog box. Click the **Themes tab** and select the **Windows XP theme** if it is not already selected. Click **OK**.

■ We prefer to work without any wallpaper (background picture) on the desktop. **Right click** the desktop, click **Properties**, then click the **Desktop tab** in the Display Properties dialog box. Click **None** as shown in Figure 7b, then click **OK**. The background disappears.

■ The Start menu is modified independently of the theme. **Right click** a blank area of the taskbar, click the **Properties command** to display the Taskbar and Start Menu Properties dialog box, then click the **Start Menu tab**.

■ Click the **Start Menu option button**. Click **OK**.

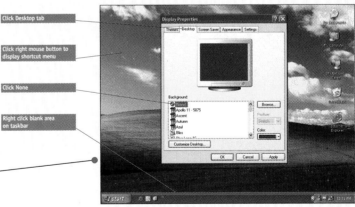

Click Desktop tab

Click right mouse button to display shortcut menu

Click None

Right click blank area on taskbar

(b) Choose the Theme and Start Menu (step 2)

FIGURE 7 Hands-on Exercise 1 (*continued*)

IMPLEMENT A SCREEN SAVER

A screen saver is a delightful way to personalize your computer and a good way to practice with basic commands in Windows XP. Right click a blank area of the desktop, click the Properties command to open the Display Properties dialog box, then click the Screen Saver tab. Click the down arrow in the Screen Saver list box, choose the desired screen saver, then set the option to wait an appropriate amount of time before the screen saver appears. Click OK to accept the settings and close the dialog box.

GETTING STARTED WITH MICROSOFT WINDOWS XP   11

New! Larger screen shots with clear callouts.

Boxed tips provide students with additional information.

MINI CASES AND PRACTICE EXERCISES

New!
We've added mini cases at the end of each chapter for expanded practice and review.

MINI CASES

The Financial Consultant

A friend of yours is in the process of buying a home and has asked you to compare the payments and total interest on a 15- and 30-year loan at varying interest rates. You have decided to analyze the loans in Excel, and then incorporate the results into a memo written in Microsoft Word. As of now, the principal is $150,000, but it is very likely that your friend will change his mind several times, and so you want to use the linking and embedding capability within Windows to dynamically link the worksheet to the word processing document. Your memo should include a letterhead that takes advantage of the formatting capabilities within Word; a graphic logo would be a nice touch.

Fun with the If Statement

Open the *Chapter 4 Mini Case—Fun with the If Statement* workbook in the Exploring Excel folder, then follow the directions in the worksheet to view a hidden message. The message is displayed by various If statements scattered throughout the worksheet, but the worksheet is protected so that you cannot see these formulas. (Use help to see how to protect a worksheet.) We made it easy for you, however, because you can unprotect the worksheet since a password is not required. Once the worksheet is unprotected, pull down the Format menu, click the Cells command, click the Protection tab, and clear the Hidden check box. Prove to your professor that you have done this successfully, by changing the text of our message. Print the completed worksheet to show both displayed values and cell formulas.

The Lottery

Many states raise money through lotteries that advertise prizes of several million dollars. In reality, however, the actual value of the prize is considerably less than the advertised value, although the winners almost certainly do not care. One state, for example, recently offered a twenty million dollar prize that was to be distributed in twenty annual payments of one million dollars each. How much was the prize actually worth, assuming a long-term interest rate of five percent? Use the PV (Present Value) function to determine the answer. What is the effect on the answer if payments to the recipient are made at the beginning of each year, rather than at the end of each year?

A Penny a Day

What if you had a rich un[...] salary each day for the n[...] prised at how quickly th[...] use the Goal Seek comm[...] (if any) will your uncle pa[...] uncle pay you on the 31s[...]

The Rule of 72

Delaying your IRA for on[...] on when you begin. Tha[...] a calculator, using the "R[...] long it takes money to [...] money earning 8% annu[...] money doubles again in [...] your IRA at age 21, rathe[...] initial contribution. Use[...] lose, assuming an 8% ra[...] determine the exact amo[...]

New!
Each project in the end-of-chapter material begins at the top of a page—now students can easily see where their assignments begin and end.

PRACTICE WITH EXCEL

1. **Theme Park Admissions:** A partially completed version of the worksheet in Figure 3.13 is available in the Exploring Excel folder as *Chapter 3 Practice 1*. Follow the directions in parts (a) and (b) to compute the totals and format the worksheet, then create each of the charts listed below.

    a. Use the AutoSum command to enter the formulas to compute the total number of admissions for each region and each quarter.

    b. Select the entire worksheet (cells A1 through F8), then use the AutoFormat command to format the worksheet. You do not have to accept the entire design, nor do you have to use the design we selected. You can also modify the design after it has been applied to the worksheet by changing the font size of selected cells and/or changing boldface and italics.

    c. Create a column chart showing the total number of admissions in each quarter as shown in Figure 3.13. Add the graphic shown in the figure for emphasis.

    d. Create a pie chart that shows the percentage of the total number of admissions in each region. Create this chart in its own chart sheet with an appropriate name.

    e. Create a stacked column chart that shows the total number of admissions for each region and the contribution of each quarter within each region. Create this chart in its own chart sheet with an appropriate name.

    f. Create a stacked column chart showing the total number of admissions for each quarter and the contribution of each region within each quarter. Create this chart in its own chart sheet with an appropriate name.

    g. Change the color of each of the worksheet tabs.

    h. Print the entire workbook, consisting of the worksheet in Figure 3.13 plus the three additional sheets that you create. Use portrait orientation for the Sales Data worksheet and landscape orientation for the other worksheets. Create a custom header for each worksheet that includes your name, your course, and your instructor's name. Create a custom footer for each worksheet that includes the name of the worksheet. Submit the completed assignment to your instructor.

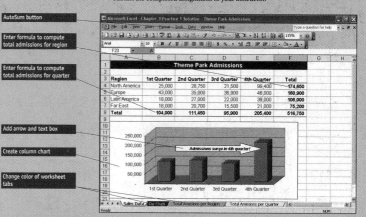

FIGURE **3.13** Theme Park Admissions (exercise 1)

INTEGRATED CASE STUDIES

New!

Each case study contains multiple exercises that use Microsoft Office applications in conjunction with one another.

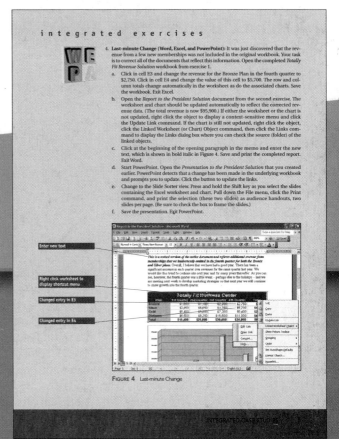

Companion Web site

New!

Updated and enhanced Companion Web site. Find everything you need— student practice files, PowerPoint lectures, online study guides, and instructor support (solutions)!

www.prenhall.com/grauer

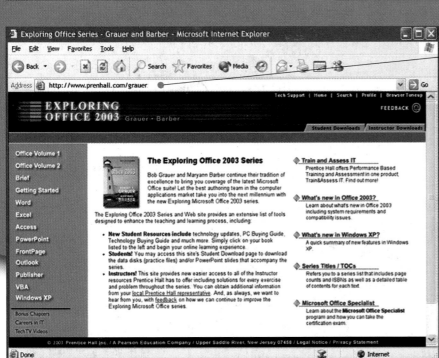

Acknowledgments

We want to thank the many individuals who have helped to bring this project to fruition. Jodi McPherson, executive acquisitions editor at Prentice Hall, has provided new leadership in extending the series to Office 2003. Cathi Profitko did an absolutely incredible job on our Web site. Shelly Martin was the creative force behind the chapter-opening case studies. Emily Knight coordinated the marketing and continues to inspire us with suggestions for improving the series. Greg Hubit has been masterful as the external production editor for every book in the series from its inception. Eileen Clark coordinated the myriad details of production and the certification process. Lynne Breitfeller was the project manager and manufacturing buyer. Lori Johnson was the project manager at The GTS Companies and in charge of composition. Chuck Cox did his usual fine work as copyeditor. Melissa Edwards was the supplements editor. Cindy Stevens, Tom McKenzie, and Michael Olmstead wrote the instructor manuals. Michael Fruhbeis developed the innovative and attractive design. We also want to acknowledge our reviewers who, through their comments and constructive criticism, greatly improved the series.

Lynne Band, Middlesex Community College
Don Belle, Central Piedmont Community College
Stuart P. Brian, Holy Family College
Carl M. Briggs, Indiana University School of Business
Kimberly Chambers, Scottsdale Community College
Jill Chapnick, Florida International University
Alok Charturvedi, Purdue University
Jerry Chin, Southwest Missouri State University
Dean Combellick, Scottsdale Community College
Cody Copeland, Johnson County Community College
Larry S. Corman, Fort Lewis College
Janis Cox, Tri-County Technical College
Douglass Cross, Clackamas Community College
Martin Crossland, Southwest Missouri State University
Bill Daley, University of Oregon
Paul E. Daurelle, Western Piedmont Community College
Shawna DePlonty, Sault College of Applied Arts and Technology
Carolyn DiLeo, Westchester Community College
Judy Dolan, Palomar College
David Douglas, University of Arkansas
Carlotta Eaton, Radford University
Judith M. Fitspatrick, Gulf Coast Community College
James Franck, College of St. Scholastica
Raymond Frost, Central Connecticut State University
Susan Fry, Boise State University
Midge Gerber, Southwestern Oklahoma State University
James Gips, Boston College
Vernon Griffin, Austin Community College
Ranette Halverson, Midwestern State University
Michael Hassett, Fort Hays State University
Mike Hearn, Community College of Philadelphia
Wanda D. Heller, Seminole Community College

Bonnie Homan, San Francisco State University
Ernie Ivey, Polk Community College
Walter Johnson, Community College of Philadelphia
Mike Kelly, Community College of Rhode Island
Jane King, Everett Community College
Rose M. Laird, Northern Virginia Community College
David Langley, University of Oregon
John Lesson, University of Central Florida
Maurie Lockley, University of North Carolina at Greensboro
Daniela Marghitu, Auburn University
David B. Meinert, Southwest Missouri State University
Alan Moltz, Naugatuck Valley Technical Community College
Kim Montney, Kellogg Community College
Bill Morse, DeVry Institute of Technology
Kevin Pauli, University of Nebraska
Mary McKenry Percival, University of Miami
Marguerite Nedreberg, Youngstown State University
Jim Pruitt, Central Washington University
Delores Pusins, Hillsborough Community College
Gale E. Rand, College Misericordia
Judith Rice, Santa Fe Community College
David Rinehard, Lansing Community College
Marilyn Salas, Scottsdale Community College
Herach Safarian, College of the Canyons
John Shepherd, Duquesne University
Barbara Sherman, Buffalo State College
Robert Spear, Prince George's Community College
Michael Stewardson, San Jacinto College—North
Helen Stoloff, Hudson Valley Community College
Margaret Thomas, Ohio University
Mike Thomas, Indiana University School of Business
Suzanne Tomlinson, Iowa State University
Karen Tracey, Central Connecticut State University
Antonio Vargas, El Paso Community College
Sally Visci, Lorain County Community College
David Weiner, University of San Francisco
Connie Wells, Georgia State University
Wallace John Whistance-Smith, Ryerson Polytechnic University
Jack Zeller, Kirkwood Community College

A final word of thanks to the unnamed students at the University of Miami who make it all worthwhile. Most of all, thanks to you, our readers, for choosing this book. Please feel free to contact us with any comments and suggestions.

Robert T. Grauer   Maryann Barber
rgrauer@miami.edu   mbarber@miami.edu
www.prenhall.com/grauer

1

Introduction to Access:
What Is a Database?

OBJECTIVES

After reading this chapter you will:

1. Define the terms field, record, table, and database.

2. Describe the objects in an Access database.

3. Download the practice files (data disk) for use in hands-on exercises.

4. Add, edit, and delete records within a table.

5. Use existing forms and reports.

6. Explain the importance of data validation in maintaining a table.

7. Apply a filter by form or selection.

8. Sort a table on one or more fields.

9. Identify the one-to-many relationships in a database.

10. Explain how changes in one table of a relational database affect other the tables in the database.

hands-on exercises

1. INTRODUCTION TO ACCESS
   Input: Bookstore database
   Output: Bookstore database (modified)

2. FILTERS AND SORTING
   Input: Employee database
   Output: Employee database (modified)

3. A LOOK AHEAD
   Input: Look Ahead database
   Output: Look Ahead database (modified)

CASE STUDY
NATALIE'S CUPPA JOE

Natalie's Cuppa Joe is a locally famous coffee shop that is known for its large and very creative selection of signature espresso drinks for coffee enthusiasts. The owner, Natalie Anderson, has always believed that variety is the spice of life and that there is much more to coffee than just cream and sugar. Natalie insists on good customer relations, and her staff is expected to know regular customers by their first name. Customers are also encouraged to submit suggestions for additional signature selections.

To make it easier on her employees, Natalie has built a database with information about her customers. New customers are asked to complete a questionnaire the first time they come into the shop as they wait for their drink to be prepared. Customers provide the standard name and address information, indicate whether they want to be included on a mailing list, and whether they wish to purchase the discount "Cuppa Card." This data is then entered into the database within three to four days.

You have just been hired by Natalie's Cuppa Joe and are expected to become knowledgeable about its customers and proficient at brewing the wild coffee drinks for which they are famous. Natalie has given you time away from the front counter to become familiar with the database, to enter recent customer information, and to generate two reports that will reflect the new data. ■

Your assignment is to read the chapter, paying special attention to each of the hands-on exercises. You will then open the *Chapter 1 Case Study— Natalie's Cuppa Joe* database, and examine each of its objects (tables, forms, queries, and reports). You will use the existing Customers form to enter data about yourself as a new customer. Indicate that you want to be on the mailing list, but that you have not yet purchased the discount card. Be sure to suggest a specialty drink in the space provided. Print the completed form containing your data, and then print both of the reports within the database. (Your name should appear on both if you followed our instructions correctly.) Submit all of the printed information to your instructor.

THE COLLEGE BOOKSTORE

Imagine, if you will, that you are the manager of a college bookstore and that you maintain data for every book in the store. Accordingly, you have recorded the specifics of each book (the title, author, publisher, price, and so on) in a manila folder, and have stored the folders in one drawer of a file cabinet.

One of your major responsibilities is to order books at the beginning of each semester, which in turn requires you to contact the various publishers. You have found it convenient, therefore, to create a second set of folders with data about each publisher—such as the publisher's phone number, address, and discount policy. You also found it necessary to create a third set of folders with data about each order—such as when the order was placed, the status of the order, which books were ordered, and how many copies.

Normal business operations will require you to make repeated trips to the filing cabinet to maintain the accuracy of the data and keep it up to date. You will have to create a new folder whenever a new book is received, whenever you contract with a new publisher, or whenever you place a new order. In similar fashion, you will have to modify the data in an existing folder to reflect changes that occur, such as an increase in the price of a book, a change in a publisher's address, or an update in the status of an order. And, lastly, you will need to remove the folder of any book that is no longer carried by the bookstore, or of any publisher with whom you no longer have contact, or of any order that was canceled.

The preceding discussion describes the bookstore of 40 years ago—before the advent of computers and computerized databases. The bookstore manager of today needs the same information as his or her predecessor. Today's manager, however, has the information readily available, at the touch of a key or the click of a mouse, through the miracle of modern technology.

Information systems have their own vocabulary. A ***field*** is a basic fact (or data element)—such as the name of a book or the telephone number of a publisher. A ***record*** is a set of fields. A ***table*** is a set of records. Every record in a table contains the same fields in the same order. A ***database*** consists of one or more tables. In our example each record in the Books table will contain the identical six fields—ISBN (a unique identifying number for the book), title, author, year of publication, price, and publisher. In similar fashion, every record in the Publishers table will have the same fields for each publisher just as every record in the Orders table has the same fields for each order.

You can think of the file cabinet in the manual system as a database. Each set of folders in the file cabinet corresponds to a table within the database. Thus, the Bookstore database consists of three separate tables—of books, publishers, and orders. Each table, in turn, consists of multiple records, corresponding to the folders in the file cabinet. The Books table, for example, contains a record for every book title in the store. The Publishers table has a record for each publisher, just as the Orders table has a record for each order.

The real power of Access is derived from a database with multiple tables—such as Books, Publishers, and Orders tables within the Bookstore database. For the time being, however, we focus on a simpler database with only one table so that you can learn the basics of Access. After you are comfortable working with a single table, we will show you how to work with multiple tables and relate them to one another.

GARBAGE IN, GARBAGE OUT

The information produced by a system is only as good as the data on which the information is based. In other words, no system, be it manual or electronic, can produce valid output from invalid input. The phenomenon is described by the acronym "GIGO"—garbage in, garbage out.

Microsoft Access, the fourth major application in the Microsoft Office suite, is used to create and manage a database such as the one for the college bookstore. Consider now Figure 1.1, which shows how Microsoft Access appears on the desktop. Our discussion assumes a basic familiarity with the Windows operating system and the user interface that is common to all Windows applications. You should recognize, therefore, that the desktop in Figure 1.1 has two open windows— an application window for Microsoft Access and a document (database) window for the database that is currently open. (Microsoft Office Access 2003 uses the Access 2000 file format by default, to maintain compatability with earlier versions of Access.)

Each window has its own title bar and Minimize, Maximize (or Restore), and Close buttons. The title bar in the application window contains the name of the application (Microsoft Access). The title bar in the document (database) window contains the name of the database that is currently open (Bookstore). The application window for Access has been maximized to take up the entire desktop, and hence the Restore button is visible. The database window has not been maximized.

A menu bar appears immediately below the application title bar. A toolbar (similar to those in other Office applications) appears below the menu bar and offers alternative ways to execute common commands.

The Database Window

The **Database window** displays the various objects in an Access database. There are seven types of objects—tables, queries, forms, reports, pages, macros, and modules. Every database must contain at least one table, and it may contain any or all (or none) of the other objects. Each object type is accessed through the appropriate button within the Database window. In this chapter we concentrate on tables, but we briefly describe the other types of objects as a preview of what you will learn as you read our book.

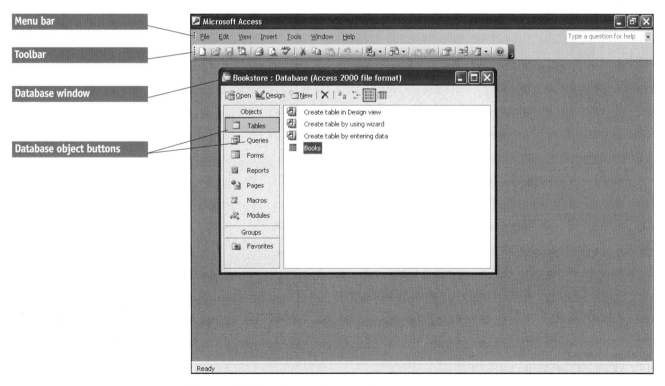

FIGURE 1.1   The Database Window

Tables

A table stores data about a physical entity such as a person, place, or thing, and it is the basic element in any database. A table is made up of records, which in turn are made up of fields. It is similar to an Excel worksheet in appearance, with each record appearing in a separate row. Each field appears in a separate column.

Access provides different ways in which to view a table. The **_Datasheet view_** is where you add, edit, and delete records of a table, and it is the view on which we concentrate throughout the chapter. The **_Design view_** is used to create (and/or modify) the table by specifying the fields it will contain and the associated properties for each field. The field type (for example, text or numeric data) and the field length are examples of field properties. (The Design view is covered in detail in Chapter 2, where we show you how to create a table.)

Access also includes two additional views that provide a convenient way to display summary information from a table. The **_PivotTable view_** is similar in concept to an Excel pivot table and provides a convenient way to summarize data about groups of records. The **_PivotChart view_** creates a chart from the associated PivotTable view. (These views are discussed further in Chapter 4 and need not concern you at this time.)

Figure 1.2 shows the Datasheet view for the Books table in our bookstore. The first row in the table displays the field names. Each additional row contains a record (the data for a specific book). Each column represents a field (one fact about a book). Every record in the table contains the same fields in the same order: ISBN number, Title, Author, Year, List Price, and Publisher.

The **_primary key_** is the field (or combination of fields) that makes each record in a table unique. The ISBN is the primary key in the Books table; it ensures that every record in a table is different from every other record, and hence it prevents the occurrence of duplicate records. A primary key is not required but is strongly recommended. (We cannot think of an example where you would not want to use a primary key.) There can be only one primary key per table.

The status bar at the bottom of Figure 1.2 indicates that there are 22 records in the table and that you are positioned on record number 13. You can work on only one record at a time. The vertical scroll bar at the right of the window indicates that there are more records in the table than can be seen at one time. The horizontal scroll bar at the bottom of the window indicates that you cannot see an entire record.

The triangle that appears to the left of the record indicates that the data in the **_current record_** has been saved. The triangle will change to a pencil as you begin to enter new data, then it will change back to a triangle after you complete the data entry and move to another record, since data is saved automatically as soon as you move from one record to the next.

| Field names | Triangle indicates data has been saved | Total number of records | Current record is record 13 |

ISBN Number	Title	Author	Year	List Price	Publisher
0-13-143487-X	Exploring PowerPoint 2003	Grauer/Barber	2003	$39.00	Prentice Hall
0-13-143490-X	Exploring Word 2003	Grauer/Barber	2003	$39.00	Prentice Hall
0-13-754193-7	Exploring Windows 98	Grauer/Barber	1998	$28.95	Prentice Hall
0-13-790817-2	COBOL: From Micro to Mainframe/3e	Grauer/Villar/Buss	1998	$52.95	Prentice Hall
0-672-30306-X	Memory Management for All of Us	Goodman	1993	$39.95	Sams Publishing
0-672-31325-1	Teach Yourself HTML in 10 Minutes	Evans	1998	$12.99	Sams Publishing
0-672-31344-8	Teach Yourself Web Publishing	Lemay	1998	$39.99	Sams Publishing
0-789-72812-5	Using Microsoft .NET Enterprise Server	Jones	2002	$44.99	Que Publishing
0-789-72818-4	MCAD/MCSD Training Guide	Gunderloy	2002	$44.99	Que Publishing
0-87835-669-X	A Guide to SQL	Pratt	1991	$24.95	Boyd & Fraser
0-940087-32-4	Looking Good in Print	Parker	1990	$23.95	Ventana Press
0-940087-37-5	The Presentation Design Book	Rabb	1990	$24.95	Ventana Press

Record: 13 of 22

FIGURE 1.2 An Access Table

Forms, Queries, and Reports

As previously indicated, an Access database contains different types of objects. A table (or set of tables) is at the heart of any database because it contains the actual data. The other objects in a database—such as forms, queries, and reports—are based on an underlying table. Figure 1.3a displays a form based on the Books table that was shown earlier.

A *form* provides a friendlier interface than does a table and it is easier to use when entering or modifying data. Note, for example, the command buttons that appear in the form to add a new record, to find or delete an existing record, to print a record, and to close the form. In short, the form provides access to all of the data maintenance operations that are available through a table. The status bar and navigation buttons at the bottom of the form are similar to those that appear at the bottom of a table.

Figure 1.3b displays a query that lists the books for a particular publisher (Prentice Hall in this example). A *query* provides information based on the data within an underlying table. The Books table, for example, contains records for many publishers, but the query in Figure 1.3b shows only the books that were published by a specific publisher. The results of the query are similar in appearance to the underlying table, except that the query contains selected records and/or selected fields for those records. The query may also list the records in a different sequence from that of the table. (A query can also be used to add new records and/or modify existing records.)

Figure 1.3c displays a *report* that contains the same information as the query in Figure 1.3b. The report, however, provides the information in a more attractive format than the query. Note, too, that a report can be based on either a table or a query. Thus, you could have based the report on the Books table, rather than the query, in which case the report would list every book in the table, as opposed to a limited subset of the records within the table.

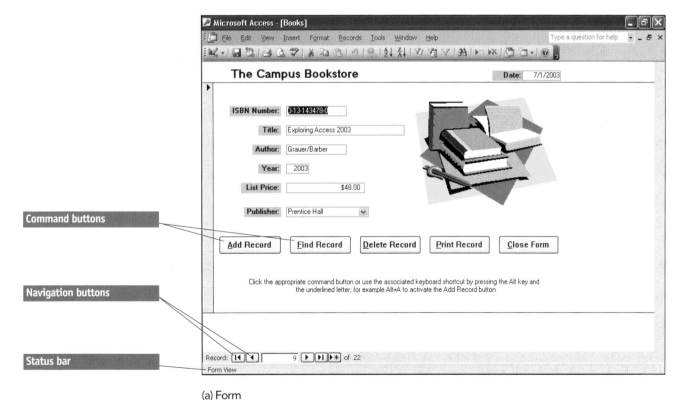

(a) Form

FIGURE 1.3 Forms, Queries, and Reports

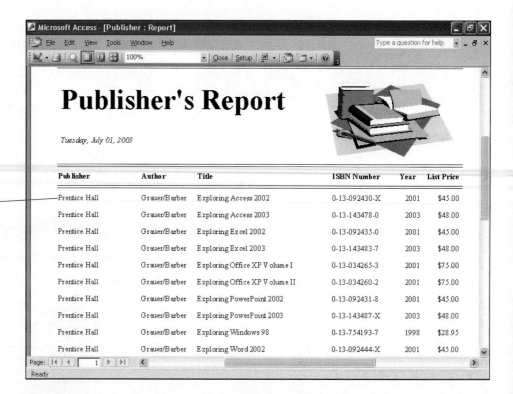

Only books published by Prentice Hall are displayed

(b) Query

Report is based on query shown in Figure 1.3b

(c) Report

FIGURE 1.3 Forms, Queries, and Reports (*continued*)

ONE FILE HOLDS EVERYTHING

All of the objects in an Access database are stored in a single file. The database can be opened from within Windows Explorer by double clicking the file name. It can also be opened from within Access through the Open command in the File menu or by clicking the Open button on the Database toolbar. The individual objects within a database are opened from the Database window.

Objective To open an existing Access database; to add, edit, and delete records within a table in that database; to open forms, queries, and reports within an existing database. Use Figure 1.4 as a guide in the exercise.

Step 1: **Log on to Windows XP**

■ Turn on the computer and all of its peripherals. The floppy drive should be empty prior to starting your machine.

■ Your system will take a minute or so to get started, after which you should see the desktop in Figure 1.4a. Do not be concerned if the appearance of your desktop is different from ours.

■ Click the icon for the user account you want to access. You may be prompted for a password, depending on the security options in effect.

■ You should be familiar with basic file management and be able to copy files from one folder to another. If not, you may want to review this material in the "Getting Started with Microsoft Windows" section in the text.

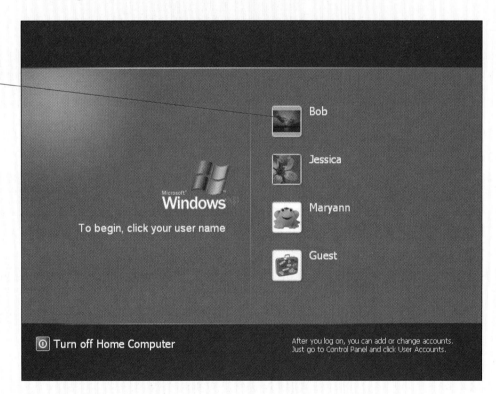

Click icon for your user account

(a) Log onto Windows XP (step 1)

FIGURE 1.4 Hands-on Exercise 1

USER ACCOUNTS

The available user names are created automatically during the installation of Windows XP, but you can add or delete users at any time. Click the Start button, click Control Panel, switch to the Category view, and select User Accounts. Choose the desired task, such as creating a new account or changing an existing account. Do not expect, however, to be able to modify accounts in a school setting.

Step 2: Obtain the Practice Files

- Start Internet Explorer, and go to **www.prenhall.com/grauer**. Click the book for **Office 2003**, which takes you to the Office 2003 home page. Click the **Student Downloads tab** (near the top of the window) to go to the Student Download page as shown in Figure 1.4b.

- Select the appropriate file to download.
  - ❏ Choose **Exploring Access** (or **Access Volume I**) if you are using a stand-alone Access text, as opposed to an Office text with multiple applications.
  - ❏ Choose **Office 2003 Volume I** (or **Office 2003 Brief**) if you are using an Office text.

- Click the link to download the file. You will see the File Download box asking what you want to do. Click the **Save button**. The Save As dialog box appears.

- Click the **down arrow** in the Save In list box and select the drive and folder where you want to save the file. Click **Save**.

- Start Windows Explorer, select the drive and folder where you saved the file, then double click the file to follow the onscreen instructions.

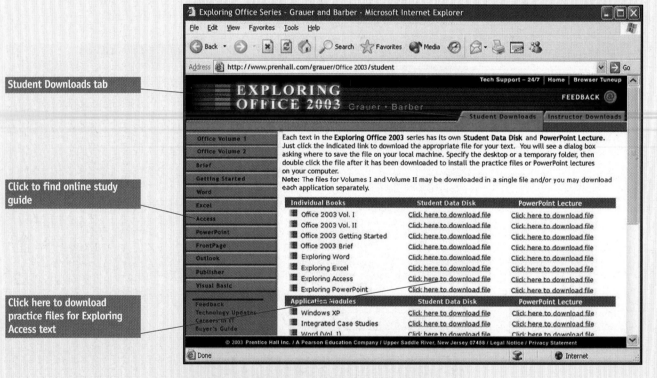

(b) Obtain the Practice Files (step 2)

FIGURE 1.4 Hands-on Exercise 1 (*continued*)

EXPLORE OUR WEB SITE

The Exploring Office Series Web site offers an online study guide (multiple-choice, true/false, and matching questions) for each individual textbook to help you review the material in each chapter. You can take practice quizzes by yourself and/or e-mail the results to your instructor. These online study guides are available via the tabs in the left navigation bar. You can return to the Student Download page at any time by clicking the tab toward the top of the window and/or you can click the link to Home to return to the home page for the Office 2003 series. And finally, you can click the Feedback button at the top of the screen to send a message directly to Bob Grauer.

Step 3: **Start Microsoft Access**

- Click the **Start button**, click the **All Programs button**, click **Microsoft Office**, then click **Microsoft Office Access 2003** to start the program.

- Pull down the **File menu** and click the **Open command** to display the Open dialog box in Figure 1.4c. (Do this even if the task pane is open.)

- Click the **down arrow** on the **Views button**, then click **Details** to change to the Details view.

- Click and drag the vertical border between columns to increase (or decrease) the size of a column.

- Click the **drop-down arrow** on the Look In list box. Click the appropriate drive (drive C is recommended rather than drive A) depending on the location of your data. Double click the **Exploring Access folder**.

- Click the down scroll arrow (if needed) to click the **Bookstore database**. Click the **Open command button** to open the database.

- Click the **Open button** within the Security Warning dialog box if you see a warning message saying that the database may contain code to harm your computer. (The message is caused by the programming statements that are behind the command buttons in the various forms within the database.)

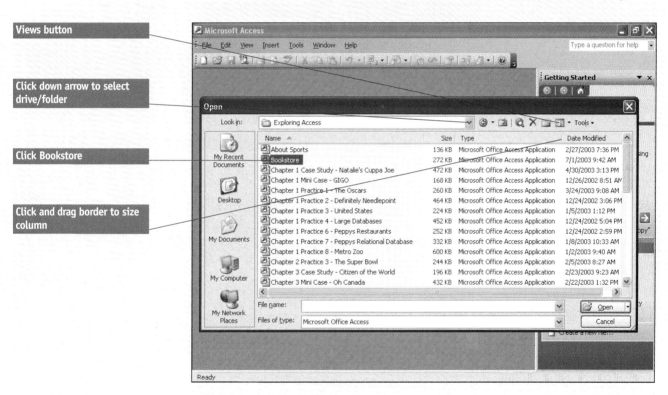

(c) Start Microsoft Access (step 3)

FIGURE 1.4   Hands-on Exercise 1 (*continued*)

FILE FORMATS

Access 2002 (Office XP) introduced a new file format that was continued in Access 2003. Access 2000, however, cannot read the new format, and thus, it is convenient to save files in the Access 2000 format to maintain compatibility with anyone using Microsoft Office 2000. Pull down the Tools menu, click Options, click the Advanced tab, and change the Default File Format to Access 2000.

Step 4: **Open the Books Table**

- If necessary, click the **Maximize button** in the application window so that Access takes the entire desktop.

- You should see the database window for the Bookstore database. Click the **Tables button**. Double click the icon next to Books to open the table as shown in Figure 1.4d.

- Click the **Maximize button** so that the Books table fills the Access window and reduces the clutter on the screen.

- Practice with the navigation buttons above the status bar to move from one record to the next. Click ► or ◄ to move forward to the next record or return to the previous record.

- Click |◄ to move to the first record in the table or ►| to move to the last record in the table.

- Click in any field of the first record. The status indicator at the bottom of the Books table indicates record 1 of 22. The triangle symbol in the record selector column indicates that the record has not changed since it was last saved.

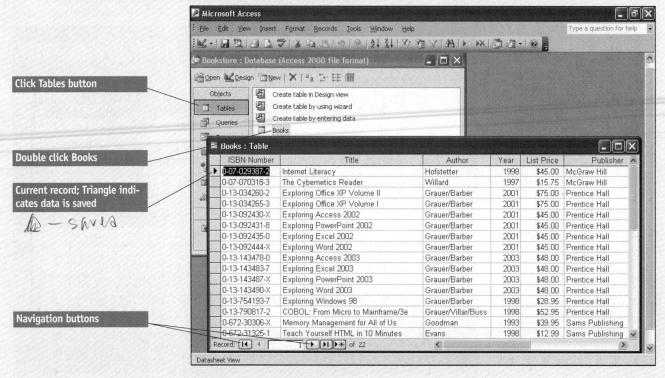

Click Tables button

Double click Books

Current record; Triangle indicates data is saved

ß̸ — saved.

Navigation buttons

(d) Open the Books Table (step 4)

FIGURE 1.4 Hands-on Exercise 1 (*continued*)

MOVING FROM FIELD TO FIELD

Press the Tab key, the right arrow key, or the Enter key to move to the next field in the current record (or the first field in the next record if you are already in the last field of the current record). Press Shift+Tab or the left arrow key to return to the previous field in the current record (or the last field in the previous record if you are already in the first field of the current record). Press Home or End to move to the first or last field, respectively.

Step 5: Add a New Record

- Pull down the **Insert** menu and click **New Record** (or click the **New Record button** on the Table Datasheet toolbar). The record selector moves to the last record (record 23). The insertion point is positioned in the first field (ISBN Number).

- Enter data for the new book (Exploring Microsoft Office 2003 Volume I) as shown in Figure 1.4e. The record selector changes to a pencil as soon as you enter the first character in the new record.

- Press **Enter** when you have entered the last field for the record. The record has been saved to the database, and the record selector changes to a triangle.

- Add another record. Enter **0-13-143442-X** as the ISBN. The title is **Exploring Microsoft Office 2003 Volume II** by **Grauer/Barber**. The price is **$79.00**. The book was published by **Prentice Hall** in **2003**. Be sure to press **Enter** when you have completed the data entry.

- There are now 24 records in the table.

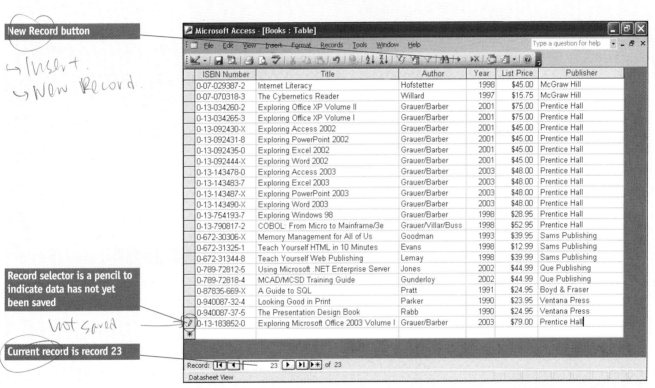

(e) Add a New Record (step 5)

FIGURE 1.4 Hands-on Exercise 1 (*continued*)

CREATE YOUR OWN SHORTHAND

Use the AutoCorrect feature that is common to all Office applications to expand abbreviations such as "PH" for Prentice Hall. Pull down the Tools menu, click AutoCorrect Options, type the abbreviation in the Replace text box and the expanded entry in the With text box. Click the Add command button, then click OK to exit the dialog box and return to the document. The next time you type PH (in uppercase) as you enter a record, it will be automatically expanded to Prentice Hall. (This feature may not work in a laboratory setting.)

Step 6: Edit a Record

- Click in the **Title field** for the first record, pull down the **Edit menu**, and click **Find** (or click the **Find button** on the toolbar) to display the dialog box in Figure 1.4f.

- Enter **COBOL** in the Find What text box. Check that the other parameters for the Find command match the dialog box in Figure 1.4f. Be sure that the **Title field** is selected in the Look In list box and **Any Part of Field** is selected in the Match text box.

- Click the **Find Next command button**. Access moves to record 14, the record containing the designated character string, and selects the matching word in the Title field for that record. Click **Cancel** to close the Find dialog box.

- Press the **Tab key** three times to move from the Title field to the Price field (or click directly in the price field). The current price ($52.95) is already selected.

- Type **$58.95**, then press the **down arrow** to move to the next record and save the data. (The changes are saved automatically; i.e., you do not have to click the Save button.)

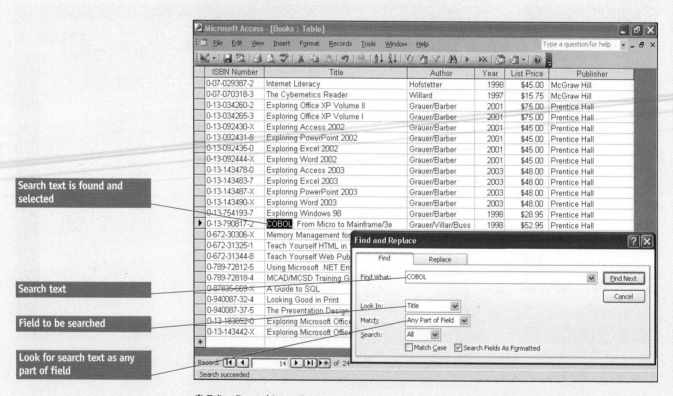

Search text is found and selected

Search text

Field to be searched

Look for search text as any part of field

(f) Edit a Record (step 6)

FIGURE 1.4 Hands-on Exercise 1 (*continued*)

USE WHAT YOU KNOW

The Find command is contained in the Edit menu of every Office application, and it is an ideal way to search for specific records within a table. You have the option to search a single field or the entire record, to match all or part of the selected field(s), to move forward or back in a table, and to specify a case-sensitive search. The Replace command can be used to substitute one value for another. Be careful, however, about using the Replace All option for global replacement because unintended replacements are far too common.

[handwritten annotations: "→ Del. key", "→ Delete Record button"]

Step 7: Delete a Record

- Use the Find command to search for the book **A Guide to SQL**. (You can click in the Title field, enter "SQL" in the Find What dialog box, then use the same search parameters as in the previous step.)

- The Find command should return the appropriate record, which is *not visible* in Figure 1.4g. (This is because we have deleted the record to display the dialog box in the figure.)

[handwritten annotation: "Edit → Select Record. ⇒ highlight."]

- Pull down the **Edit menu** and click the **Select Record command** to highlight the entire record. You can also click the **record selector column** (the box immediately to the left of the first field) to select the record without having to use a pull-down menu.

- Press the **Del key** (or click the **Delete Record button** on the toolbar) to delete the record. You will see the dialog box in Figure 1.4g indicating that you are about to delete a record and asking you to confirm the deletion. Click **Yes** to delete the record.

- Pull down the **Edit menu**. The Undo command is dim, indicating that you cannot undelete a record. Press **Esc** to continue working.

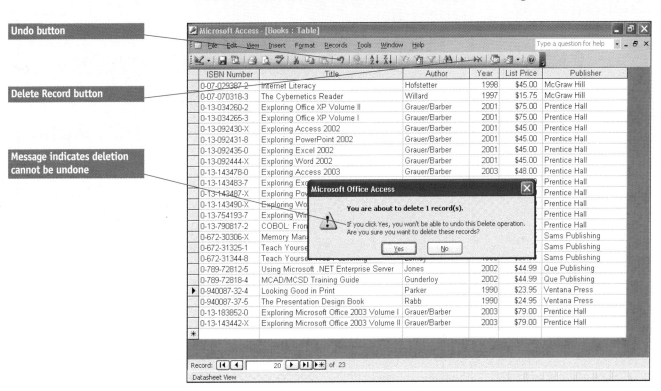

(g) Delete a Record (step 7)

FIGURE 1.4 Hands-on Exercise 1 (*continued*)

THE UNDO COMMAND

The Undo command is common to all Office applications, but it is implemented differently in Access. Word, Excel, and PowerPoint let you undo the last several operations. Access, however, because it saves changes automatically as soon as you move to the next record, lets you undo only the last command that was executed. Even this is limited, because once you delete a record, you cannot undo the deletion; that is, the record is permanently deleted.

Step 8: Print the Table

- Pull down the **File menu** and click the **Print Preview command** to see the table prior to printing. The status bar indicates that you are viewing page 1 (and further, the active scroll buttons indicate that there are additional pages).

- Click the **Setup button** on the Print Preview toolbar to display the Page Setup dialog box as shown in Figure 1.4h.

- Click the **Page tab**. Click the **Landscape option button**. Click **OK** to accept the settings and close the dialog box.

- The table should now fit on one page. (If it still does not fit on one page, click the Setup button on the Print Preview toolbar to display the Page Setup dialog box, click the **Margins tab**, and make the margins smaller.)

- Click the **Print button** to print the table. Alternatively, you can pull down the File menu, click **Print** to display the Print dialog box, click the **All options button**, then click **OK**.

- Click **Close** to close the Print Preview window. Close the table.

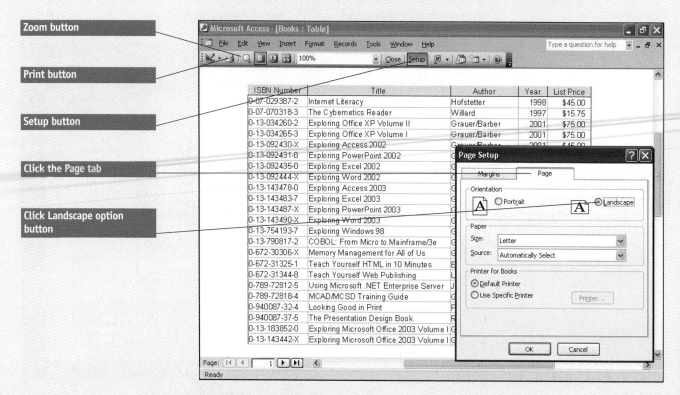

(h) Print the Table (step 8)

FIGURE 1.4 Hands-on Exercise 1 (*continued*)

THE PRINT PREVIEW TOOLBAR

The Print Preview toolbar is displayed automatically when you preview a report prior to printing. Click the Zoom button to toggle back and forth between fitting the entire page in the window and viewing the report at 100% magnification. Click the one, two, and multiple page buttons, to view different portions of the report in reports that extend over multiple pages. Use the Setup button to change the margins and/or orientation. Click the Close button to exit Print Preview.

Step 9:   Open the Books Form

■ Click the **Forms button** in the Database window. Double click the **Books form** to open the form, and if necessary, maximize the form so that it takes the entire window.

■ Click the **Add Record command button**, or use the keyboard shortcut, **Alt+A**. (Each command button has a different underlined letter to indicate the keyboard shortcut.)

■ Click in the text box for **ISBN number**, then use the **Tab key** to move from field to field as you enter data for the book as shown in Figure 1.4i.

■ Enter text in the **Price field** to view the data validation that is built into Access. Click **OK** when you see the error message, then enter the indicated price. Click the **drop-down arrow** on the Publisher's list box to display the available publishers and to select the appropriate one. The use of a combo box ensures that you cannot misspell a publisher's name.

■ Click the button to **Print Record** (or press **Alt+P**) to print the form for the record that you just added.

■ Close the Books form to return to the Database window.

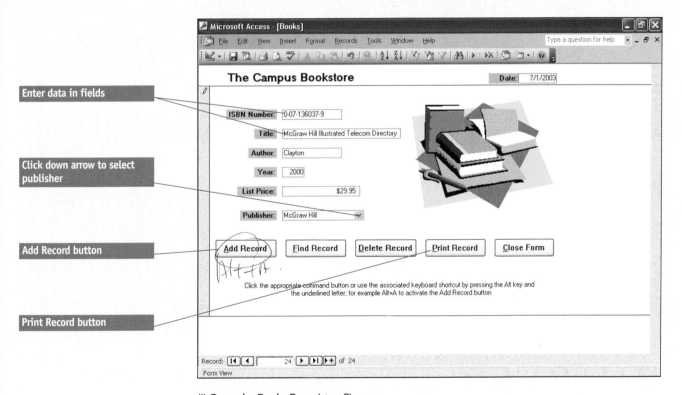

(i) Open the Books Form (step 9)

FIGURE 1.4   Hands-on Exercise 1 (*continued*)

DATA VALIDATION

No system, no matter how sophisticated, can produce valid output from invalid input. Thus, good systems are built to anticipate errors in data entry and to reject those errors prior to saving a record. Access will automatically prevent you from adding records with a duplicate primary key or entering invalid data into a numeric or date field. Other types of validation, such as requiring the author's name, are implemented by the database developer.

Step 10: Run a Query

- Click the **Queries button** in the Database window. Double click the **Publisher query** to run the query. You will see a dialog box asking you to enter the name of a publisher.

- Type **McGraw Hill** and press **Enter** to see the results of the query, which should contain three books by this publisher. (If you do not see any books, it is because you spelled the publisher incorrectly. Close the query to return to the Database window, then rerun the query.)

- You can use a query to display information, as was just done, and/or you can modify data in the underlying table. Click in the **Publisher field** for the blank record in the last row (the record selector is an asterisk). Type **McGraw Hill** to begin entering the data for a new record as shown in Figure 1.4j.

- You can enter data for any publisher within the query, but you must satisfy the requirements for data validation. See what happens if you omit the ISBN number or Author's name, or enter alphabetic data for the year or price. (The missing ISBN is **0-07-561585-1**.)

- Click the **Close button** to close the query and return to the Database window.

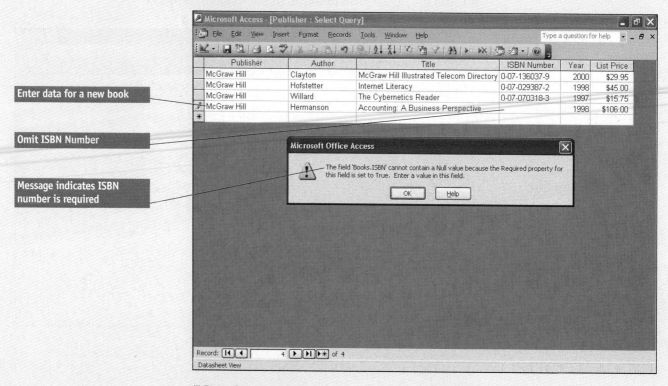

(j) Run a Query (step 10)

FIGURE 1.4 Hands-on Exercise 1 (*continued*)

FORMAT A DATASHEET

Format your tables and/or queries to make the results stand out. Click anywhere in a table or query (in Datasheet view), pull down the Format menu, and click the Datasheet command to display the Format Datasheet dialog box. You can change the style of the table to sunken or raised, change the color of the gridlines or suppress them altogether. The Format command also enables you to change the row height or column width and/or to hide columns. See practice exercise 4 at the end of the chapter.

Step 11: Open a Report

- Click the **Reports button** in the Database window to display the available reports. Double click the icon for the **Publisher report**. Type **McGraw Hill** in the Parameter dialog box. Press **Enter**.

- Click the **Maximize button** in the Report Window so that the report takes the entire screen as shown in Figure 1.4k.

- Click the **Zoom button** to toggle to 100% so that you can read the report, which should contain four records.

- Two books were in the original database. One book was entered through a form in step 9. The other book was entered through a query in step 10. All of the books in the report are published by McGraw Hill, which is consistent with the parameter you entered at the beginning of this step.

- Click the **Print button** on the Report toolbar. Click the **Close button** to close the Report window.

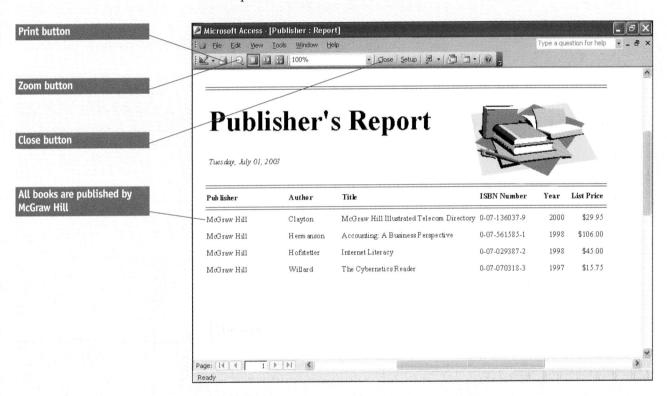

Print button

Zoom button

Close button

All books are published by McGraw Hill

Publisher's Report

Tuesday, July 01, 2003

Publisher	Author	Title	ISBN Number	Year	List Price
McGraw Hill	Clayton	McGraw Hill Illustrated Telecom Directory	0-07-136037-9	2000	$29.95
McGraw Hill	Hermanson	Accounting: A Business Perspective	0-07-561585-1	1998	$106.00
McGraw Hill	Hofstetter	Internet Literacy	0-07-029387-2	1998	$45.00
McGraw Hill	Willard	The Cybernetics Reader	0-07-070318-3	1997	$15.75

(k) Open a Report (step 11)

FIGURE 1.4   Hands-on Exercise 1 (*continued*)

TIP OF THE DAY

Pull down the Help menu, click the command to Show the Office Assistant, click the Office Assistant when it appears, then click the Options button to display the Office Assistant dialog box. Click the Options tab, check the box to Show the Tip of the Day at Startup, and then click OK. The next time you start Access, you will be greeted by the Assistant, who will offer you the tip of the day. (You can display a Tip of the Day for the other Office applications in similar fashion.)

Step 12: Help with Access

- There are several different ways to request help, but in any event, the best time to obtain help is when you don't need any. Try any of the following:
  - ❏ Pull down the **Help menu** and click the command to **Show the Office Assistant**. Click the **Assistant**, then enter the question, "**What is a table?**" in the Assistant's balloon and click **Search**, or
  - ❏ Type the question directly in the **Ask a Question list box** in the upper right of the Access window and press **Enter**, or
  - ❏ Pull down the **Help menu**, click **Microsoft Access Help** to display the task pane, enter the question in the **Search box**, and click the **Start Searching arrow**.

- Regardless of the technique you choose, Access will display a message indicating that it is searching Microsoft Office Online. (Help is not available locally, and this can be a problem with a slow Internet connection.)

- You should see a task pane with the results of the search as shown in Figure 1.4l. Click the link that is most appropriate (e.g., **About tables** in this example).

- A new window opens containing the detailed help information. Close the Help window. Close the task pane. Hide the Office Assistant.

- Exit Access if you do not want to continue with the next exercise at this time.

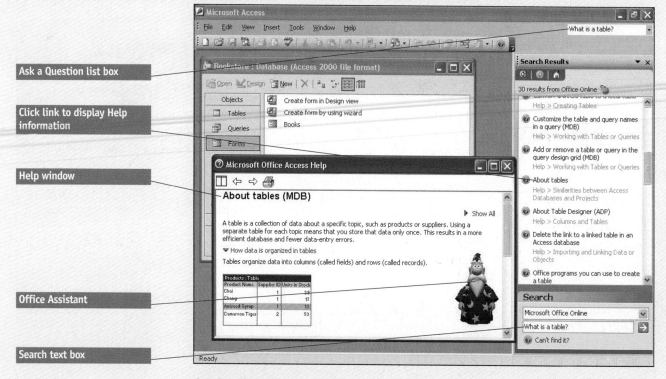

(l) Help with Access (step 12)

FIGURE 1.4 Hands-on Exercise 1 (*continued*)

CHOOSE YOUR OWN ASSISTANT

Pull down the Help menu, click the command to Show the Office Assistant, click the Office Assistant when it appears, then click the Options button to display the Office Assistant dialog box. Click the Gallery tab, then click the Next button repeatedly to cycle through the available characters. Click OK to accept the character of your choice. You're still in control, however. Pull down the Help menu and click the command to Hide the Office Assistant if it becomes annoying.

The exercise just completed described how to use an existing report to obtain information from the database. But what if you are in a hurry and don't have the time to create the report? There is a faster way. You can open the table in the Datasheet view, then apply a filter and/or a sort to the table to display selected records in any order. A *filter* displays a subset of records from the table according to specified criteria. A *sort* lists those records in a specific sequence, such as alphabetically by last name or by EmployeeID. We illustrate both of these concepts in conjunction with Figure 1.5.

Figure 1.5a displays an employee table with 14 records. Each record has 8 fields. The records in the table are displayed in sequence according to the EmployeeID, which is also the primary key (the field or combination of fields that uniquely identifies a record). The status bar indicates that there are 14 records in the table. What if, however, you wanted a partial list of those records, such as employees with a specific title?

Figure 1.5b displays a filtered view of the same table in which we see only the Account Reps. The status bar shows that this is a filtered list, and that there are 8 records that satisfy the criteria. (The employee table still contains the original 14 records, but only 8 records are visible with the filter in effect.) The table has also been sorted so that the selected employees are displayed in alphabetical order, as opposed to EmployeeID order.

Two operations are necessary to go from Figure 1.5a to Figure 1.5b—filtering and sorting, and they can be performed in either order. The easiest way to implement a filter is to click in any cell that contains the value of the desired criterion (such as any cell that contains "Account Rep" in the Title field), then click the *Filter by Selection* button on the Database toolbar. To sort the table, click in the field on which you want to sequence the records (the LastName field in this example), then click the *Sort Ascending* button on the Database toolbar. The *Sort Descending* button is appropriate for numeric fields such as salary, if you want to display the records with the highest value listed first.

The operations can be done in any order; that is, you can filter a table to show only selected records, then you can sort the filtered table to display the records in a different order. Conversely, you can sort a table and then apply a filter. It does not matter which operation is performed first, and indeed, you can go back and forth between the two. You can also filter the table further, by applying a second (or third) criterion; for example, click in a cell containing "Good," then click the Filter by Selection button a second time to display the Account Reps with good performance. You can also click the *Remove Filter* button at any time to display all of the records in the complete table.

Figure 1.5c illustrates an alternate and more powerful way to apply a filter known as *Filter by Form*, in which you can select the criteria from a drop-down list, and/or apply multiple criteria simultaneously. However, the real advantage of the Filter by Form command extends beyond these conveniences to two additional capabilities. First, you can specify relationships within a criterion; for example, you can select employees with a salary greater than (or less than) $40,000. Filter by Selection, on the other hand, requires you to specify criteria equal to an existing value. Figure 1.5d displays the filtered table of Chicago employees earning more than $40,000.

A second advantage of the Filter by Form command is that you can specify alternative criteria (such as employees in Chicago *or* employees who are account reps) by clicking the Or tab. (The latter capability is not implemented in Figure 1.5.) Suffice it to say, however, that the availability of the various filter and sort commands enables you to obtain information from a database quickly and easily without having to create a query or report.

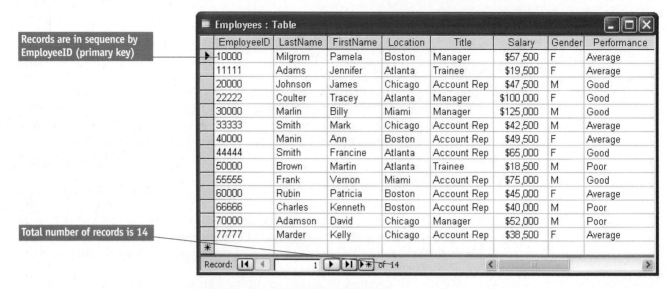

Records are in sequence by EmployeeID (primary key)

Total number of records is 14

(a) The Employees Table (by EmployeeID)

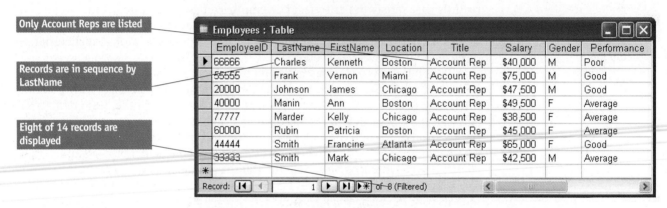

Only Account Reps are listed

Records are in sequence by LastName

Eight of 14 records are displayed

(b) Filtered List (Account Rep by last name)

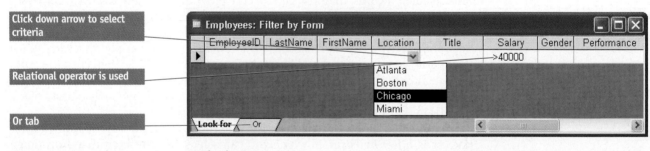

Click down arrow to select criteria

Relational operator is used

Or tab

(c) Filter by Form

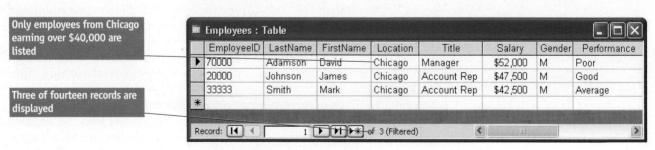

Only employees from Chicago earning over $40,000 are listed

Three of fourteen records are displayed

(d) Filtered List (Chicago employees earning more than $40,000)

FIGURE 1.5 Filters and Sorting

2 Filters and Sorting

Objective To display selected records within a table by applying the Filter by Selection and Filter by Form criteria; to sort the records in a table. Use Figure 1.6 as a guide in the exercise.

Step 1: **Open the Employees Table**

- Start Access as you did in the previous exercise, but this time you will open a different database. Pull down the **File menu** and click the **Open command** to display the Open dialog box.

- Click the **down arrow** in the Look In box to select the drive (**drive C** is recommended rather than drive A) and folder (**Exploring Access**) that contains the **Employee database**.

- Click the **Open button** in the Open dialog box to open the database, then click the **Open button** within the Security Warning dialog box if you see a warning message.

- Click the **Forms button** in the Database window, then double click the **Employees form** to open the form as shown in Figure 1.6a. Click the **Maximize button** so that the Employee form fills the Access window.

- Click the **Add Record button**, then enter data for yourself, using **12345** as the EmployeeID, and your first and last name. You have been hired as an **Account Rep**. Your salary is **$40,000**, you will work in **Miami**, and your performance is **Good**.

- Click the **Print Record button** to print the record containing your data. Click the **Close Form button** to return to the Database window.

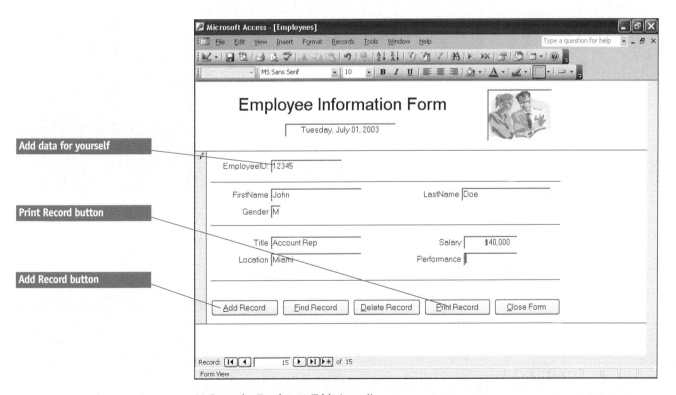

(a) Open the Employees Table (step 1)

FIGURE 1.6 Hands-on Exercise 2

Step 2: **Filter by Selection**

Click field → Filter by Selection

- Click the **Tables button** in the Database window. Double click the **Employees table** to open the table, which should contain 15 records, including the record you added for yourself.

- Click in the Title field of any record that contains the title **Account Rep**, then click the **Filter by Selection button**.

- You should see 9 employees, all of whom are Account Reps, as shown in Figure 1.6b. The status bar indicates that there are 9 records (as opposed to 15) and that there is a filter condition in effect.

- Click in the performance field of any employee with a Good performance (we clicked in the Performance field of the first record), then click the **Filter by Selection button** a second time.

- This time you see 4 employees, each of whom is an Account Rep with a performance evaluation of Good. The status bar indicates that 4 records satisfy this filter condition.

- Click the **Print button** to print the filtered table.

Filter by Form button

Print button

Filter by Selection button

Click in Performance field where entry is Good

Nine records are listed of 15 total records

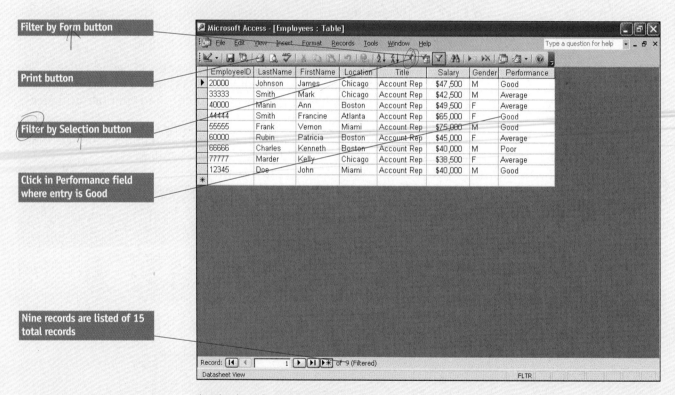

(b) Filter by Selection (step 2)

FIGURE 1.6 Hands-on Exercise 2 *(continued)*

FILTER EXCLUDING SELECTION

The Filter by Selection button on the Database toolbar selects all records that meet the designated criterion. The Filter Excluding Selection command does just the opposite and displays all records that do not satisfy the criterion. First, click the Remove Filter button to remove any filters that are in effect, then click in the appropriate field of any record that contains the value you want to exclude. Pull down the Records menu, click (or point to) the Filter command, then click the Filter Excluding Selection command to display the records that do not meet the criterion.

Step 3: Filter by Form

■ Click the **Filter by Form button** to display the form in Figure 1.6c, where you can enter or remove criteria in any sequence. Each time you click in a field, a drop-down list appears that displays all of the values for the field that occur within the table.

■ Click in the columns for **Title** and **Performance** to remove the criteria that were entered in the previous step. Select the existing entries individually and press the **Del key** as each entry is selected.

■ Click in the cell underneath the **Salary field** and type **>30000** (as opposed to selecting a specific value). Click in the cell underneath the **Location Field**, click the **down arrow**, and select **Chicago**.

■ Click the **Apply Filter button** to display the records that satisfy these criteria. (You should see 4 records.)

■ Click the **Print button** to print the table.

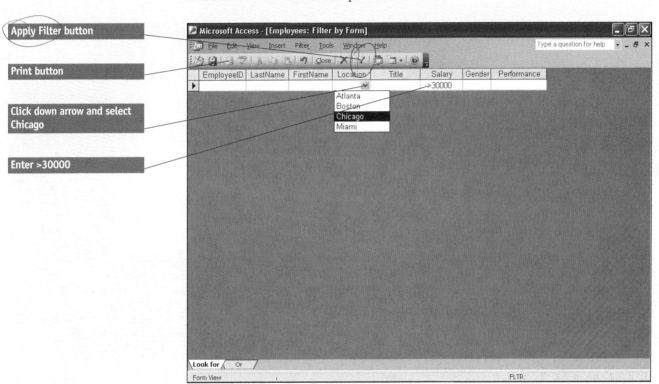

(c) Filter by Form (step 3)

FIGURE 1.6 Hands-on Exercise 2 (*continued*)

FILTER BY FORM VERSUS FILTER BY SELECTION

The Filter by Form command has all of the capabilities of the Filter by Selection command, and provides two additional capabilities. First, you can use relational operators such as >, >=, <, or <=, as opposed to searching for an exact value. Second, you can search for records that meet one of several conditions (the equivalent of an "Or" operation). Enter the first criterion as you normally would, then click the Or tab at the bottom of the window to display a second form in which you enter the alternate criteria. (To delete an alternate criterion, click the associated tab, then click the Delete button on the toolbar.)

Step 4: Sort the Table

- Click the **Remove Filter button** to display the complete table, which contains 15 employee records.

- Click in the **LastName field** of any record, then click the **Sort Ascending button**. The records are displayed in alphabetical (ascending) order by last name as shown in Figure 1.6d.

- Click in the **Salary field** of any record, then click the **Sort Descending button**. The records are in descending order of salary; that is, the employee with the highest salary is listed first.

- Click in the **Location field** of any record, then click the **Sort Ascending button** to display the records by location, although the employees within a location are not in any specific order.

- You can sort on two fields at the same time, provided the fields are next to each other, as described in the next step.

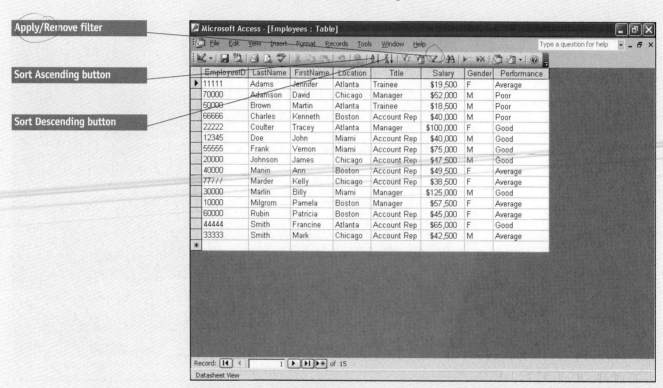

(d) Sort the Table (step 4)

FIGURE 1.6 Hands-on Exercise 2 (*continued*)

THE SORT OR FILTER—WHICH IS FIRST?

It doesn't matter whether you sort a table and then apply a filter, or filter first and then sort. The operations are cumulative. Thus, once a table has been sorted, any subsequent display of filtered records for that table will be in the specified sequence. Alternatively, you can apply a filter, then sort the filtered table by clicking in the desired field and clicking the appropriate sort button. Remember, too, that all filter commands are cumulative, and hence you must remove the filter to see the original table.

Step 5: Sort on Two Fields

- Click the header for the **Location field** to select the entire column. Click and drag the **Location header** so that the Location field is moved to the left of the LastName field.

- Click anywhere to deselect the column, then click on the **Location header** and click and drag to select both the Location header and the LastName Header as shown in Figure 1.6e.

- Click the **Sort Ascending button**. The records are sorted by location and alphabetically within location. (You could extend the sort to three fields such as Location, LastName, and FirstName by selecting all three fields prior to clicking the Sort button.)

- Print the table for your instructor. Close the table, saving the changes when prompted to do so.

> **Click Location header area and drag to select LastName as well**
>
> **Sort Ascending button**

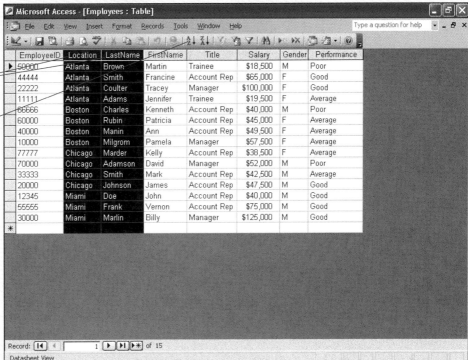

(e) Sort on Two Fields (step 5)

FIGURE 1.6 Hands-on Exercise 2 (*continued*)

REMOVING VERSUS DELETING A FILTER

Removing a filter displays all of the records that are in a table, but it does not delete the filter because the filter is stored permanently with the table. To delete the filter entirely is more complicated than simply removing it. Pull down the Records menu, click Filter, then click the Advanced Filter/Sort command to display a grid containing the criteria for the filter. Clear the Sort and Criteria rows by clicking in any cell containing an entry and deleting that entry, then click the Apply Filter button when all cells are clear to return to the Datasheet view. The Apply Filter button should be dim, indicating that the table does not contain a filter.

Step 6: Print a Report

- Click the **Reports button** in the Database window. Double click the icon for **Employees by Location report**.

- Click the **Maximize button** in the Report Window so that the report takes the entire screen as shown in Figure 1.6f.

- Click the **Zoom button** to toggle to 100% so that you can read the report. The report displays the employees in the same order as the sorted table from step 5. (The sequence for the report is contained in its design specification and does not depend on the sequence of the underlying table.)

- Click the **Print button** on the Report toolbar to print the report for your instructor. Submit all of the printed information to your instructor:
  - ❑ The employee form from step 1
  - ❑ The filtered table from steps 2 and 3
  - ❑ The sorted table from step 5
  - ❑ The Employees by Location report from this step

- Close the report. Exit Access if you do not want to continue with the next exercise at this time.

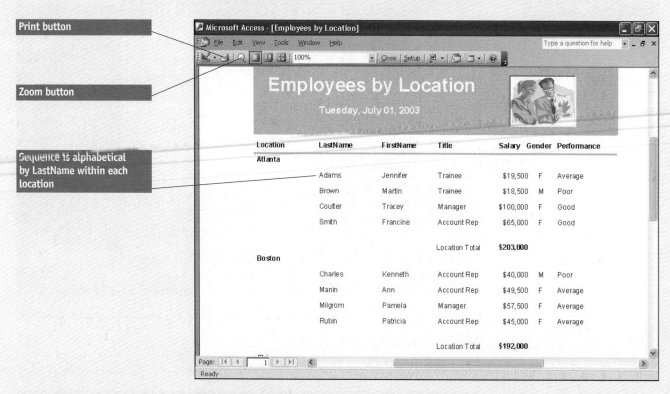

(f) Print a Report (step 6)

FIGURE 1.6 Hands-on Exercise 2 (*continued*)

DATA VERSUS INFORMATION

Data and information are not synonymous although the terms are often used interchangeably. Data is the raw material and consists of the table (or tables) that comprise a database. Information is the finished product. Data is converted to information by selecting (filtering) records, by sequencing (sorting) the selected records, and/or by summarizing data from multiple records. Decisions in an organization are based on information that is compiled from multiple records, as opposed to raw data.

The Bookstore and Employee databases are both examples of simple databases in that they each contained only a single table. The real power of Access, however, is derived from multiple tables and the relationships between those tables. This type of database is known as a *relational database* and is illustrated in Figure 1.7. This figure expands the original Employee database by adding two tables, for locations and titles, respectively.

The Employees table in Figure 1.7a is the same table we used at the beginning of the previous exercise, except for the substitution of a LocationID and TitleID for the location and title, respectively. The Locations table in Figure 1.7b has all of the fields that pertain to each location: LocationID, Location, Address, State, Zipcode, and OfficePhone. One field, the LocationID, appears in both Employees and Locations tables and links the two tables to one another. In similar fashion, the Titles table in Figure 1.7c has the information for each title: the TitleID, Title, Description, EducationRequired, and Minimum and MaximumSalary. The TitleID appears in both the Employees and Titles tables to link those tables to one another.

EmployeeID	LastName	FirstName	LocationID	TitleID	Salary	Gender	Performance
10000	Milgrom	Pamela	L02	T02	$57,500	F	Average
11111	Adams	Jennifer	L01	T03	$19,500	F	Average
20000	Johnson	James	L03	T01	$47,500	M	Good
22222	Coulter	Tracey	L01	T02	$100,000	F	Good
30000	Marlin	Billy	L04	T02	$125,000	M	Good
33333	Smith	Mark	L03	T01	$42,500	M	Average
40000	Manin	Ann	L02	T01	$49,500	F	Average
44444	Smith	Francine	L01	T01	$65,000	F	Good
50000	Brown	Mark	L01	T03	$18,500	M	Poor
55555	Frank	Vernon	L04	T01	$75,000	M	Good
60000	Rubin	Patricia	L02	T01	$45,000	F	Average
66666	Charles	Kenneth	L02	T01	$40,000	M	Poor
70000	Adamson	David	L03	T02	$52,000	M	Poor
77777	Marder	Kelly	L03	T01	$38,500	F	Average

(a) The Employees Table

LocationID	Location	Address	State	Zipcode	OfficePhone
L01	Atlanta	450 Peachtree Road	GA	30316	(404) 333-5555
L02	Boston	3 Commons Blvd	MA	02190	(617) 123-4444
L03	Chicago	500 Loop Highway	IL	60620	(312) 444-6666
L04	Miami	210 Biscayne Blvd	FL	33103	(305) 787-9999

(b) The Locations Table

TitleID	Title	Description	EducationRequired	MinimumSalary	MaximumSalary
T01	Account Rep	A marketing ...	Four year degree	$25,000	$75,000
T02	Manager	A supervisory ...	Four year degree	$50,000	$150,000
T03	Trainee	An entry-level ...	Two year degree	$18,000	$25,000

(c) The Titles Table

FIGURE 1.7 A Relational Database

To obtain information about a specific employee's title or location, you go to the Employees table, then use the LocationID and TitleID to locate the appropriate records in the Locations and Titles tables, respectively. The tables are color coded to emphasize the relationships between them. It sounds complicated, but it is really quite simple and very elegant. More importantly, it enables you to obtain detailed information about any employee, location, or title. To show how it works, we will ask a series of questions that require you to look in one or more tables for the answer. Consider:

Query: At which location does Pamela Milgrom work? What is the phone number of her office?

Answer: Pamela works in the Boston office, at 3 Commons Blvd., Boston, MA, 02190. The phone number is (617) 123-4444.

Did you answer the question correctly? You had to search the Employees table for Pamela Milgrom to obtain the LocationID (L02 in this example) corresponding to her office. You then searched the Locations table for this LocationID to obtain the address and phone number for that location. The process required you to use both the Locations and Employees tables, which are linked to one another through a ***one-to-many relationship***. One location can have many employees, but a specific employee can work at only one location. Let's try another question:

Query: Which employees are managers?

Answer: There are four managers: Pamela Milgrom, Tracey Coulter, Billy Marlin, and David Adamson.

The answer to this question is based on the one-to-many relationship that exists between titles and employees. One title can have many employees, but a given employee has only one title. To answer the query, you search the Titles table for "manager" to determine its TitleID (T02). You then go to the Employees table and select those records that have this value in the TitleID field.

The design of a relational database enables us to extract information from multiple tables in a single query. Equally important, it simplifies the way data is changed in that modifications are made in only one place. Consider:

Query: Which employees work in the Boston office? What is their phone number?

Answer: There are four employees in Boston: Pamela Milgrom, Ann Manin, Patricia Rubin, and Kenneth Charles, each with the same number (617-123-4444).

Once again, we draw on the one-to-many relationship between locations and employees. Thus, we begin in the Locations table where we search for "Boston" to determine its LocationID (L02) and phone number (617 123-4444). Then we go to the Employees table to select those records with this value in the LocationID field.

Query: What change(s) are necessary to accommodate a new telephone number for the Boston office?

Answer: Only one change is necessary. One would open the Locations table, locate the record for Boston, and change the phone number.

This query illustrates the ease with which changes are made to a relational database. There are four employees in Boston, but each employee record contains the LocationID (L02), rather than the actual information for the Boston office. Thus, changing the contents of the appropriate record in the Locations table automatically changes the information for the employees in that location.

We're ready for our next hands-on exercise in which we illustrate the true power of an Access database and its ability to work with multiple tables in a relational database. (The exercise uses the same data as the tables in Figure 1.7.)

3   A Look Ahead

Objective   To open a database with multiple tables; to identify the one-to-many relationships within the database; and to produce reports based on those relationships. Use Figure 1.8 as a guide in the exercise.

Step 1:   **Open the Relationships Window**

- Start Access. Pull down the **File menu** and click the **Open command**. Open the **Look Ahead database** in the **Exploring Access folder**.
- Pull down the **Tools menu** and click the **Relationships command** to open the Relationships window as shown in Figure 1.8a. Pull down the **Relationships menu** and click the **Show Table command** to display the Show Table dialog box.
- Click (select) the **Locations table** (within the Show Table dialog box), then click the **Add button** to add this table to the Relationships window.
- Double click the **Titles** and **Employees tables** to add these tables to the Relationships window. Close the Show Table dialog box.

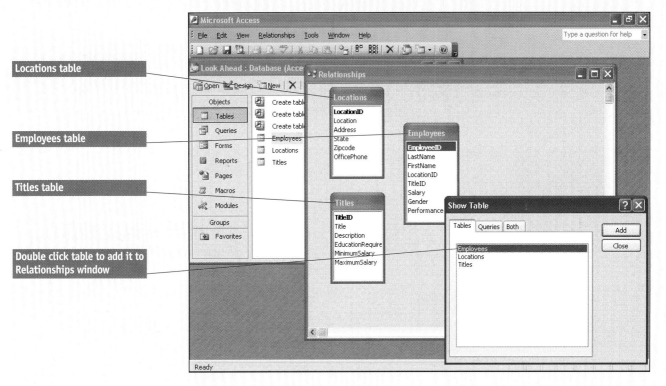

Locations table

Employees table

Titles table

Double click table to add it to Relationships window

(a) Open the Relationships Window (step 1)

FIGURE 1.8   Hands-on Exercise 3

WORK ON DRIVE C

Even in a lab setting, it is preferable to work on the local hard drive, as opposed to a floppy disk. The hard drive is much faster, which is significant when working with the large files associated with Access. More importantly, the capacity of the floppy disk is limited, so that you are likely to crash as the database expands. Work on drive C throughout the exercise, then use Windows Explorer at the end of the exercise to copy the database to a floppy disk that you can take with you.

Step 2: Create the Relationships

- Maximize the Relationships windows so that you have more room in which to work. Click and drag the title bar of each table so that the positions of the tables match those in Figure 1.8b.

- Click and drag the bottom (and/or right) border of each table so that you see all of the fields in each table.

- Click and drag the **LocationID field** in the Locations table field list to the **LocationID field** in the Employees field list. Release the mouse button. You will see the Edit Relationships dialog box.

- Check the box to **Enforce Referential Integrity**. Click the **Create button** to create the relationship.

- Click and drag the **TitleID field** in the Titles table field list to the **TitleID field** in the Employees field list. Release the mouse button. You will see the Edit Relationships dialog box.

- Check the box to **Enforce Referential Integrity** as shown in Figure 1.9b. Click the **Create button** to create the relationship.

- Click the **Save button** on the Relationships toolbar to save the Relationships window, then close the Relationships window.

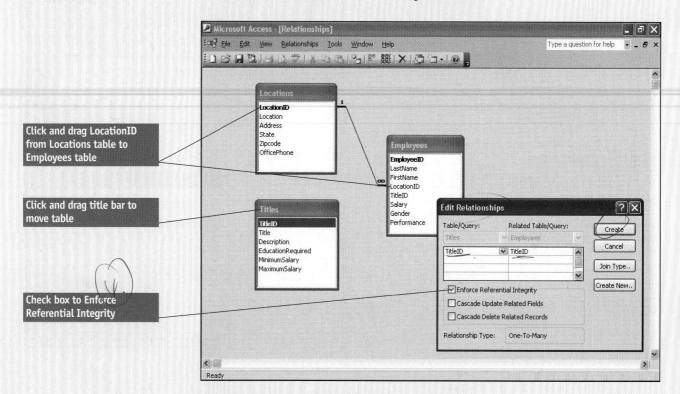

(b) Create the Relationships (step 2)

FIGURE 1.8   Hands-on Exercise 3 (continued)

THE RELATIONSHIPS ARE VISUAL

The tables in an Access database are created independently, then related to one another through the Relationships window. The number 1 and the infinity symbol (∞) appear at the ends of the lines to indicate the nature of the relationship—for example, a one-to-many relationship between the Locations and Employees tables.

Step 3: Referential Integrity

- Double click the **Employees table** to open the table. Maximize the window. Pull down the **Insert** menu and click the **New Record command** (or click the **New Record button** on the Table Datasheet toolbar).

- Enter data for yourself, using <u>12345</u> as the EmployeeID, and your first and last name as shown in Figure 1.8c. Enter an invalid LocationID (e.g., **L44**), then complete the record as shown in the figure.

- Press the **Enter key** when you have completed the data entry, then click **OK** when you see the error message. Access prevents you from entering a location that does not exist.

- Click in the **LocationID field** and enter **L04**, the LocationID for Miami. Press the **down arrow key** to move to the next record, which automatically saves the current record.

- Close the Employees table.

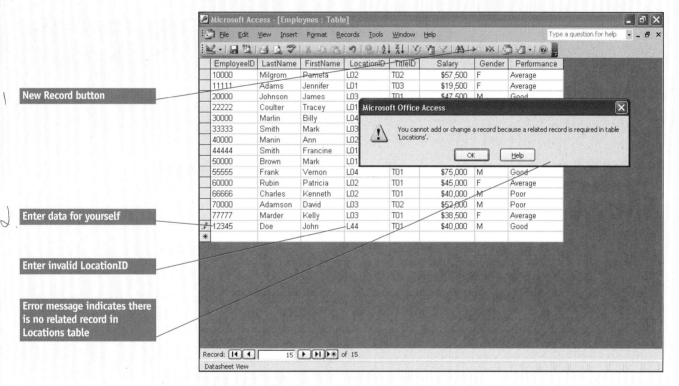

New Record button

Enter data for yourself

Enter invalid LocationID

Error message indicates there is no related record in Locations table

(c) Referential Integrity (step 3)

FIGURE 1.8 Hands-on Exercise 3 (*continued*)

REFERENTIAL INTEGRITY

The tables in a database must be consistent with one another, a concept known as referential integrity. Thus, Access automatically implements certain types of data validation to prevent such errors from occurring. You cannot, for example, enter a record in the Employees table that contains an invalid value for either the LocationID or the TitleID. Nor can you delete a record in the Locations or Titles table if it has related records in the Employees table. Think for a moment what the consequences would be if this type of validation was not imposed on the database.

Step 4: <u>Simplified Data Entry</u>

- Click the **Forms button** in the Database window, then double click the **Employees form** to open this form as shown in Figure 1.8d.

- Click the **Add Record button** (or use the **Alt+A** keyboard shortcut), then click in the text box for the EmployeeID.

- Enter the data for **Bob Grauer** one field at a time, pressing the **Tab key** to move from one field to the next. Click the **down arrow** when you come to the location field to display the available locations, then select (click) **Miami**.

- Press the **Tab key** to move to the Title field, click the **down arrow**, and choose **Account Rep**.

- Complete the data for Bob's record by entering **$150,000**, **M**, and **Excellent** in the Salary, Gender, and Performance fields, respectively.

- Click the **Close Form button** (or use the **Alt+C** keyboard shortcut) when you have finished entering the data.

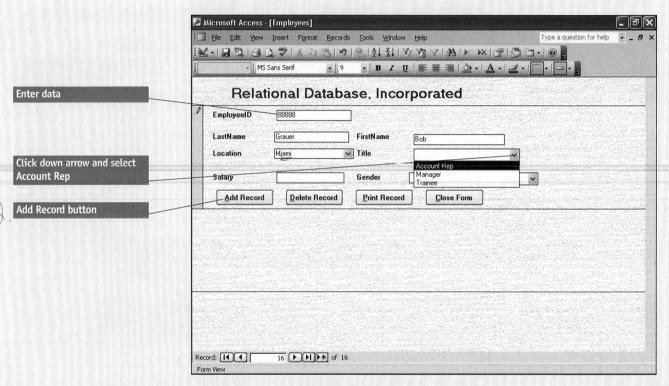

(d) Simplified Data Entry (step 4)

FIGURE 1.8 Hands-on Exercise 3 (*continued*)

SIMPLIFIED DATA ENTRY

The success of any system depends on the accuracy of its data as well as its ease of use. Both objectives are met through a well-designed form that guides the user through the process of data entry and simultaneously rejects invalid responses. The drop-down list boxes for the Location, Title, and Performance fields ensure that the user can enter only valid values in these fields. Data entry is also simplified in these fields in that you can enter just the first letter of a field, then press the Tab key to move to the next field. The command buttons at the bottom of the form provide easy access to basic commands.

Step 5: Print the Employee Master List

Open →

■ Click the **Reports button** in the Database window. Double click the **Employee Master List** report to open the report as shown in Figure 1.8e.

■ Click the **Maximize button** in the Report window so that the report takes the entire desktop. Click the **Zoom button** to view the report at **100%**.

■ The report displays selected fields for every employee in the Employees table. The two new employees, you and Bob Grauer, appear in alphabetical order. Both employees are in the Miami office.

■ The fields for each employee are taken from different tables in the database:
  ❑ The values for last name, first name, salary, and performance are from the Employees table.
  ❑ The name of the location and the office phone are from the Locations table, which is related to the Employees table through the LocationID field that appears in both tables.
  ❑ The employee's title is taken from the Titles table, which is related to the Employees table through the TitleID field that appears in both tables.

■ Click the **Print button** to print the report. Close the Report window.

Ask a Question list box

Print button

Zoom button

Your record and Bob Grauer's record reflect the Miami office

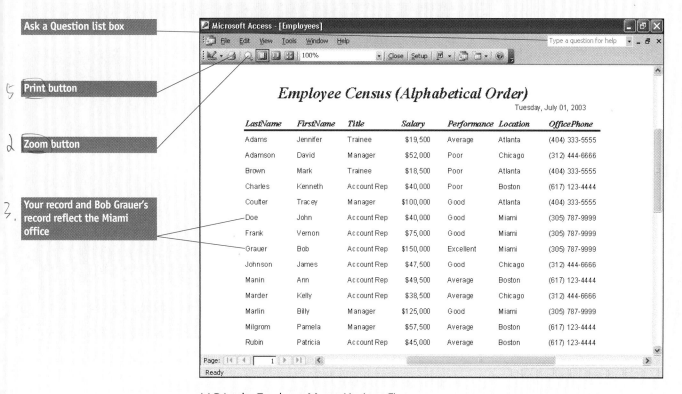

(e) Print the Employee Master List (step 5)

FIGURE 1.8   Hands-on Exercise 3 (continued)

ASK A QUESTION

Click in the "Ask a Question" list box that appears at the right of the document window, enter the text of a question such as "How do I print a report?", press Enter, and Access returns a list of potential Help topics. Click any topic that appears promising to display the detailed information. You can ask multiple questions during an Access session, then click the down arrow in the list box to return to an earlier question, which will return you to the Help topics.

Step 6: Change the Locations Table

open 1.
- Click the **Tables button** in the Database window, then double click the **Locations table** to open this table as shown in figure 1.8f. Maximize the window if necessary.

2
- Click the **plus sign** next to location L04 (Miami) to view the employees in this office. The plus sign changes to a minus sign as the employee records for this location are shown.

3
- Your name appears in this list as does Bob Grauer's. Click the **minus sign** and the list of related records disappears.

4
- Click and drag to select **Miami** (the current value in the Location field). Type **Orlando** and press the **Tab key**. Enter the corresponding values for the other fields: **1000 Kirkman Road, FL, 32801**, and **(407) 555-5555** for the address, state, zip code, and office phone, respectively.

5
- Close the **Locations table**. You have effectively moved the Miami Office to Orlando; i.e., all employees who were assigned to the Miami Office are now working out of Orlando.

Record for Miami is expanded to show related records in Employees table

Change Miami to Orlando

4.
tab.

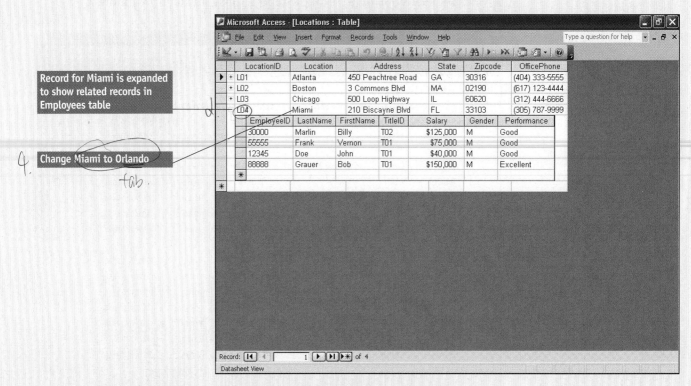

(f) Change the Locations Table (step 6)

FIGURE 1.8 Hands-on Exercise 3 (*continued*)

ADD AND DELETE RELATED RECORDS

Take advantage of the one-to-many relationship between locations and employees (or titles and employees) to add and/or delete records in the Employees table. Open the Locations table, then click the plus sign next to the location where you want to add or delete an employee record. To add a new employee, click in any employee record, click the New Record navigation button, then add the new data. To delete a record, click the record, then click the Delete Record button on the Table Datasheet toolbar. Click the minus sign to close the employee list.

Step 7: Print the Employees by Title Report

- Click the **Reports button** in the Database window, then double click the **Employees by Title report** to open the report shown in Figure 1.8g.

- Click the **Maximize button** in the Report window so that the report takes the entire desktop. Click the **Zoom button** to view the report at **100%**.

- This report lists employees by title, rather than alphabetically. Note that you and Bob Grauer are both listed as Account Reps in the Orlando office; that is, the location of the office was changed in the Locations table, and that change is automatically reflected for all employees assigned to that office.

- Pull down the **File menu** and click the **Page Setup command**. Click the **Margins tab**, then change the left and right margins to **.75 inch** each, so that the report fits on one page. Click **OK**. Print the report for your instructor to show you completed the exercise.

- Close the Report window. Close the Database window. Exit Access. Welcome to the world of relational databases.

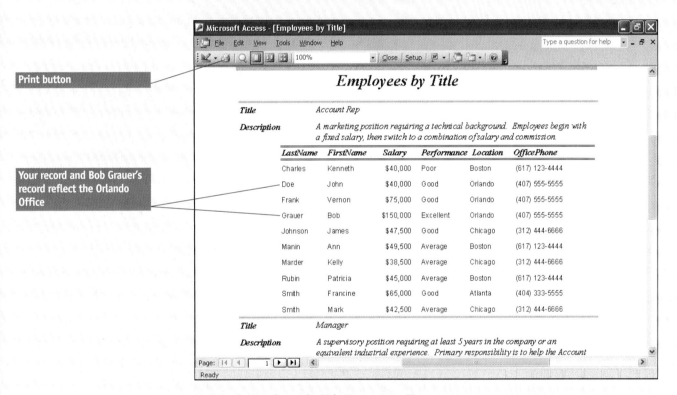

Print button

Your record and Bob Grauer's record reflect the Orlando Office

(g) Print the Employees by Title Report (step 7)

FIGURE 1.8 Hands-on Exercise 3 (*continued*)

BACK UP YOUR WORK

We cannot overemphasize the importance of adequate backup and urge you to back up your important files at every opportunity. Exit Access, start Windows Explorer, then copy the database from drive C to a floppy disk, CD, or zip drive. Remember, you can always get another copy of Microsoft Office, but your data files are irreplaceable. Make duplicate copies of any files that you cannot afford to lose, and then store those files away from your computer. Develop a backup strategy and follow it faithfully!

SUMMARY

An Access database has seven types of objects—tables, forms, queries, reports, pages, macros, and modules. The database window displays these objects and enables you to open an existing object or create a new object.

Each table in the database is composed of records, and each record is in turn composed of fields. Every record in a given table has the same fields in the same order. The primary key is the field (or combination of fields) that makes every record in a table unique. A table can have only one primary key.

A table is displayed in multiple views. The Design view is used to define the table initially and to specify the fields it will contain. The Datasheet view is the view you use to add, edit, or delete records. The PivotTable view is similar in concept to an Excel pivot table and provides a convenient way to summarize data about groups of records. The PivotChart view creates a chart from the associated PivotTable view. (The PivotTable and PivotChart views are discussed in Chapter 4.)

A record selector symbol is displayed next to the current record in Datasheet view and signifies the status of that record. A triangle indicates that the record has been saved. A pencil indicates that the record has not been saved and that you are in the process of entering (or changing) the data. An asterisk appears next to the blank record present at the end of every table, where you add a new record to the table.

Access automatically saves any changes in the current record as soon as you move to the next record or when you close the table. The Undo Current Record command cancels (undoes) the changes to the previously saved record.

A filter is a set of criteria that is applied to a table to display a subset of the records in that table. Microsoft Access lets you filter by selection or filter by form. The application of a filter does not remove the records from the table, but simply suppresses them from view. The records in a table can be displayed in ascending or descending sequence by clicking the appropriate button on the Database toolbar.

No system, no matter how sophisticated, can produce valid output from invalid input. Data validation is thus a critical part of any system. Access automatically imposes certain types of data validation during data entry. Additional checks can be implemented by the user.

A relational database contains multiple tables and enables you to extract information from those tables in a single query. The related tables must be consistent with one another, a concept known as referential integrity. Thus, Access automatically implements additional data validation to ensure the integrity of a database.

Adequate backup is essential when working with an Access database (or any other Office application). A duplicate copy of the database should be created at the end of every session and stored off site (away from the computer).

KEY TERMS

MULTIPLE CHOICE

1. Which sequence represents the hierarchy of terms, from smallest to largest?

   (a) Database, table, record, field
   (b) Field, record, table, database
   (c) Record, field, table, database
   (d) Field, record, database, table

2. Which of the following is true regarding movement within a record (assuming you are not in the first or last field of that record)?

   (a) Press Tab or the right arrow key to move to the next field
   (b) Press Shift+Tab or the left arrow key to return to the previous field
   (c) Both (a) and (b)
   (d) Neither (a) nor (b)

3. You're performing routine maintenance on a table within an Access database. When should you execute the Save command?

   (a) Immediately after you add, edit, or delete a record
   (b) Periodically during a session—for example, after every fifth change
   (c) Once at the end of a session
   (d) None of the above since Access automatically saves the changes as they are made

4. Which of the following objects are contained within an Access database?

   (a) Tables and forms
   (b) Queries and reports
   (c) Macros and modules
   (d) All of the above

5. Which of the following is true about the views associated with a table?

   (a) The Design view is used to create a table
   (b) The Datasheet view is used to add or delete records
   (c) Both (a) and (b)
   (d) Neither (a) nor (b)

6. Which of the following is true of an Access database?

   (a) Every record in a table has the same fields as every other record
   (b) Every table contains the same number of records as every other table
   (c) Both (a) and (b)
   (d) Neither (a) nor (b)

7. Which of the following is *false* about the Open Database command?

   (a) It can be executed from the File menu
   (b) It can be executed by clicking the Open button on the Database toolbar
   (c) It loads a database from disk into memory
   (d) It opens the selected table from the Database window

8. Which of the following is true regarding the record selector symbol?

   (a) A pencil indicates that the current record has already been saved
   (b) A triangle indicates that the current record has not changed
   (c) An asterisk indicates the first record in the table
   (d) All of the above

9. Which view is used to add, edit, and delete records in a table?

   (a) The Design view
   (b) The Datasheet view
   (c) Either (a) or (b)
   (d) Neither (a) nor (b)

10. What does GIGO stand for?

    (a) Gee, I Goofed, OK
    (b) Global Input, Global Output
    (c) Garbage In, Garbage Out
    (d) Gospel In, Gospel Out

... continued

11. Which of the following will be accepted as valid during data entry?

    (a) Adding a record with a duplicate primary key

    (b) Entering text into a numeric field

    (c) Entering numbers into a text field

    (d) Omitting a required field

12. The find and replace values in a Replace command must be:

    (a) The same length

    (b) The same case

    (c) Both (a) and (b)

    (d) Neither (a) nor (b)

13. An Access table containing 10 records, and 10 fields per record, requires two pages for printing. What, if anything, can be done to print the table on one page?

    (a) Print in Landscape rather than Portrait mode

    (b) Decrease the left and right margins

    (c) Both (a) and (b)

    (d) Neither (a) nor (b)

14. Which of the following capabilities is available through Filter by Selection?

    (a) The imposition of a relational condition

    (b) The imposition of an alternate (OR) condition

    (c) Both (a) and (b)

    (d) Neither (a) nor (b)

15. Which of the following best describes the relationship between locations and employees as implemented in the Look Ahead database within the chapter?

    (a) One to one

    (b) One to many

    (c) Many to many

    (d) Impossible to determine

16. A corporate database has a one-to-many relationship between its branch offices and its employees. The Atlanta branch, which currently has 50 employees, is relocating. Where do you enter the new address and phone number?

    (a) In the employee record of the Atlanta branch manager

    (b) In the employee record of every employee who works in Atlanta

    (c) In the Atlanta record in the Branch Office table

    (d) All of the above

17. Which of the following commands can be used to replace all existing occurrences of the abbreviation CIS with Computer Information Systems?

    (a) Find and Replace

    (b) AutoCorrect

    (c) Both AutoCorrect and Find and Replace

    (d) Neither AutoCorrect nor Find and Replace

18. You are looking at an Employee table in Datasheet view. Which of the following requires an ascending sort?

    (a) To list the employees alphabetically by their last name

    (b) To list the employees according to their age with the youngest employee appearing first (an employee's birth date is stored in the table rather than the employee's age)

    (c) Both (a) and (b)

    (d) Neither (a) nor (b)

ANSWERS

1. b	7. d	13. c
2. c	8. b	14. d
3. d	9. b	15. b
4. d	10. c	16. c
5. c	11. c	17. a
6. a	12. d	18. a

PRACTICE WITH ACCESS

1. **The Oscars:** The Academy Awards®, also known as the Oscars®, are given out each year to honor the best efforts in motion pictures for the previous year. We enjoy the movies and we have created a database that contains the Oscar winners in the major categories. Your first task is to update the table in our database to include any additional awards since the publication of our text. Proceed as follows:

   a. Open the *Chapter 1 Practice 1* database in the Exploring Access folder. Click the Forms button and open the Award Winners form shown in Figure 1.9. Maximize the form. Use the navigation bar at the bottom of the form to go to the last record to determine the last year in our table.

   b. Skip this step if the database is current; otherwise, click the hyperlink in the Award Winners form to go to the Oscars site and determine the winners for the years since we published our text. Use the existing form to enter the winners for the six major awards (best picture, best actor and actress, best director, and best supporting actor and actress) into the Award Winners table.

   c. The form should display the most recent year for which data is available. Click the selection area at the left of the form to select this record. Pull down the File menu, click the Print command, then click the option button to print the selected record. Click OK. (You can also click the Print button on the form to print only the current record.) Close the form.

   d. Return to the Database window, click the Tables button and open the Award Winners table. Adjust the column widths (if necessary) so that you see all of the information for each field in each column. Pull down the File menu, click the Page Setup command, and change to landscape printing with one-half-inch margins all around. Use the Print Preview button to see how the table will appear prior to actually printing the table. Unless you change to a font that is too small to read, the data for one year will not fit on one page. Do not print the table. Close the Print Preview window, then close the table.

   e. Return to the Database window. Click the Reports button. Open the Major Winners by Year report and print the first page. (All of the data for a given year appears on the same page.) Close the report.

   f. Add a cover sheet, then submit the form and report to your instructor.

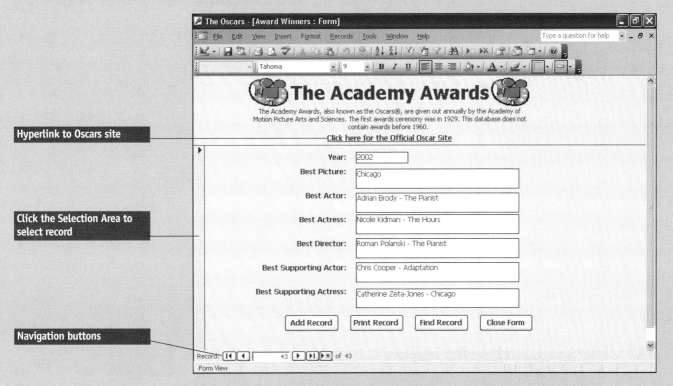

FIGURE 1.9 The Oscars (exercise 1)

2. **Definitely Needlepoint:** The Definitely Needlepoint boutique is owned and operated by four friends who wanted a friendly place to sit and stitch. They opened their store three years ago and it has grown quickly. The friends created a simple database to maintain custom records. It is your job to test the various objects in that database. Open the *Chapter 1 Practice 2* database in the Exploring Access folder and proceed as follows:

   a. Open the Customers form, maximize the form, and click the Add Record button. Enter data for yourself (even if you are not interested in needlepoint) as shown in Figure 1.10. Use customer number C1000 as shown in the figure. Indicate that you are a guild member and that you want to receive all mailings. Print the completed form for your instructor.

   b. Open the Guild Members query and uncheck the Guild Member box for Diane Battle, indicating that she is no longer a guild member. Delete the record for Anita Brockway. Close the query.

   c. Run the Guild Members report, which is based on the modified Guild Members query. Diane Battle is not listed on the report, as she is no longer a guild member. Anita Brockway is not listed either because her record has been permanently deleted from the table. Print the report for your instructor. Close the report.

   d. Open the Customers table. Filter the list by selection so that only the customers from Coral Gables are displayed. Sort the filtered list so that the customers are displayed in alphabetical order by last name. Print the filtered list. Further filter the list so that only the customers from Coral Gables who are priority 1 on the mailing list are displayed. Print this list as well. Submit both filtered lists to your instructor.

   e. Click the Filter by Form tool and delete the existing filters. Use the Filter by Form to filter the list so that only mailing list priority 1 or 2 is shown, but not priority 3. Sort the filtered list in ascending order by zip code. Print the filtered list for your instructor.

   f. Add a cover sheet to identify the assignment and submit all items to your instructor to show you completed the assignment.

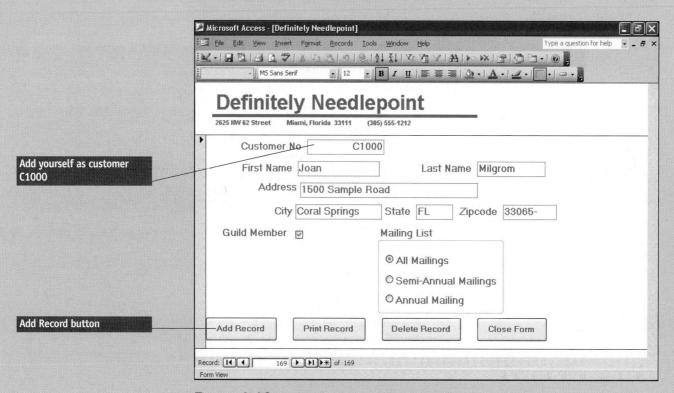

FIGURE 1.10   Definitely Needlepoint (exercise 2)

practice exercises

3. **The United States:** Figure 1.11 displays a table from the *Chapter 1 Practice 3* database in the Exploring Access folder. The database contains statistical data about all 50 states and enables you to create various reports such as the 10 largest states in terms of population or area.

a. Open the *Chapter 1 Practice 3* database, and then open the States table, as shown in Figure 1.11. Pull down the File menu and click the Page Setup command to display the associated dialog box. Select landscape printing and decrease the left and right margins to half an inch. Click the Print Preview button to check that all of the fields for one record fit on one page. Print the table with all fifty records. (The table itself will take two pages because there are 50 records in the table.)

b. Return to the Datasheet view. Click in the Population field of any state, and then click the Sort Descending button to list the states in descending order by population. Click and drag to select the first ten records so that you have selected the ten most populous states.

c. Change to landscape printing, and then click the Print Preview button to check that all of the fields for one record fit on one page. Pull down the File menu, click the Print command, then click the option button to print the selected records (the ten states with the largest population).

d. Return to the table and print the 10 states with the largest area. Which states (if any) appear on both listings? Close the table.

e. Click the Queries button and open the Population Density Query. Which field is present in the query that is not present in the underlying States table? How is this field computed? How many records are displayed? What is the sequence for the displayed records? Close the query.

f. Click the Reports button and print the Population Density Report. How does the information in this report compare to the Population Density Query? Which format do you prefer? Close the report.

g. Print any other reports that are in the database. Are these reports based on a table or a query?

h. Create a cover sheet. Submit the table of all 50 states, the 10 largest states by population, the 10 largest states by area, the Population Density report, as well as any additional reports that were in the database.

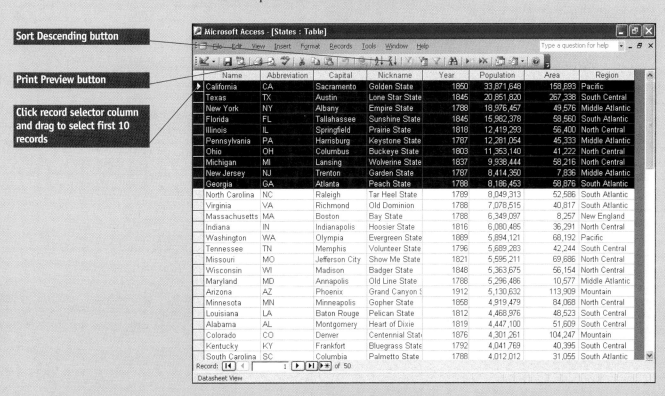

FIGURE 1.11 The United States (exercise 3)

4. **Large Databases:** Figure 1.12 displays a filtered list from the *Chapter 1 Practice 4* database that is found in the Exploring Access folder. The database is similar to the Employee database that was used in the second hands-on exercise, except that it contains more than 300 records. The purpose of this exercise, however, is to provide experience working with a larger database. It also introduces the Format Datasheet command to change the default formatting for an Access table.

   a. Open the *Chapter 1 Practice 4* database and add your name as the last record in the Employees table. Assume that you are employed as an Account Rep in Boston. Your salary is $55,000, and your performance has been rated excellent. Use your own name and an EmployeeID of 99999.

   b. Filter the Employee table to display only the employees who are Account Reps in Boston as shown in Figure 1.12. Sort the filtered list by last name.

   c. Pull down the Format menu and click the Datasheet command to display the Format Datasheet dialog box in Figure 1.12. Note that the default formatting provides for both horizontal and vertical gridlines in silver. Clear the box to print vertical gridlines, and then change the color of the gridlines to dark blue. Click OK to apply the changes to the table.

   d. Pull down the File menu, click the Page Setup command, click the Page tab, and then change to landscape printing. Click the Print Preview button to be sure that the filtered table will fit on a single sheet of paper. Print the table.

   e. Remove the existing filter, then impose a new filter to display only those employees who are managers. Sort this filtered list in alphabetical order by employee number. Print the list of managers.

   f. Pull down the Format menu and explore the additional commands that are available to change the appearance of a table. How do these commands compare to similar commands in Excel? Do you think that the additional formatting enhances the appearance of a table, or are you better off to stick with the default formatting?

   g. Create a cover sheet for this assignment. Submit the printed tables together with your responses to the discussion question to your instructor.

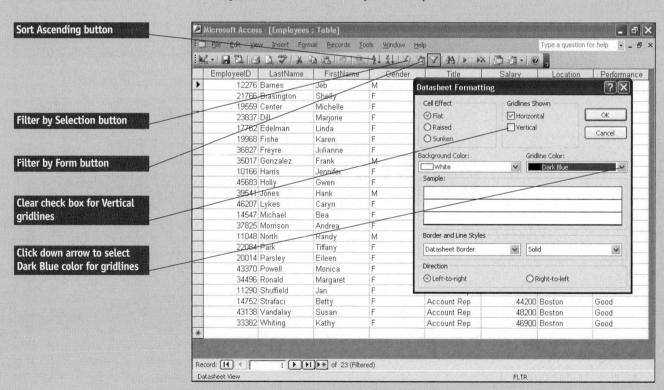

FIGURE 1.12 Large Databases (exercise 4)

5. **The Look Ahead Database:** The Look Ahead database that was introduced at the end of the chapter is a relational database that contains three tables—for employees, locations, and titles. This type of database facilitates data entry in that any change to a specific location or title is made in only one place, in the Locations or Titles tables, respectively, as opposed to having to change every employee record individually. Complete the third hands-on exercise in the chapter, and then make the following additional changes to the database.

a. Open the *Look Ahead* database, open the Locations table, and add a new location. Use L05, Los Angeles, 1000 Rodeo Drive, CA, 90210, and (213) 666-6666 for the LocationID, Location, Address, State, ZipCode, and OfficePhone fields, respectively. Close the Locations table.

b. Open the Titles table and change the title "Manager" to "Supervisor". Change the education requirement for a supervisor to a graduate degree. Close the Titles table.

c. Open the Employees table. Delete the records for Kenneth Charles and David Adamson. Change the location for Bob Grauer and Francine Smith to the Los Angeles Office (location L05). Change Bob's title code to T02 so that Bob becomes the supervisor of the new office. Close the Employees table.

d. Open the Employees form and use it to add two employees, Linda Laquer and Paul Frank, to the Los Angeles office. Both employees are Account Reps and start at $50,000. These are new employees, so no performance data is available. Assign a unique EmployeeID to each person. Is it easier to use the Employees table or the Employees form to modify data?

e. Print all three reports in the database after the changes to the various tables have been made. (The second page of the Employees by Location report is shown in Figure 1.13 after the changes to the various tables have been made.) Submit all three reports to your instructor.

f. Create a new report that displays the relationships within the database. Pull down the Tools menu and click Relationships to open the Relationships window, then pull down the File menu and click the Print Relationships command to display the Print Preview screen of a report that displays the contents of the Relationships window. Print this report for your instructor.

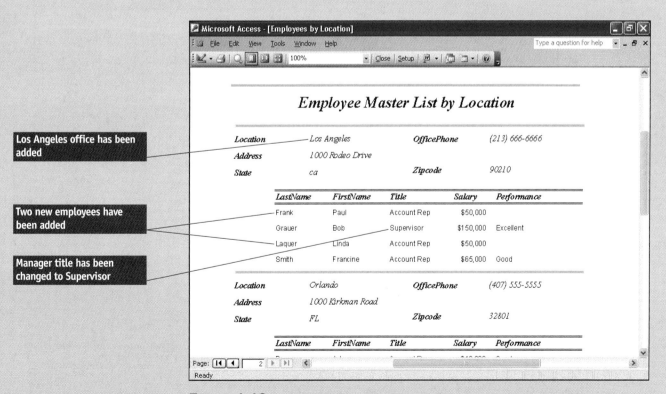

FIGURE 1.13 The Look Ahead Database (exercise 5)

6. **Peppy's Restaurants:** The Peppy's Restaurant chain is operated by individual franchisees throughout the state of Florida. Each restaurant offers the same menu, but differs in the size of the restaurant and the type of service offered. The data about all of the restaurants is maintained at corporate headquarters in an Access database. Your assignment is to open the *Chapter 1 Practice 6* database in the Exploring Access folder and test the various objects. Proceed as follows:

a. Open the Restaurants form as shown in Figure 1.14. Add R0011 to the table, entering your name as the franchisee. Use any data that you think is appropriate. Print the record that you just added for your restaurant by clicking the Print button within the form. Close the form.

b. Open the Restaurants table. Change the annual sales for restaurant R0003 to $1,000,000. Delete restaurant R0007.

c. Print the Restaurants table for your instructor. Does all of the information for each restaurant fit on one page? Close the table. Return to the Database window, click the Report tab, and print the All Restaurants report. Does all of the information for each restaurant fit on one page? Do you see the restaurant that you just added in both places? Close the report.

d. Click the Queries button in the Database window, then open both queries. Do both queries display all of the records in the Restaurants table? Does either query contain a field that is not present in the Restaurants table? Close the queries.

e. Click the Reports button and print the two reports that correspond to the queries in part (d) for your instructor. Which is the more attractive way to display information, a query or a report?

f. Return to the Database window. Pull down the File menu, click the Database Properties command, and then click the Contents tab. Which objects are in the database? How does this information compare to the information that is displayed in the Database Window?

g. Submit all of the printed information to your instructor together with your answers to the discussion questions. Add a cover sheet to complete the assignment.

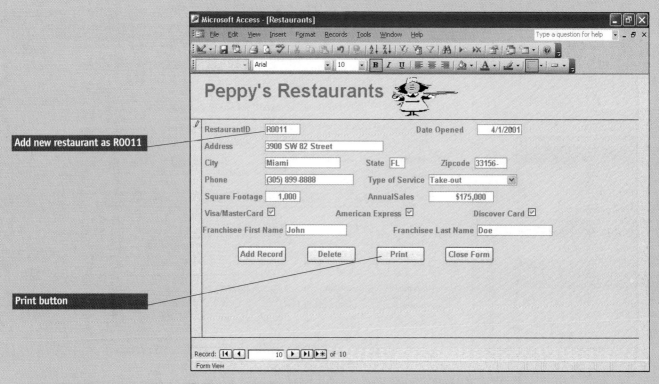

FIGURE 1.14   Peppy's Restaurants (exercise 6)

7. **Peppy's Relational Database:** The Peppy's Restaurant chain has replaced the database from the previous exercise with a relational database that contains separate tables for restaurants and franchisees. We have created a new database for you, as opposed to asking you to convert the previous database to a relational format. Nevertheless, there is still work for you to do. Accordingly, open the *Chapter 1 Practice 7* database and do the following:

a. Create the one-to-many relationship between franchisees (i.e., owners) and restaurants as shown in Figure 1.15. The company encourages individuals to operate more than one restaurant, but a specific restaurant is run by only one franchisee.

b. Open the Franchisees form and add yourself as Franchisee F008. Use any data that you deem appropriate. (You do not have to enter the same information as in the previous problem.)

c. Open the Restaurants form and add restaurant R0011, using any data that you deem appropriate. You must, however, assign yourself (F008) as the franchisee.

d. Change the FranchiseeID in restaurants 9 and 10 to F008 so that you will be associated with these restaurants as well.

e. Print the Master Restaurant List report, which displays all restaurants in order of Restaurant ID. Print the Restaurant by Franchisee report, which lists the franchisees in order together with the restaurants they operate. Submit both reports to your instructor as proof you did the exercise.

f. Create a new report that displays the relationships within the database. Pull down the Tools menu and click Relationships to open the Relationships window, then pull down the File menu and click the Print Relationships command to display the Print Preview screen of a report that displays the contents of the Relationships window. Print this report for your instructor.

g. What is referential integrity and how does it pertain to Peppy's Relational Database? What happens if you assign a restaurant to a franchisee that does not exist? What happens if you attempt to delete a franchisee who owns multiple restaurants? Submit all of the printed information to your instructor together with the answers to the discussion questions.

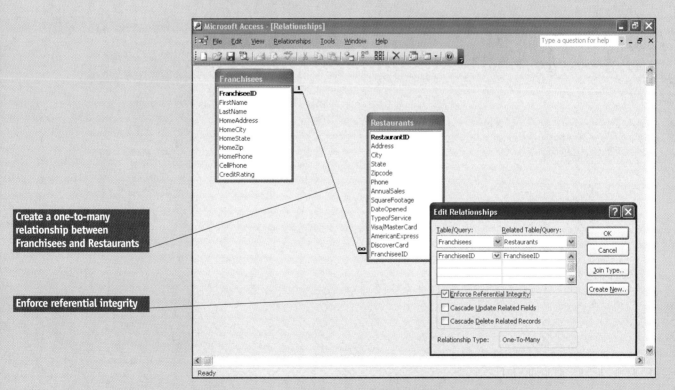

FIGURE 1.15 Peppy's Relational Database (exercise 7)

8. **Metro Zoo:** The newly opened Metro Zoo is the pride of your city. A relational database has been created with three tables: exhibits, trainers, and animals. There is a one-to-many relationship between exhibits and animals. One exhibit can have many different animals, but a specific animal is assigned to only one exhibit. A one-to-many relationship also exists between trainers and animals. One trainer can have many animals, but a specific animal has only one trainer. Open the *Chapter 1 Practice 8* database and proceed as follows:

a. Pull down the Tools menu, click the Relationships command, and create the one-to-many relationships that exist in the system. Be sure to enforce referential integrity for both relationships.

b. Open the Trainers form. Add yourself as a new trainer, using any information you deem appropriate. (Do not enter the TrainerID as this number is entered automatically.)

c. Open the Animals form to add the record for the mountain tapir as shown in Figure 1.16. (Do not enter the AnimalID as this value is entered automatically.) Assign the tapir to the Americas exhibit and assign yourself as the trainer. Locate the Galapagos tortoise, black rhinoceros, and gorilla (AnimalID of 3, 11, and 12, respectively), and assign yourself as the trainer for these animals as well. Close the form.

d. Click the Reports button in the database and print all four reports to verify that you have entered the data correctly. Which of these reports is based on data from more than one table?

e. Create a fifth report that displays the relationships within the database. Pull down the Tools menu and click Relationships to open the Relationships window, then pull down the File menu and click the Print Relationships command to display the Print Preview screen of a report that displays the contents of the Relationships window. Print this report for your instructor.

f. What is referential integrity, and how does it apply to the Metro Zoo database? What happens, for example, if you attempt to assign an animal to an exhibit that does not exist? What happens if you attempt to delete a trainer who has several employees? Submit all of the printed information to your instructor.

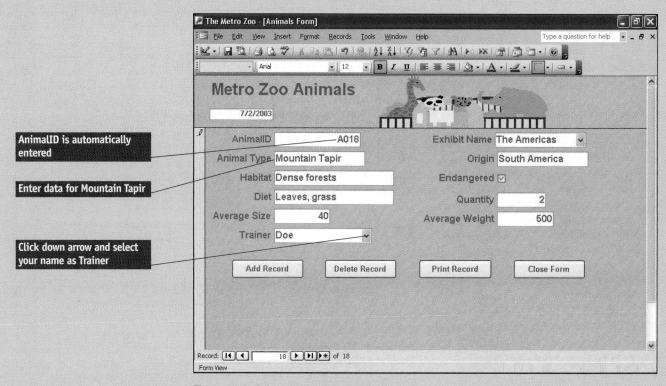

FIGURE 1.16   Metro Zoo (exercise 8)

Planning for Disaster

This exercise has nothing to do with databases per se, but it is perhaps the most important assignment of all, as it deals with the question of backup. Do you have a backup strategy? Do you even know what a backup strategy is? You had better learn, because eventually you will wish you had one. You will erase a file, your system may become infected by a virus, or worse yet suffer a hardware failure in which you are unable to access the hard drive. The problem always seems to occur the night before an assignment is due. Describe in 250 words or less the backup strategy you plan to implement in conjunction with your work in this course.

Your First Consultant's Job

Go to a real installation, such as a doctor's or an attorney's office, the company where you work, or the computer lab at school. Determine the backup procedures that are in effect, then write a one-page report indicating whether the policy is adequate, and if necessary, offering suggestions for improvement. Your report should be addressed to the individual in charge of the business, and it should cover all aspects of the backup strategy—that is, which files are backed up and how often, and what software is used for the backup. Smaller organizations and professional offices (e.g., physicians and attorneys) are apt to be the installations that are most in need of assistance.

Changing Menus and Toolbars

Microsoft Office enables you to display a series of short menus that contain only basic commands. The additional commands are made visible by clicking the chevron that appears at the bottom of the menu. New commands are added to the menu as they are used, and conversely, other commands are removed if they are not used. A similar strategy is followed for the Standard and Formatting toolbars that are displayed on a single row, and thus do not show all of the buttons at one time. The intent is to simplify Office for the new user by limiting the number of visible commands. The consequence, however, is that the individual is not exposed to the new commands, and hence may not use Office to its full potential. Which set of menus do you prefer? How do you switch from one set to the other? Summarize your thoughts in a short note to your instructor.

Garbage In, Garbage Out

Your excellent work in this course has earned you an internship in the registrar's office. Your predecessor has created a student database that appears to work well, but in reality it has several problems in that the report on student grade point averages does not produce the expected information. Open the *Chapter 1 Mini Case GIGO* database in the Exploring Access folder and print the existing report. Study the results and see if you can determine the errors in the underlying data that create the erroneous output. What would you do in the future to prevent similar errors from reoccurring?

The Common User Interface

One of the most significant benefits of the Office environment is the common user interface, which provides a sense of familiarity when you go from one application to another—for example, when you go from Excel to Access. How many similarities can you find between these two applications? Which menus are common to both? Which keyboard shortcuts? Which formatting conventions? Which toolbar icons? Which shortcut menus?

Tables and Forms:
Design, Properties, Views, and Wizards

CASE STUDY
KAHAKAI VILLAS

Kahakai Villas, owned and operated by Kahakai Development, Inc. in Kona, Hawaii, has just broken ground on the construction of a 156-unit condominium. Kahakai Villas promises its future residents the ultimate in oceanside living, with unobstructed ocean views from every unit, in a lush tropical setting to create a true spirit of aloha. Residents choose from one, two, or three bedrooms. The base price ranges from $150,000 to $350,000, with the final price determined by the location and amenities selected. A carport is standard, whereas a garage is optional. Approximately half of the villas are adjacent to the private beach owned by the development company. The complex will also contain a spectacular swimming pool with units close to the pool paying a premium.

Joseph Murray, the project sales manager, wants to create an Access database to track the sales prospects who visit the site. He has created a simple questionnaire to capture demographic data (name, address, telephone, and so on) as well as the client's preferences in a villa. Joseph inquires about the client's price range, preferred floor, number of bedrooms, if they want a garage or carport, how soon they would be interested in moving (6 months, 9 months, 1 year, and 1 year plus), and if they would be living in the villa year-round or would be interested in offering their villa up for rental. He also leaves a space to make notes for himself. ■

Your assignment is to read the chapter and create a database for Mr. Murray. You can use the Table Wizard as the basis of your Customers (Prospects) table, but you will have to modify the table to include all of the required data as per the case description, and further to set the properties of the individual fields as appropriate. You will also need to create a form in which to enter the data. The Form Wizard is a good place to start, but you will have to modify the result to include command buttons, a suitable piece of clip art in the form header, and appropriate formatting throughout. Use the completed form to enter information about your instructor and the villa that he or she desires.

This chapter introduces a new case study, that of a student database, which we use to present the basic principles of table and form design. Tables and forms are used to input data into a system from which information can be produced. The value of that information depends entirely on the quality of the underlying data, which must be both complete and accurate. We begin, therefore, with a conceptual discussion emphasizing the importance of proper design and develop essential guidelines that are used throughout the book.

After the design has been developed, we turn our attention to implementing that design in Access. We show you how to create a table using the Table Wizard, then show you how to refine its design by changing the properties of various fields within the table. We also stress the importance of data validation during data entry.

The second half of the chapter introduces forms as a more convenient way to enter and display data. We introduce the Form Wizard to create a basic form, then show you how to modify that form to include command buttons, a list box, a check box, and an option group.

As a student you are well aware that your school maintains all types of data about you. They have your Social Security number. They have your name and address and phone number. They know whether or not you are receiving financial aid. They know your major and the number of credits you have completed. Think for a moment about the information your school requires, then write down all of the data needed to produce that information. This is the key to the design process. You must visualize the output the end user will require to determine the input to produce that output. Think of the specific fields you will need. Try to characterize each field according to the type of data it contains (such as text, numbers, or dates) as well as its size (length).

Our solution is shown in Figure 2.1, which may or may not correspond to what you have written down. The order of the fields within the table is not significant. Neither are the specific field names. What is important is that the table contain all necessary fields so that the system can perform as intended.

Field Name	Type
SSN	Text
FirstName	Text
LastName	Text
Address	Text
City	Text
State	Text
PostalCode	Text
PhoneNumber	Text
Major	Text
BirthDate	Date/Time
FinancialAid	Yes/No
Gender	Text
Credits	Number
QualityPoints	Number
DateAdmitted	Date/Time
E-mail	Text
International	Yes/No
HomePage	Hyperlink

FIGURE 2.1 The Students Table

Figure 2.1 may seem obvious upon presentation, but it does reflect the results of a careful design process based on three essential guidelines:

1. Include all of the necessary data

2. Store data in its smallest parts

3. Do not use calculated fields

Each guideline is discussed in turn. As you proceed through the text, you will be exposed to many applications that help you develop the experience necessary to design your own systems. Design is an important skill. Yes, you want to learn how to use Access, but you must first understand how to design a database and its tables if you are to use Access effectively.

Include the Necessary Data

How do you determine the necessary data? The best way is to create a rough draft of the reports you will need, then design the table so that it contains the fields necessary to create those reports. In other words, ask yourself what information will be expected from the system, then determine the data required to produce that information. Consider, for example, the type of information that can and cannot be produced from the table in Figure 2.1:

- You can contact a student by mail or by telephone. You cannot, however, contact the student's parents if the student lives on campus or has an address different from that of his or her parents.

- You can calculate a student's grade point average (GPA) by dividing the quality points by the number of credits. You cannot produce a transcript listing the courses a student has taken.

- You can calculate a student's age from his or her date of birth. You cannot determine how long the student has been at the university because the date of admission is not in the table.

Whether or not these omissions are important depends on the objectives of the system. Suffice it to say that you must design a table carefully, so that you are not disappointed when the database is implemented. *You must be absolutely certain that the data entered into a system is sufficient to provide all necessary information.* Think carefully about all of the reports you are likely to want, then be sure to capture the data to create those reports.

DESIGN FOR THE NEXT 100 YEARS

Your system will not last 100 years, but it is prudent to design as though it will. It is a fundamental law of information technology that systems evolve continually and that information requirements will change. Try to anticipate the future needs of the system, then build in the flexibility to satisfy those demands. Include the necessary data at the outset, and be sure that the field sizes are large enough to accommodate future expansion.

Store Data in Its Smallest Parts

The design in Figure 2.1 divides a student's name into two fields (first name and last name) to reference each field individually. You might think it easier to use a single field consisting of both the first and last name, but that approach is inadequate. Consider, for example, the list shown on the next page in which the student's name is stored as a single field:

List is in alphabetical order by first name

Allison Foster
Brit Reback
Carrie Graber
Danielle Ferrarro
Evelyn Adams
Frances Coulter

The first problem in this approach is one of flexibility, in that you cannot separate a student's first name from her last name. You could not, for example, create a salutation of the form "Dear Allison" or "Dear Ms. Foster" because the first and last name are not accessible individually. (In actuality you could write a procedure to divide the name field in two, but that is well beyond the capability of the Access novice.)

A second difficulty is that the list of students cannot be put into true alphabetical order because the last name begins in the middle of the field. Indeed, whether you realize it or not, the names in the list are already in alphabetical order (according to the design criteria of a single field) because sorting always begins with the leftmost position in a field. Thus the "A" in Allison comes before the "B" in Brit, and so on. The proper way to sort the data is on the last name, which can be done only if the last name is stored as a separate field. This illustrates the importance of storing data in its smallest parts.

CITY, STATE, AND ZIP CODE: ONE FIELD OR THREE?

The city, state, and zip code should always be stored as separate fields. Any type of mass mailing requires you to sort on zip code to take advantage of bulk mail. Other applications may require you to select records from a particular state or zip code, which can be done only if the data is stored as separate fields. The guideline is simple—store data in its smallest parts.

Avoid Calculated Fields

A *calculated field* is a field whose value is derived from a formula or function that references an existing field or combination of fields. Calculated fields should not be stored in a table because they are subject to change, waste space, and are otherwise redundant.

A student's Grade Point Average (GPA) is an example of a calculated field since it is computed by dividing the number of quality points by the number of credits. Thus it is unnecessary to store GPA in the Students table, because the table contains the fields on which the GPA is based. In other words, Access is able to calculate the GPA from these fields whenever it is needed, which is much more efficient than doing it manually. Imagine, for example, having to manually enter new values for credits and quality points and then having to recalculate the GPA for 10,000 students each semester.

BIRTH DATE VERSUS AGE

A person's age and date of birth provide equivalent information, as one is calculated from the other. It might seem easier, therefore, to store the age rather than the birth date, and thus avoid the calculation. That would be a mistake because age changes continually (and would need to be updated continually), whereas the date of birth remains constant. Similar reasoning applies to an employee's length of service versus date of hire.

CREATING A TABLE

There are two ways to create a table. The easier way is to use the *Table Wizard*, an interactive coach that lets you choose from many predefined tables. The Table Wizard asks you questions about the fields you want to include in your table, then creates the table for you. Alternatively, you can create a table yourself by defining every field in the table. Regardless of how a table is created, you can modify it to include a new field or to delete an existing field.

Every field has a *field name* to identify the data that is entered into the field. The field name should be descriptive of the data and can be up to 64 characters in length, including letters, numbers, and spaces. We do not, however, use spaces in our field names, but use uppercase letters to distinguish the first letter of a new word. This is consistent with the default names provided by Access in its predefined tables.

Every field also has a *data type* that determines the type of data that can be entered and the operations that can be performed on that data. Access recognizes nine data types:

- A *Number field* contains a value that can be used in a calculation, such as the number of credits a student has earned. The contents of a number field are restricted to numbers, a decimal point, and a plus or minus sign.

- A *Text field* stores alphanumeric data, such as a student's name or address. It can contain alphabetic characters, numbers, and/or special characters (e.g., an apostrophe in O'Malley). Fields that contain only numbers but are not used in a calculation (e.g., Social Security Number, telephone number, or zip code) should be designated as text fields. A text field can hold up to 255 characters.

- A *Memo field* can be up to 65,535 characters long. Memo fields are used to hold lengthy, descriptive data (several sentences or paragraphs).

- A *Date/Time field* holds formatted dates or times (e.g., mm/dd/yy) and allows the values to be used in date or time arithmetic.

- A *Currency field* can be used in a calculation and is used for fields that contain monetary values.

- A *Yes/No field* (also known as a Boolean or Logical field) assumes one of two values, such as Yes or No, or True or False, or On or Off.

- An *OLE Object field* contains an object created by another application. OLE objects include pictures, sounds, or graphics.

- An *AutoNumber field* is a special data type that causes Access to assign the next consecutive number each time you add a record. The value of an AutoNumber field is unique for each record in the file, and thus AutoNumber fields are frequently used as the primary key.

- A *Hyperlink field* stores a Web address (URL). All Office documents are Web-enabled so that you can click a hyperlink and display the associated Web page.

Primary Key

The *primary key* is a field (or combination of fields) that makes each record in a table unique. The primary key is not required, but is highly recommended. There can be only one primary key per table.

A person's name is not used as the primary key because names are not unique. A Social Security Number, on the other hand, is unique and is a frequent choice for the primary key, as in the Students table in this chapter. The primary key emerges naturally in many applications, such as a part number in an inventory system, or the ISBN in the Books table of Chapter 1. If there is no apparent primary key, a new field can be created with the AutoNumber field type.

Views

A table has multiple views. The Datasheet view is the view you used in Chapter 1 to add, edit, and delete records. The Design view is the view you will use in this chapter to create (and modify) a table. The ***PivotTable view*** provides a convenient way to summarize data about groups of records. The ***PivotChart view*** displays a chart of the associated PivotTable view. (The PivotTable view and PivotChart view were introduced in Access 2002 and did not exist in previous versions. Both views are discussed in detail in Chapter 4.)

Figure 2.2a shows the Datasheet view corresponding to the table in Figure 2.1. (The horizontal scroll bar indicates that not all of the fields are visible.) The ***Datasheet view*** displays the record selector symbol for the current record (a pencil or a triangle). It also displays an asterisk in the record selector column next to the blank record at the end of the table.

Figure 2.2b shows the Design view of the same table. The ***Design view*** displays the field names in the table, the data type of each field, and the properties of the selected field. The Design view also displays a key indicator next to the field (or combination of fields) designated as the primary key.

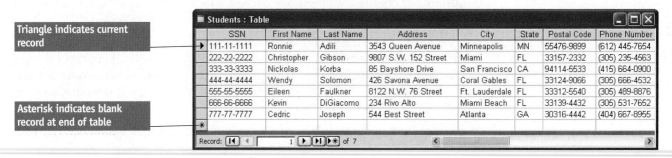

Triangle indicates current record

Asterisk indicates blank record at end of table

(a) Datasheet View

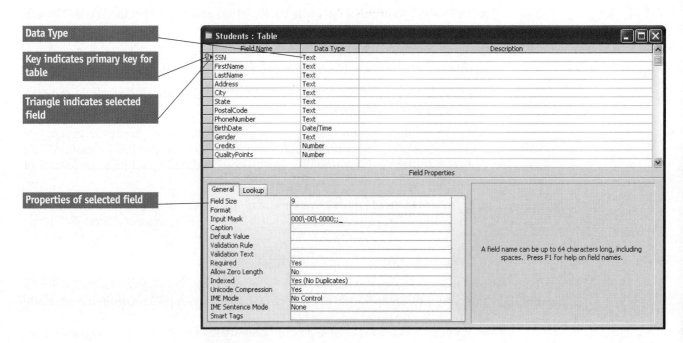

Data Type

Key indicates primary key for table

Triangle indicates selected field

Properties of selected field

(b) Design View

FIGURE 2.2 The Views of a Table

Properties

A ***property*** is a characteristic or attribute of an object that determines how the object looks and behaves. Every Access object (tables, forms, queries, and reports) has a set of properties that determine the behavior of that object. The properties for an object are displayed and/or changed in a ***property sheet***, which is described in more detail later in the chapter.

Each field has its own set of properties that determine how the data in the field is stored and displayed. The properties are set to default values according to the data type, but can be modified as necessary. The properties are displayed in the Design view and described briefly below:

- The ***Field Size property*** adjusts the size of a text field or limits the allowable value in a number field. Microsoft Access uses only the amount of space it needs even if the field size allows a greater number.

- The ***Format property*** changes the way a field is displayed or printed, but does not affect the stored value.

- The ***Input Mask property*** facilitates data entry by displaying literal characters, that are displayed but not stored, such as hyphens in a Social Security number or slashes in a date. It also imposes data validation by ensuring that the data entered by the user fits within the mask.

- The ***Caption property*** specifies a label other than the field name for forms and reports.

- The ***Default Value property*** automatically enters a designated (default) value for the field in each record that is added to the table.

- The ***Validation Rule property*** rejects any record in which the data entered does not conform to the specified rules for data entry.

- The ***Validation Text property*** specifies the error message that is displayed when the validation rule is violated.

- The ***Required property*** rejects any record that does not have a value entered for this field.

- The ***Allow Zero Length property*** allows text or memo strings of zero length.

- The ***Indexed property*** increases the efficiency of a search on the designated field. (The primary key in a table is always indexed.)

- The ***Unicode Compression property*** is set to "Yes" by default for Text, Memo, and Hyperlink fields to store the data more efficiently.

- The ***IME Mode*** and ***IME Sentence Mode properties*** refer to the Input Method Editor for East Asian languages and are not discussed further.

There is no need to memorize the list of properties because they are readily available in the Design view of a table. And, as you may have guessed, it's time for our next hands-on exercise, in which you create a new database. We begin with the Table Wizard, then switch to the Design view to add additional fields and modify selected properties of various fields within the table.

CHANGE THE DEFAULT FOLDER

The default folder is the folder Access uses to retrieve (and save) a database unless it is otherwise instructed. To change the default folder, pull down the Tools menu, click Options, then click the General tab in the Options dialog box. Enter the name of the default database folder (e.g., C:\Exploring Access), then click OK to accept the settings and close the Options dialog box. The next time you access the File menu, the default folder will reflect the change.

1   Creating a Table

Objective   To create a new database; to use the Table Wizard to create a table; to add and delete fields of an existing table. Use Figure 2.3 as a guide.

Step 1:   **Create a New Database**

- Click the **Start button**, click the **All Programs button**, click **Microsoft Office**, then click **Microsoft Access** to start the program.

- Click **Create a new file** at the bottom of the Getting Started task pane, then click **Blank database** in the New File task pane. (If the task pane is not open, click the **New button** on the toolbar.)

- You should see the File New Database dialog box shown in Figure 2.3a.

- Click the **drop-down arrow** on the Save In list box and select the appropriate drive. Double click the **Exploring Access folder**.

- Click in the **File Name text box** and drag to select **db1**. Type **My First Database** as the name of the database you will create. Click the **Create button**.

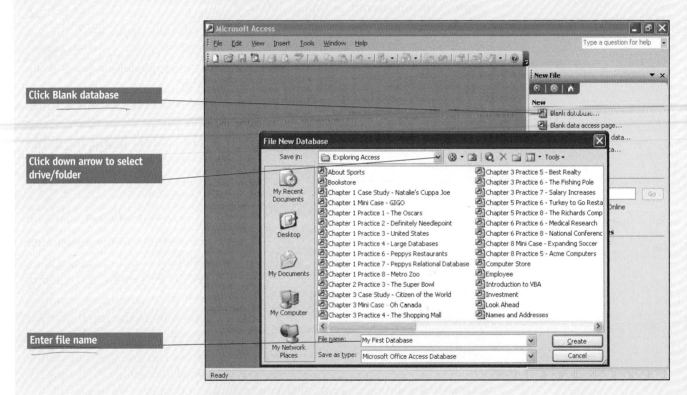

(a) Create a New Database (step 1)

FIGURE 2.3   Hands-on Exercise 1

FILE FORMATS

Access 2002 (Office XP) introduced a new file format that was continued in Access 2003. Access 2000, however, cannot read the new format; thus, it is convenient to save files in the older Access 2000 format to maintain compatibility with anyone using Microsoft Office 2000. Pull down the Tools menu, click Options, click the Advanced tab, and change the Default File Format to Access 2000. Use Help to learn about converting from one file format to another.

Step 2: The Table Wizard

- The Database window for My First Database should appear on your monitor. The Tables button is selected by default.
- Double click the icon to **Create table by using wizard** to start the Table Wizard as shown in Figure 2.3b. Click the **Business option button**.
- Click the **down arrow** on the Sample Tables list box to scroll through the available tables until you can select (click) the **Students table**. (The Students table is found near the bottom of the list.)
- The **StudentID field** is already selected in the Sample Fields list box. Click the **> button** to enter this field into the list of fields for the new table.
- Enter the additional fields for the new table by selecting the field and clicking the **> button** (or by double clicking the field). The fields to enter are **FirstName, LastName, Address, City**, and **StateOrProvince**.
- Click the **Rename Field button** after adding the StateOrProvince field to display the Rename Field dialog box. Enter **State** to shorten the name of this field. Click **OK** to accept the new name and close the dialog box.

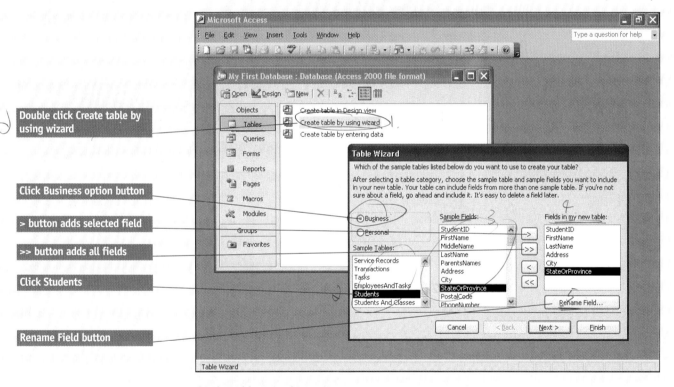

Double click Create table by using wizard

Click Business option button

> button adds selected field

>> button adds all fields

Click Students

Rename Field button

(b) The Table Wizard (step 2)

FIGURE 2.3 Hands-on Exercise 1 (*continued*)

WIZARDS AND BUTTONS

Many wizards present you with two open list boxes and expect you to copy some or all fields from the list box on the left to the list box on the right. The > and >> buttons work from left to right. The < and << buttons work in the opposite direction. The > button copies the selected field from the list box on the left to the box on the right. The >> button copies all of the fields. The < button removes the selected field from the list box on the right. The << removes all of the fields.

Step 3: The Table Wizard Continued

and 1
- Add **PostalCode** and **PhoneNumber** (you may need to click the **down arrow** to scroll). Click **Next**.

2
- The next screen in the Table Wizard asks you to name the table and determine the primary key.
  - ❑ Accept the Wizard's suggestion of **Students** as the name of the table.
  - ❑ Make sure that the option button **Yes, set a primary key for me** is selected as shown in Figure 2.3c.
  - ❑ Click **Next** to accept both of these options.

-finish . 3
- The final screen in the Table Wizard asks what you want to do next.
  - ❑ Click the option button to **Modify the table design**.
  - ❑ Click the **Finish command button**.

"student" -save . 4
table .
- The Students table should appear in Design view. Pull down the **File menu** and click **Save** (or click the **Save button** on the Table Design toolbar) to save the table within the database.

- The Table Wizard provided an easy way to create the table initially. You can now modify the table in Design view as described in the next several steps.

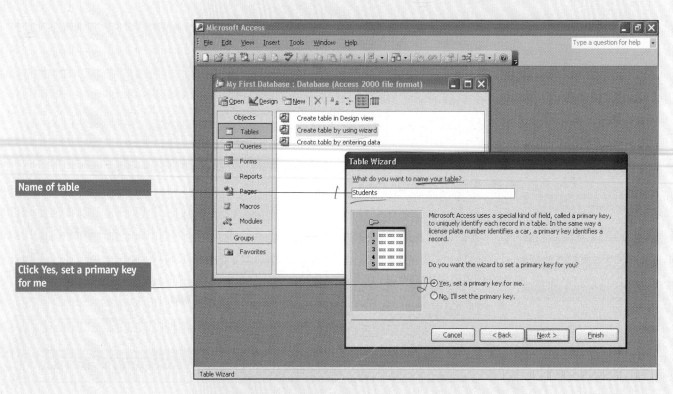

Name of table

Click Yes, set a primary key for me

(c) The Table Wizard Continued (step 3)

FIGURE 2.3   Hands-on Exercise 1 *(continued)*

YOU DON'T HAVE TO USE THE TABLE WIZARD

There is no requirement to use the Table Wizard, especially if you are creating a table that is very different from those available through the wizard. Go to the Database window, click the Tables button, then double click the option to Create Table in Design view. Enter the field name for the first field, select the field type, then modify the field properties as necessary. Continue to work in this fashion as you enter the remaining fields into the table. See practice exercises 4, 6, and 8 at the end of the chapter.

Modify table.

Step 4: Add the Additional Fields

- Add fields.
  ↳ BirthDATE.

1. ■ Click the **Maximize button** to give yourself more room to work. Click the cell immediately below the last field in the table (PhoneNumber). Type **BirthDate** as shown in Figure 2.3d.

move to 'data column'

2. ■ Press the **Tab key** to move to the Data Type column. Click the **down arrow** on the drop-down list box. Click **Date/Time.** (You can also type the first letter of the field type such as **D** for Date/Time, **T** for Text, or **N** for number.)

- Add fields.

3. ■ Add the remaining fields to the Students table.
   - ❏ Add **Gender** as a Text field.
   - ❏ Add **Credits** as a Number field.
   - ❏ Add **QualityPoints** as a Number field. (There is no space in the field name.)

4. ■ The additional fields are unique to our application and were not available in the wizard.

Save

5. ■ Click the **Save button** to save the table.

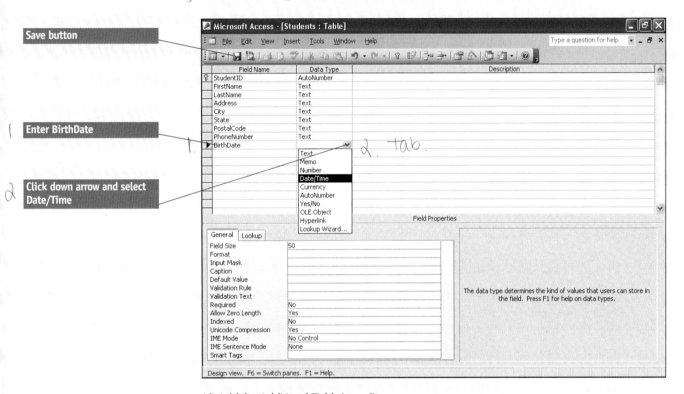

Save button

Enter BirthDate

Click down arrow and select Date/Time

(d) Add the Additional Fields (step 4)

FIGURE 2.3 Hands-on Exercise 1 (*continued*)

NUMBERS AS TEXT FIELDS

The numeric field type should be restricted to fields on which you perform calculations, such as a student's credits or quality points. This implies that fields such as Social Security number, zip code, and telephone number are defined as text fields even though they contain numbers, as opposed to alphabetic characters. Look closely within the Students table that was created by the Table Wizard and you will see that PostalCode and PhoneNumber have been defined as text fields. (The additional characters that appear within a field, such as hyphens in a Social Security number, are entered as an input mask and are not stored within the field.)

Step 5: Change the Primary Key

right click

— Add field
(↓ SNN)

↓ insert
Rows

- Point to the first field in the table and click the **right mouse button** to display the shortcut menu in Figure 2.3e. Click **Insert Rows**.

- Click the **Field Name column** in the newly inserted row. Type **SSN** (for Social Security Number) as the name of the new field. Press **Enter**. The data type will be set to Text by default.

- Click the **Required box** in the Properties area. Click the **drop-down arrow** and select **Yes**.

- Click in the Field Name column for **SSN**, then click the **Primary Key button** on the Table Design toolbar to change the primary key to Social Security Number. The primary key symbol has moved to SSN.

Delete fields

- Point to the **StudentID field** in the second row. Click the **right mouse button** to display the shortcut menu. Click **Delete Rows** to remove this field from the table definition.

- Save the table.

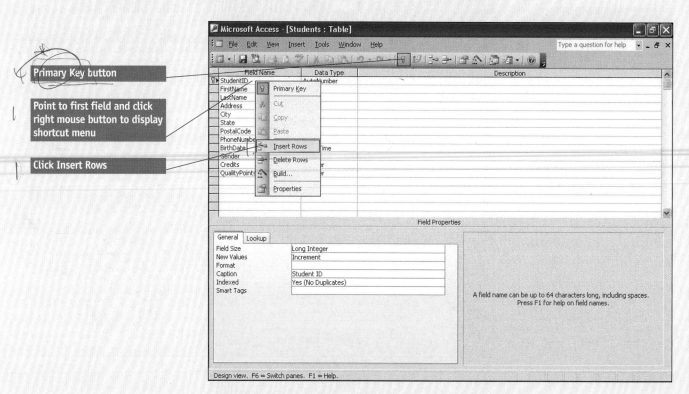

(e) Change the Primary Key (step 5)

FIGURE 2.3 Hands-on Exercise 1 (*continued*)

INSERTING OR DELETING FIELDS

To insert or delete a field, point to an existing field, then click the right mouse button to display a shortcut menu. Click Insert Rows or Delete Rows to add or remove a field as appropriate. To insert (or delete) multiple fields, point to the field selector to the left of the field name, click and drag the mouse over multiple rows to extend the selection, then click the right mouse button to display a shortcut menu.

Step 6: Create an Input Mask

- Click the field selector column for **SSN**. Click the **Input Mask box** in the Properties area. (The box is currently empty.)

- Click the **Build button** to display the Input Mask Wizard. Click **Yes** if asked to save the table. Click **Social Security Number** in the Input Mask Wizard dialog box as shown in Figure 2.3f.

- Click the **Try It** text box and enter a Social Security number to see how the mask works. If necessary, press the **left arrow key** until you are at the beginning of the text box, then enter a Social Security number (digits only). Click the **Finish command button** to accept the input mask. Click in the text box for the Field Size property and change the field size to **9**.

- Click the field selector column for **BirthDate**, then follow the steps detailed above to add an input mask. (Choose the **Short Date** format.) Click **Yes** if asked whether to save the table.

- Set an appropriate input mask for the telephone number as well. Change the field size to **10**.

- Save the table.

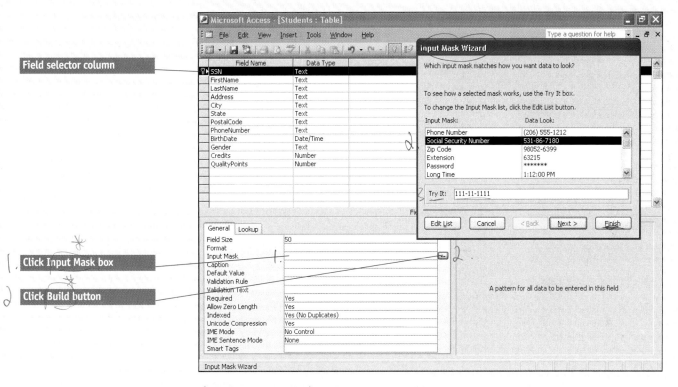

(f) Create an Input Mask (step 6)

FIGURE 2.3 Hands-on Exercise 1 (*continued*)

CREATE YOUR OWN INPUT MASK

The Input Mask imposes character-by-character data validation by requiring that data be entered in a specific way. The Social Security mask, for example, 000\-00\-0000, specifies a zero to require a numeric value from 0 to 9. The character following the slash (a hyphen in this example) is an insertion character and appears within the field during data entry but is not stored. You can create your own input masks for text fields by using the characters "L" to require a letter, or "A" to require either a letter or a digit. Use the Help command for additional information.

Step 7: Change the Field Properties

- Click the field selector column for the **FirstName field**. Click in the text box for the **Field Size property** and change the field size to **15**. Change the **Required property** to **Yes**.

- Select the **LastName field**. Set the **Field Size property** to **20** and the **Required property** to **Yes**.

- Select the **State field.** Set the **Field Size property** to two. Click the **Format box** in the Properties Area. Type a > sign to display the data in uppercase as shown in Figure 2.3g. Click in the **InputMask property** and type **LL** to require letters, as opposed to digits.

- Select the **Credits field**. Click the **Field Size box** in the Properties area, click the **down arrow** to display the available field sizes, then click **Integer**. Click in the **Default property box** and delete the default value of zero.

- Set the Field Size and Default properties for the **QualityPoints field** to match those of the Credits field.

- Save the table.

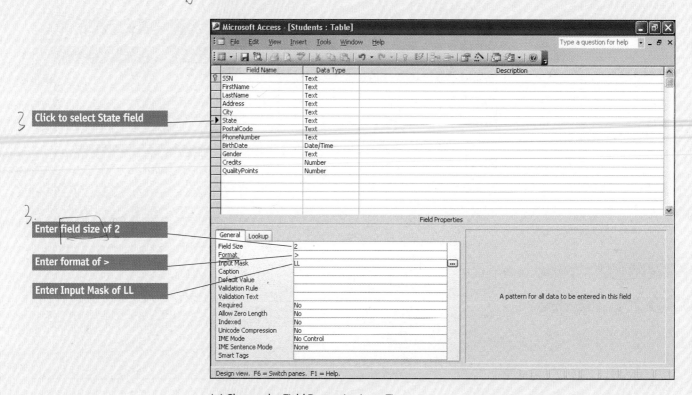

(g) Change the Field Properties (step 7)

FIGURE 2.3 Hands-on Exercise 1 (continued)

THE FIELD SIZE PROPERTY

The field size property should be set to the smallest possible setting because smaller data sizes are processed more efficiently. A text field can hold from 0 to 255 characters (50 is the default). Number fields which do not contain a decimal value can be set to Byte, Integer, or Long Integer field sizes, which hold values up to 255, 32,767, or 2,147,483,647, respectively. (Click in the Field Size box for a Number field and press F1 for more information.)

Step 8: Add a Validation Rule

- Data validation is implemented in several ways. You can set the Required property to Yes to ensure that a value is entered and/or you can create an input mask to accept only certain characters. You can also set the Validation Rule property.

- Select the **Gender field** as shown in Figure 2.3h. Click the **Field Size box** and change the field size to **1**.

- Click the **Format box** in the Properties area. Type a > sign to display the data in uppercase letters.

- Click the **Validation Rule box**. Type =**"M" or "F"** to accept only these values on data entry. Click the **Validation Text box**, and type **You must specify M or F**. (This message explains the error to the user.)

- Check that the required property is set to "No" so that gender is not required. If the user enters a value, however, it must be "M" or "F".

- Save the table.

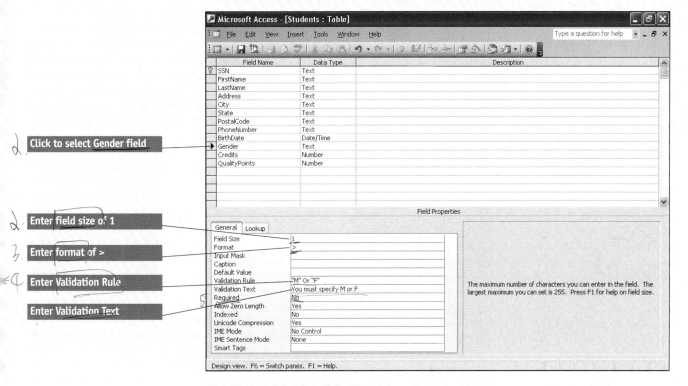

Click to select Gender field

Enter field size of 1

Enter format of >

Enter Validation Rule

Enter Validation Text

(h) Add a Validation Rule (step 8)

FIGURE 2.3 Hands-on Exercise 1 (*continued*)

VALIDATE THE INCOMING DATA

No system, no matter how sophisticated, can produce valid output from invalid input—in other words, "garbage in, garbage out." It is absolutely critical, therefore, that you take the time to validate the data as it is entered to ensure the quality of the output. Some validation is already built in by Access. You cannot, for example, enter duplicate values for a primary key, nor can you enter text into a numeric field. Other validation is built in at the initiative of the developer by setting various field properties in Design view.

Step 9: Print the Students Table

- Pull down the **View menu** and click **Datasheet View** to change to the Datasheet view as shown in Figure 2.3i. Enter data for yourself. Note the input masks that appear in conjunction with the Social Security number, phone number, and birth date.

- Pull down the **File menu** and click the **Page Setup command** to display the Page Setup dialog box. Click the **Page tab** and change to **Landscape printing**.

- Click the **Margins tab**. Change the left and right margins to **.5 inch**. Click **OK**.

- Click the **Print Preview button** to view the table to check that it fits on one page. (If not, return to the Datasheet view and reduce the column widths as necessary.)

- Pull down the **File menu**, click the **Print command**, and click **OK** to print the table. Close the Print Preview window. Close the Students table. Click **Yes** if prompted to save the changes to the table.

- Pull down the **File menu** and click the **Exit command** if you do not want to continue with the next exercise at this time.

Print Preview button

Enter data for yourself

Click and drag border to change width of column

Change left and right margins to 0.5″

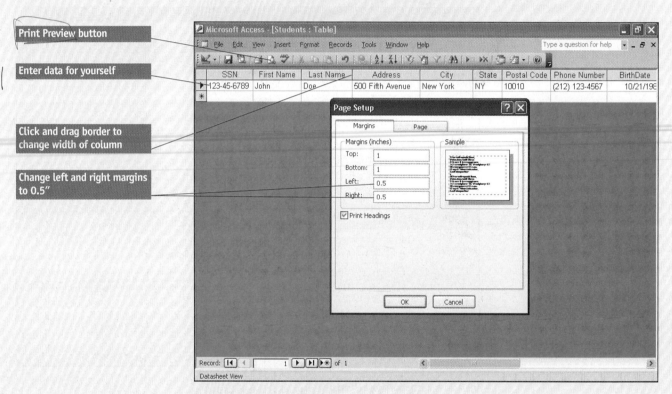

(i) Print the Students Table (step 9)

FIGURE 2.3 Hands-on Exercise 1 *(continued)*

CHANGE THE FIELD WIDTH—ACCESS AND EXCEL

Drag the border between field names to change the displayed width of a column. You can also double click the right border of a field name to change the width of the column to accommodate the widest entry in that column. This is the same convention that is followed in Microsoft Excel. Look for other similarities between the two applications. For example, you can click within a field, then click the Sort Ascending or Sort Descending buttons (in tables with multiple records) on the toolbar to display the records in the indicated sequence.

FORMS

A *form* provides an easy way to enter and display the data stored in a table. You type data into a form, such as the one in Figure 2.4, and Access stores the data in the corresponding (underlying) table in the database. One advantage of using a form (as opposed to entering records in the Datasheet view) is that you can see all of the fields in a single record without scrolling. A second advantage is that a form can be designed to resemble a paper form, and thus provide a sense of familiarity for the individuals who actually enter the data.

A form has different views, as does a table. The ***Form view*** in Figure 2.4a displays the completed form and is used to enter or modify the data in the underlying table. The ***Design view*** in Figure 2.4b is used to create or modify the form. A form also provides access to the PivotTable view and PivotChart view.

All forms contain ***controls*** (objects) that accept and display data, perform a specific action, decorate the form, or add descriptive information. There are three types of controls—bound, unbound, and calculated. A ***bound control*** (such as the text boxes in Figure 2.4a) has a data source (a field in the underlying table) and is used to enter or modify the data in that table.

An ***unbound control*** has no data source. Unbound controls are used to display titles, labels, lines, graphics, or pictures. Note, too, that every bound control in Figure 2.4a is associated with an unbound control (or label to identify the control). The bound control for Social Security number, for example, is preceded by a label (immediately to the left of the control) that indicates to the user the value that is to be entered. An unbound control is also used for the title of the form.

A ***calculated control*** has as its data source an expression rather than a field. An ***expression*** is a combination of operators (e.g., +, −, *, and /), field names, constants, and/or functions. A student's Grade Point Average (GPA in Figure 2.4a) is an example of a calculated control because it is computed by dividing the number of quality points by the number of credits.

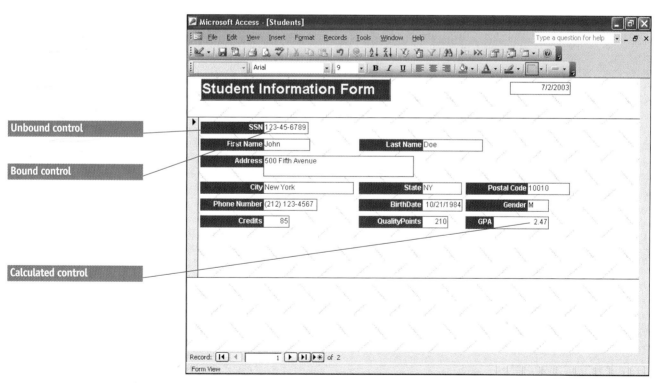

(a) Form View

FIGURE 2.4   Forms

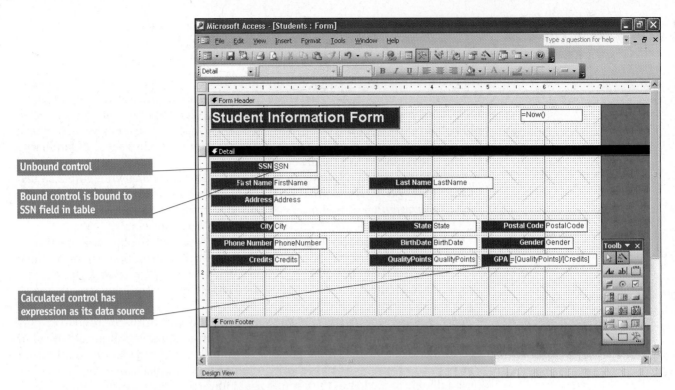

Unbound control

Bound control is bound to SSN field in table

Calculated control has expression as its data source

(b) Design View

FIGURE 2.4   Forms *(continued)*

Properties

As previously stated, a property is a characteristic or attribute of an object that determines how the object looks and behaves. Every control in a form has its own set of properties, just as every field in a table has its own set of properties. The properties for a control are displayed in a property sheet, as shown in Figure 2.5.

Figure 2.5a displays the property sheet for the Form Header Label. There are many different properties (note the vertical scroll bar) that control every aspect of the label's appearance. The properties are determined automatically as the object is created; that is, as you move and size the label on the form, the properties related to its size and position (Left, Top, Width, and Height in Figure 2.5a) are established for you.

Other actions, such as various formatting commands, set the properties that determine the font name and size (Arial and 18 point in Figure 2.5a). You can change the appearance of an object in two ways—by executing a command to change the object on the form, which in turn changes the property sheet, *or* by changing the property within the property sheet, which in turn changes the object's appearance on the form.

Figure 2.5b displays the property sheet for the bound SSN control. The name of the control is SSN. The source for the control is the SSN field in the Students table. Thus, various properties of the SSN control, such as the input mask, are inherited from the SSN field in the underlying table. Note, too, that the list of properties in Figure 2.5b, which reflects a bound control, is different from the list of properties in Figure 2.5a for an unbound control. Some properties, however (such as Left, Top, Width, and Height, which determine the size and position of an object), are present for every control and determine its location on the form.

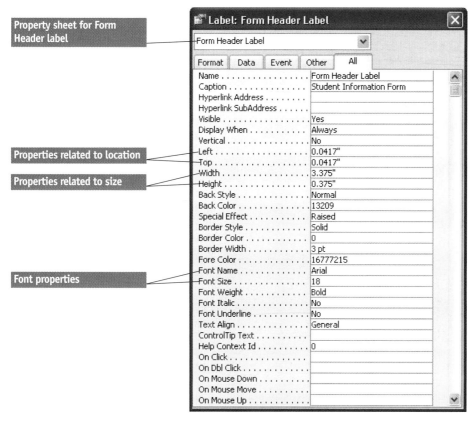

Property sheet for Form Header label

Properties related to location

Properties related to size

Font properties

(a) From Header Label (unbound control)

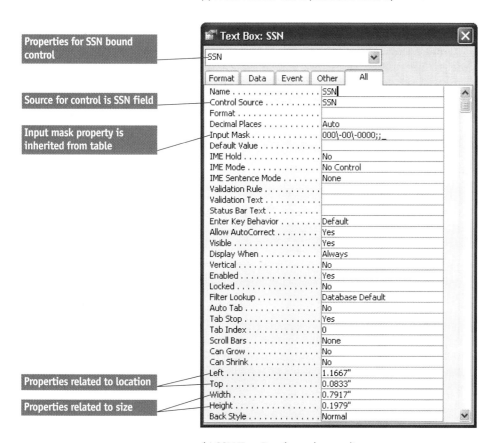

Properties for SSN bound control

Source for control is SSN field

Input mask property is inherited from table

Properties related to location

Properties related to size

(b) SSN Text Box (bound control)

FIGURE 2.5 Property Sheets

AutoForms and the Form Wizard

The easiest way to create a form is by selecting one of several predefined *AutoForms*. Double click the Columnar Autoform, for example, and you are presented with a form that contains all of the fields in the underlying table or query. (Queries are discussed in Chapter 3.) The *Form Wizard* gives you greater flexibility because you can select the fields you want and/or choose a different style from the default style provided by the AutoForm. The wizard asks you a series of questions, then builds the form according to your answers.

Figure 2.6a displays the New Form dialog box, where you choose AutoForm or select the Form Wizard, but either way you have to specify the underlying table or query. If you choose one of the AutoForm layouts, you're finished; that is, the form will be created automatically, and you can go right to the Design view to customize the form. Choosing the Form Wizard provides greater flexibility because you can select the fields you want in Figure 2.6b, the layout in Figure 2.6c, and the style in Figure 2.6d. It is at that point that you go to the Design view to further customize the form.

Modifying a Form

The Form Wizard (or an AutoForm) provides an excellent starting point, but you typically need to customize the form by adding other controls (e.g., the calculated control for GPA) and/or by modifying the controls that were created by the wizard. Each control is treated as an object, and moved or sized like any other Windows object. In essence, you select the control, then click and drag to resize the control or position it elsewhere on the form. You can also change the properties of the control through buttons on the various toolbars or by displaying the property sheet for the control and changing the appropriate property. Consider:

- *To select a bound control and its associated label (an unbound control),* click either the control or the label. If you click the control, the control has sizing handles and a move handle, but the label has only a move handle. If you click the label, the opposite occurs; that is, the label will have both sizing handles and a move handle, but the control will have only a move handle.

- *To size a control,* click the control to select the control and display the sizing handles, then drag the sizing handles in the appropriate direction. Drag the handles on the top or bottom to size the box vertically. Drag the handles on the left or right side to size the box horizontally. Drag the handles in the corner to size both horizontally and vertically.

- *To move a control and its label,* click and drag the border of either object. To move either the control or its label, click and drag the move handle (a tiny square in the upper left corner) of the appropriate object.

- *To change the properties of a control,* point to the control, click the right mouse button to display a shortcut menu, then click Properties to display the property sheet. Click the text box for the desired property, make the necessary change, then close the property sheet.

- *To select multiple controls,* press and hold the Shift key as you click each successive control. The advantage of selecting multiple controls is that you can modify the selected controls at the same time rather than working with them individually.

There is a learning curve, and it may take you a few extra minutes to create your first form. Everything you learn about forms, however, is also applicable to reports. Subsequent exercises will go much faster. And, as you may have guessed, it's time for our next hands-on exercise.

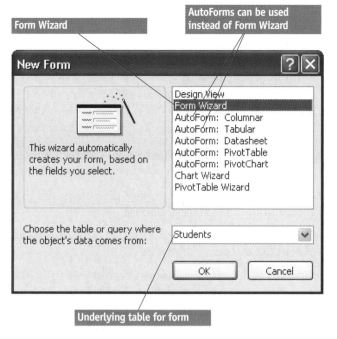

(a) Specify the Underlying Table

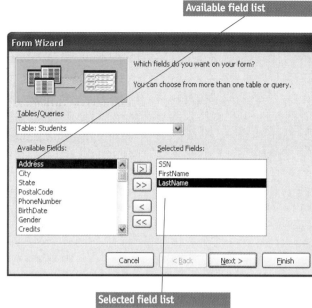

(b) Select the Fields

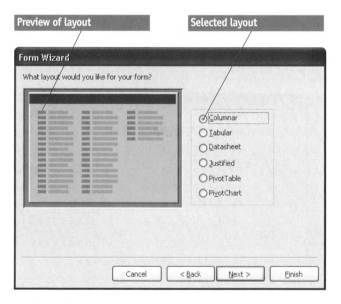

(c) Choose the Layout

(d) Choose the Style

FIGURE 2.6 The Form Wizard

TRY THE AUTOFORM FIRST

Go to the Database window, click the Forms button, then click the New button to display the New Form dialog box. Click the drop-down arrow in the Table or Query list box to select the object on which the form is based, then double click one of the AutoForm entries to create the form. If you don't like the result, don't bother to save the form. You have lost all of 30 seconds and can start again with the Form Wizard.

2 Creating a Form

Objective To use the Form Wizard to create a form; to move and size controls within a form; to use the completed form to enter data into the associated table.

Step 1: **Open the Database**

- Start Access. The **My First database** from the previous exercise should appear in the list of databases in the Open section in the task pane. Click the link to open the database.

- If the database is not listed or the task pane is not open, pull down the **File menu**, and click the **Open command** to open the database.

- Click the **Forms button** in the Database window. Click the **New command button** to display the New Form dialog box as shown in Figure 2.7a.

- Click **Form Wizard** in the list box. Click the **drop-down arrow** to display the available tables and queries in the database on which the form can be based.

- Click **Students** to select the table from the previous exercise. Click **OK**.

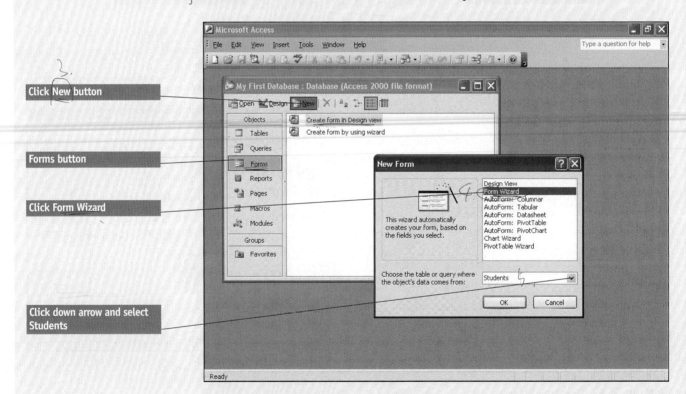

Click New button

Forms button

Click Form Wizard

Click down arrow and select Students

(a) Open the Database (step 1)

FIGURE 2.7 Hands-on Exercise 2

ANATOMY OF A FORM

A form is divided into one or more sections. Virtually every form has a detail section to display or enter the records in the underlying table. You can, however, increase the effectiveness or visual appeal of a form by adding a header and/or footer. Either section may contain descriptive information about the form, such as a title, instructions for using the form, or a graphic or logo.

Step 2: The Form Wizard

- You should see the dialog box in Figure 2.7b, which displays all of the fields in the Students table. Click the **>> button** to enter all of the fields in the table on the form. Click the **Next command button**.

- The **Columnar layout** is already selected. (The various layouts correspond to the different AutoForms.) Click the **Next command button**.

- Click **Industrial** as the style for your form. Click the **Next command button**.

- The Form Wizard will ask you for the title of the form and what you want to do next.
  - ❏ The Form Wizard suggests **Students** as the title of the form. Keep this entry.
  - ❏ Click the option button to **Modify the form's design**.

- Click the **Finish command button** to display the form in Design view. The wizard has created the initial form for you. You will now modify the form in Design view as described in the next several steps.

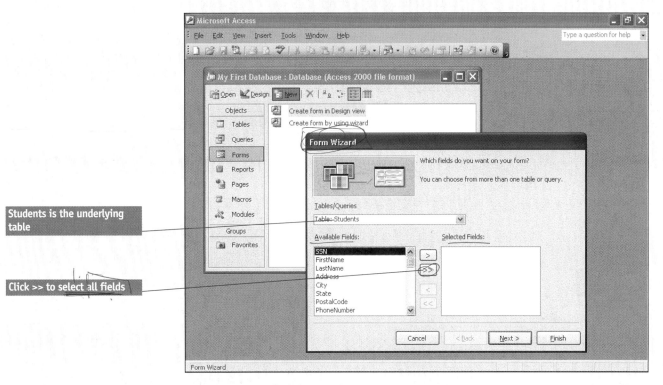

Students is the underlying table

Click >> to select all fields

(b) The Form Wizard (step 2)

FIGURE 2.7   Hands-on Exercise 2 (*continued*)

FLOATING TOOLBARS

A toolbar is typically docked (fixed) along the edge of the application window, but it can be displayed as a floating toolbar within the application window. To move a docked toolbar, drag the toolbar background (or the toolbar's move handle). To move a floating toolbar, drag its title bar. To size a floating toolbar, drag any border in the direction you want to go. And finally, you can double click the background of any floating toolbar to dock it.

Step 3: Move the Controls

- If necessary, click the **Maximize button** so that the form takes the entire screen as shown in Figure 2.7c. Close the field list. The Form Wizard has arranged the controls in columnar format, but you need to rearrange the controls.

- Click the **Credits control** to select it. Press the **Shift key** as you click the **QualityPoints control** to select it as well. Click and drag the border of either control (the pointer changes to a hand) to move them out of the way.

- Click the **LastName control** to select the control and display the sizing handles. (Be sure to select the text box and *not* the attached label.) Click and drag the **border** of the control (the pointer changes to a hand) so that the LastName control is on the same line as the FirstName control. Use the grid to space and align the controls.

- Click and drag the **Address control** under the FirstName control (to take the space previously occupied by the last name).

- Click and drag the **right border** of the form to **7 inches** so that the City, State, and PostalCode controls will fit on the same line. (Click and drag the title bar of the Toolbox toolbar to move the toolbar out of the way.)

- Click and drag the **State control** so that it is next to the City control, then click and drag the **PostalCode control** so that it is on the same line as the other two. Press and hold the **Shift key** as you click the **City**, **State**, and **PostalCode controls** to select all three, then click and drag the selected controls under the Address control.

- Place the controls for **PhoneNumber**, **BirthDate**, and **Gender** on the same line. Move the controls under City, State, PostalCode.

- Place the controls for **Credits** and **QualityPoints** on the same line. Move the controls under PhoneNumber.

- Save the form.

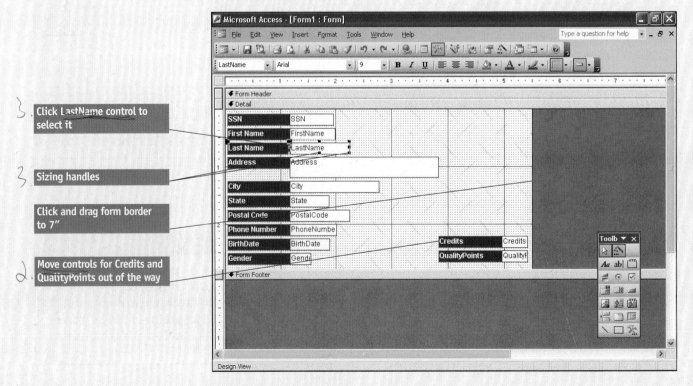

Click LastName control to select it

Sizing handles

Click and drag form border to 7"

Move controls for Credits and QualityPoints out of the way

(c) Move the Controls (step 3)

FIGURE 2.7 Hands-on Exercise 2 (*continued*)

Step 4: Add a **Calculated Control** (GPA)

- Click the **Text Box tool** in the toolbox as shown in Figure 2.7d. The mouse pointer changes to a tiny crosshair with a text box attached.

- Click and drag in the form where you want the text box (the GPA control) to go. Release the mouse. You will see an Unbound control and an attached label containing a field number (e.g., Text24) as shown in Figure 2.7d.

- Click in the **text box** of the control. The word Unbound will disappear. Enter **=[QualityPoints]/[Credits]** to calculate a student's GPA. You must enter the field names *exactly* as they were defined in the table; that is, do *not* include a space between Quality and Points.

- Select the attached label (**Text24**), then click and drag to select the text in the attached label. Type **GPA** as the label for this control and press **Enter**.

- Size the label appropriately for GPA. Size the bound control as well. Move either control as necessary.

- Save the form.

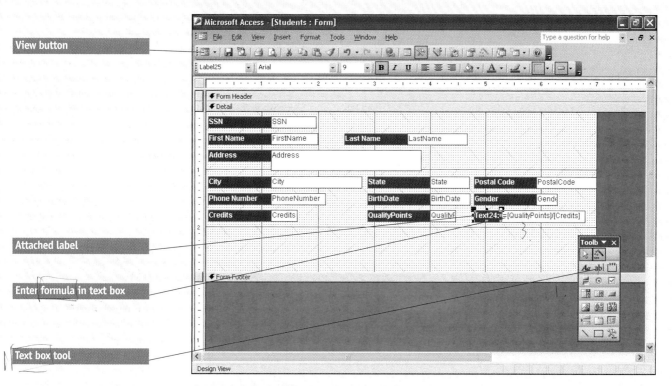

(d) Add a Calculated Control (step 4)

FIGURE 2.7 Hands-on Exercise 2 (*continued*)

SIZING OR MOVING A CONTROL AND ITS LABEL

A bound and/or an unbound control is created with an attached label. Select (click) the control, and the control has sizing handles and a move handle, but the label has only a move handle. Select the label (instead of the control), and the opposite occurs; the control has only a move handle, but the label will have both sizing handles and a move handle. To move a control and its label, click and drag the border of either object. To move either the control or its label, click and drag the move handle (a tiny square in the upper left corner) of the appropriate object.

Step 5: Modify the Property Sheet

- Point to the GPA bound control and click the **right mouse button** to display a shortcut menu. Click **Properties** to display the Properties dialog box.

- If necessary, click the **All tab** as shown in Figure 2.7e. The Control Source text box contains the entry =[QualityPoints]/[Credits] from the preceding step.

- Click the **Name text box**. Replace the original name (e.g., Text24) with **GPA**.

- Click the **Format box**. Click the **drop-down arrow**, then scroll until you can select **Fixed**.

- Click the box for the **Decimal places**. Click the **drop-down arrow** and select **2** as the number of decimal places.

- Close the Properties dialog box to accept these settings and return to the form.

- Save the form.

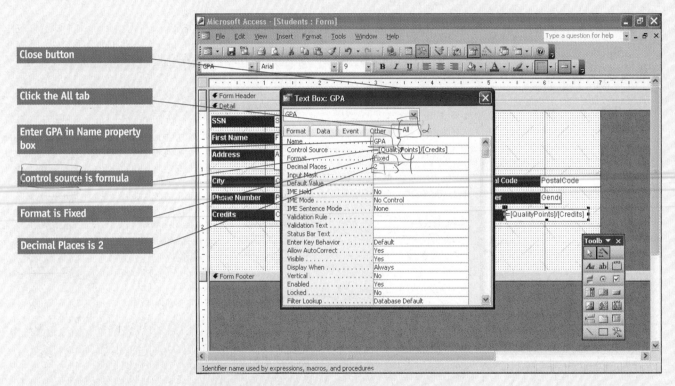

(e) Modify the Property Sheet (step 5)

FIGURE 2.7 Hands-on Exercise 2 (*continued*)

USE THE PROPERTY SHEET

You can change the appearance or behavior of a control in two ways—by changing the actual control on the form itself or by changing the underlying property sheet. Anything you do to the control automatically changes the associated property, and conversely, any change to the property sheet is reflected in the appearance or behavior of the control. In general, you can obtain greater precision through the property sheet, but we find ourselves continually switching back and forth between the two techniques. Every object in an Access database has its own property sheet.

Step 6: **Align the Controls**

- Click the label for SSN, then press and hold the **Shift key** as you click the labels for the other controls on the form. This enables you to select multiple controls at the same time to apply uniform formatting to the selected controls.

- All labels should be selected as shown in Figure 2.7f. Click the **Align Right button** on the Formatting toolbar to move the text to the right so that the text in each label is closer to its associated control.

- Click anywhere on the form to deselect the controls, then fine-tune the form as necessary to make it more attractive. (Use the Undo command anytime the results of a command are not what you expect.)

- Make additional changes as necessary. We moved LastName to align it with State. We also made the PostalCode and GPA controls smaller.

- Save the form.

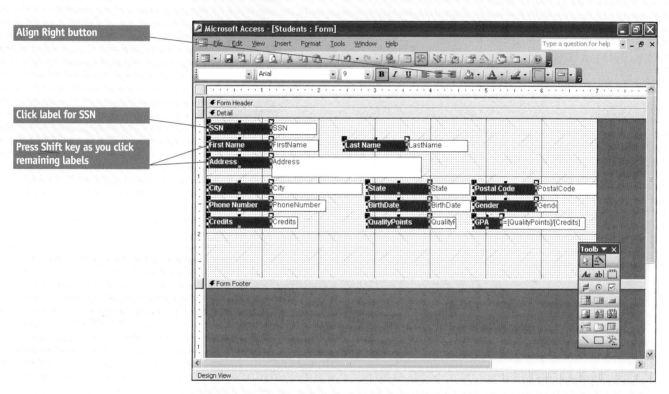

(f) Align the Controls (step 6)

FIGURE 2.7 Hands-on Exercise 2 (*continued*)

ALIGN THE CONTROLS

To align controls in a straight line (horizontally or vertically), press and hold the Shift key and click the labels of the controls to be aligned. Pull down the Format menu, click Align, then select the edge to align (Left, Right, Top, and Bottom). Click the Undo command if you are not satisfied with the result. It takes practice to master the Design view, but everything you learn about forms also applies to reports. (Reports are covered in Chapter 3.)

Step 7: Create the Form Header

- Click and drag the line separating the border of the Form Header and Detail sections to provide space for a header as shown in Figure 2.7g.

- Click the **Label tool** on the Toolbox toolbar (the mouse pointer changes to a cross hair combined with the letter A). Click and drag the mouse pointer to create a label within the header. The insertion point (a flashing vertical line) is automatically positioned within the label.

- Type **Student Information Form**. Do not be concerned about the size or alignment of the text at this time. Click outside the label when you have completed the entry, then click the control to select it.

- Click the **drop-down arrow** on the **Font Size list box** on the Formatting toolbar. Click **18**. The size of the text changes to the larger point size.

- Click the **drop-down arrow** next to the **Special Effect button** on the Formatting toolbar to display the available effects. Click the **Raised button** to highlight the label. Click outside the label to deselect it.

- Click the **Textbox tool** on the Toolbox toolbar. The mouse pointer changes to a tiny crosshair with a text box attached.

- Click and drag in the form where you want the text box for the date, then release the mouse.

- You will see an Unbound control and an attached label containing a number (e.g., Text27). Click in the text box, and the word Unbound will disappear. Type **=Now( )** to enter the current date. Click the attached label. Press the **Del key** to delete the label.

- Right click the newly created control to display a context-sensitive menu. Click the **Properties command** and change the format to **Short Date**. Close the Properties sheet.

- Save the form.

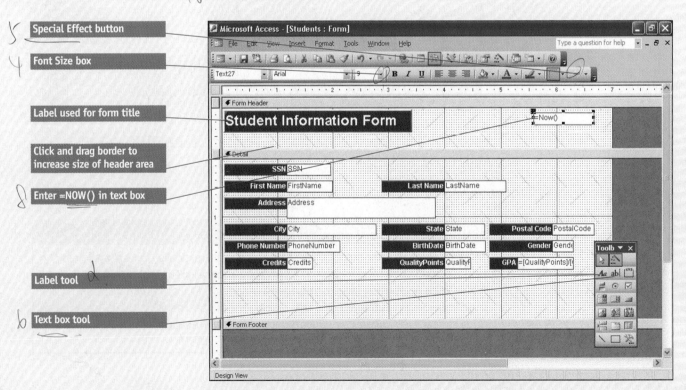

Special Effect button

Font Size box

Label used for form title

Click and drag border to increase size of header area

Enter =NOW() in text box

Label tool

Text box tool

(g) Create the Form Header (step 7)

FIGURE 2.7 Hands-on Exercise 2 (*continued*)

Step 8: The Finished Form

- Click the **View button** to switch to the Form view. You will see the first record in the table that was created in the previous exercise.

- Click the **New Record button** to move to the end of the table to enter a new record as shown in Figure 2.7h. Enter data for a classmate:
  - ❏ The record selector symbol changes to a pencil as you begin to enter data as shown in Figure 2.7h.
  - ❏ Press the **Tab key** to move from one field to the next within the form. All properties (masks and data validation) have been inherited from the Students table created in the first exercise.
  - ❏ There are now two records in the table.

- Pull down the **File menu** and click **Close** to close the form. Click **Yes** if asked to save the changes to the form.

- Pull down the **File menu** and click **Close** to close the database and remain in Access. Pull down the **File menu** a second time and click **Exit** if you do not want to continue with the next exercise at this time.

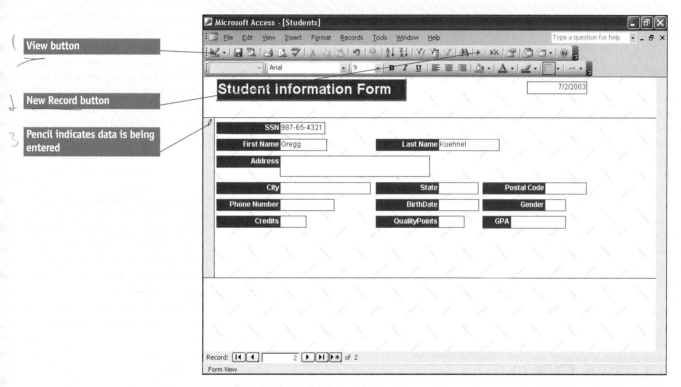

(h) The Finished Form (step 8)

FIGURE 2.7   Hands-on Exercise 2 (*continued*)

ERROR MESSAGES—#NAME? OR #ERROR?

The most common reason for either message is that the control source references a field that no longer exists, or a field whose name is misspelled. Go to the Design view, right click the control, click the Properties command, then click the All tab within the Properties dialog box. Look at the Control Source property and check the spelling of every field. Be sure there are brackets around each field in a calculated control—for example, =[QualityPoints]/[Credits].

The Form Wizard provides an excellent starting point but stops short of creating the form you really want. The exercise just completed showed you how to add controls to a form that were not in the underlying table, such as the calculated control for the GPA. The exercise also showed how to move and size existing controls to create a more attractive and functional form.

Consider now Figure 2.8, which further improves on the form from the previous exercise. Three additional controls have been added—for major, financial aid, and campus—to illustrate other ways to enter data than through a text box. The student's major is selected from a *drop-down list box*. The indication of financial aid (a Yes/No field) is entered through a *check box*. The student's campus is selected from an *option group*, in which you choose one of three mutually exclusive options.

The form in Figure 2.8 also includes clip art in the header. The way in which clip art is added to a form (or report) in Access differs from the way it is done in the other Office applications, in that the Insert Picture command does not link to the Clip Organizer as it does with Word, Excel, and PowerPoint. Execution of the command in Access is more limited and requires you to specify the file that contains the clip art image. (You can, however, start the Clip Organizer as a separate application, copy the clip art to the clipboard, then paste the contents of the clipboard into Access.)

Command buttons have also been added to the bottom of the form to facilitate the way in which the user carries out certain procedures. To add a record, for example, the user simply clicks the Add Record command button, as opposed to having to click the New Record button on the Database toolbar or having to pull down the Insert menu. Additional buttons have been added to find or delete a record and to close the form. The next exercise has you retrieve the form you created in Hands-on Exercise 2 to add these enhancements.

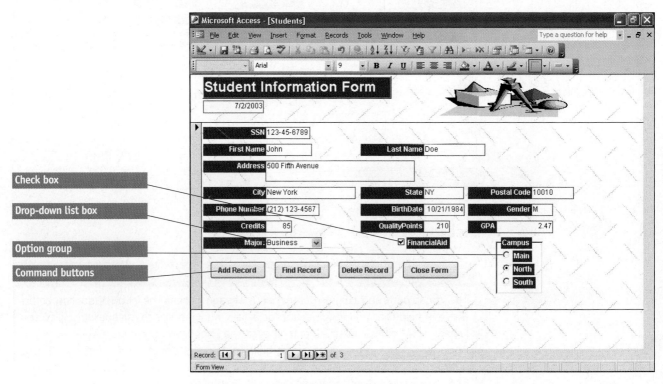

FIGURE 2.8 A More Sophisticated Form

3 A More Sophisticated Form

Objective To add fields to an existing table; to use the Lookup Wizard to create a combo box; to add controls to an existing form to demonstrate inheritance; to add command buttons to a form. Use Figure 2.9 as a guide in the exercise.

Step 1: ## Modify the Table

■ Open **My First Database** that we have been using throughout the chapter. If necessary, click the **Tables button** in the Database window. The **Students table** is already selected since that is the only table in the database.

■ Click the **Design command button** to open the table in Design view as shown in Figure 2.9a. (The FinancialAid, Campus, and Major fields have not yet been added.) Maximize the window.

■ Click the **Field Name box** under QualityPoints. Enter **FinancialAid** as the name of the new field. Press the **Enter (Tab, or right arrow) key** to move to the Data Type column. Type **Y** (the first letter in a Yes/No field) to specify the data type.

■ Click the **Field Name box** on the next row. Type **Campus**. (There is no need to specify the Data Type since Text is the default.)

■ Press the **down arrow key** to move to the Field Name box on the next row. Enter **Major**. Press the **Enter (Tab, or right arrow) key** to move to the Data Type column. Click the **drop-down arrow** to display the list of data types as shown in Figure 2.9a. Click **Lookup Wizard**.

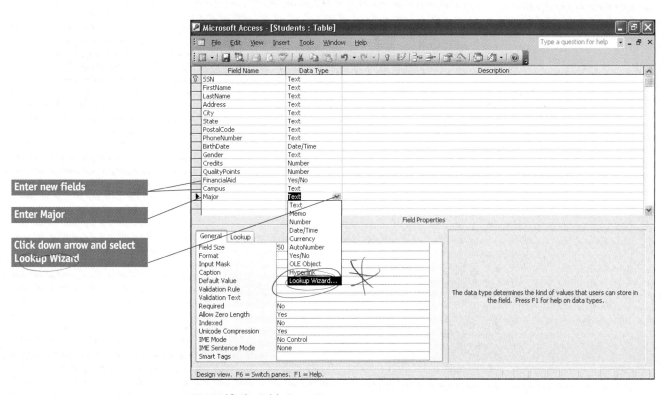

(a) Modify the Table (step 1)

FIGURE 2.9 Hands-on Exercise 3

Step 2:   The Lookup Wizard

- The first screen in the Lookup Wizard asks how you want to look up the data. Click the option button that indicates **I will type in the values that I want**. Click **Next**.

- You should see the dialog box in Figure 2.9b. The number of columns is already entered as 1. Click the **text box** to enter the first major. Type **Business**. Press **Tab** or the **down arrow key** (do *not* press the Enter key) to enter the next major.

- Complete the entries shown in Figure 2.9b. Click **Next**. The wizard asks for a label to identify the column. (Major is already entered.)

- Click **Finish** to exit the wizard and return to the Design view.

- The data type has been set to Text as a result of the entries you made using the Lookup Wizard.

- Click the **Save button** to save the table. Close the table.

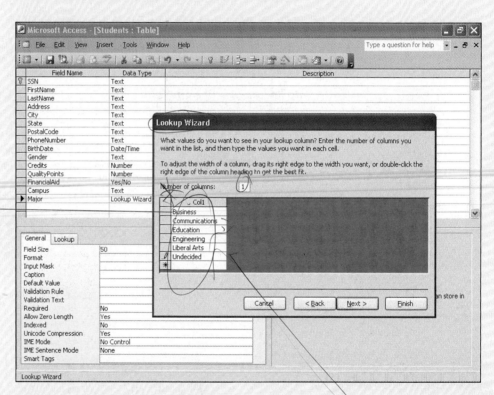

(b) The Lookup Wizard (step 2)

FIGURE 2.9   Hands-on Exercise 3 (*continued*)

RELATIONAL DATABASES—MORE SOPHISTICATED APPLICATIONS

The simplest way to use the Lookup Wizard is to type the potential values directly into the associated field. It's more powerful, however, to instruct the wizard to look up the values in a table, which in turn necessitates the creation of that table, in effect creating a relational database. Indeed, the true power of Access comes from databases with multiple tables, as was demonstrated in the Look Ahead database of Chapter 1. We develop this topic further, beginning in Chapter 4 and continue through the remaining chapters in the text.

Step 3: Add the New Controls

- Click the **Forms button** in the Database window. If necessary, click the **Students form** to select it.

- Click the **Design command button** to open the form from the previous exercise. If necessary, click the **Maximize button** so that the form takes the entire window.

- If the field list is not displayed, pull down the **View menu**. Click **Field List** to display the field list for the table on which the form is based. You can move and size the field list just like any other Windows object.
  - ❏ Click and drag the **title bar** of the field list to the position in Figure 2.9c.
  - ❏ Click and drag a **corner** or **border** of the field list so that you can see all of the fields at the same time.

- Fields can be added to the form from the field list in any order. Click and drag the **Major field** from the field list to the form. The Major control is created as a combo box because of the lookup list in the underlying table.

- Click and drag the **FinancialAid field** from the list to the form. The FinancialAid control is created as a check box because FinancialAid is a Yes/No field in the underlying table.

- Move and size the labels and bound controls as necessary. Save the form.

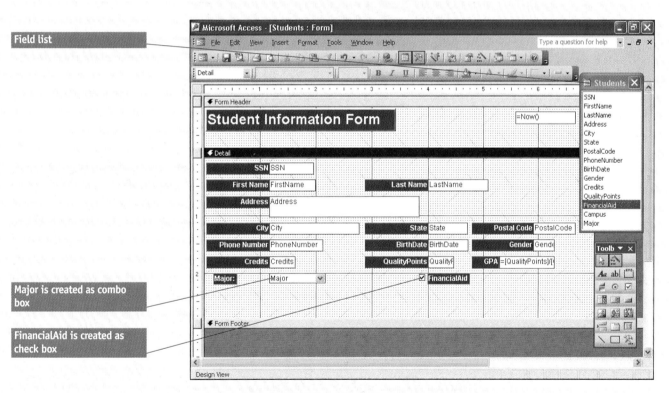

Field list

Major is created as combo box

FinancialAid is created as check box

(c) Add the New Controls (step 3)

FIGURE 2.9 Hands-on Exercise 3 (*continued*)

Yes/No field (table)
(form)
 ↳ check box
lookup wizard (table)
 ↳ dropdown (form)

INHERITANCE

A bound control inherits its properties from the associated field in the underlying table. A check box, for example, appears automatically for any field that was defined as a Yes/No field. In similar fashion, a drop-down list appears for any field that was defined through the Lookup Wizard. All of the other properties of the control are also inherited from the underlying table.

Step 4: **Create an Option Group**

- Click the **Option Group button** on the Toolbox toolbar. The mouse pointer changes to a tiny crosshair. Click and drag in the form where you want the option group to go, then release the mouse.

- You should see the Option Group Wizard as shown in Figure 2.9d. Enter **Main** as the label for the first option, then press the **Tab key** to move to the next line. Type **North** and press **Tab** to move to the next line. Enter **South** as the third and last option. Click **Next**.

- The option button to select Main (the first label that was entered) as the default is selected. Click **Next**.

- Main, North, and South will be assigned the values 1, 2, and 3, respectively. (Numeric entries are required for an option group.) Click **Next**.

- Click the **drop-down arrow** to select the field in which to store the value selected through the option group, then scroll until you can select **Campus**. Click **Next**.

- Make sure the Option button is selected as the type of control.

- Click the Option button for the **Sunken style** to match the other controls on the form. Click **Next**.

- Enter **Campus** as the caption for the group. Click the **Finish command button** to create the option group on the form. Click and drag the option group to position it on the form under the GPA control.

- Point to the border of the option group on the form, click the **right mouse button** to display a shortcut menu, and click **Properties**. Click the **All tab**. Change the name to **Campus**.

- Click the label for the **Option Group** (Campus). Click the **Fill Color button** on the Formatting toolbar to change the fill color to match that of the other labels.

- Close the dialog box. Close the field list. Save the form.

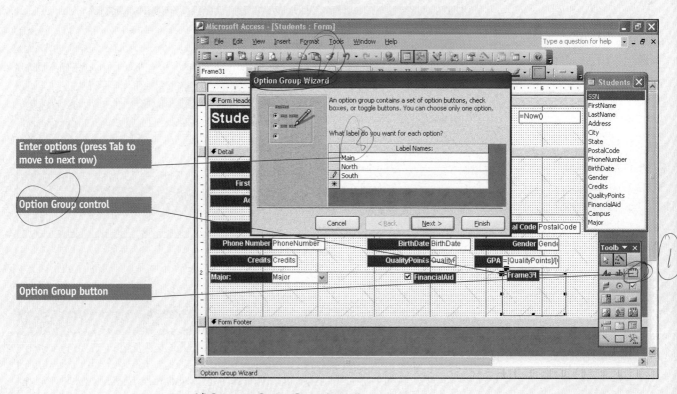

(d) Create an Option Group (step 4)

FIGURE 2.9 Hands-on Exercise 3 (*continued*)

82   CHAPTER 2: TABLES AND FORMS

Step 5: **Add the Command Buttons**

■ Click the **Command Button tool**. The mouse pointer changes to a tiny crosshair that is attached to a command button when you point anywhere in the form.

■ Click and drag in the form where you want the button to go, then release the mouse. This draws a button and simultaneously opens the Command Button Wizard as shown in Figure 2.9e. (The number in your button may be different from ours.)

■ Click **Record Operations** in the Categories list box. Choose **Add New Record** as the operation. Click **Next**.

■ Click the **Text option button** in the next screen. Click **Next**.

■ Type **Add Record** as the name of the button, then click the **Finish command button**. The completed command button should appear on your form.

■ Repeat these steps to add the command buttons to find a record (Record Navigation), to delete a record (Record Operations), and to close the form (Form Operations). We will adjust the size and alignment of all four buttons in the next step.

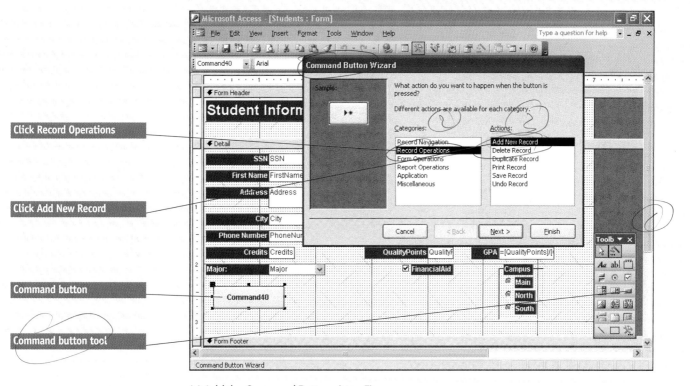

(e) Add the Command Buttons (step 5)

FIGURE 2.9 Hands-on Exercise 3 (*continued*)

WINDOWS THEMES AND ROUNDED COMMAND BUTTONS

It's a subtle difference, but we prefer the sleeker look of rounded command buttons in our forms, as opposed to the rectangular buttons that are created by default. Pull down the Tools menu, click the Options command, click the Forms/Reports tab, and check the box to use Windows Themed Controls on forms. Click the Apply button, then close the dialog box. Save the form you are working on, close the form, and then reopen it. You should see rounded buttons.

Step 6: Align the Command Buttons

- Select the four command buttons that were created in the previous step by pressing and holding the **Shift key** as you click each button. Release the Shift key when all buttons are selected.

- Pull down the **Format menu**. Click **Size** to display the cascade menu shown in Figure 2.9f. (Click the **double arrow** at the bottom of the menu if you don't see the Size command.) Click **To Widest** to set a uniform width.

- Pull down the **Format menu** a second time, click **Size**, then click **To Tallest** to set a uniform height.

- Pull down the **Format menu** again, click **Horizontal Spacing**, then click **Make Equal** so that each button is equidistant from the other buttons.

- Pull down the **Format menu** a final time, click **Align**, then click **Bottom** to complete the alignment.

- Save the form.

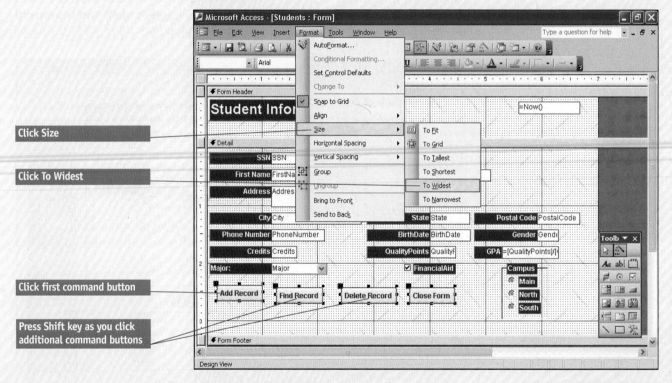

(f) Align the Command Buttons (step 6)

FIGURE 2.9 Hands-on Exercise 3 (*continued*)

MULTIPLE CONTROLS AND PROPERTIES

Press and hold the Shift key as you click one control after another to select multiple controls. To view or change the properties for the selected controls, click the right mouse button to display a shortcut menu, then click Properties to display a property sheet. If the value of a property is the same for all selected controls, that value will appear in the property sheet; otherwise the box for that property will be blank. Changing a property when multiple controls are selected changes the property for all selected controls.

Step 7: Reset the Tab Order

- Click anywhere in the Detail section. Pull down the **View menu**. Click **Tab Order** to display the Tab Order dialog box in Figure 2.9g. (Click the **double arrow** at the bottom of the menu if you don't see the Tab Order command.)

- Click the **Auto Order command button** so that the Tab key will move to fields in left-to-right, top-to-bottom order as you enter data in the form. Click **OK** to close the Tab Order dialog box.

- Right click the **GPA control**, click **Properties** to display the Properties sheet, click the **All tab**, set the **Tab Stop** property to **No**, and close the property sheet.

- Check the form one more time to make any last-minute changes. (We had to right align the label for major.)

- Save the form.

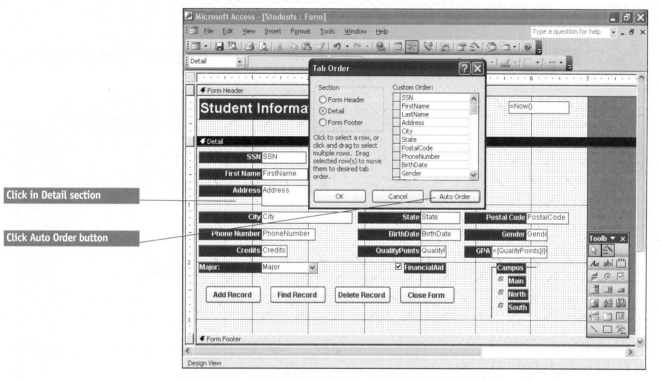

Click in Detail section

Click Auto Order button

(g) Reset the Tab Order (step 7)

FIGURE 2.9 Hands-on Exercise 3 (*continued*)

THE TAB STOP PROPERTY

The Tab key provides a shortcut in the finished form to move from one field to the next. Calculated controls, such as GPA, are not entered explicitly, however, and can be bypassed by setting the Tab Stop property to no. AutoNumber fields can be bypassed in similar fashion. Note, too, that the order in which fields are selected corresponds to the sequence in which the controls were entered onto the form, and need not correspond to the physical appearance of the actual form. To restore a left-to-right, top-to-bottom sequence, pull down the View menu, click Tab Order, select AutoOrder, then click OK to close the Tab Order dialog box.

Step 8:   **Insert the Clip Art**

- Click in the Form Header area. Pull down the **Insert menu** and click the **Picture command** to display the Insert Picture dialog box as shown in Figure 2.9h.

- Change to the **Exploring Access folder**. Click the **Views button** repeatedly until you see the **Thumbnails Views**.

- Select (click) a picture, then click **OK** to insert the picture on the form. Right click the newly inserted object to display a shortcut menu, then click **Properties** to display the Properties dialog box.

- Select the **Size Mode property** and select **Stretch** from the associated list. Close the dialog box.

- Click and drag the sizing handles on the frame to size the object appropriately for the header area. Size the form header as necessary. Move the picture and other controls in the header until you are satisfied with its appearance.

- Save the form.

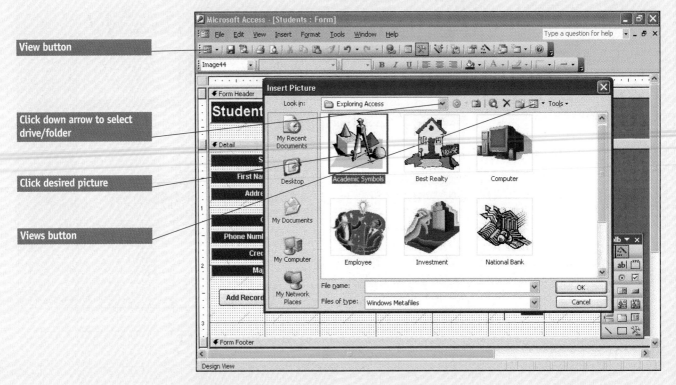

(h) Insert the Clip Art (step 8)

FIGURE 2.9   Hands-on Exercise 3 (*continued*)

MISSING TASK PANE

The Insert Picture command functions differently in Access than in the other Office applications since it does not display the Clip Art task pane. You can still search for clip art explicitly, however, by starting the Clip Organizer as a separate application. Click the Start button, click the All Programs button, click Microsoft Office Tools, then start the Clip Organizer. Select a clip art image from within the Clip Organizer, and click the Copy button. Use the Windows taskbar to return to Access, open the form in Design view, and click the Paste button.

Step 9: **The Completed Form**

■ Click the **View button** to switch to the Form view. Click the **Add Record command button** to create a new record. Click the text box for **Social Security Number**. Add the record shown in Figure 2.9i.

■ Click the **selection area** (the thin vertical column to the left of the form) to select the current record. The record selector changes to an arrow. The selection area is shaded to indicate that the record has been selected.

■ Pull down the **File menu**. Click **Print** to display the Print dialog box. Click the option button to print **Selected Record**. Click **OK**.

■ Examine your printed output to be sure that the form fits on a single page.

■ If it doesn't, you need to adjust the margins of the form itself and/or change the margins using the Page Setup command in the File menu, then print the form a second time.

■ Click the **Close Form command button** on the form after you have printed the record for your instructor.

■ Click **Yes** if you see a message asking to save changes to the form design.

■ Pull down the **File menu**. Click **Exit** to leave Access.

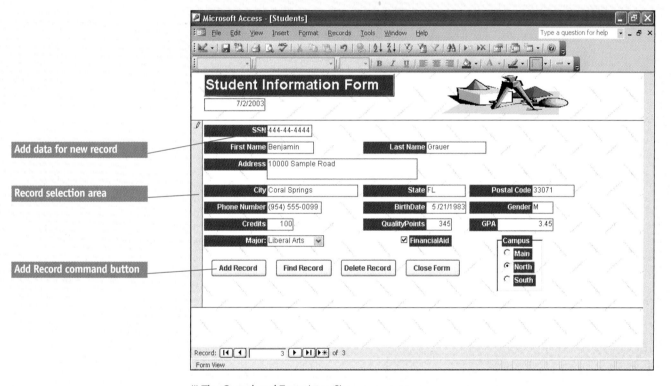

(i) The Completed Form (step 9)

FIGURE 2.9 Hands-on Exercise 3 (*continued*)

KEYBOARD SHORTCUTS

You can point and click to enter data within a form, but it's faster to use the keyboard. Use Tab (or Shift+Tab) to move forward (or backward) from field to field. Press the space bar to toggle a check box on and off. Type the first letter(s) of the desired value from a combo box to enter the value—for example "B" for "Business" within the list box for Major. These are universal shortcuts and apply to any Windows application.

SUMMARY

Access should be considered as a means to an end, rather than an end in itself. The real objective is to obtain useful information from a database, and that can be accomplished only if the database contains the necessary data to produce that information. Thus, one starts with a list of desired reports (or output), then determines the data (or input) to produce that information, after which the table can be created. The data within a table should be divided into the smallest possible units, such as separate fields for first and last name. Calculated fields should be avoided.

A table has different views—the Design view and the Datasheet view. The Design view is used to create the table and determine the fields within the table, as well as the data type and properties of each field. The Datasheet view is used after the table has been created to add, edit, and delete records. (The PivotTable view and PivotChart view display summary data and are discussed in Chapter 4.)

The Table Wizard is the easiest way to create a table. It lets you choose from a series of business or personal tables, asks you questions about the fields you want, then creates the table for you. The wizard creates the initial table for you, after which you can modify the table in Design view.

A form provides a user-friendly way to enter and display data, in that it can be made to resemble a paper form. AutoForms and the Form Wizard are easy ways to create a form. The Design view enables you to modify an existing form.

A form consists of objects called controls. A bound control has a data source such as a field in the underlying table. An unbound control has no data source. A calculated control contains an expression. Controls are selected, moved, and sized the same way as any other Windows object.

A property is a characteristic or attribute of an object that determines how the object looks and behaves. Every Access object (e.g., tables, fields, forms, and controls) has a set of properties that determine the behavior of that object. The properties for an object are displayed in a property sheet.

KEY TERMS

MULTIPLE CHOICE

1. Which of the following is true?

   (a) The Table Wizard must be used to create a table
   (b) The Form Wizard must be used to create a form
   (c) Both (a) and (b)
   (d) Neither (a) nor (b)

2. Which of the following is implemented automatically by Access?

   (a) Rejection of a record with a duplicate value of the primary key
   (b) Rejection of numbers in a text field
   (c) Both (a) and (b)
   (d) Neither (a) nor (b)

3. Social Security number, phone number, and zip code should be designated as:

   (a) Number fields
   (b) Text fields
   (c) Yes/No fields
   (d) Any of the above depending on the application

4. Which of the following is true of the primary key?

   (a) Its values must be unique
   (b) It must be defined as a text field
   (c) It must be the first field in a table
   (d) It can never be changed

5. Social Security number rather than name is used as a primary key because:

   (a) The Social Security number is numeric, whereas the name is not
   (b) The Social Security number is unique, whereas the name is not
   (c) The Social Security number is a shorter field
   (d) All of the above

6. Which of the following is true regarding buttons within the Form Wizard?

   (a) The > button copies a selected field from a table onto a form
   (b) The < button removes a selected field from a form
   (c) Both (a) and (b)
   (d) Neither (a) nor (b)

7. Which of the following was *not* a suggested guideline for designing a table?

   (a) Include all necessary data
   (b) Store data in its smallest parts
   (c) Avoid calculated fields
   (d) Designate at least two primary keys

8. Which of the following are valid parameters for use with a form?

   (a) Portrait orientation, a width of 6 inches, left and right margins of 1¼ inch
   (b) Landscape orientation, a width of 9 inches, left and right margins of 1 inch
   (c) Both (a) and (b)
   (d) Neither (a) nor (b)

9. Which view is used to add, edit, or delete records in a table?

   (a) The Datasheet view
   (b) The Design view
   (c) The PivotTable view
   (d) The PivotChart view

10. Which of the following is true?

   (a) Any field added to a table after a form has been created is automatically added to the form as a bound control
   (b) Any calculated control that appears in a form is automatically inserted into the underlying table
   (c) Every bound and unbound control in a form has an underlying property sheet
   (d) All of the above

11. In which view will you see the record selector symbols of a pencil and a triangle?

   (a) Only the Datasheet view
   (b) Only the Form view
   (c) The Datasheet view and the Form view
   (d) The Form view, the Design view, and the Datasheet view

... continued

12. To move a control (in the Design view), you select the control, then:

    (a) Point to a border (the pointer changes to an arrow) and click and drag the border to the new position

    (b) Point to a border (the pointer changes to a hand) and click and drag the border to the new position

    (c) Point to a sizing handle (the pointer changes to an arrow) and click and drag the sizing handle to the new position

    (d) Point to a sizing handle (the pointer changes to a hand) and click and drag the sizing handle to the new position

13. Which fields are commonly defined with an input mask?

    (a) Social Security Number and phone number

    (b) First name, middle name, and last name

    (c) City, state, and zip code

    (d) All of the above

14. Which data type appears as a check box in a form?

    (a) Text field

    (b) Number field

    (c) Yes/No field

    (d) All of the above

15. Which properties would you use to limit a user's response to two characters, and automatically convert the response to uppercase?

    (a) Field Size and Format

    (b) Input Mask, Validation Rule, and Default Value

    (c) Input Mask and Required

    (d) Field Size, Validation Rule, Validation Text, and Required

16. Which of the following is true with respect to an individual's hire date and years of service, both of which appear on a form that is based on an employee table?

    (a) Hire date should be a calculated control; years of service should be a bound control

    (b) Hire date should be a bound control; years of service should be a calculated control

    (c) Both should be bound controls

    (d) Both should be calculated controls

17. What is the best way to store an individual's name in a table?

    (a) As a single field consisting of the last name, first name, and middle initial, in that order

    (b) As a single field consisting of the first name, last name, and middle initial, in that order

    (c) As three separate fields for first name, last name, and middle initial

    (d) All of the above are equally suitable

18. Which of the following would *not* be a good primary key?

    (a) Student Number

    (b) Social Security Number

    (c) An e-mail address

    (d) A 9-digit zip code

ANSWERS

1. d	7. d	13. a
2. a	8. c	14. c
3. b	9. a	15. a
4. a	10. c	16. b
5. b	11. c	17. c
6. c	12. b	18. d

PRACTICE WITH ACCESS

April 12 ✓ 1. **A Modified Student Form:** Open the *My First Database* used in the chapter and modify the Student form created in the hands-on exercises to match the form in Figure 2.10. (The form contains three additional controls that must be added to the Students table, prior to modifying the form.)

a. Open the Students table in Design view. Add DateAdmitted and EmailAddress as a date and a text field, respectively. Add a Yes/No field to indicate whether the student is an international student.

b. Open the Students form in Design view. Add controls for the additional fields as shown in Figure 2.10.

c. Modify the State field in the underlying Students table to use the Lookup Wizard, and set CA, FL, NJ, and NY as the values for the list box. (These are the most common states in the student population.) The control in the form will not, however, inherit the list box because it was added to the table after the form was created. Hence, you have to delete the existing control in the form, display the field list, then click and drag the State field from the field list to the form.)

d. Add a hyperlink in the form header that contains the Web address of your school or university. It's easy—just click the Insert Hyperlink button on the Form Design toolbar, then enter the text and associated address in the ensuing dialog box. Click and drag the control containing the hyperlink to the appropriate place on the form.

e. Change the Caption property in each command button to include an ampersand in front of the underlined letter (e.g., &Add Record). The resulting command button is shown with an underline under the letter (e.g., Add Record). This in turn lets you use a shortcut, Alt+A (where A is the underlined letter), to activate the command button.

f. Resize the control in the Form Header so that *Your School or University Student Information Form* takes two lines. Press Ctrl+Enter to force a line break within the control. Resize the Form Header.

g. Change the tab order to reflect the new fields in the form.

h. Use the Page Setup command to change the margins and/or orientation of the page to be sure that the form fits on one page. Click the record selector column to select your record, then print the form for your instructor.

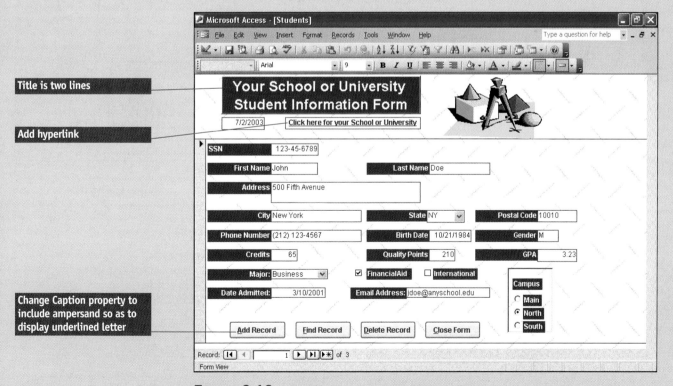

FIGURE 2.10 Modified Student Form (exercise 1)

2. **The United States Database:** This assignment builds on the United States database that was used for an earlier exercise in Chapter 1. Your assignment is to build a form similar to the one in Figure 2.11. You do not have to match our form exactly. You do, however, have to duplicate the functionality. Proceed as follows:

a. Open the *Chapter 1 Practice 3* database in the Exploring Access folder. Click the Tables button in the Database window and open the States table in Design view. Insert a new field at the end of the table, using WebPage and hyperlink as the field name and field type, respectively.

b. Use the Form Wizard to create the form initially, based on the States table (select all of the fields). Select a column layout and choose any style. Open the form in Design view to complete the form. Move and size the various controls as shown in Figure 2.11.

c. Add clip art to the form header that contains an image representing the United States. (Change the Size Mode property of the clip art to Stretch.) Insert a hyperlink to the White House (www.whitehouse.gov) underneath the image. Add your name and date in the form header.

d. Create a calculated control for the population density (population/area). Set the Tab Stop property to No.

e. Add the indicated command buttons, using the Caption property to implement the keyboard shortcut; for example, &Find Record will underline the letter "F" and enable the Alt+F keyboard shortcut to activate the button.

f. Pull down the View menu, click the Tab Order command to display the Tab Order dialog box, and then click the Auto Order button to set the tab order to match the physical arrangement of the controls in the form.

g. Go to the Form view. Use the navigation buttons to locate your home state (or any state if you are an international student). Enter the address of the state's Web page, using an address of the form www.state.*abbreviation*.us (e.g., www.state.fl.us for Florida).

h. Use the Page Setup command to change the margins and/or orientation of the page to be sure that the form fits on one page. Click the record selector column to select your state and print this record for your instructor. Click the hyperlink for your state's Web page and print that page for your instructor as well.

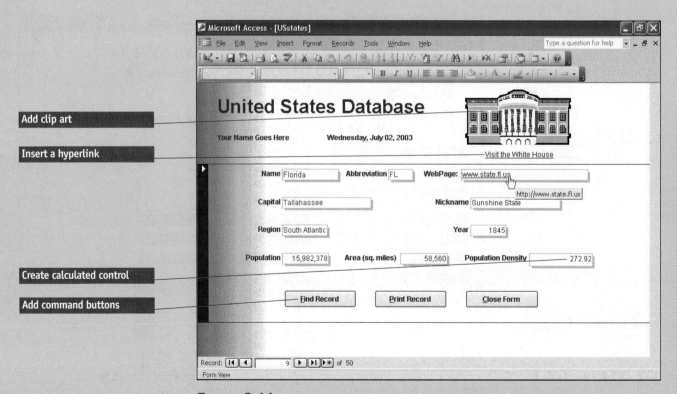

FIGURE 2.11 The United States Database (exercise 2)

3. **The Super Bowl:** Figure 2.12 displays a Web page (or Data Access page) that can be used to view and/or enter data in an underlying Access database. Look closely and you will see that the form is displayed in Internet Explorer, as opposed to Access, because the form was created as a Web page within Access. Proceed as follows:

a. Open the *Chapter 2 Practice 3* database in the Exploring Access folder. Click the Pages tab in the Database window, and then double click the option to create the Data Access page using the wizard. The wizard will prompt you for the information it needs in a series of screens. The first screen asks you to choose the table or query (Previous Games) and the fields within that table (All). Click Next.

b. You do not need grouping or sorting, but you should check the box to apply a theme (to make the form more attractive). End the wizard by viewing the page in Design view. Enter a title as indicated by the Click here prompt. Insert a hyperlink to the Super Bowl Web site (www.superbowl.com).

c. Pull down the File menu, click the Save command, then save the page in the Exploring Access folder. You will be warned that you have specified an absolute path and that the network may not be able to reconnect in the future. Click OK.

d. Close the database and exit Access. Go to the Exploring Access folder and open the Web page (HTML document) that you just created to view the records in the Super Bowl table as shown in Figure 2.12. (The HTML document exists as a separate document outside of the Access database.)

e. Click the New button to add a record for any games that are not in our table. (You can click the link to the Super Bowl Web site to obtain the scores of the additional games.) Print the record of the most recent game from Internet Explorer. Close Internet Explorer.

f. Start Access and reopen the *Chapter 2 Practice 3* database. Click the Tables button, open the Previous Games table, and go to the last record in the table, which should contain the data that you just entered. Now think about what you have accomplished. You were able to add a record to an Access database using a Web page as the "front end" for the database. You can continue to add, edit, or delete records using the Web page, and all changes will be reflected in the underlying Access table.

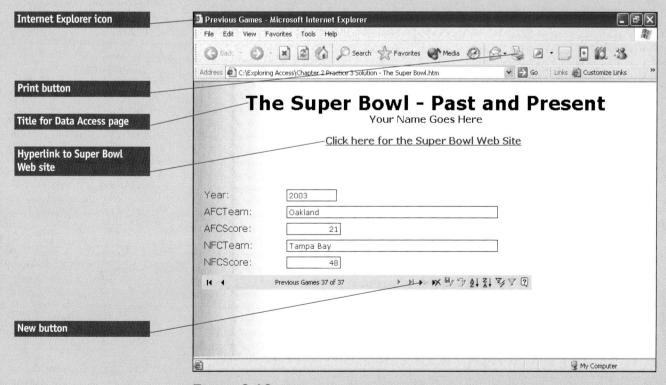

FIGURE 2.12 The Super Bowl (exercise 3)

4. **The Fishing Pole:** You have been asked by a marine hardware store to create a database that will be used to track its customers. In essence, you are to create the table in Figure 2.13 without benefit of the Table Wizard. Proceed as follows:

a. Start Access and create a new (blank) database. Click the Tables button in the Database window and double click the option to create a new table in Design view. To enter a new field, click in the Field Name column and type the name of the field (do not use spaces in the field name). Move to the Data Type column and choose the field type.

b. Create all of the fields in Figure 2.13. (The BoatType should be specified using the Lookup Wizard, and include Fishing, Power, and Sail as the boat types to be listed.) Save the table as Customers.

c. The CustomerNumber is to be the primary key. It should be an AutoNumber data type, and the Format should be \C0000, which will automatically produce a Customer Number that begins with the letter C, followed by a four-digit number each time a record is added to the table.

d. Establish input masks for the customer's zip code and phone number, as well as the initial purchase date. The initial purchase date should also have a short date format.

e. Use the Format property so that the state is displayed in uppercase letters, regardless of how it is entered.

f. Set appropriate field sizes for all text fields. Eliminate the default value of 0 and set a currency format with 2 decimal places for the initial purchase amount.

g. Set the Required property for the LastName and FirstName fields to Yes.

h. Set the Validation Rule property for the MailingList field to restrict values to 1, 2, or 3. Set the Validation Text property to display an appropriate message if the user attempts to enter invalid data.

i. Enter one record into the completed table, entering your name as the customer name. Print the table only if you are not doing the next exercise. The table will require two pages, even if you change to landscape printing.

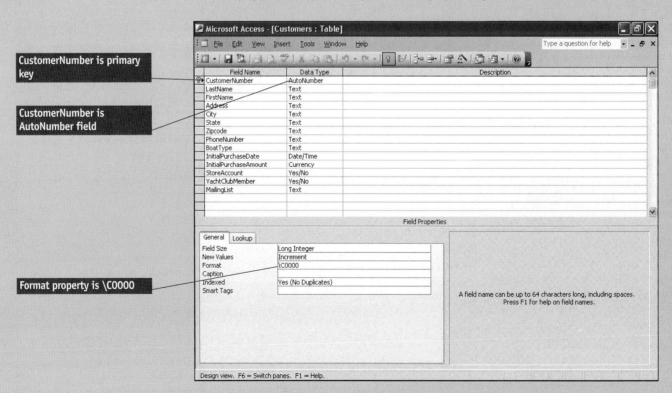

FIGURE 2.13 The Fishing Pole (exercise 4)

5. **A Form for the Fishing Pole:** Your assignment is to create a form similar to the one in Figure 2.14 that is based on the Fishing Pole database created in the previous exercise. The design of your form can be different from ours, but you must duplicate the functionality in our figure. Start with the Form Wizard, and then modify the resulting form as necessary so that your finished form accommodates all of the following:

a. The form should contain a control for every field in the underlying table. Move, format, align, and size the controls as necessary. Change the tab order of the controls so that the user tabs through the controls from left to right, top to bottom. Set the Tab Stop property of the Customer Number to No because the user does not input this value.

b. Use a different background color for the required fields (such as the customer's first and last name) to emphasize that these fields must be entered. Include a note at the bottom of the form to explain the color change.

c. Insert a form header with clip art (you do not have to use the same clip art as in our figure) and an appropriate title as shown in Figure 2.14. Set the Size Mode property of the clip art to Stretch.

d. Add command buttons as indicated. The command buttons should be a uniform size with equal spacing between them. Test each command button to be sure that it works as intended.

e. Use the Page Setup command to be sure that the form will fit on a single page when printed. Change the margins and/or orientation of the form as necessary. The completed form should display the data that you entered for yourself when you created the table in the previous problem. Print this form for your instructor.

f. Click the Add Record button to add a new record to the Customers table. Use your instructor's name as the customer's name, and supply other information as you see fit. Click the record selector column to select your instructor's record. Pull down the File menu, click the Print command, then select the option button to print the selected record. Submit both forms to your instructor to show that you completed this assignment.

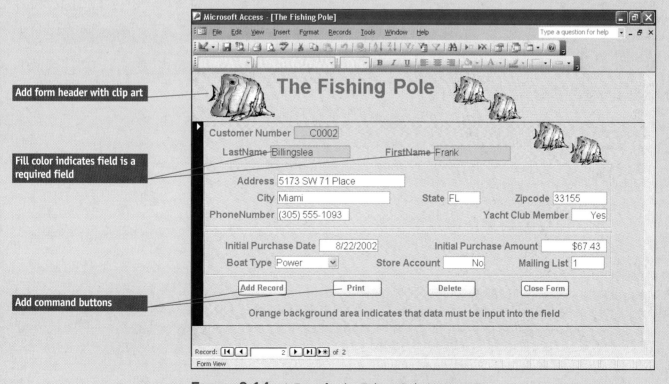

FIGURE 2.14 A Form for the Fishing Pole (exercise 5)

practice exercises

6. **The Shopping Mall:** You have been hired as a consultant for a shopping mall to create a database that is to track all of the stores in the mall. You have met with the mall manager several times and have decided on the various fields that need to be included in the Stores table. The results of your discussion can be summarized by the Design view of the table as shown in Figure 2.15.

a. Create the table without benefit of the Table Wizard. Start Access and specify that you will create a new database. The database should be called Shopping Mall and it should be stored in your Exploring Access folder.

b. Click the Tables button in the Database window and double click the option to create a new table in Design view. To enter a new field, click in the Field Name column and type the name of the field (do not use spaces in the field name). Move to the Data Type column and choose the field type. The fields in your table should match those in Figure 2.15.

c. The StoreID is to be the primary key. Use the validation rule that is specified in the figure, which requires that the file begin with the letter S followed by four digits to indicate the store unit number.

d. The StoreType should be specified using the Lookup Wizard, and include Clothing, Jewelry, Furniture, Home Accessories, Restaurant, and Shoes as the store types to be listed.

e. Establish input masks for the manager's phone number, as well as the lease start date and lease end date. The latter two fields require short date formats.

f. Set appropriate field sizes for all text fields. Eliminate the default values of 0 and set appropriate formats for the currency fields. The PricePerSquareFt is the rent per square foot and should allow two decimal places. The StoreRevenue field should be formatted without any decimal places.

g. The StoreID, StoreName, and StoreType are required fields.

h. Enter one record into the completed table. Use StoreID S0001 and use your name as the manager. Change to landscape printing and adjust the column width and/or the margins, so that the records fit on a single sheet of paper. Print this record for your instructor.

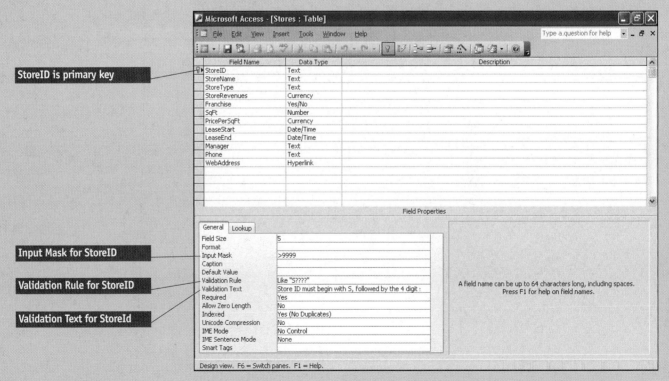

FIGURE 2.15   The Shopping Mall (exercise 6)

7. **A Form for the Shopping Mall:** Your assignment is to create a form similar to the one in Figure 2.16 that is based on the Shopping Mall database created in the previous exercise. The design of your form can be different from ours, but you must duplicate the functionality in our figure. Start with the Form Wizard, and then modify the resulting form as necessary so that your finished form accommodates all of the following:

a. The form should contain a control for every field in the underlying table. Format, move, size, and align the controls as necessary. Change the tab order of the controls so that the user tabs through the controls from left to right, top to bottom.

b. Include a calculated control to determine the monthly rent, which is equal to the number of square feet times the price per square foot. Change the format of this control to currency. Set the Tab Stop property to No.

c. Use a different background for the required fields (such as the StoreID and StoreType) to emphasize that the data for these fields is required. Include a note at the bottom of the form that explains the color change.

d. Insert a form header with clip art (you do not have to use the same clip art as in our figure) and an appropriate title. Set the Size Mode property of the clip art to Stretch.

e. Add command buttons as indicated. The command buttons should be a uniform size with equal spacing between them. Test each command button to be sure that it works as intended.

f. Use the Page Setup command to be sure that the form will fit on a single page when printed. The completed form should display the data that you entered for store number S0001 when you created the table in the previous problem. Print this form for your instructor.

g. Click the Add Record button to add a new record with StoreID S0002. Use your instructor's name as the store manager, and supply other information as you see fit. Click the record selector column to select your instructor's record. Pull down the File menu, click the Print command, then select the option button to print the selected record. Submit both forms to your instructor to show that you completed this assignment.

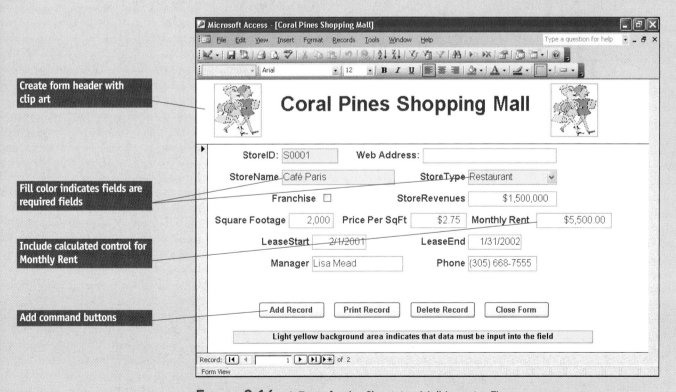

FIGURE 2.16 A Form for the Shopping Mall (exercise 7)

8. **Best Realty:** Best Realty is a real estate agency that specializes in the listing/selling of homes, including single-family dwellings as well as multiple-family dwellings. You have recently been hired by Best Realty to develop a database to track their property listings. After much thought and planning, you have decided upon the fields shown in Figure 2.17. Proceed as follows:

a. Create the table shown *without* using the Table Wizard. After you start Access, specify that you will create a new database—then assign the name Best Realty and save it in the Exploring Access folder.

b. Click the Tables button in the Database window and double click the option to create a new table in the Design view. To enter a new field, click in the Field Name column and type the name of the field (do not use spaces in the field name). Move to the Data Type column and choose the field type. The fields in your table should match those in Figure 2.17.

c. The PropertyID should be designated as the primary key. Be sure to include a validation rule that specifies that the ID should be composed of the letter P followed by four digits.

d. The PropertyType should be created using the Lookup Wizard, and include Single-Family, Townhome, Duplex, and Condominium.

e. Set appropriate field sizes for all text fields. Eliminate the default values of 0 and set appropriate formats for the number fields.

f. Create an input mask and format for the DateListed and DateSold fields.

g. The PropertyID, Address, AskingPrice, and AgentLastName should be specified as required fields.

h. Enter one record into the completed table. Use P0001 as the PropertyID and use your name as the agent. Change to landscape printing and adjust the column width and/or the margins so that the record fits on a single sheet of paper. Print this record for your instructor.

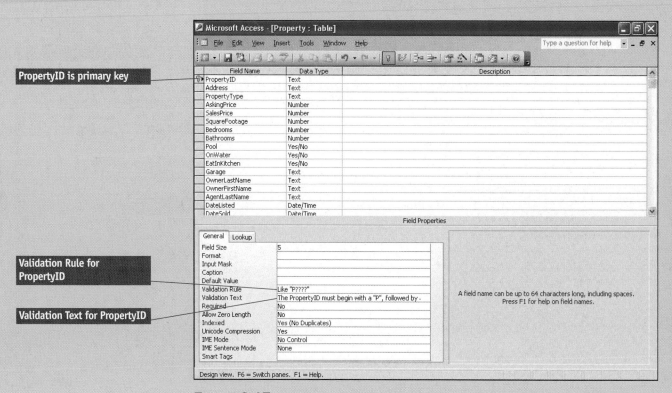

FIGURE 2.17 Best Realty (exercise 8)

9. **A Form for Best Realty:** Your assignment is to create a form similar to the one in Figure 2.18 that is based on the Best Realty database created in the previous exercise. The design of your form can be different from ours, but you must duplicate the functionality in our figure. Start with the Form Wizard, and then modify the resulting form as necessary so that your finished form accommodates all of the following:

a. The form should contain a control for every field in the underlying table. Format, move, size, and align the controls as necessary. Change the tab order of the controls so that the user tabs through the controls from left to right, top to bottom.

b. Add a calculated control to determine the price per square foot, which is equal to the sales price divided by the number of square feet. Change the format of this control to currency. Set the Tab Stop property to No.

c. Use a different background for the required fields (such as the PropertyID and Address) to emphasize that the data for these fields is required. Include a note at the bottom of the form to explain the color change.

d. Insert a form header with clip art (you do not have to use the same clip art as in our figure) and an appropriate title. Set the Size Mode property of the clip art to Stretch.

e. Add command buttons as indicated. The command buttons should be a uniform size with equal spacing between them. Test each command button to be sure that it works as intended.

f. Use the Page Setup command to be sure that the form will fit on a single page when printed. The completed form should display the data that you entered for the first property when you created the table in the previous problem. Print this form for your instructor.

g. Click the Add Record button to add a new record with PropertyID P0002. Use your instructor's name as the owner, and supply other information as you see fit. Click the record selector column to select this record. Pull down the File menu, click the Print command, then select the option button to print the selected record. Submit both forms to your instructor to show that you completed this assignment.

FIGURE 2.18   A Form for Best Realty (exercise 9)

10. **About Our Students:** Figure 2.19 illustrates a form that we create for all of our databases that appears automatically when the database is opened. The form is not based on a table within the database; that is, the form contains descriptive information about the database such as a version number, serial number, logo, and/or copyright notice. You can use our design and wording and/or you can modify either element as you see fit. Proceed as follows:

a. Open the *My First Database* that you have used throughout the chapter. Click the Forms button, then double click the command to create a form in Design view. Click and drag the borders of the form so that the size of the form is approximately 3½ inches by 3½ inches.

b. Display the Toolbox toolbar. Use the Label tool to add the various text boxes that appear on the form. We suggest an 8-point sans serif typeface (Arial, Tahoma, or MS Sans Serif).

c. Insert the clip art logo that you used earlier for the Students form. (Set the Size Mode property to Stretch so that the clip art is not truncated.)

d. Use the Command Button Wizard to insert a button to close the form. Change the text of the button to "OK" as shown in Figure 2.19.

e. You have to change the properties of the form itself to suppress the scroll bars, record selector, and navigation buttons because the form is not based on an underlying table. Go to Design view, right click the Form Selector button (the tiny square in the upper-left corner) to display a context-sensitive menu, choose Properties to display the Property sheet for the form, and then look for the appropriate properties.

f. Save the form as About Our Students. (The name of the form will appear automatically in the title bar when the form is displayed.) Go to the Form view to see the completed form. Return to Design view to make changes as necessary. Print the completed form for your instructor.

g. The Startup property can be used to display the form automatically when the database is open. Pull down the Tools menu, click the Startup command, select About Our Students in the Display Form/Page list box, and click OK. Close the database, then reopen it to see your form.

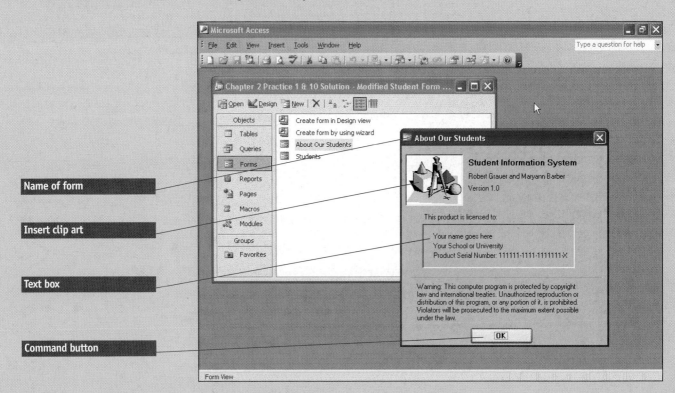

FIGURE 2.19 About Our Students (exercise 10)

MINI CASES

Employee Compensation

You have been hired as the Personnel Director for a medium-sized firm (500 employees) and are expected to implement a system to track employee compensation. You want to be able to calculate the age of every employee as well as the length of service. You want to know each employee's most recent performance evaluation. You want to be able to calculate the amount of the most recent salary increase, both in dollars and as a percentage of the previous salary. You also want to know how long the employee had to wait for that increase—that is, how much time elapsed between the present and previous salary. Design a table capable of providing this information. Create a supporting form.

The Stockbroker

A good friend has come to you for help. He is a new stockbroker whose firm provides computer support for existing clients, but does nothing in the way of data management for prospective clients. Your friend wants to use a PC to track the clients he is pursuing. He wants to know when he last contacted a person, how the contact was made (by phone or through the mail), and how interested the person was. He also wants to store the investment goals of each prospect, such as growth or income, and whether a person is interested in stocks, bonds, and/or a retirement account. And finally, he wants to record the amount of money the person has to invest. Design a table suitable for the information requirements. Create a supporting form, then use that form to enter data for two clients.

Form Design

Collect several examples of such real forms as a magazine subscription, auto registration, or employment application. Choose the form you like best and implement the design in Access. Start by creating the underlying table (with some degree of validation), then use the Form Wizard to create the form. How closely does the form you create resemble the paper form with which you began? To what extent does the data validation ensure the accuracy of the data?

File Compression

Access databases get very large very quickly. Accordingly, you might want to consider acquisition of a file compression program to facilitate copying large documents to a floppy disk in order to transport your documents to and from school, home, or work. You can download an evaluation copy of the popular WinZip program at www.winzip.com. Investigate the subject of file compression, then submit a summary of your findings to your instructor.

Information from the Database:
Reports and Queries

CASE STUDY
CITIZEN OF THE WORLD

Jodi McPherson, a student intern at the World Health Organization, was asked to conduct a study on overcrowding in countries around the world. The premise of the study is that we share one planet, that we are all "citizens of the world," and that we must work together to develop a global environmental policy. The study is to focus on population density, which is defined as the number of people per square kilometer. Jodi's supervisor has asked for a report that shows the twenty countries with the highest population density in descending order of that statistic. He has also requested two additional reports that show the twenty largest countries by area and the twenty largest countries by population. All three reports are to have a similar design with attractive formatting and a uniform logo.

Thus far, Jodi's internship has been terrific. She has a nicely equipped cubicle with a beautiful view and a state-of-the art computer with the latest version of Microsoft Access. She spent the first two weeks of her internship gathering data about each country, including its capital, area, and population. Once this was accomplished, Jodi entered the data into a table within an Access database and now needs to create various reports to analyze the data she has collected. ■

Your assignment is to put yourself in Jodi's place and develop the required reports based on the Access database, *Chapter 3 Case Study—Citizen of the World*. The database also contains an "About Citizen of the World" form that cites the source of the data. You are to read the chapter and pay special attention to Hands-on Exercises 2 and 3 that describe how to create a select query and how to create a report based on that query. Your next task will be to create a query that contains population density as a calculated field and that sorts the records in descending order of population density. You can then set the Top Values property to display the twenty countries with the highest population density. (In actuality, you will need three queries, one for each report.) Print a copy of each report for your instructor.

[handwritten margin notes: table form; overview. → ask que; Report .→ summary info.]

Chapters 1 and 2 described how to enter and maintain data through the use of tables and forms. This chapter shows how to convert the data into information through queries and reports. Queries enable you to ask questions about the database. Reports provide presentation quality output and display detail as well as summary information about the records in a database.

As you read the chapter, you will see that the objects in an Access database (tables, forms, reports, and queries) have many similar characteristics. We use these similarities to build on what you have learned in previous chapters. You already know, for example, that the controls in a form inherit their properties from the corresponding fields in a table. The same concept applies to the controls in a report. You also know that there are three types of controls—bound controls, unbound controls, and calculated controls. And since you know how to move and size controls within a form, you also know how to move and size the controls in a report. As you read the chapter, look for these similarities to apply your existing knowledge to new material.

[handwritten margin note: Report wizard →]

Reports

A *report* is a printed document that displays information from a database. Figure 3.1 shows several sample reports, each of which will be created in this chapter. The reports were created with the ***Report Wizard*** and are based on the Students table that was presented in Chapter 2. (The table has been expanded to 24 records.) As you view each report, ask yourself how the data in the table was rearranged to produce the information in the report.

The ***columnar (vertical) report*** in Figure 3.1a is the simplest type of report. It lists every field for every record in a single column (one record per page) and typically runs for many pages. The records in this report are displayed in the same sequence (by Social Security number) as the records in the table on which the report is based.

The ***tabular report*** in Figure 3.1b displays fields in a row rather than in a column. Each record in the underlying table is printed in its own row. Unlike the previous report, only selected fields are displayed, so the tabular report is more concise than the columnar report of Figure 3.1a. Note, too, that the records in the report are listed in alphabetical order rather than by Social Security number.

The report in Figure 3.1c is also a tabular report, but it is very different from the report in Figure 3.1b. The report in Figure 3.1c lists only a selected set of students (those students with a GPA of 3.50 or higher), as opposed to the earlier reports, which listed every student. The students are listed in descending order according to their GPA.

The report in Figure 3.1d displays the students in groups, according to their major, then computes the average GPA for each group. The report also contains summary information (not visible in Figure 3.1d) for the report as a whole, which computes the average GPA for all students. The individual fields within a student record are considered data. A list of students on the Dean's list, however, is information that has been produced from the data about the individual students. In similar fashion, the average GPA for each major is also information rather than data.

DATA VERSUS INFORMATION

Data and information are not synonymous although the terms are often interchanged. Data is the raw material and consists of the table (or tables) that comprise a database. Information is the finished product. Data is converted to information by selecting records, performing calculations on those records, and/or changing the sequence in which the records are displayed. Decisions in an organization are based on information rather than raw data.

Student Roster

SSN	111-11-1111
First Name	Ronnie
Last Name	Adili
Address	3543 Queen Avenue
City	Minneapolis
State	MN
Postal Code	55476-9899
Phone Number	(612) 445-7654
BirthDate	6/1/1985
Gender	F
Credits	60
QualityPoints	155
FinancialAid	No
Campus	3
Major	Business

Sunday, July 06, 2003   Page 1 of 24

(a) Columnar Report

Student Master List

Last Name	First Name	Phone Number	Major
Adili	Ronnie	(612) 445-7654	Business
DiGiacomo	Kevin	(305) 531-7652	Business
Gibson	Christopher	(305) 235-4563	Business
Ramsay	Robert	(212) 223-9889	Business
Watson	Ana	(305) 561-2334	Business
Faulkner	Eileen	(305) 489-8876	Communications
Joseph	Cedric	(404) 667-8955	Communications
Ortiz	Frances	(303) 575-3211	Communications
Price	Lori	(310) 961-2323	Communications
Slater	Erica	(312) 545-6978	Communications
Korba	Nickolas	(415) 664-0900	Education
Zimmerman	Kimberly	(713) 225-3434	Education
Berlin	Jared	(803) 223-7868	Engineering
Heltzer	Peter	(305) 753-4533	Engineering
Solomon	Wendy	(305) 666-4532	Engineering
Camejo	Oscar	(716) 433-3321	Liberal Arts
Parulis	Christa	(410) 877-6565	Liberal Arts
Watson	Ana	(305) 595-7877	Liberal Arts
Weissman	Kimberly	(904) 388-8605	Liberal Arts
Coe	Bradley	(415) 235-6543	Undecided
Cornell	Ryan	(404) 755-4490	Undecided
Frazier	Steven	(410) 995-8755	Undecided
Huerta	Carlos	(212) 344-5654	Undecided
Zacco	Michelle	(617) 884-3434	Undecided

7/6/2003   Page 1 of 1

(b) Tabular Report

Dean's List

First Name	Last Name	Major	Credits	Quality Points	GPA
Peter	Heltzer	Engineering	25	100	4.00
Cedric	Joseph	Communications	45	170	3.78
Erica	Slater	Communications	105	390	3.71
Kevin	DiGiacomo	Business	105	375	3.57
Wendy	Solomon	Engineering	50	175	3.50

Sunday, July 06, 2003   Page 1 of 1

(c) Dean's List

GPA by Major

Major	Last Name	First Name	GPA
Business			
	Adili	Ronnie	2.58
	DiGiacomo	Kevin	3.57
	Gibson	Christopher	1.71
	Ramsay	Robert	3.24
	Watson	Ana	2.50
	Average GPA for major		2.72
Communications			
	Faulkner	Eileen	2.67
	Joseph	Cedric	3.78
	Ortiz	Frances	2.14
	Price	Lori	1.75
	Slater	Erica	3.71
	Average GPA for major		2.81
Education			
	Korba	Nickolas	1.66
	Zimmerman	Kimberly	3.29
	Average GPA for major		2.48
Engineering			
	Berlin	Jared	2.50
	Heltzer	Peter	4.00
	Solomon	Wendy	3.50
	Average GPA for major		3.33
Liberal Arts			
	Camejo	Oscar	2.80
	Parulis	Christa	1.80
	Watson	Ana	2.79
	Weissman	Kimberly	2.63
	Average GPA for major		2.51
Undecided			
	Coe	Bradley	2.75
	Cornell	Ryan	1.78
	Frazier	Steven	1.29
	Huerta	Carlos	2.67
	Zacco	Michelle	3.24
	Average GPA for major		2.35

Sunday, July 06, 2003   Page 1 of 2

(d) Summary Report

FIGURE 3.1   Report Types

Anatomy of a Report

All reports are based on an underlying table or query within the database. (Queries are discussed later in the chapter.) A report, however, displays the data or information in a more attractive fashion because it contains various headings and/or other decorative items that are not present in either a table or a query.

The easiest way to learn about reports is to compare a printed report with its underlying design. Consider, for example, Figure 3.2a, which displays the tabular report, and Figure 3.2b, which shows the underlying design. The latter shows how a report is divided into sections, which appear at designated places when the report is printed. There are seven types of sections, but a report need not contain all seven.

The *Report Header* appears once, at the beginning of a report. It typically contains information describing the report, such as its title and the date the report was printed. (The report header appears above the page header on the first page of the report.) The *Report Footer* appears once at the end of the report, above the page footer on the last page of the report, and displays summary information for the report as a whole.

The *Page Header* appears at the top of every page in a report and can be used to display page numbers, column headings, and other descriptive information. The *Page Footer* appears at the bottom of every page and may contain page numbers (when they are not in the page header) or other descriptive information.

A *Group Header* appears at the beginning of a group of records to identify the group. A *Group Footer* appears after the last record in a group and contains summary information about the group. Group headers and footers are used only when the records in a report are sorted (grouped) according to a common value in a specific field. These sections do not appear in the report of Figure 3.2, but were shown earlier in the report of Figure 3.1d.

The *Detail section* appears in the main body of a report and is printed once for every record in the underlying table (or query). It displays one or more fields for each record in columnar or tabular fashion, according to the design of the report.

The Report Wizard

The Report Wizard is the easiest way to create a report, just as the Form Wizard is the easiest way to create a form. The Report Wizard asks you questions about the report you want, then builds the report for you. You can accept the report as is, or you can customize it to better suit your needs.

Figure 3.3a displays the New Report dialog box, from which you can select the Report Wizard. The Report Wizard, in turn, requires you to specify the table or query on which the report will be based. The report in this example will be based on an expanded version of the Students table that was created in Chapter 2.

After you specify the underlying table, you select one or more fields from that table, as shown in Figure 3.3b. The Report Wizard then asks you to select a layout (e.g., Tabular in Figure 3.3c.) and a style (e.g., Soft Gray in Figure 3.3d). This is all the information the Report Wizard requires, and it proceeds to create the report for you. The controls on the report correspond to the fields you selected and are displayed in accordance with the specified layout.

Apply What You Know

The Report Wizard provides an excellent starting point, but typically does not create the report exactly as you would like it to be. Accordingly, you can modify a report created by the Report Wizard, just as you can modify a form created by the Form Wizard. The techniques are the same, and you should look for similarities between forms and reports so that you can apply what you already know. Knowledge of one is helpful in understanding the other.

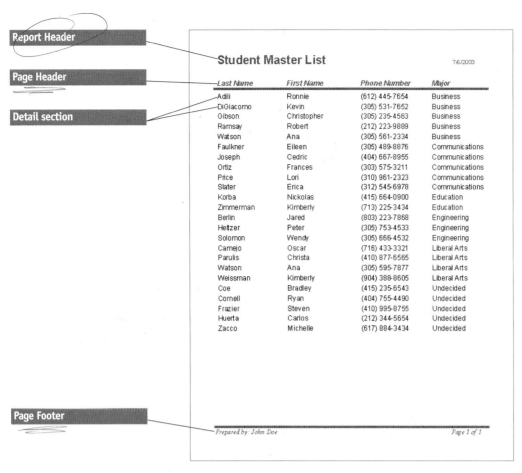

(a) The Printed Report

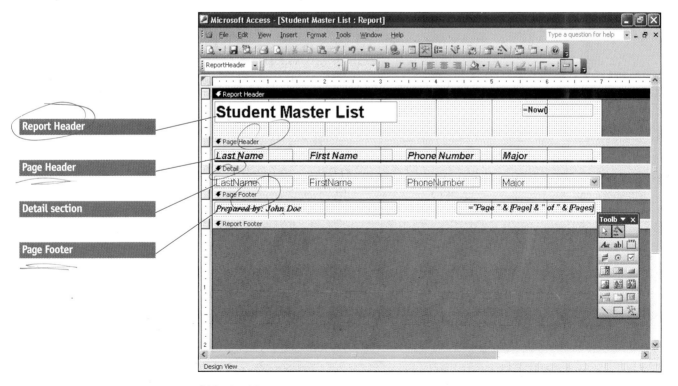

(b) Design View

FIGURE 3.2 Anatomy of a Report

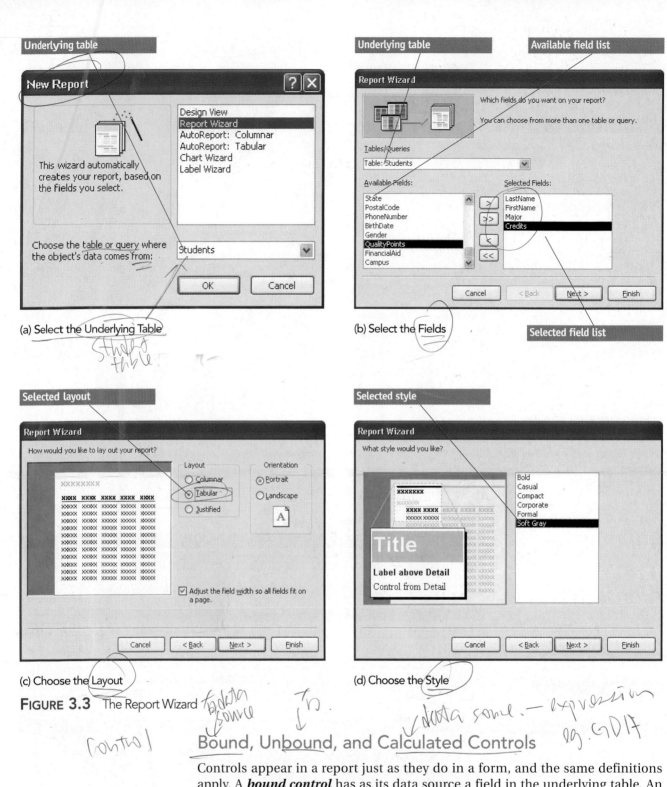

(a) Select the Underlying Table

(b) Select the Fields

Selected field list

Selected layout

Selected style

(c) Choose the Layout

(d) Choose the Style

FIGURE 3.3 The Report Wizard

Bound, Unbound, and Calculated Controls

Controls appear in a report just as they do in a form, and the same definitions apply. A **_bound control_** has as its data source a field in the underlying table. An **_unbound control_** has no data source and is used to display titles, labels, lines, rectangles, and graphics. A **_calculated control_** has as its data source an expression rather than a field. A student's Grade Point Average is an example of a calculated control since it is computed by dividing the number of quality points by the number of credits. The means for selecting, sizing, moving, aligning, and deleting controls are the same, regardless of whether you are working on a form or a report. And, as you may have guessed, it is time for our next hands-on exercise.

1   The Report Wizard

Objective   To use the Report Wizard to create a new report; to modify an existing report by adding, deleting, and/or modifying its controls. Use Figure 3.4 as a guide in the exercise.

Step 1:   **Open the Our Students Database**

- Start Access. Pull down the **File menu** and click the **Open command** or click the link to **More . . .** if the task pane is open.

- Open the **Our Students database** in the Exploring Access folder. Click **Open** in response to the security warning.

- The Our Students database has the identical design as the database you created in Chapter 2. We have, however, expanded the Students table so that it contains 24 records to enable you to create more meaningful reports and queries from the database.

- Click the **Reports button** in the Database window, then click the **New command button** to display the New Report dialog box in Figure 3.4a. Select the **Report Wizard** as the means of creating the report.

- Click the **drop-down arrow** to display the tables and queries in the database in order to select the one on which the report will be based. (There are currently two tables and no queries.)

- Click **Students**, then click **OK** to start the Report Wizard, which prompts you for the information it needs to create a report.

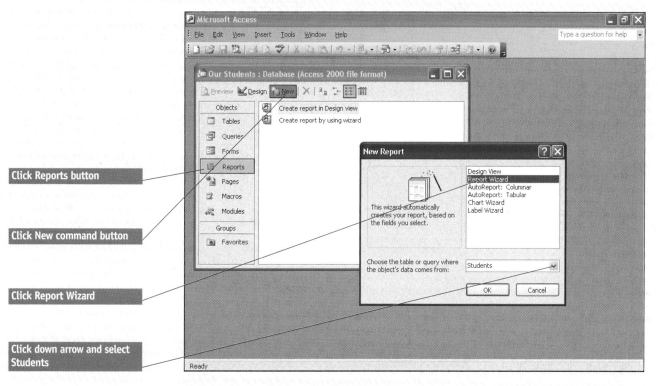

(a) Open the Our Students Database (step 1)

FIGURE 3.4   Hands-on Exercise 1

Step 2:   The Report Wizard

- You should see the dialog box in Figure 3.4b, which displays all of the fields in the Students table. Double click the **LastName field** in the Available Fields list box, as shown in Figure 3.4b.

- Enter the remaining fields (**FirstName**, **PhoneNumber**, and **Major**) one at a time by double clicking the field name. Click **Next**.

- The Report Wizard displays several additional screens asking about the report you want to create. The first screen asks whether you want to choose any grouping levels. Click **Next** without specifying a grouping level.

- The next screen asks whether you want to sort the records. Click the **drop-down arrow** to display the available fields, then select **LastName**. Click **Next**.

- The **Tabular layout** is selected, as is **Portrait orientation**. Be sure the box is checked to **Adjust field width so all fields fit on a page**. Click **Next**.

- Choose **Corporate** as the style. Click **Next**.

- Enter **Student Master List** as the title for your report. The option button to **Preview the Report** is already selected.

- Click the **Finish button** to exit the Report Wizard and view the report.

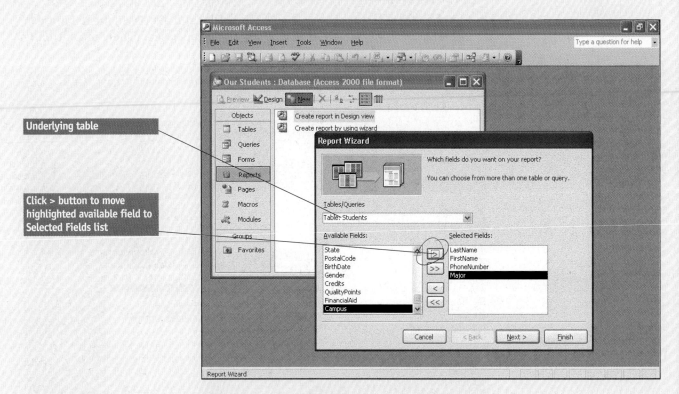

Underlying table

Click > button to move highlighted available field to Selected Fields list

(b) The Report Wizard (step 2)

FIGURE 3.4   Hands-on Exercise 1 (*continued*)

WHAT THE REPORT WIZARD DOESN'T TELL YOU

The fastest way to select a field is by double clicking; that is, double click a field in the Available Fields list box, and it is automatically moved to the Selected Fields list for inclusion in the report. The process also works in reverse; that is, you can double click a field in the Selected Fields list to remove it from the report.

Step 3: Preview the Report

- Click the **Maximize button** so the report takes the entire window as shown in Figure 3.4c.
  - ❏ There is a Report Header (the title of the report) at the beginning of the report, a Page Header (column headings) at the top of the page, and a Page Footer at the bottom of the page.
  - ❏ There is also a detail line for every record in the underlying table.

- Click the **drop-down arrow** on the Zoom box so that you can view the report at different magnifications. We chose 75%.

- Click the **scroll arrows** on the vertical scroll bar to view the names of additional students. Click and drag the horizontal scroll bar to position the report within the window.

- Click the **Close button** to close the Print Preview window and change to the Report Design view. The next step describes how to modify the report so that the controls are spaced more attractively.

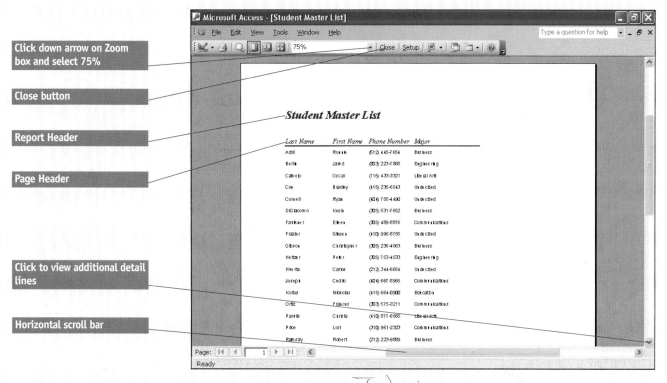

Click down arrow on Zoom box and select 75%

Close button

Report Header

Page Header

Click to view additional detail lines

Horizontal scroll bar

(c) Preview the Report (step 3)   Tabular.

FIGURE 3.4 Hands-on Exercise 1 (*continued*)

THE PRINT PREVIEW WINDOW

The Print Preview window enables you to preview a report in various ways. Click the One Page, Two Pages, or Multiple Pages buttons for different views of a report. Use the Zoom button to toggle between the full page and zoom (magnified) views, or use the Zoom box to choose a specific magnification. The Navigation buttons at the bottom of the Print Preview window enable you to preview a specific page, while the vertical scroll bar at the right side of the window lets you scroll within a page.

Step 4: **Modify an Existing Control**

- Click the **Major control** in the Detail section, then press the **Shift key** as you click its label in the Page Header. Point to the border of either control, then drag the controls to the right. Move the **PhoneNumber** and **FirstName** controls in similar fashion so that the fields are spaced attractively across the width of the report.

- Click the **blue line** in the Page Header to select the line. Press the **Shift key** (to retain a horizontal line) as you drag the sizing handle to the right side of the page.

- Click and drag the border of the control containing the **Now function** from the Report Footer to the Report Header as shown in Figure 3.4d.

- Size the control as necessary, then check that the control is still selected and click the **Align Right button** on the Formatting toolbar.

- Point to the control, then click the **right mouse button** to display a shortcut menu, and click **Properties** to display the Properties sheet.

- Click the **Format tab** in the Properties sheet, click the **Format property**, then click the **drop-down arrow** to display the available formats. Click **Short Date**, then close the Properties sheet.

- Pull down the **File menu** and click **Save** (or click the **Save button**) to save the modified design

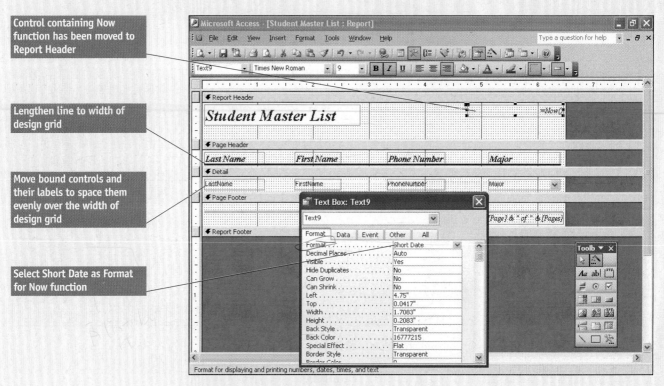

Control containing Now function has been moved to Report Header

Lengthen line to width of design grid

Move bound controls and their labels to space them evenly over the width of design grid

Select Short Date as Format for Now function

(d) Modify an Existing Control (step 4)

FIGURE **3.4** Hands-on Exercise 1 (*continued*)

THE REPORT WIZARD, FUNCTIONS, AND FIELDS

The Report Wizard automatically inserts the Now function and the Page and Pages fields to enhance the appearance of a report. The Now function returns the current date and time. The Page and Pages fields return the specific page number and the total number of pages, respectively. You can also add these controls explicitly by creating a text box, then replacing the default unbound control by an equal sign, followed by the function or field—for example, =Now() to insert the current date and time.

Step 5: Add an Unbound Control

- Click the **Label tool** on the Toolbox toolbar, then click and drag in the Report Footer where you want the label to go and release the mouse. You should see a flashing insertion point inside the label control. (If you see the word *Unbound* instead of the insertion point, it means you selected the Text Box tool rather than the Label tool; delete the text box and begin again.)

- Type **Prepared by** followed by your name as shown in Figure 3.4e. Press **Enter** to complete the entry and also select the control.

- You will see a green triangle in the upper-left corner of the control and an exclamation point icon to indicate a potential error. Point to the icon, click the **down arrow** to display the list of potential errors, then click **Ignore Error**.

- Point to the control, click the **right mouse button** to display the shortcut menu, then click **Properties** to display the Properties dialog box.

- Click the **down arrow** on the scroll bar, then scroll until you see the Font Size property. Click in the **Font Size box**, click the **drop-down arrow**, then scroll until you can change the font size to **9**. Close the Property sheet.

- Save the report.

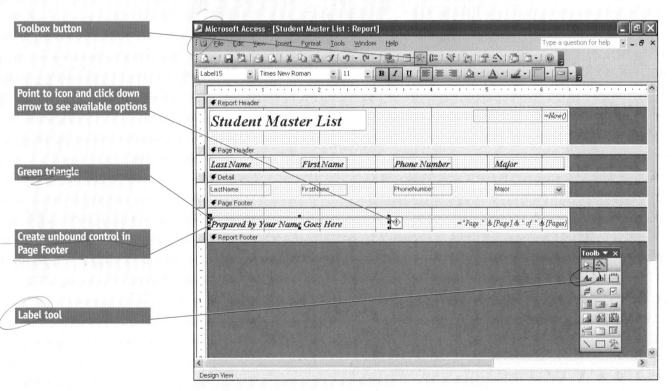

Toolbox button

Point to icon and click down arrow to see available options

Green triangle

Create unbound control in Page Footer

Label tool

(e) Add an Unbound Control (step 5)

FIGURE 3.4 Hands-on Exercise 1 (*continued*)

MISSING TOOLBARS

The Report Design, Formatting, and Toolbox toolbars appear by default in the Report Design view, but any (or all) of these toolbars may be hidden at the discretion of the user. If any of these toolbars does not appear, point to any visible toolbar, click the right mouse button to display a shortcut menu, then click the name of the toolbar you want to display. You can also click the Toolbox button on the Report Design toolbar to display (hide) the Toolbox toolbar.

Step 6: **Change the Sort Order**

- Pull down the **View menu**. Click the **Sorting and Grouping command** to display the Sorting and Grouping dialog box in Figure 3.4f. The students are currently sorted by last name.

- Click the **drop-down arrow** in the Field Expression box. Click **Major**. (The ascending sequence is selected automatically.)

- Click on the next line in the Field Expression box, click the **drop-down arrow** to display the available fields, then click **LastName** to sort the students alphabetically within major.

- Close the Sorting and Grouping dialog box. The students will now be listed by major and alphabetically by last name within each major when you view the report in step 7.

- Save the report.

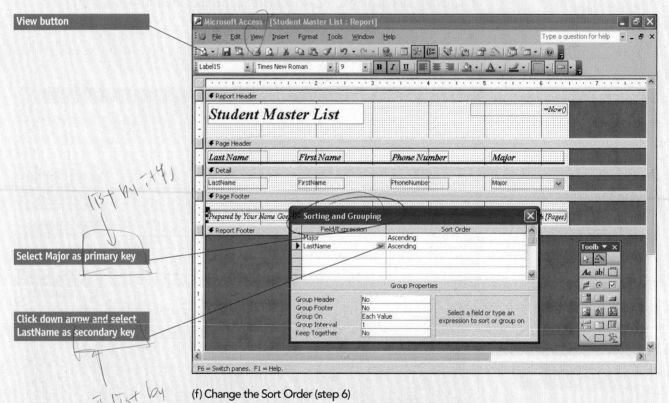

(f) Change the Sort Order (step 6)

FIGURE 3.4 Hands-on Exercise 1 (*continued*)

ADDING A GROUP HEADER OR FOOTER

You can add or remove a Group Header or Footer after a report has been created. Pull down the View menu and click the Sorting and Grouping command to display the associated dialog box. Click the line containing the field for which you want to add or remove the element, then enter Yes or No, respectively, in the Group Properties area and close the dialog box. The newly created header or footer is initially empty, and thus you will have to insert the necessary controls to complete the report.

Step 7: View the Modified Report

- Click the **View button** to preview the finished report. If necessary, click the **Zoom button** on the Print Preview toolbar so that the display on your monitor matches Figure 3.4g. The report has changed so that:
  - ❑ The date appears in the Report Header (as opposed to the Report Footer). The format of the date has changed to a numbered month, and the day of the week has been eliminated.
  - ❑ The controls are spaced attractively across the page.
  - ❑ The students are listed by major and, within each major, alphabetically according to last name.
  - ❑ Your name appears in the Report Footer. Click the **down arrow** on the vertical scroll bar to move to the bottom of the page to see your name.

- Click the **Print button** to print the report and submit it to your instructor. Click the **Close button** to exit the Print Preview window.

- Click the **Close button** in the Report Design window. Click **Yes** if asked whether to save the changes to the Student Master List report.

- Close the database. Exit Access if you do not want to continue with the next exercise at this time.

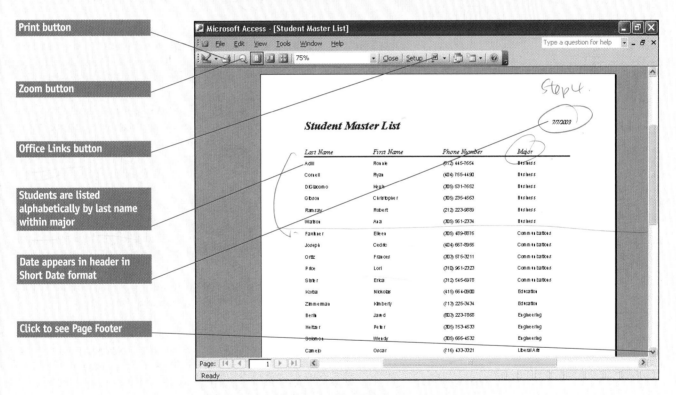

(g) View the Modified Report (step 7)

FIGURE 3.4 Hands-on Exercise 1 (*continued*)

LINK TO WORD OR EXCEL

Click the down arrow on the Office Links button to display links to Word and Excel. Click either link to start the associated application, where you can take advantage of the extended editing or analysis (including chart) capabilities in Word and Excel, respectively. You can save the report as either a Word document or Excel workbook, but any subsequent changes to the Access report are static and will not be reflected in the other applications.

INTRODUCTION TO QUERIES

The report you just created displayed every student in the underlying table. What if, however, we wanted to see just the students who are majoring in Business? Or the students who are receiving financial aid? Or the students who are majoring in Business *and* receiving financial aid? The ability to ask questions such as these, and to see the answers to those questions, is provided through a query. Queries represent the real power of a database.

A *query* lets you see the data you want in the sequence that you want it. It lets you select specific records from a table (or from several tables) and show some or all of the fields for the selected records. It also lets you perform calculations to display data that is not explicitly stored in the underlying table(s), such as a student's GPA.

The query is created by the *Simple Query Wizard* or directly in Design view. The results of the query are displayed in a *dynaset*, which contains the records that satisfy the criteria specified in the query.

A dynaset looks and acts like a table, but it isn't a table; it is a *dyna*mic sub*set* of a table that selects and sorts records as specified in the query. A dynaset is similar to a table in appearance and, like a table, it enables you to enter a new record or modify or delete an existing record. Any changes made in the dynaset are automatically reflected in the underlying table.

Figure 3.5a displays the Students table we have been using throughout the chapter. (We omit some of the fields for ease of illustration.) Figure 3.5b contains the design grid used to select students whose major is "Undecided" and further, to list those students in alphabetical order. (The design grid is explained in the next section.) Figure 3.5c displays the answer to the query in the form of a dynaset.

The table in Figure 3.5a contains 24 records. The dynaset in Figure 3.5c has only five records, corresponding to the students who are undecided about their major. The table in Figure 3.5a has 15 fields for each record (some of the fields are hidden). The dynaset in Figure 3.5c has only four fields. The records in the table are in Social Security Number order (the primary key), whereas the records in the dynaset are in alphabetical order by last name.

The query in Figure 3.5 is an example of a *select query*, which is the most common type of query. A select query searches the underlying table (Figure 3.5a in the example) to retrieve the data that satisfies the query. The data is displayed in a dynaset (Figure 3.5c), which can be modified to update the data in the underlying table(s). The specifications for selecting records and determining which fields will be displayed for the selected records, as well as the sequence of the selected records, are established within the design grid of Figure 3.5b.

The design grid consists of columns and rows. Each field in the query has its own column and contains multiple rows. The *Field row* displays the field name. The *Sort row* enables you to sort in *ascending* or *descending sequence*. The *Show row* controls whether or not the field will be displayed in the dynaset. The *Criteria row(s)* determines the records that will be selected, such as students with an undecided major.

REPORTS, QUERIES, AND TABLES

Every report is based on either a table or a query. The design of the report may be the same with respect to the fields that are included, but the actual reports will be very different with respect to the information they provide. A report based on a table contains every record in the table. A report based on a query contains only the records that satisfy the criteria in the query.

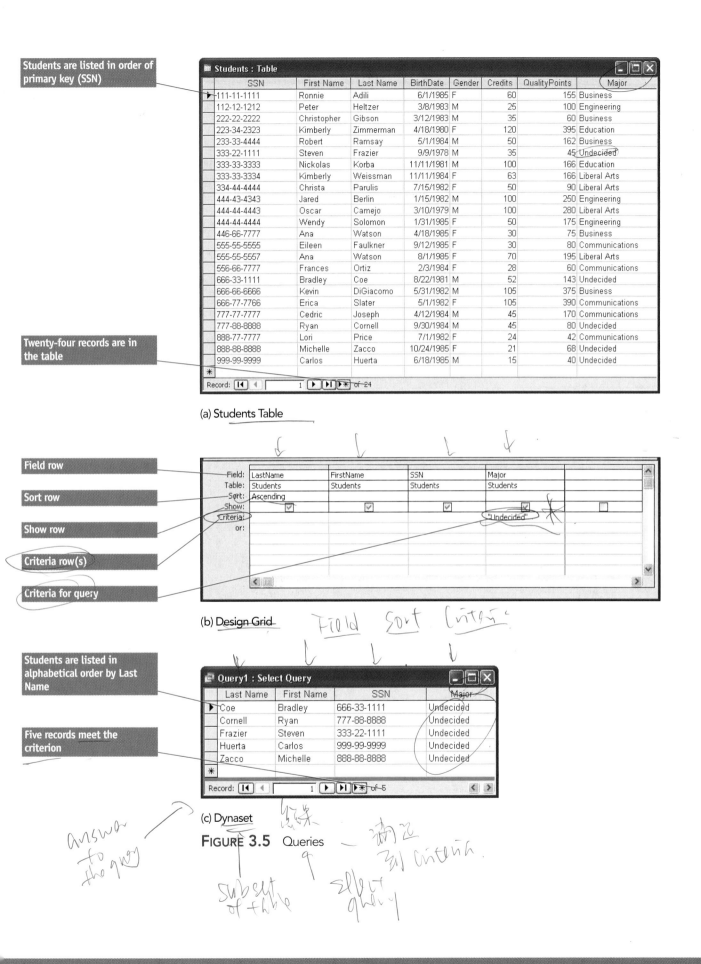

Students are listed in order of primary key (SSN)

Students : Table

SSN	First Name	Last Name	BirthDate	Gender	Credits	QualityPoints	Major
111-11-1111	Ronnie	Adili	6/1/1985	F	60	155	Business
112-12-1212	Peter	Heltzer	3/8/1983	M	25	100	Engineering
222-22-2222	Christopher	Gibson	3/12/1983	M	35	60	Business
223-34-2323	Kimberly	Zimmerman	4/18/1980	F	120	395	Education
233-33-4444	Robert	Ramsay	5/1/1984	M	50	162	Business
333-22-1111	Steven	Frazier	9/9/1978	M	35	45	Undecided
333-33-3333	Nickolas	Korba	11/11/1981	M	100	166	Education
333-33-3334	Kimberly	Weissman	11/11/1984	F	63	166	Liberal Arts
334-44-4444	Christa	Parulis	7/15/1982	F	50	90	Liberal Arts
444-43-4343	Jared	Berlin	1/15/1982	M	100	250	Engineering
444-44-4443	Oscar	Camejo	3/10/1979	M	100	280	Liberal Arts
444-44-4444	Wendy	Solomon	1/31/1985	F	50	175	Engineering
446-66-7777	Ana	Watson	4/18/1985	F	30	75	Business
555-55-5555	Eileen	Faulkner	9/12/1985	F	30	80	Communications
555-55-5557	Ana	Watson	8/1/1985	F	70	195	Liberal Arts
556-66-7777	Frances	Ortiz	2/3/1984	F	28	60	Communications
666-33-1111	Bradley	Coe	8/22/1981	M	52	143	Undecided
666-66-6666	Kevin	DiGiacomo	5/31/1982	M	105	375	Business
666-77-7766	Erica	Slater	5/1/1982	F	105	390	Communications
777-77-7777	Cedric	Joseph	4/12/1984	M	45	170	Communications
777-88-8888	Ryan	Cornell	9/30/1984	M	45	80	Undecided
888-77-7777	Lori	Price	7/1/1982	F	24	42	Communications
888-88-8888	Michelle	Zacco	10/24/1985	F	21	68	Undecided
999-99-9999	Carlos	Huerta	6/18/1985	M	15	40	Undecided

Twenty-four records are in the table

Record: ◄◄ ◄ 1 ► ►► ►* of 24

(a) Students Table

Field row
Sort row
Show row
Criteria row(s)
Criteria for query

Field:	LastName	FirstName	SSN	Major	
Table:	Students	Students	Students	Students	
Sort:	Ascending				
Show:	☑	☑	☑	☑	☐
Criteria:				"Undecided"	
or:					

(b) Design Grid

Students are listed in alphabetical order by Last Name

Query1 : Select Query

Last Name	First Name	SSN	Major
Coe	Bradley	666-33-1111	Undecided
Cornell	Ryan	777-88-8888	Undecided
Frazier	Steven	333-22-1111	Undecided
Huerta	Carlos	999-99-9999	Undecided
Zacco	Michelle	888-88-8888	Undecided

Five records meet the criterion

Record: ◄◄ ◄ 1 ► ►► ►* of 5

(c) Dynaset

FIGURE 3.5 Queries

Query Design View

A select query is created by the Simple Query Wizard and/or in Design view as shown in Figure 3.6. The upper portion of the Design View window contains the field list for the table(s) on which the query is based (the Students table in this example). The lower portion of the window displays the ***design grid***, which is where the specifications for the select query are entered. A field is added to the design grid by dragging it from the field list.

The data type of a field determines the way in which the criteria are specified for that field. The criterion for a text field is enclosed in quotation marks. The criteria for number, currency, and counter fields are shown as digits with or without a decimal point. (Commas and dollar signs are not allowed.) Dates are enclosed in pound signs and are entered in the mm/dd/yy format. The criterion for a Yes/No field is entered as Yes (or True) or No (or False).

Access accepts values for text and date fields in the design grid in multiple formats. The value for a text field can be entered with or without quotation marks (Undecided or "Undecided"). A date can be entered with or without pound signs (1/1/97 or #1/1/97#). Access converts your entries to standard format as soon as you move to the next cell in the design grid. Thus, text entries are always shown in quotation marks, and dates are enclosed in pound signs.

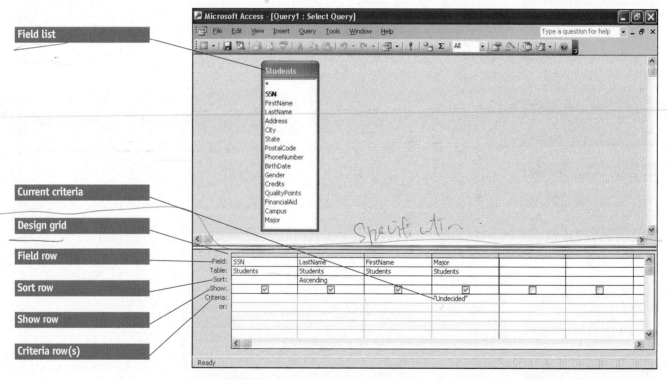

FIGURE 3.6 Query Design View

WILD CARDS

Select queries recognize the question mark and asterisk wild cards that enable you to search for a pattern within a text field. A question mark stands for a single character in the same position as the question mark; thus H?ll will return Hall, Hill, and Hull. An asterisk stands for any number of characters in the same position as the asterisk; for example, S*nd will return Sand, Stand, and Strand.

Selection Criteria

To specify selection criteria in the design grid, enter a value or expression in the Criteria row of the appropriate column. Figure 3.7 contains several examples of simple criteria and provides a basic introduction to select queries.

The criterion in Figure 3.7a selects the students majoring in Business. The criteria for text fields are case insensitive. Thus, *"Business"* is the same as *"business"* or *"BUSINESS"*.

Values entered into multiple columns of the same Criteria row implement an **AND condition** in which the selected records must meet *all* of the specified criteria. The criteria in Figure 3.7b select students who are majoring in Business *and* who are from the state of Florida. The criteria in Figure 3.7c select Communications majors who are receiving financial aid.

Values entered into different Criteria rows are connected by an **OR condition** in which the selected records may satisfy *any* of the indicated criteria. The criteria in Figure 3.7d select students who are majoring in Business *or* who are from Florida or both.

Field:	LastName	State	Major	BirthDate	FinancialAid	Credits
Sort:						
Show:	☑	☑	☑	☑	☑	☑
Criteria:			"Business"			
or:						

(a) Business Majors

Field:	LastName	State	Major	BirthDate	FinancialAid	Credits
Sort:						
Show:	☑	☑	☑	☑	☑	☑
Criteria:		"FL"	"Business"			
or:						

(b) Business Majors from Florida

Field:	LastName	State	Major	BirthDate	FinancialAid	Credits
Sort:						
Show:	☑	☑	☑	☑	☑	☑
Criteria:			"Communications"		Yes	
or:						

(c) Communications Majors Receiving Financial Aid

Field:	LastName	State	Major	BirthDate	FinancialAid	Credits
Sort:						
Show:	☑	☑	☑	☑	☑	☑
Criteria:		"FL"				
or:			"Business"			

(d) Business Majors or Students from Florida

FIGURE 3.7   Selection Criteria

Relational operators (>, <, >=, <=, =, and <>) are used with date or number fields to return records within a designated range. The criteria in Figure 3.7e select Engineering majors with fewer than 60 credits.

Criteria can grow more complex by combining multiple AND and OR conditions. The criteria in Figure 3.7f select Engineering majors with fewer than 60 credits *or* Communications majors who were born on or after April 1, 1974.

Other functions enable you to impose still other criteria. The **Between function** selects records that fall within a range of values. The criterion in Figure 3.7g selects students who have between 60 and 90 credits. The **NOT function** selects records that do not contain the designated value. The criterion in Figure 3.7h selects students with majors other than Liberal Arts.

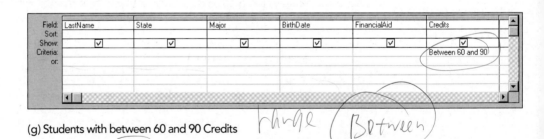

Field:	LastName	State	Major	BirthDate	FinancialAid	Credits
Sort:						
Show:	✓	✓		✓	✓	✓
Criteria:			"Engineering"			<60
or:						

(e) Engineering Majors with Fewer than 60 Credits

Field:	LastName	State	Major	BirthDate	FinancialAid	Credits
Sort:						
Show:	✓	✓		✓	✓	✓
Criteria:			"Engineering"			<60
or:			Communications	>=#4/1/74#		

(f) Engineering Majors with Fewer than 60 Credits or Communications Majors Born on or after April 1, 1974

Field:	LastName	State	Major	BirthDate	FinancialAid	Credits
Sort:						
Show:	✓	✓	✓	✓	✓	✓
Criteria:						Between 60 and 90
or:						

(g) Students with between 60 and 90 Credits

Field:	LastName	State	Major	BirthDate	FinancialAid	Credits
Sort:						
Show:	✓	✓	✓	✓	✓	✓
Criteria:			Not "Liberal Arts"			
or:						

(h) Students with Majors Other than Liberal Arts

FIGURE 3.7 Selection Criteria (*continued*)

hands-on exercise

2

Creating a Select Query

Objective To create a select query using the Simple Query Wizard; to show how changing values in a dynaset changes the values in the underlying table; to create a report based on a query. Use Figure 3.8 as a guide in the exercise.

Step 1: **The Simple Query Wizard**

- Start Access and open the **Our Students database** from the previous exercise. Click **Open** in response to the security warning.

- Click the **Queries button** in the Database window. Double click the icon next to **Create query by using wizard** to start the Simple Query Wizard as shown in Figure 3.8a.

- The Students table should be already selected from the Tables/Queries list box. (If not, click the **drop-down arrow** in this list box and select the **Students table**.)

- Select the **LastName field** from the field list at the left, then click the **> button** to add this field to the Selected Fields list. (Use the **< button** if necessary to remove a field from the Selected Fields list.)

- Add the **FirstName**, **PhoneNumber**, **Major**, and **Credits fields** in that order to the Selected Fields list. (You can double click a field name to add it to the field list.) Click **Next**.

- The option button for a **Detail query** is selected. Click **Next**.

- Enter **Undecided Major** as the name of the query. Click the option button that says you want to **Modify the query design**. Click **Finish**.

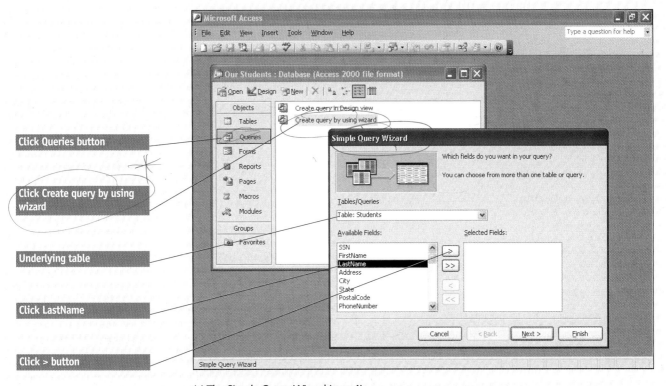

(a) The Simple Query Wizard (step 1)

FIGURE 3.8 Hands-on Exercise 2

Step 2: **Complete the Query**

■ You should see the Query Design window as shown in Figure 3.8b. (Your query has not yet been completed, however, and so your figure does not match ours at this time.) Click the **Maximize button** so that the Design window takes the entire screen.

■ Click and drag the border between the upper and lower portions of the window to give you more room in the upper half. Click and drag the bottom of the field list so that you can see all of the fields in the Students table.

■ Check that you have all of the necessary fields in the lower half of the window. You can click and drag any missing field from the field list to the grid, and/or you can select a column, then drag it within the grid to rearrange the order of the fields.

■ Click the **Criteria row** for **Major**. Type **Undecided**.

■ Click the **Sort row** under the LastName field, click the **drop-down arrow**, then select **Ascending** as the sort sequence.

■ Click the **Save button** to save the query.

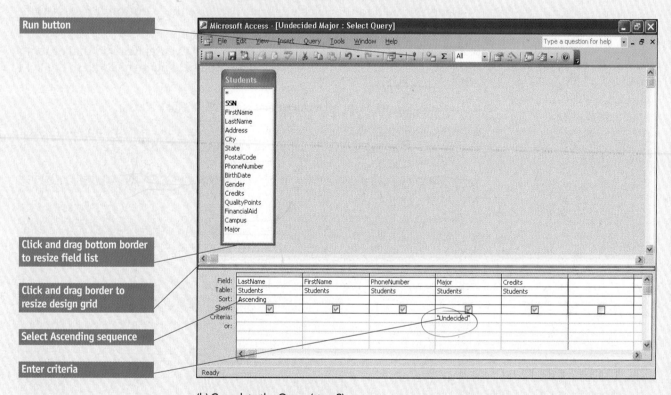

(b) Complete the Query (step 2)

FIGURE 3.8 Hands-on Exercise 2 (continued)

CUSTOMIZE THE QUERY WINDOW

The Query window displays the field list and design grid in its upper and lower halves, respectively. To increase (decrease) the size of either portion of the window, drag the line dividing the upper and lower sections. Drag the title bar to move a field list. You can also size a field list by dragging a border just as you would size any other window. Press the F6 key to toggle between the upper and lower halves as you work in the Design view.

Step 3: **Run the Query**

- Pull down the **Query menu** and click **Run** (or click the **Run button**) to run the query and change to the Datasheet view.

- You should see the five records in the dynaset of Figure 3.8c. Change Ryan Cornell's major to Business by clicking in the **Major field**, clicking the **drop-down arrow**, then choosing **Business** from the drop-down list.

- Click the **View button** to return to the Design view in order to rerun the query. Click the **Run button**.

- You should now see four students. Ryan Cornell no longer appears because he has changed his major.

- Change to the Design view.

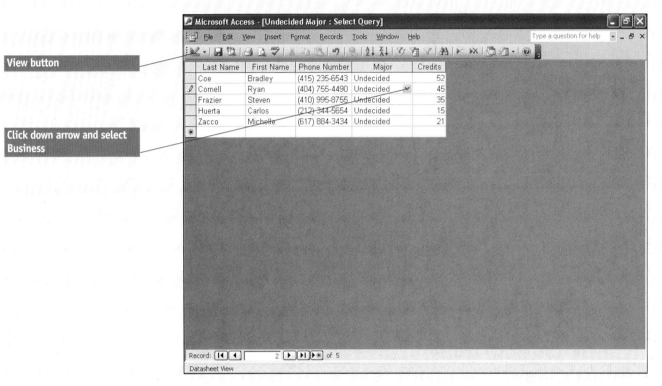

(c) Run the Query (step 3)

FIGURE 3.8 Hands-on Exercise 2 (*continued*)

THE DYNASET

A query represents a question and an answer. The question is developed by using the design grid in the Query Design view. The answer is displayed in a dynaset that contains the records that satisfy the criteria specified in the query. A dynaset looks and acts like a table, but it isn't a table; it is a dynamic subset of a table that selects and sorts records as specified in the query. A dynaset is like a table in that you can enter a new record or modify or delete an existing record. It is dynamic because the changes made to the dynaset are automatically reflected in the underlying table.

Step 4: Modify the Query

- Click the **Show check box** in the Major field to remove the check as shown in Figure 3.8d. The Major field will be used to select students, but it will not appear in the dynaset.

- Click the **Criteria row** under credits. Type **>30** to select only the Undecided majors with more than 30 credits.

- Click the **Save button** to save the revised query. Click the **Run button** to run the revised query.

- This time there are only two records (Bradley Coe and Steven Frazier) in the dynaset, and the major is no longer displayed.

- Carlos Huerta and Michelle Zacco do not appear because they do not have more than 30 credits.

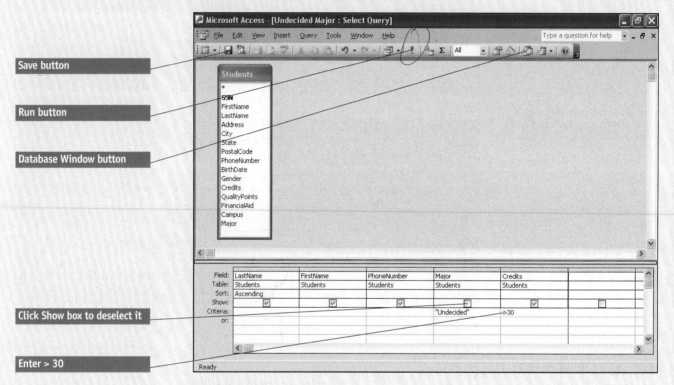

Save button

Run button

Database Window button

Click Show box to deselect it

Enter > 30

(d) Modify the Query (step 4)

FIGURE 3.8 Hands-on Exercise 2 (*continued*)

FLEXIBLE CRITERIA

Access offers a great deal of flexibility in the way you enter the criteria for a text field. Quotation marks and/or an equal sign are optional. Thus, "Undecided", Undecided, =Undecided, or ="Undecided" are all valid, and you may choose any of these formats. Access will convert your entry to standard format ("Undecided" in this example) after you have moved to the next cell. Numeric fields, however, are always entered without quotation marks.

Step 5: Create a Report

■ Pull down the **Window menu** and click **1 Our Students: Database** (or click the **Database window button** on the toolbar). You will see the Database window in Figure 3.8e.

■ Click the **Reports button**, then double click the icon next to **Create report by using wizard**.

■ Click the **drop-down arrow** on the **Tables/Queries** list box and select **Query:Undecided Major**. All of the visible fields (major has been hidden) are displayed. Click the **>>button** to select all of the fields in the query for the report. Click **Next**.

■ You do not want to choose additional grouping levels. Click **Next** to move to the next screen.

■ There is no need to specify a sort sequence. Click **Next**.

■ The **Tabular layout** is selected, as is **Portrait orientation**. Be sure the box is checked to **Adjust field width so all fields fit on a page**. Click **Next**.

■ Choose **Soft Gray** as the style. Click **Next**.

■ If necessary, enter **Undecided Major** as the title for your report. The option button to **Preview the report** is already selected. Click the **Finish command button** to exit the Report Wizard and view the report.

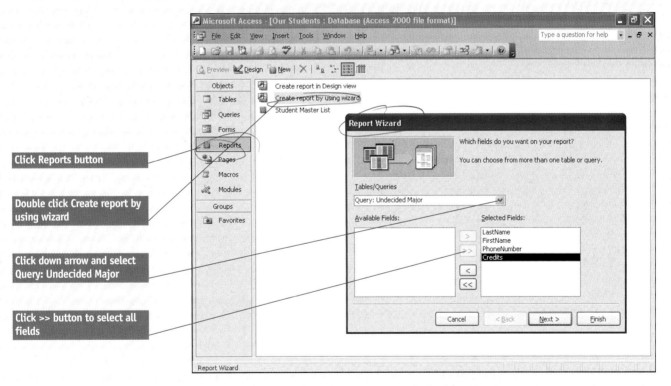

Click Reports button

Double click Create report by using wizard

Click down arrow and select Query: Undecided Major

Click >> button to select all fields

(e) Create a Report (step 5)

FIGURE 3.8 Hands-on Exercise 2 (*continued*)

THE BACK BUTTON

The Back button is present on every screen within the Report Wizard and enables you to recover from mistakes or simply to change your mind about how you want the report to look. Click the Back button at any time to return to the previous screen, then click it again if you want to return to the screen before that.

Step 6: **The Completed Report**

- If necessary, click the **Maximize button** to see the completed report as shown in Figure 3.8f. If necessary, return to the Design view to space the fields and their labels attractively across the page. Save the design changes.

- Click the **Print button** to print the report. Click the **Close button** to exit the Print Preview window. Close the Report design window.

- Switch to the Query window, then close the Query window.

- If necessary, click the **Database Window button** on the toolbar to return to the Database window. Click the **Maximize button**:
  - ❑ Click the **Queries button** to display the names of the queries in the Our Students database. You should see the *Undecided Major* query created in this exercise.
  - ❑ Click the **Reports button**. You should see two reports: *Student Master List* and *Undecided Major*.

- Close the **Our Students database** and exit Access if you do not wish to continue with the next exercise at this time.

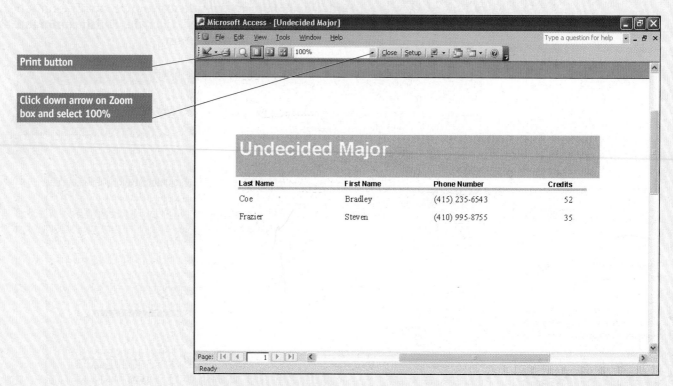

(f) The Completed Report (step 6)

FIGURE 3.8   Hands-on Exercise 2 (*continued*)

THE BORDER PROPERTY

The Border property enables you to display a border around any type of control. Point to the control (in the Design view), click the right mouse button to display a shortcut menu, then click Properties to display the Properties dialog box. Select the Format tab, click the Border Style property, then choose the type of border you want (e.g., solid to display a border or transparent to suppress a border). Use the Border Color and Border Width properties to change the appearance of the border.

ACCESS FUNCTIONS AND CALCULATED CONTROLS

A report, and/or the query on which it is based, can be enhanced through the use of Access functions to create calculated controls. Figure 3.9a displays a query in Design view, whereas Figure 3.9b shows (a portion of) the corresponding dynaset. The students appear in alphabetical order according to their major, and then alphabetically by last name within each major. Three of the controls in the query (Major, QualityPoints, and Credits) are from the underlying Students table as can be seen from the corresponding entries in the Table row. The other controls (Name, GPA, and Distinction) are calculated and thus, are not contained in an underlying table; that is, the entries in the Table row for these fields are blank.

Syntactically, the name of a calculated control is followed by a colon, a space, and then the expression. The first calculated control, Name, uses the ampersand to *concatenate* (join together) three components of a student's name: the last name, a comma followed by a space, and the first name. The result can be seen in the dynaset—for example, "Adili, Ronnie" for the first student in the table. Notice how the concatenated field is more visually appealing than displaying the two name fields individually.

The next calculated control, GPA, uses simple division (the quality points divided by the number of credits) to compute a student's grade point average. Jared Berlin, for example, has quality points and credits of 250 and 100, respectively, resulting in a calculated GPA of 2.50.

An *Immediate IF (IIF) function* is used in the last calculated control (Distinction) to determine if a student is on the Dean's list. The IIF function has three arguments—a condition that is either true or false, the result when the condition is true, and an (optional) result when the condition is false. Thus, in this example, if the GPA is greater than or equal to 3.50, the function returns the expression "Dean's List". If, however, the condition is not true, the function does not return any value; that is, the control will be left blank in the resulting data set. The query in Figure 3.9 will be the basis of the report described in the next section as well as the hands-on exercise that follows.

Concatenated fields
Calculated control
Immediate IF function

(a) Design View

Students are listed alphabetically by last name within major

Student's last name and first name have been concatenated

GPA has been calculated to 2 decimals

Dean's List is indicated only where GPA is >= 3.5

Major	Name	QualityPoints	Credits	GPA	Distinction
Business	Adili, Ronnie	155	60	2.58	
Business	Cornell, Ryan	80	45	1.78	
Business	DiGiacomo, Kevin	375	105	3.57	Dean's List
Business	Gibson, Christopher	60	35	1.71	
Business	Ramsay, Robert	162	50	3.24	
Business	Watson, Ana	75	30	2.50	
Communications	Faulkner, Eileen	80	30	2.67	
Communications	Joseph, Cedric	170	45	3.78	Dean's List
Communications	Ortiz, Frances	60	28	2.14	
Communications	Price, Lori	42	24	1.75	
Communications	Slater, Erica	390	105	3.71	Dean's List
Education	Korba, Nickolas	166	100	1.66	

(b) Dynaset

FIGURE 3.9 Access Functions

GROUPING RECORDS

The report in Figure 3.10 is based on the query just discussed; that is, look closely, and you will see that the report contains the same business majors as previously. The GPA is calculated as before, and it illustrates **conditional formatting**; that is, the format (in this case, the font color) depends on the value of the GPA control. A GPA greater than 3.5 is printed in blue, a GPA less than 2.0 is printed in red, and all other values are printed in black.

The report in Figure 3.10a, for example, groups students according to their major, sorts them alphabetically according to last name within each major, then calculates the average GPA for all students in each major. A Group Header appears before each group of students to identify the group and display the major. A Group Footer appears at the end of each group and displays the average GPA for students in that major.

Figure 3.10b displays the Design view of the report in Figure 3.10a, which determines the appearance of the printed report. Look carefully at the design to relate each section to the corresponding portion of the printed report:

- The **Report Header** contains the title of the report and appears once, at the beginning of the printed report.

- The **Page Header** contains the column headings that appear at the top of each page. The column headings are labels (or unbound controls) and are formatted in bold.

- The **Group Header** consists of a single bound control that displays the value of the major field prior to each group of detail records.

- The **Detail section** consists of bound controls that appear directly under the corresponding heading in the Page Header. The Detail section is printed once for each record in each group.

- The **Group Footer** appears after each group of detail records. It consists of an unbound control (Average GPA for Major:) followed by a calculated control that computes the average GPA for each group of students.

- The **Page Footer** appears at the bottom of each page and contains the date, page number, and total number of pages in the report.

- The **Report Footer** appears at the end of the report. It consists of an unbound control (Average GPA for All Students:) followed by a calculated control that computes the average GPA for all students.

Grouping records within a report enables you to perform calculations on each group, as was done in the Group Footer of Figure 3.10. The calculations in our example made use of the **Avg function**, but other types of calculations are possible:

- The **Sum function** computes the total for a specific field for all records in the group.

- The **Min function** determines the minimum value for all records in the group.

- The **Max function** determines the maximum value for all records in the group.

- The **Count function** counts the number of records in the group.

Look closely at the page footer to see the inclusion of three additional functions—Now, Page, and Pages—that display the current date, the current page, and total number of pages, respectively. The Report Wizard builds the Page Footer automatically, but you can learn from the wizard and incorporate these functions in other reports that you create.

The following exercise has you create the report in Figure 3.10. The Report Wizard is used to design the basic report, but additional modifications are necessary to create the Group Header and Group Footer.

Major	Name	Gender	FinancialAid	GPA	Distinction
GPA by Major					
Your Name Goes Here					
Business					
	Adili, Ronnie	F	No	2.58	
	Cornell, Ryan	M	No	1.78	
	DiGiacomo, Kevin	M	Yes	3.57	Dean's List
	Gibson, Christopher	M	Yes	1.71	
	Ramsay, Robert	M	Yes	3.24	
	Watson, Ana	F	No	2.50	
	Average GPA for Major			2.56	
Communications					
	Faulkner, Eileen	F	No	2.67	
	Joseph, Cedric	M	Yes	3.78	Dean's List
	Ortiz, Frances	F	Yes	2.14	
	Price, Lori	F	Yes	1.75	
	Slater, Erica	F	Yes	3.71	Dean's List
	Average GPA for Major			2.81	
Education					
	Korba, Nickolas	M	No	1.66	
	Zimmerman, Kimberly	F	No	3.29	
	Average GPA for Major			2.48	
Engineering					
	Berlin, Jared	M	Yes	2.50	
	Heltzer, Peter	M	No	4.00	Dean's List
	Solomon, Wendy	F	No	3.50	Dean's List
	Average GPA for Major			3.33	

Monday, July 07, 2003   Page 1 of 2

Major	Name	Gender	FinancialAid	GPA	Distinction
Liberal Arts					
	Camejo, Oscar	M	Yes	2.80	
	Parulis, Christa	F	No	1.80	
	Watson, Ana	F	Yes	2.79	
	Weissman, Kimberly	F	Yes	2.63	
	Average GPA for Major			2.51	
Undecided					
	Coe, Bradley	M	No	2.75	
	Frazier, Steven	M	No	1.29	
	Huerta, Carlos	M	No	2.67	
	Zacco, Michelle	F	No	3.24	
	Average GPA for Major			2.49	
	Average GPA for All Students			2.68	

Monday, July 07, 2003   Page 2 of 2

(a) The Printed Report

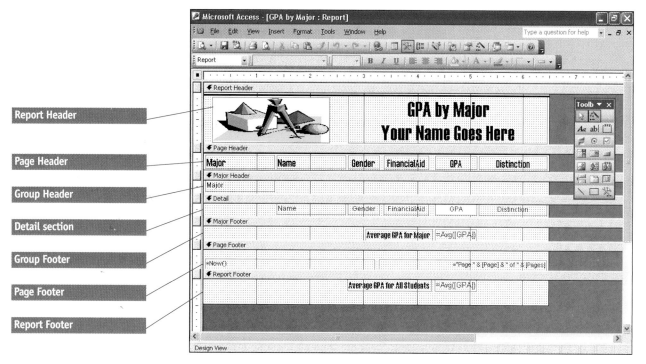

(b) Design View

FIGURE 3.10   The Summary Report

3 Grouping Records

Objective To create a query containing a calculated control, then create a report based on that query; to use the Sorting and Grouping command to add a Group Header and Group Footer to a report. Use Figure 3.11 as a guide.

Step 1: **Create the Query**

- Start Access and open the **Our Students database** from the previous exercise. Click **Open** in response to the security warning.
- Click the **Queries button** in the Database window. Double click **Create query in Design view** to display the Query Design window and bypass the Simple Query Wizard.
- The Show Table dialog box appears; the **Tables tab** is already selected, as is the **Students table**. Click the **Add button** to add the table to the query. Click **Close** to close the Show Table dialog box.
- Click the **Maximize button** so that the window takes up the entire screen as shown in Figure 3.11a. Drag the border between the upper and lower portions of the window to give yourself more room in the upper portion. Make the field list larger, to display more fields at one time.
- Scroll (if necessary) within the field list, then click and drag the **Major field** from the field list to the query. Click and drag the **Gender**, **FinancialAid**, **QualityPoints**, and **Credits fields** (in that order).
- Click the **Sort row** for the Major field. Click the **down arrow** to open the drop-down list box. Click **Ascending**.
- Click **Save** to display the dialog box in Figure 3.11a. Enter **GPA by Major** as the query name. Click **OK**.

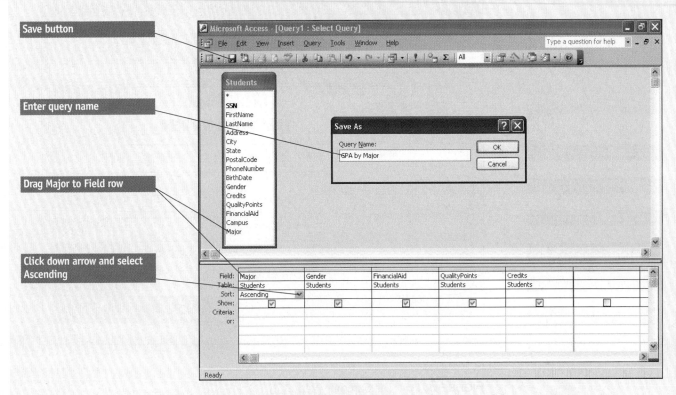

(a) Create the Query (step 1)

FIGURE 3.11 Hands-on Exercise 3

Step 2: **Add the Calculated Controls**

- Click anywhere in the **Gender column**. Pull down the **Insert menu** and click **Columns** to insert a blank column to the left of the Gender field.

- Click in the **Field row** of the newly inserted column to enter a calculated control. Type **Name: LastName & ", " & FirstName**, and press **Enter**. The ampersand concatenates (joins together) the various components in the name field.

- Be sure to spell the fields correctly (there are no spaces in "LastName" or "FirstName"). You are concatenating (joining together) the last name, a comma and a space, and the first name into a single field called Name.

- Click in the **Sort row** under the newly created Name control. Click the **down arrow** and choose an **Ascending** sequence as shown in Figure 3.11b.

- Click in the **Field row** of the first blank column. Type **GPA: QualityPoints/Credits**, and press **Enter**. Be sure to spell the field names correctly.

- Change the column widths as necessary to see the field contents. Save the query.

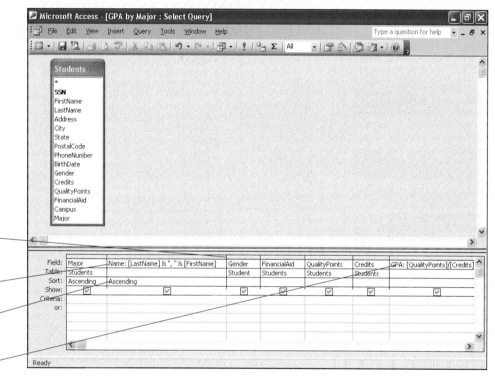

Click and drag border to change column width

Click in Field row and enter calculated control for Name

Select Ascending sequence

Click in Field row and enter calculated control for GPA

(b) Add the Calculated Controls (step 2)

FIGURE 3.11 Hands-on Exercise 3 (*continued*)

THE TOP VALUES PROPERTY

The Top Values property lets you display a specified percentage or number of the top or bottom records in a list. Remove any sort keys in the query, then sort the table according to the desired sequence, ascending or descending, to get the lowest or highest values, respectively. Click the down arrow in the Top Values list box to choose the number of records, such as 5 or 5% to show the top five or five percent, respectively. Save the query, then run it. See practice exercise 3 at the end of the chapter.

Step 3: Run the Query

- Pull down the **Query menu** and click **Run** (or click the **Run button** on the Query Design toolbar). You will see the dynaset in Figure 3.11c, which displays the records that satisfy the query.

- Students are listed by major and alphabetically by last name within major. (Access sorts from left to right according to the way in which the fields appear in the Design grid. Thus, the Major field must appear to the left of the LastName field within the Design view.)

- Change column widths as necessary by dragging the border between adjacent column headings.

- A total of seven fields appear in the dynaset, corresponding to the controls that were added to the design grid in Design view. The GPA is displayed to too many decimal places.

- Click the **View button** to modify the query.

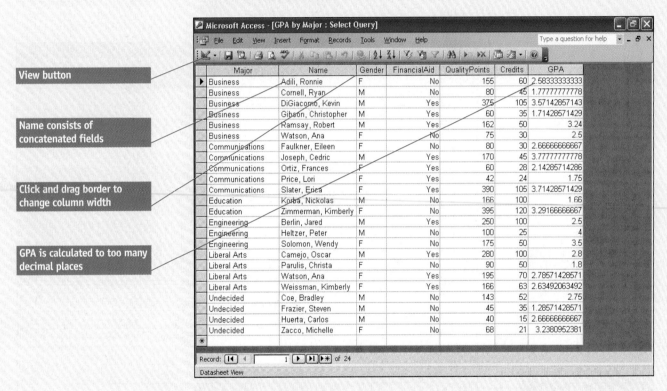

(c) Run the Query (step 3)

FIGURE 3.11 Hands-on Exercise 3 (*continued*)

ADJUST THE COLUMN WIDTH

Point to the right edge of the column you want to resize, then drag the mouse in the direction you want to go; drag to the right to make the column wider or to the left to make it narrower. Alternatively, you can double click the column selector line (right edge) to fit the longest entry in that column. Adjusting the column width in the Design view does not affect the column width in the Datasheet view, but you can use the same technique in both views.

Step 4: Modify the Query

- Point to the GPA column and click the **right mouse button** to display a shortcut menu. Click the **Properties command** to display the Field Properties dialog box in Figure 3.11d.

- Click the **General tab** if necessary. Click the **Format text box**. Click the **drop-down arrow** to display the available formats. Click **Fixed**. Close the Field Properties dialog box.

- We will add another calculated control that will display "Dean's List" if the student has earned this distinction. Click in the **Field row** in the first blank column of the design grid.

- Enter **Distinction: IIF(GPA>=3.5, "Dean's List")** for the new control as shown in Figure 3.11d. This expression will display the literal "Dean's List" if the student has a GPA greater than or equal to 3.5.

- Click the **Save button** to save the modified query.

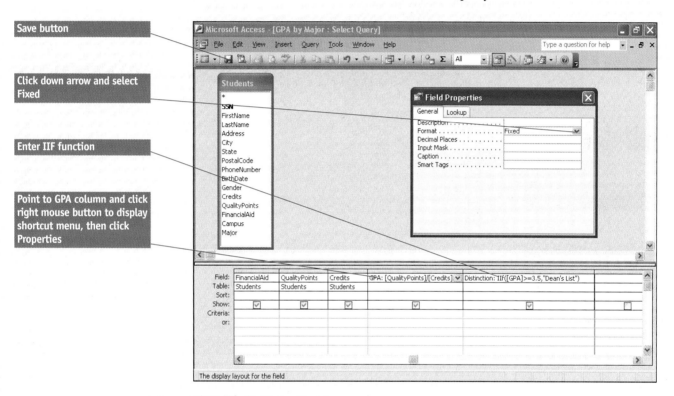

(d) Modify the Query (step 4)

FIGURE 3.11 Hands-on Exercise 3 (continued)

NESTED IF STATEMENTS

A "nested If" (or an If within an If) is a common logic structure in every programming language. It could be used in this example to implement more complicated logic such as displaying either "Dean's List" or "Probation", depending on the GPA. The IIF function has three arguments—a condition, the result if the condition is true, and the result if the condition is false. A nested If replaces either condition with another If. Thus, you could enter IIF(GPA>=3.5, "Dean's List", IIF(GPA<2.0, "Probation","N/A")).

Step 5: Rerun the Query

- Click the **Run button** to run the modified query. You will see a new dynaset corresponding to the modified query as shown in Figure 3.11e. Resize the column widths (as necessary) within the dynaset.
  - ❏ Students are still listed by major and alphabetically within major.
  - ❏ The GPA is calculated to two decimal places and appears under the GPA field.
  - ❏ Dean's List is indicated for those students with a GPA of 3.5 or above.

- Click the **QualityPoints field** for Christopher Gibson. Replace 60 with **70**. Press **Enter**. The GPA changes automatically to 2.

- Pull down the **Edit menu** and click **Undo Current Field/Record** (or click the **Undo button** on the Query toolbar). The GPA returns to its previous value.

- Tab to the **GPA field** for Christopher Gibson. Type **2**. Access will beep and prevent you from changing the GPA because it is a calculated field as indicated on the status bar.

- Click the **Close button** to close the query and return to the Database window. Click **Yes** if asked whether to save the changes.

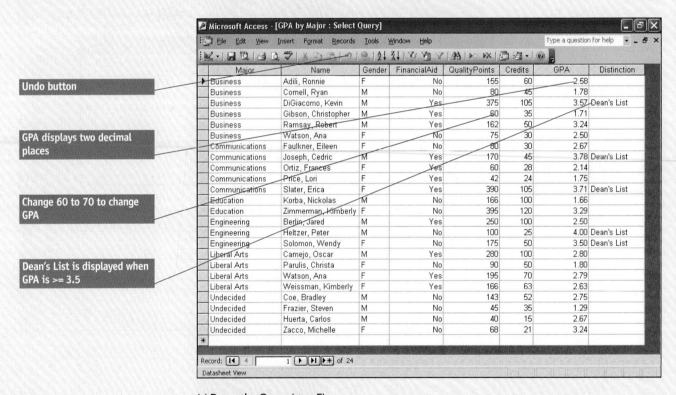

Undo button

GPA displays two decimal places

Change 60 to 70 to change GPA

Dean's List is displayed when GPA is >= 3.5

(e) Rerun the Query (step 5)

FIGURE 3.11 Hands-on Exercise 3 (*continued*)

USE WHAT YOU KNOW

An Access table or dynaset not only resembles an Excel worksheet in appearance, but it also accepts many of the same commands and operations. The Sort Ascending and Sort Descending buttons function identically to their Excel counterparts. You can also double click the right border of a column heading to adjust the column width. The Format menu enables you to change the row width or column height, hide or unhide columns, or freeze and unfreeze columns.

Step 6: The Report Wizard

- You should see the Database window. Click the **Reports button**, then double click **Create report by using the wizard** to start the Report Wizard.

- Select **GPA by Major** from the Tables/Queries drop-down list. The Available Fields list displays all of the fields in the GPA by Major query.
  - ❏ Click the **Major field** in the Available Fields list box. Click the **>** button.
  - ❏ Add the **Name**, **Gender**, **FinancialAid**, **GPA**, and **Distinction fields** one at a time. The easiest way to add a field is to double click the field name.
  - ❏ Do not include the QualityPoints or Credits fields. Click **Next**.

- You should see the screen asking whether you want to group the fields. Click the **Major field**, then click the **>** button to display the screen in Figure 3.11f.

- The Major field appears above the other fields to indicate that the records will be grouped according to the value of the Major field. Click **Next**.

- The next screen asks you to specify the order for the detail records. Click the **drop-down arrow** on the list box for the first field. Click **Name** to sort the records alphabetically by last name within each major. Click **Next**.

- The **Stepped Option button** is already selected for the report layout, as is **Portrait orientation**. Be sure the box is checked to **Adjust field width so all fields fit on a page**. Click **Next**.

- Choose **Compact** as the style. Click **Next**.

- **GPA by Major** (which corresponds to the name of the underlying query) is already entered as the name of the report. Click the Option button to **Modify the report's design**.

- Click **Finish** to exit the Report Wizard.

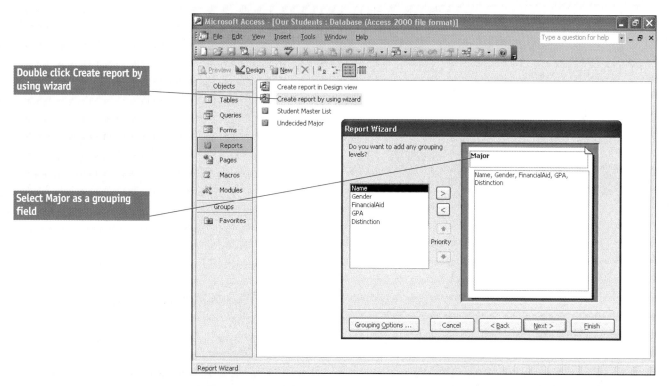

(f) The Report Wizard (step 6)

FIGURE 3.11 Hands-on Exercise 3 (*continued*)

Step 7: Sorting and Grouping

- Click and drag the right border of the label in the Report Header to the left to increase the size of the label. Press **Shift+Enter** to force a line break. Enter your name as shown in Figure 3.11g.

- Click the **Center button** to center the text within the unbound control. Click outside the label, then click and drag the label to the right.

- Move, size, and align the column headings and bound controls. You may have to go back and forth between Design view and Report Preview until you are satisfied.

- Pull down the **View menu**. Click **Sorting and Grouping** to display the Sorting and Grouping dialog box.

- The **Major field** should already be selected. Click the **Group Footer** property, click the **drop-down arrow**, then click **Yes** to create a Group Footer for the Major field. Close the dialog box.

- Click the down arrow for the **Keep Together** property. Click **Whole Group**. The Major footer has been added to the report.

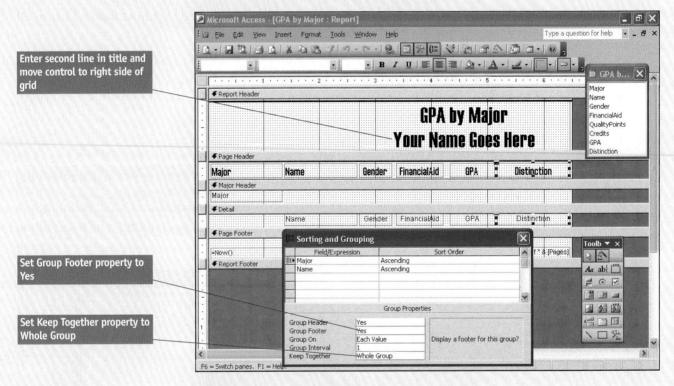

Enter second line in title and move control to right side of grid

Set Group Footer property to Yes

Set Keep Together property to Whole Group

(g) Sorting and Grouping (step 7)

FIGURE 3.11 Hands-on Exercise 3 (continued)

SELECTING MULTIPLE CONTROLS

Select (click) a column heading in the Page Header, then press and hold the Shift key as you select the corresponding bound control in the Detail section. This selects both the column heading and the bound control and enables you to move and size the objects in conjunction with one another. Continue to work with both objects selected as you apply formatting through various buttons on the Formatting toolbar, or change properties through the property sheet. Click anywhere on the report to deselect the objects when you are finished.

Step 8:   Create the Group and Report Footers

- Click the **Text Box button** on the Toolbox toolbar. The mouse pointer changes to a tiny crosshair with a text box attached.

- Click and drag in the Group Footer where you want the text box (which will contain the average GPA) to go. Release the mouse.

- You will see an Unbound control and an attached label containing a field number (e.g., Text 18).

- Click in the **text box** control (Unbound will disappear). Enter **=Avg(GPA)** to calculate the average of the GPA for all students in this group as shown in Figure 3.11h.

- Click in the attached unbound control, click and drag to select the text (Text 18), then type **Average GPA for Major** as the label for this control. Size, move, and align the label as shown in the figure. (See the boxed tip on sizing or moving a control and its label.)

- Point to the **Average GPA control**, click the **right mouse button** to display a shortcut menu, then click **Properties** to display the Properties dialog box.

- Click the **Format tab**. Change the format to **Fixed** and the number of decimal places to **2**. Close the Properties sheet.

- Click and drag the bottom of the Report Footer down to create space for the Report Footer. Press and hold the **Shift key** as you select the label and associated control in the Major (Group) footer. Click the **Copy Button**.

- Click in the Report Footer, then click the **Paste button** to copy the controls to the report footer. Click and drag both controls to align them under the corresponding controls in the Major footer.

- Change the text of the label in the Report Footer to reflect **all students** as shown in Figure 3.11h. Move and size the label as necessary. Save the report.

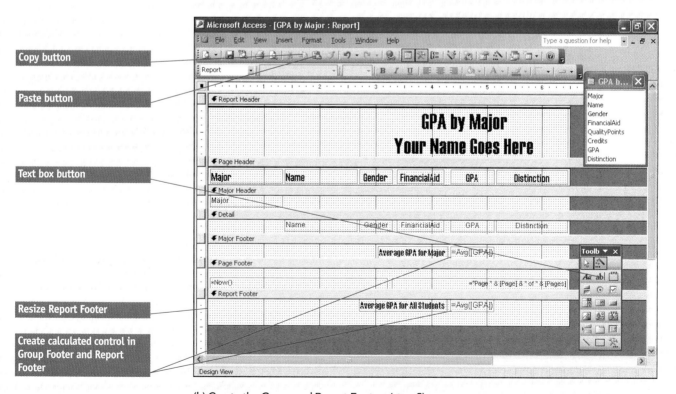

(h) Create the Group and Report Footers (step 8)

FIGURE 3.11   Hands-on Exercise 3 (*continued*)

Step 9: The Finishing Touches

- Click in the Report Header. Pull down the **Insert menu** and click the **Picture command** to display the Insert Picture dialog box. Change to the **Exploring Access folder**. Select the **Academic Symbols picture**, then click **OK**.

- **Right click** the picture to display a context-sensitive menu, then click **Properties** to display the Properties Dialog box. Click the **Size Mode property**, click the **down arrow**, and click **Stretch**. Close the Properties sheet.

- Click and drag to size the picture. Resize the Report Header as appropriate.

- Select the **GPA control** in the Detail section. Pull down the **Format menu** and click the **Conditional Formatting command** to display the associated dialog box.

- Enter the first condition as shown in Figure 3.11i. Click the **down arrow** on the font color button and click **blue**.

- Click the **Add button**, then enter the second condition, this time selecting a font color of **red**. Click **OK** to accept both conditions and close the dialog box.

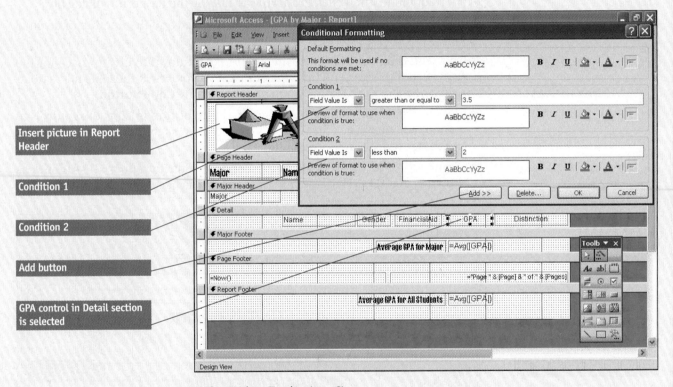

(i) The Finishing Touches (step 9)

FIGURE 3.11 Hands-on Exercise 3 (*continued*)

MISSING TASK PANE

The Insert Picture command functions differently in Access than in the other Office applications because it does not display the Clip Art task pane. You can still search for clip art explicitly, however, by starting the Clip Organizer as a separate application. Click the Start button, click the All Programs button, click Microsoft Office, click Microsoft Office Tools, then start the Microsoft Clip Organizer. Select a clip art image from within the Clip Organizer, and click the Copy button. Use the Windows taskbar to return to Access, open the form or report in Design view, and click the Paste button.

Step 10: **The Completed Report**

- Click the **Print Preview button** to view the completed report as shown in Figure 3.11j. The status bar shows you are on Page 1 of the report.

- Click the **Zoom button** to see the entire page. Click the **Zoom button** a second time to return to the higher magnification, which lets you read the report.

- Be sure that you are satisfied with the appearance of the report and that all controls align properly with their associated labels. If necessary, return to the Design view to modify the report.

- Pull down the **File menu** and click **Print** (or click the **Print button**) to display the Print dialog box. The **All option button** is already selected under Print Range. Click **OK** to print the report.

- Pull down the **File menu** and click **Close** to close the GPA by Major report. Click **Yes** if asked to save design changes to the report.

- Close the **Our Students database**. Exit Access if you do not want to continue with the next exercise at this time.

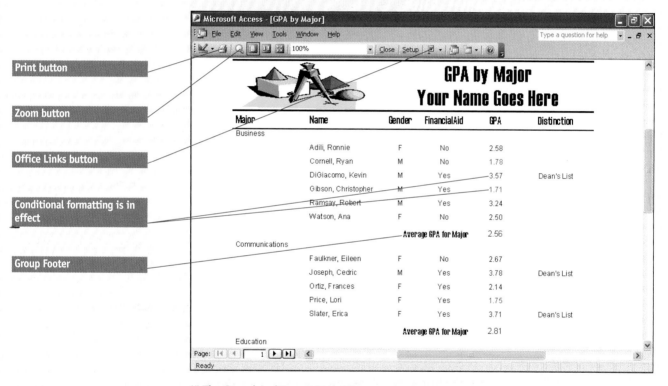

(j) The Completed Report (step 10)

FIGURE 3.11 Hands-on Exercise 3 (*continued*)

THE PRINT PREVIEW TOOLBAR

The Print Preview toolbar has several useful tools to preview a report. Click the One page, Two pages, or Multiple pages buttons, to see the indicated number of pages, and/or use the Zoom button to toggle between different magnifications. And finally, you can use the Office Links button to convert the report to a Word document or Excel workbook.

CROSSTAB QUERIES

A ***crosstab query*** consolidates data from an Access table and presents the information in a row and column format (similar to a pivot table in Excel). Figure 3.12 shows a crosstab query that displays the average GPA for all students by major and gender. A crosstab query aggregates (sums, counts, or averages) the values of one field (e.g., GPA), then groups the results according to the values of another field listed down the left side of the table (major), and a set of values listed across the top of the table (gender).

A crosstab query can be created in the Query Design view, but it is easier to use the Crosstab Query Wizard, as you will see in the next hands-on exercise. The wizard allows you to choose the table (or query) on which the crosstab query is based, then prompts you for the fields to be used for the row and column values (major and gender in our example). You then select the field that will be summarized (GPA), and choose the desired calculation (average). It's easy and you get a chance to practice in the hands-on exercise that follows shortly.

Major is in the rows

Gender is in the columns

Calculation is average GPA

GPA by Major_Crosstab : Crosstab Query		
Major	F	M
Business	2.54	2.66
Communications	2.57	3.78
Education		1.66
Engineering	3.50	3.25
Liberal Arts	2.41	2.80
Undecided	2.96	2.23

Record: 3 of 6

FIGURE 3.12 Crosstab Query

ACTION QUERIES

Queries are generally used to extract information from a database. A special type of query, however, known as an ***action query***, enables you to update the database by changing multiple records in a single operation. There are four types of action queries: update, append, delete, and make-table.

An ***update query*** changes multiple records within a table. You could, for example, create an update query to raise the salary of every employee by 10 percent. You can also use criteria in the update query; for example, you can increase the salaries of only those employees with a specified performance rating.

An ***append query*** adds records from one table to the end of another table. It could be used in the context of the student database to add transfer students to the Students table, given that the transfer records were stored originally in a separate table. An append query can include criteria, so that it adds only selected records from the other table, such as those students with a designated GPA.

A ***delete query*** deletes one or more records from a table according to designated criteria. You could, for example, use a delete query to remove employees who are no longer working for a company, students who have graduated, or products that are no longer kept in inventory.

A ***make-table query*** creates a new table from records in an existing table. This type of query is especially useful prior to running a delete query in that you can back up (archive) the records you are about to delete. Thus, you could use a make-table query to create a table containing those students who are about to graduate (e.g., those with 120 credits or more), then run a delete query to remove the graduates from the Students table. You're ready for another hands-on exercise.

4 Crosstab and Action Queries

Objective To use action queries to modify a database; to create a crosstab query to display summarized values from a table. Use Figure 3.13 as a guide in completing the exercise.

Step 1: Create the Make-Table Query

- Start Access and open the **Our Students database**. Click **Open** in response to the security warning. Click the **Queries button** in the Database window, then double click **Create query in Design view**.

- The Show Table dialog box appears automatically with the Tables tab already selected. If necessary, select the **Students table**, then click the **Add button** to add the table to the query as shown in Figure 3.13a. Close the Show Table dialog box. Maximize the query window, then resize the top portion of the window as well as the field list.

- Click the **SSN** (the first field) in the Students table. Press and hold the **Shift key**, then scroll (if necessary) until you can click **Major** (the last field) in the table. Click and drag the selected fields (i.e., every field in the table) from the field list to the design grid in Figure 3.13a.

- Scroll in the design grid until you can see the Credits field. Click in the **Criteria row** for the Credits field and enter **>=120**.

- Click the **drop-down arrow** next to the **Query Type button** on the toolbar and select (click) the **Make-Table query** as shown in Figure 3.13a. Enter **Graduating Seniors** as the name of the table you will create.

- Verify that the option button for Current Database is selected, then click **OK**.

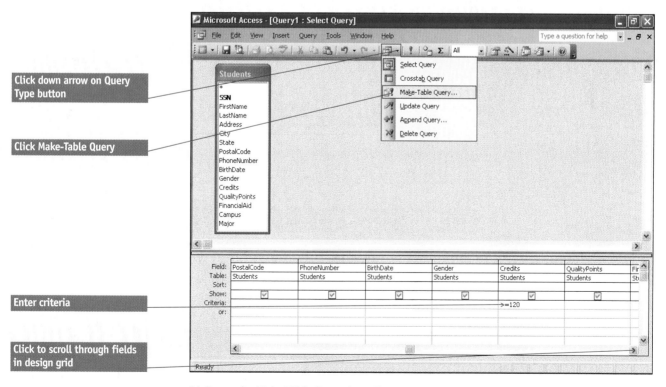

(a) Create the Make-Table Query (step 1)

FIGURE 3.13 Hands-on Exercise 4

Step 2: Run the Make-Table Query

- Click the **Run button** to run the Make-Table query. Click **Yes** in response to the message in Figure 3.13b indicating that you are about to paste one record (for the graduating seniors) into a new table.

- Do not be concerned if you do not see the Graduating Seniors table at this time; unlike a select query, you remain in the Design view after executing the Make-Table query.

- Close the Make-Table query. Save the query as **Archive Graduating Seniors**.

- Click the **Tables button** in the Database window, then open the **Graduating Seniors table** you just created. The table should contain one record (for Kim Zimmerman) with 120 or more credits.

- Close the table.

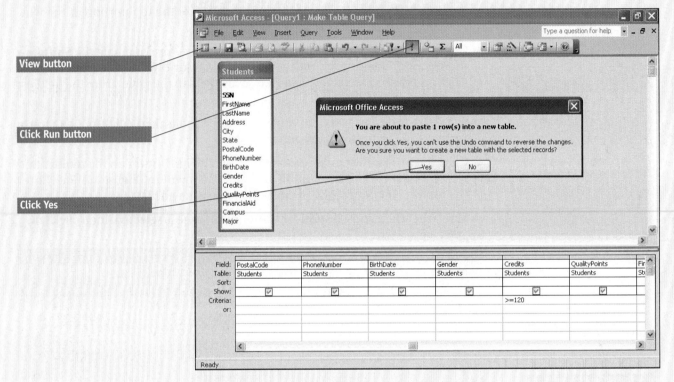

(b) Run the Make-Table Query (step 2)

FIGURE 3.13 Hands-on Exercise 4 (*continued*)

LOOK BEFORE YOU LEAP

The result of an action query is irreversible; that is, once you click Yes in the dialog box displayed by the query, you cannot undo the action. You can, however, preview the result before creating the query by clicking the View button at the left of the Query Design toolbar. Click the button and you see the results of the query displayed in a dynaset, then click the View button a second time to return to the Design view. Click the Run Query button to execute the query, but now you can click Yes with confidence since you have seen the result.

Step 3: Create the Delete Query

- Click the **Queries button** in the Database window, then click the **Archive Graduating Seniors query** to select the query.

- Pull down the **Edit menu** and click **Copy** to copy the query to the clipboard. (You can also click the Copy button on the Database toolbar.)

- Pull down the **Edit menu** a second time, then click the **Paste command** to display the Paste As dialog box in Figure 3.13c. (You can also click the Paste button on the Database toolbar.)

- Type **Purge Graduating Seniors** as the name of the query, then click **OK**.

- The Database window contains the original query (Archive Graduating Seniors) as well as the copied version (Purge Graduating Seniors) that you just created.

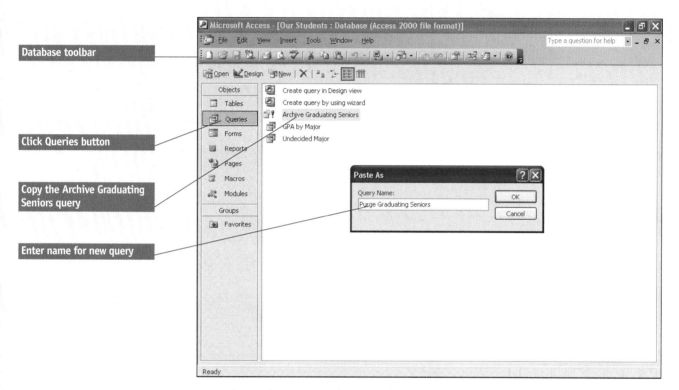

Database toolbar

Click Queries button

Copy the Archive Graduating Seniors query

Enter name for new query

(c) Create the Delete Query (step 3)

FIGURE 3.13 Hands-on Exercise 4 *(continued)*

COPY, RENAME, OR DELETE AN ACCESS OBJECT

Use the Copy and Paste commands in the Database window to copy any object in an Access database. To copy an object, select the object, pull down the Edit menu, and click Copy (or use the Ctrl+C keyboard shortcut). Pull down the Edit menu a second time and select the Paste command (or use the Ctrl+V shortcut), then enter a name for the copied object. To delete or rename an object, point to the object, then click the right mouse button to display a shortcut menu and select the desired operation.

Step 4: Complete and Run the Delete Query

- Open the newly created query in the Design view. Maximize the window. Click the **drop-down arrow** next to the **Query Type button** on the toolbar and select (click) the **Delete Query**.

- Click and drag the box on the horizontal scroll bar until you can see the **Credits field** as shown in Figure 3.13d. The criterion, >= 120, is already entered because the Delete query was copied originally from the Make-Table query, and the criteria are identical.

- Click the **Run button** to execute the query. Click **Yes** when warned that you are about to delete one record from the specified table. Once again, you remain in the Design view after the query has been executed.

- Close the Query window. Click **Yes** if asked to save the changes.

- Open the **Students table**. The record for Kim Zimmerman is no longer there.

- Close the Students table.

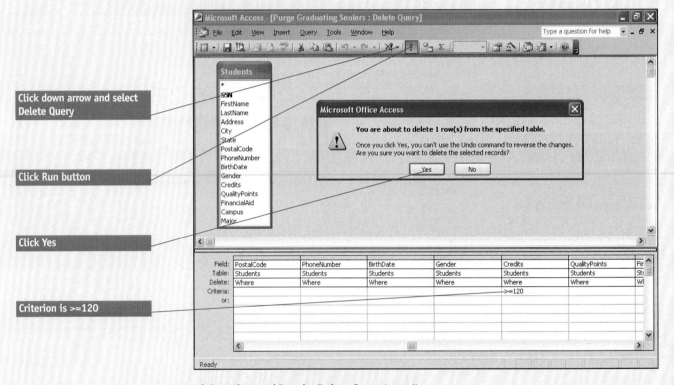

(d) Complete and Run the Delete Query (step 4)

FIGURE 3.13 Hands-on Exercise 4 (*continued*)

PLAN FOR THE UNEXPECTED

Deleting records is cause for concern in that once the records are removed from a table, they cannot be restored. This may not be a problem, but it is comforting to have some means of recovery. Accordingly, we always execute a Make-Table query, with the identical criteria as in the Delete query, prior to running the latter. The deleted records from the original table can be restored through an Append query should it be necessary.

Step 5: **Create the Append Query**

- Click the **Queries button**, then double click **Create query in Design view**. The Show Tables dialog box opens and contains the following tables:
  - ❏ The Students table that you have used throughout the chapter.
  - ❏ The Graduating Seniors table that you just created.
  - ❏ The Transfer Students table that will be appended to the Students table.

- Select the **Transfer Students table**, then click the **Add button** to add this table to the query. Close the Show Table dialog box. Maximize the window. Click and drag the **asterisk** from the field list to the **Field row** in the query design grid.

- Click the **drop-down arrow** next to the **Query Type button** on the toolbar and select (click) **Append Query** to display the Append dialog box. Click the **drop-down arrow** on the Append to Table Name list box and select the **Students table** as shown in Figure 3.13e. Click **OK**.

- Click the **Run button**. Click **Yes** when warned that you are about to add 4 rows (from the Transfer Students table) to the Students table.

- Save the query as **Append Transfer Students**. Close the query window.

- Open the **Students table**. Four records have been added (Liquer, Thomas, Rudolph, Milgrom). Close the table.

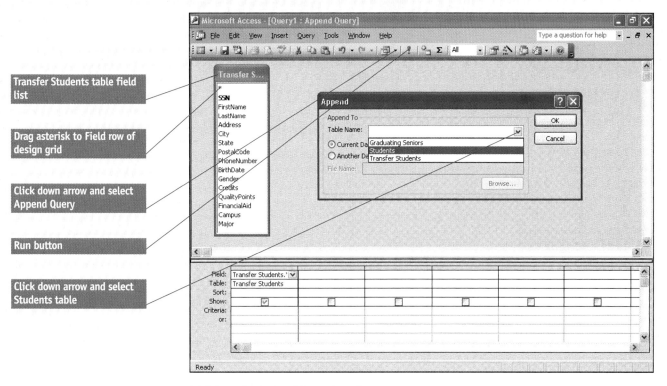

(e) Create the Append Query (step 5)

FIGURE 3.13 Hands-on Exercise 4 (*continued*)

THE ASTERISK VERSUS INDIVIDUAL FIELDS

Click and drag the asterisk in the field list to the design grid to add every field in the underlying table to the query. The advantage to this approach is that it is quicker than selecting the fields individually. The disadvantage is that you cannot sort or specify criteria for individual fields.

Step 6:   Create an Update Query

- Click the **Queries button** in the Database window. Select (click) the **GPA by Major query**, press **Ctrl+C** to copy the query, then press **Ctrl+V** to display the Paste As dialog box. Enter **Update Financial Aid**. Click **OK**.

- Open the newly created query in the Design view as shown in Figure 3.13f. Click the **drop-down arrow** next to the **Query Type button** on the toolbar and select (click) **Update Query**. The design grid changes to include an Update To row, and the Sort row disappears.

- Click in the **Criteria row** for the **GPA field** and enter **>=3**. Click in the **Update To row** for the **FinancialAid field** and enter **Yes**. The combination of these entries will change the value of the Financial Aid field to "yes" for all students with a GPA of 3.00 or higher.

- Click the **Run button** to execute the query. Click **Yes** when warned that you are about to update nine records. Close the query window.

- Click **Yes** if asked whether to save the changes.

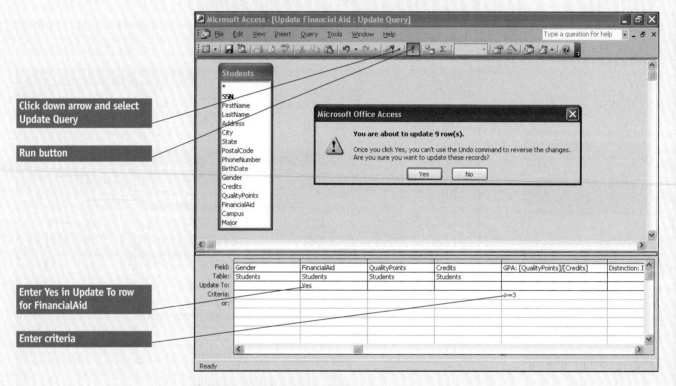

(f) Create an Update Query (step 6)

FIGURE 3.13   Hands-on Exercise 4 (*continued*)

VERIFY THE RESULTS OF THE UPDATE QUERY

You have run the Update Query, but are you sure it worked correctly? Press the F11 key to return to the Database window, click the Queries button, and rerun the GPA by Major query that was created earlier. Click in the GPA field for the first student, then click the Sort Descending button to display the students in descending order by GPA. Every student with a GPA of 3.00 or higher should be receiving financial aid.

Step 7: Check Results of the Action Queries

- Click the **Tables button** in the Database window. Open (double click) the **Students, Graduating Seniors**, and **Transfer Students tables** one after another. You have to return to the Database window each time you open a table.

- Pull down the **Window menu** and click the **Tile Vertically command** to display the tables as shown in Figure 3.13g. The arrangement of your tables may be different from ours.

- Check your progress by comparing the tables to one another:
  - ❏ Check the first record in the Transfer Students table, Lindsey Liquer, and note that it has been added to the Students table via the Append Transfer Students query.
  - ❏ Check the record in the Graduating Seniors table, Kim Zimmerman, and note that it has been removed from the Students table via the Purge Graduating Seniors query.
  - ❏ The Students table reflects the current student database. The other two tables function as backup.

- Close the Students, Transfer Students, and Graduating Seniors tables.

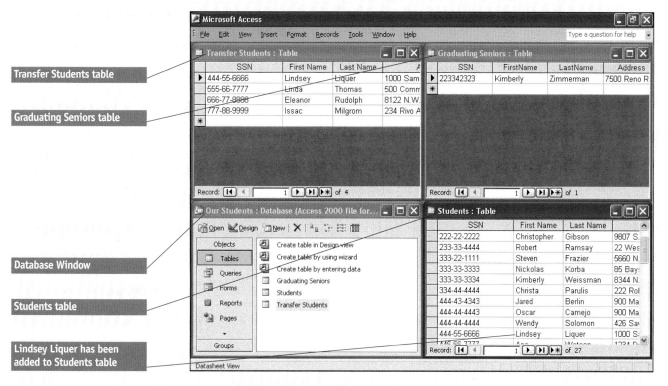

(g) Check Results of the Action Queries (step 7)

FIGURE 3.13   Hands-on Exercise 4 (*continued*)

DATABASE PROPERTIES

The buttons within the Database window display the objects within a database, but show only one type of object at a time. You can, for example, see all of the reports or all of the queries, but you cannot see the reports and queries at the same time. There is another way. Pull down the File menu, click Database Properties, then click the Contents tab to display the contents (objects) in the database.

Step 8: **Create a Crosstab Query**

- Click the **Queries button** in the Database window, click **New**, click the **Crosstab Query Wizard** in the New Query dialog box, and click **OK** to start the wizard.

- Click the **Queries option button** and select the **GPA by Major query**. Click **Next** to continue.
  - ❏ Click **Major** in the Available Fields list, then click **>** to place it in the Selected Fields list. Click **Next**.
  - ❏ Click **Gender** as the field for column headings. Click **Next**.
  - ❏ Click **GPA** as the field to calculate and select the **Avg function** as shown in Figure 3.13h. Clear the check box to include row sums. Click **Next**.
  - ❏ The name of the query is suggested for you, as is the option button to view the query. Click **Finish**.

- The results of the crosstab query are shown. The query lists the average GPA for each combination of major and gender. The display is awkward, however, in that the GPA is calculated to an unnecessary number of decimal places.

- Click the **View button** to display the Design view for this query. Right click in the **GPA column** to display a context-sensitive menu, click **Properties** to display the Field Properties dialog box, click in the **Format row**, and select **Fixed**. Set the number of decimals to **two**.

- Click the **Run button** to re-execute the query. This time the GPA is displayed to two decimal places. Save the query. Close the Query window.

- Close the Our Students database.

- Exit Access.

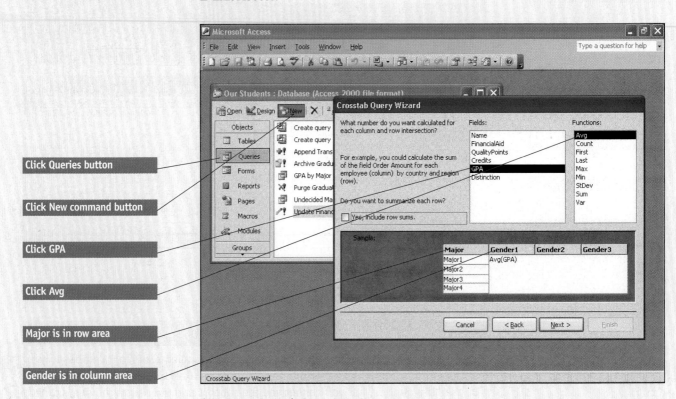

(h) Create a Crosstab Query (step 8)

FIGURE 3.13 Hands-on Exercise 4 (*continued*)

SUMMARY

Data and information are not synonymous although the terms are often interchanged. Data is the raw material and consists of the table (or tables) that comprise a database. Information is the finished product. Data is converted to information by selecting records, performing calculations on those records, and/or changing the sequence in which the records are displayed. Decisions in an organization are based on information rather than raw data.

A report is a printed document that displays information from the database. Reports are created through the Report Wizard, then modified as necessary in the Design view. A report is divided into sections. The Report Header (Footer) occurs at the beginning (end) of the report. The Page Header (Footer) appears at the top (bottom) of each page. The Detail section is found in the main body of the report and is printed once for each record in the report.

Each section is composed of objects known as controls. A bound control has a data source such as a field in the underlying table. An unbound control has no data source. A calculated control contains an expression. Controls are selected, moved, and sized the same way as any other Windows object.

Every report is based on either a table or a query. A report based on a table contains every record in that table. A report based on a query contains only the records satisfying the criteria in the query.

A query enables you to select records from a table (or from several tables), display the selected records in any order, and perform calculations on fields within the query. A select query is the most common type of query. It is created using the Simple Query Wizard and/or in Design view. A select query displays its output in a dynaset that can be used to update the data in the underlying table(s).

The records in a report are often grouped according to the value of a specific field within the record. A Group Header appears before each group to identify the group. A Group Footer appears at the end of each group and can be used to display the summary information about the group.

An action query modifies one or more records in a single operation. There are four types of action queries: update, append, delete, and make-table. An update query changes multiple records within a table. An append query adds records from one table to the end of another table. A delete query deletes one or more records from a table according to designated criteria. A make-table query creates a new table from records in an existing table.

A crosstab query displays aggregated information, as opposed to individual records. It can be created directly in the Query Design view, but is created more easily through the Crosstab Query Wizard.

KEY TERMS

1. Why might a report be based on a query rather than a table?

    (a) To limit the report to selected records
    (b) To include a calculated field in the report
    (c) Both (a) and (b)
    (d) Neither (a) nor (b)

2. An Access database may contain:

    (a) One or more tables
    (b) One or more queries
    (c) One or more reports
    (d) All of the above

3. Which of the following is true regarding the names of objects within an Access database?

    (a) A form or report may have the same name as the underlying table
    (b) A form or report may have the same name as the underlying query
    (c) Both (a) and (b)
    (d) Neither (a) nor (b)

4. The dynaset created by a query may contain:

    (a) A subset of records from the associated table
    (b) A subset of fields from the associated table for every record
    (c) Both (a) and (b)
    (d) Neither (a) nor (b)

5. Which toolbar contains a button to display the properties of a selected object?

    (a) The Query Design toolbar
    (b) The Report Design toolbar
    (c) Both (a) and (b)
    (d) Neither (a) nor (b)

6. Which of the following does *not* have a Design view and a Datasheet view?

    (a) Tables
    (b) Forms
    (c) Queries
    (d) Reports

7. Which of the following is true regarding the wild card character?

    (a) A question mark stands for a single character in the same position as the question mark
    (b) An asterisk stands for any number of characters in the same position as the asterisk
    (c) Both (a) and (b)
    (d) Neither (a) nor (b)

8. Which of the following will print at the top of every page?

    (a) Report header
    (b) Group header
    (c) Both (a) and (b)
    (d) Neither (a) nor (b)

9. Which of the following must be present in every report?

    (a) A report header and a report footer
    (b) A page header and a page footer
    (c) Both (a) and (b)
    (d) Neither (a) nor (b)

10. A query, based on the Our Students database within the chapter, contains two fields from the Student table (QualityPoints and Credits) as well as a calculated field (GPA). Which of the following is true?

    (a) Changing the value of Credits or QualityPoints in the query's dynaset automatically changes these values in the underlying table
    (b) Changing the value of GPA automatically changes its value in the underlying table
    (c) Both (a) and (b)
    (d) Neither (a) nor (b)

... continued

multiple choice

11. Which of the following may be included in a report as well as in a form?

   (a) Bound control

   (b) Unbound control

   (c) Calculated control

   (d) All of the above

12. The navigation buttons ▶ and ◀ will:

   (a) Move to the next or previous record in a table

   (b) Move to the next or previous page in a report

   (c) Both (a) and (b)

   (d) Neither (a) nor (b)

13. Assume that you created a query based on an Employee table, and that the query contains fields for Location and Title. Assume further that there is a single criteria row and that New York and Manager have been entered under the Location and Title fields, respectively. The dynaset will contain:

   (a) All employees in New York

   (b) All managers

   (c) Only the managers in New York

   (d) All employees in New York and all managers

14. You have decided to modify the query from the previous question to include a second criteria row. The Location and Title fields are still in the query, but this time New York and Manager appear in *different* criteria rows. The dynaset will contain:

   (a) All employees in New York

   (b) All managers

   (c) Only the managers in New York

   (d) All employees in New York and all managers

15. Which of the following is true about a query that lists employees by city and alphabetically within city?

   (a) The design grid should specify a descending sort on both city and employee name

   (b) The City field should appear to the left of the employee name in the design grid

   (c) Both (a) and (b)

   (d) Neither (a) nor (b)

16. Which of the following is *not* an example of an action query?

   (a) Delete query

   (b) Append query

   (c) Select query

   (d) Make-table query

17. You want to create a query that will select all managers in New York earning less than $80,000, and all managers in San Francisco earning less than $60,000. How many criteria rows will you need in the Design grid?

   (a) 1

   (b) 2

   (c) 3

   (d) 4

18. Which of the following expressions will display a student's last name, a comma and a space, followed by the student's first name?

   (a) LastName, FirstName

   (b) "LastName, FirstName"

   (c) LastName & ", " & FirstName

   (d) LastName, ", " FirstName

ANSWERS

1. c	**7.** c	**13.** c
2. d	**8.** d	**14.** d
3. c	**9.** d	**15.** b
4. c	**10.** a	**16.** c
5. d	**11.** d	**17.** b
6. d	**12.** c	**18.** c

PRACTICE WITH ACCESS

1. **The Oscars:** Figure 3.14 displays the first of three reports that you are to create for the Oscars database, which was introduced in Chapter 1. Your first task is to update the database to include the additional awards (if any) since the publication of our text. Open the *Chapter 1 Practice 1* database, open the existing form, and go to the last record to see if the data is current. If not, go to the Oscars Web site (www.oscar.com) to obtain the winners in the six major categories—Best Picture, Best Director, Best Actor and Actress, and Best Supporting Actor and Actress—for any years that are not in the database. You can then create the required reports. Proceed as follows:

   a. Use the Report Wizard to create the report in Figure 3.14, which is based on the Awards Winners table. The wizard creates a basic report with four sections—the Report Header, Page Header, Detail, and Page Footer. It will ask whether you want to group the records (no) and whether to sort the records (select year, then click the Ascending button to change to a descending sort.) Choose any layout, style, and title when prompted.

   b. Exit the wizard and go to Design view. You do not have to duplicate our design exactly, but you are to use a clip art image in the Report Header. The width of your report should not exceed 6½ inches. Close the report.

   c. Go to the Database window and select the report that you just created. Press Ctrl+C to copy the report, then press Ctrl+V to display the Paste As dialog box. Enter *Best Actor and Actress* as the name of the new report.

   d. Open *Best Actor and Actress* report in Design view (which currently has the best picture and director information). Change the labels in the Report and Page Headers as necessary. Delete the Best Picture and Best Director controls from the Detail section. Pull down the View menu and click the Field List command to display the Award Winners table. Click and drag the BestActor control to its appropriate place in the Detail section, then delete the associated label. Click and drag the BestActress control in similar fashion. Move and size the controls as needed.

   e. Close the report. Return to the Database window. Copy the *Best Actor and Actress* report that you just created to a new *Best Supporting Actor and Actress* report, then modify that report accordingly. Print all three reports for your instructor.

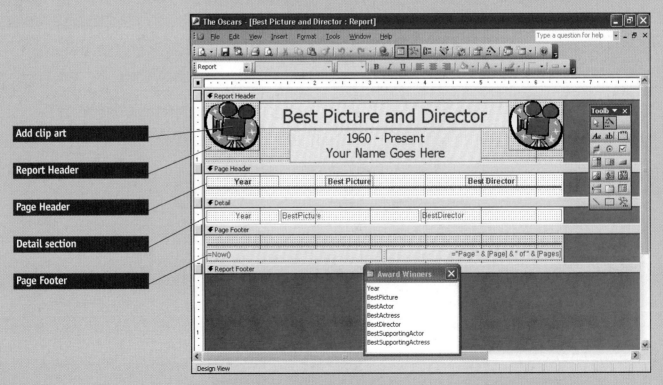

FIGURE 3.14   The Oscars (exercise 1)

2. **The United States:** The report in Figure 3.15 contains one example of every type of report section (a Report Header and Report Footer, a Page Header and Page footer, a Group header and Group footer, and a Detail section). It is based on the United States database from Chapter 1, and it computes the population and area totals for each region of the country. The report also contains a population density field that divides a state's population by its area. Open the *Chapter 1 Practice 3* database and proceed as follows:

a. Use the Report Wizard to create the report in Figure 3.15, which is based on the Population Density query that is already in the database. The report is to be sorted by region and then sorted by the name of each state within each region. Click the Summary Options button (in the same step where you specify the sorting sequence), check the boxes to sum the Population and Area fields, and click the option button for Detail and Summary information. Check the box to adjust field width so that all fields fit on one page. Choose a stepped layout and soft gray as the style. Name the report United States by Region, click the option button to modify the report's design, then click Finish.

b. You will see a report similar to Figure 3.15, but there is a lot of work to do. Start in the Region footer and change the contents to match Figure 3.15. You will have to delete an existing label, add new labels, increase font sizes, and move and align the various controls. You will have to further modify the footer so that it displays the average population density for each region. Click the Text Box tool, create an unbound control, then click in the control and enter the formula, =Sum([Population])/Sum([Area]). Click the button to preview the report. If you entered the formula correctly, the density for the Middle Atlantic region should be 396.54 (after you change the formatting properties of the control).

c. Enter a similar control =Sum([Population])/Sum([Area]) in the Report Footer to compute the population density for the country as a whole.

d. Change the formatting of the report and/or the contents of the various labels as you see fit. You do not have to match our design exactly, but be sure to add your name to the Report Header. Print the completed report for your instructor. The width of the report should not exceed 6½ inches.

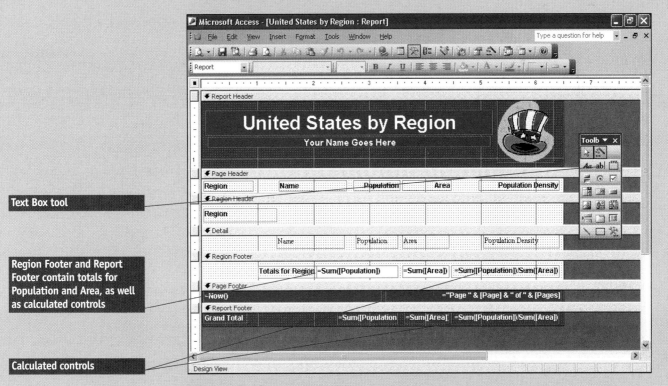

FIGURE 3.15 The United States

practice exercises

3. **The Super Bowl:** Figure 3.16 displays a History of the Super Bowl report that will be the basis of two subsequent reports that you will create in this exercise. Your first task is to update the database to include the additional games (if any) since the publication of our text. The database was introduced in Chapter 2 when we asked you to create a Web page for data entry. Proceed as follows:

   a. Open the *Chapter 2 Practice 3* database, open the existing table, and see if the data is current. If not, go to the Super Bowl Web site (www.superbowl.com) to obtain the results for any years that are not in the database.

   b. Go to the Database window. Click the Reports button. Modify the existing History of the Super Bowl report to include your name. Print this report.

   c. Click the Queries Button. Select the History of the Super Bowl query, press Ctrl+C to copy the query, then press Ctrl+V to display the Paste As dialog box. Enter Biggest Blowouts as the name of the query, then open the query in Design view. Change the sort sequence to display the records in descending sequence by margin of victory. Click in the Margin column, then click the down arrow on the Top Value list box and choose 5 (to list the five games with the highest margin.) Run the query to be sure it is correct.

   d. Click the Reports button. Select the History of the Super Bowl report, press Ctrl+C to copy the report, then press Ctrl+V to display the Paste As dialog box. Enter Biggest Blowouts as the name of the report. Open the report in Design view. Change the report properties so that the report is based on the Biggest Blowouts query. (Right click the Report Selector box in the upper left corner, click Properties to display the property sheet for the report as a whole, and click the All tab. Click the down arrow in the Record Source box and select the Biggest Blowouts query. Close the property sheet.) Change the report title to The Super Bowl's Biggest Blowouts. Print this report for your instructor.

   e. Repeat the process in steps (c) and (d) to create a query and associated report that shows the games in which your favorite team participated. Print this report. Add a cover sheet, then submit all three reports (History of the Super Bowl, Biggest Blowouts, and My Favorite Team) to your instructor.

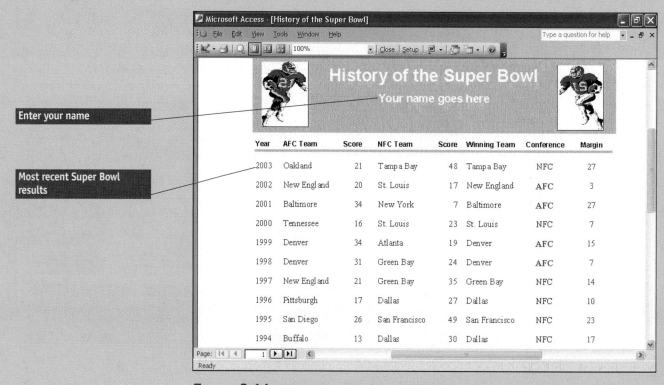

FIGURE 3.16 The Super Bowl (exercise 3)

4. **The Shopping Mall:** The partially completed *Chapter 3 Practice 4* database contains our version of the Shopping Mall database from Chapter 2. You will find a Stores table with 10 to 15 records, a form to enter data, and a form that describes the Shopping Mall database. Your assignment is to create the various reports that are described below. Each of the reports is based on an underlying query that contains a calculated control, selection criteria, and/or a sorting sequence. You should create the query first, display the associated dynaset to be sure the information is correct, then proceed to create the report. Use the Report Wizard to create the initial report, then modify the result in Design view. Proceed as follows:

   a. Create the report in Figure 3.17 that lists all stores with a monthly rental greater than $5,000. The stores are to be listed in descending order of the monthly rent. Your report should contain all of the fields that appear in our report, but you need not match the design.

   b. Create a report that shows all stores whose leases end in 2005. The stores are to be listed in chronological order by the ending date, with the earliest date shown first. Use the same design for your report as in Figure 3.17 and include all of the following fields: StoreID, StoreName, StoreType, LeaseStartDate, and LeaseEndDate.

   c. Create a report that displays all clothing stores in alphabetical order. Include the store revenue, monthly rent, manager's name, and phone number.

   d. Create a report listing those stores for which no manager has been assigned. List the stores in alphabetical order by the name of the store. The report should include the StoreID, the name of the store, whether or not it is a franchise, and the lease start and end dates.

   e. Print each of the reports and turn them in to your instructor. You may need to change the page orientation and/or margins to ensure that each report fits on one page. Add a cover sheet to complete the assignment.

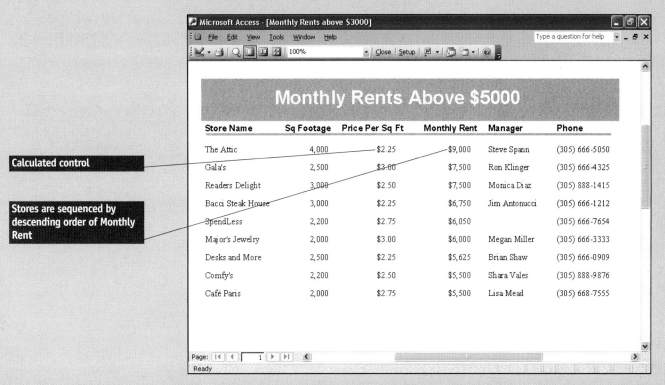

FIGURE 3.17   The Shopping Mall (exercise 4)

5. **Best Realty:** The partially completed *Chapter 3 Practice 5* database contains our version of the Best Realty database from Chapter 2. You will find a Property table with 10 to 15 records, a form to enter data, and a form that describes the Best Realty database. Your assignment is to create the various reports that are described below:

a. The report in Figure 3.18 that shows all properties that have been sold to date. The report is based on a query that contains two calculated fields: the price per square foot (based on the selling price, as opposed to the asking price) and the number of days that the property was on the market. Your report should contain all of the fields that appear in our report, but you need not match the design.

b. A report listing properties with an asking price of more than $250,000. The properties are to be listed from most expensive to least expensive. Include the Asking Price, PropertyID, Address, Agent's Last Name, Property Type, and Date Listed. This report should contain only properties that are available (i.e., properties that have not been sold).

c. A report listing the available properties that are on the water. List the properties in alphabetical order by the owner's last name. Include in the report the owner's last name, the address, the asking price, the number of bedrooms and bathrooms, and whether or not the property has a pool.

d. A report listing the available properties that have more than 3 bedrooms. List the properties in order from the one with the most to fewest bedrooms. The report should include the number of bedrooms, the agent's last name, the address, the property type, the garage information, and the date listed.

e. Choose a different format for each report to experiment with the different designs that are available. You may need to change the page orientation and/or margins to ensure that each report fits on one page.

f. Print each of the reports and turn them in to your instructor. Add a cover sheet to complete the assignment.

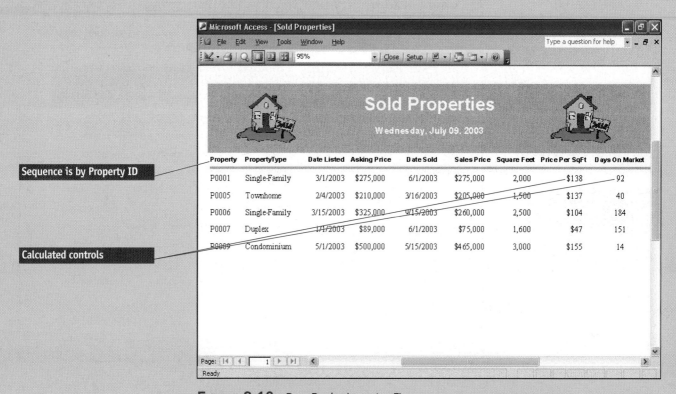

FIGURE 3.18   Best Realty (exercise 5)

6. **The Fishing Pole:** The partially completed *Chapter 3 Practice 6* database builds on an earlier example from Chapter 2. Your present assignment is to create the various reports that are described below, each of which requires its own query. We provide a Customers table with 60 records. Proceed as follows:

a. Create a report similar to Figure 3.19 that lists all customers whose initial purchase was more than $500. The customers are to be listed in descending order of the initial purchase amount. Your report should contain all of the fields that appear in our report, but you need not match our design exactly. We suggest you start with the Report Wizard, and then modify the report in Design view.

b. Create a report that shows all customers who own a fishing boat, listing the customers in alphabetical order by last name. Your report should include the customer's first and last name, the boat type, phone number, store account, and an indication of whether the customer is a yacht club member.

c. Create a report that displays all the long-term customers (people who have been customers for at least two years). This report is based on an underlying query that contains a calculated field to determine the number of years since the customer's initial purchase. (You will need to use the integer function to truncate the decimal portion of the field.) The report should include the customer's name, address (on two lines), and initial purchase date, as well as the number of years since the initial purchase.

d. Create a report that groups customers by mailing list priority. List the customers in alphabetical order by last name within each group. (The mailing list priority will appear in the group header.) The Detail section should include the customer's number, name, address, city, state, zip code, and phone number.

e. Print each of the reports and turn them in to your instructor. Change the page orientation and/or margins if necessary to ensure that all of the fields for one record fit on one page.

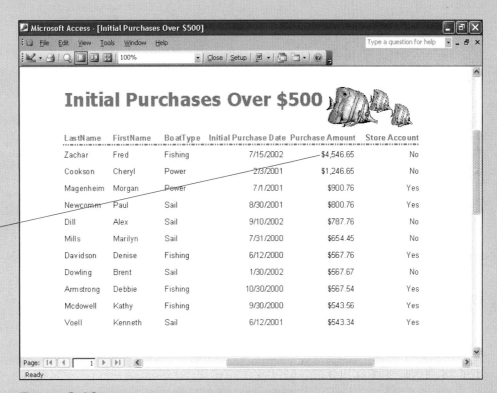

Sequence is by descending order of Purchase Amount

FIGURE 3.19 The Fishing Pole (exercise 6)

7. **Salary Increases:** The report in Figure 3.20 displays salary information for employees grouped by the location where they work. The easiest way to create this report is to use the Report Wizard, then modify the result in the Design view as necessary. You don't have to match our design exactly, but you are to include the identical information in your report. Proceed as follows:

a. Open the *Chapter 3 Practice 7* database in the Exploring Access folder. Use the Report Wizard to create the initial version of the report in Figure 3.20. Group the data by location, and sort the records by last name. Do not specify summary options at this time. Choose a stepped layout and any style that appeals to you.

b. Go to the Design view. Pull down the View menu, click the Sorting and Grouping command, select Location in the Field/Expression list box, then click Yes to display the Group Footer. Click in the location footer, then use the Text box to add an unbound control with the formula, =Sum(Salary). Change the label of the control to "Total Salaries for Location". Copy these controls to the Report Footer.

c. Add clip art to the Report Header. You can copy the clip art that appears in the Report Header from either the Employees form or the Employee Census report that is included in the database. Open either object in Design view, select the clip art, and click the Copy button. Open the Employee by Location report in Design view, click in the Report Header, click the Paste button, then move and size the image as necessary. Save the report. Print the report.

d. Create a parallel report that displays employees by title rather than location. The easiest way to create this report is to copy the location report, then modify the copied report as necessary. Go to the Database window and click the Reports button. Select the Employees by Location report. Press Ctrl+C to copy the report, then press Ctrl+V to duplicate the report as Employees by Title.

e. Open the Employees by Title report in Design view. Pull down the View menu, click the Sorting and Grouping command, and change the grouping order from location to title. Modify the report title, column headings, and bound controls within the report as necessary. Save the report, then print it for your instructor. Add a cover sheet to complete the assignment.

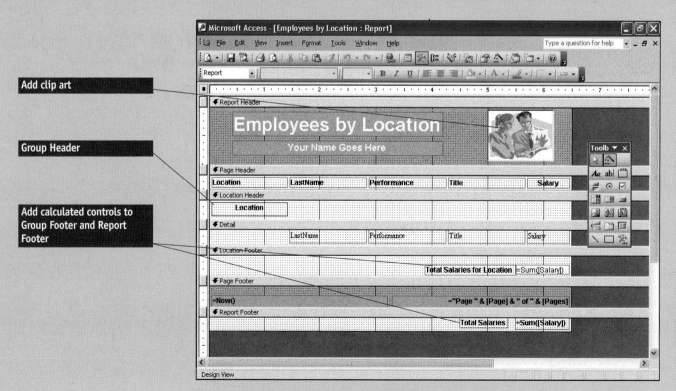

FIGURE 3.20 Salary Increases (exercise 7)

8. **Action Queries:** This problem asks you to create several action queries, after which you are to rcrun a report from the previous exercise to see the effects of the action queries on the original data. Realize, however, that action queries will modify the original Employees table, and hence it is good practice to duplicate the table before you begin. Proceed as follows:

a. Open the *Chapter 3 Practice 7* database in the Exploring Access folder. Go to the Database window, select the Employees table, pull down the Edit menu, and click the Copy command (or use the Ctrl+C keyboard shortcut). Pull down the Edit menu and click the Paste command (or use the Ctrl+V shortcut). Click the option button to copy the data and the structure. Name the copied table "Original Employees" and keep it as backup should you need to return to the original data.

b. Create a Delete query (based on the Employees table) to delete all employees with poor performance. Run the query.

c. Create an Update query to give all employees with Average performance a 5% raise. (The Update To row in the Salary column should contain the entry [Salary]*1.05). Be sure to run this query only once.

d. Create two additional Update queries to give employees who had a performance of Good or Excellent, increases of 10% and 15%, respectively. Be sure to run each query only once. (If there are no employees that satisfy the criteria, the query will not update any records.)

e. Use the Crosstab Query Wizard to create the query in Figure 3.21, which displays the total salary for each location-gender-title combination, after all of the action queries have been run. Print the query for your instructor.

f. Rerun the Employee by Location report from the previous exercise and compare the results to the earlier version. The Atlanta manager now has a salary of $110,000, which reflects the 10% increase for Good performance. Note, too, there is only one sales coordinator in Atlanta (Bowles). Her salary is $31,500, which reflects a 5% raise ($1,500) for Average performance. Brown, the other sales coordinator in Atlanta (in the previous exercise) was terminated because of Poor performance.

g. Add a cover sheet and submit all printouts to your instructor.

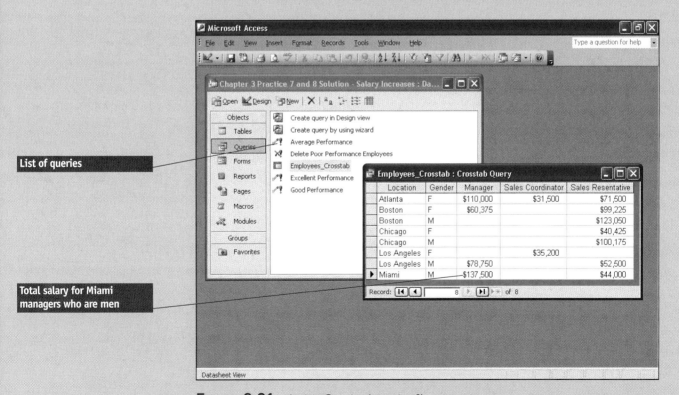

FIGURE 3.21 Action Queries (exercise 8)

MINI CASES

Mail Merge

A mail merge takes the tedium out of sending form letters, as it creates the same letter many times, changing the name, address, and other information as appropriate from letter to letter. The form letter is created in a word processor (e.g., Microsoft Word), but the data file may be taken from an Excel workbook or an Access table or query. Use the *Our Students* database that you have worked with throughout the chapter as the basis for two different form letters that are to be sent to two different groups of students. The first letter is to congratulate students on the Dean's list (GPA of 3.50 or higher). The second letter is a warning to students on academic probation (GPA of less than 2.00).

We have created the form letters for you as the Word documents *Chapter 3 Mini Case Study—Probation Letter* and *Chapter 3 Mini Case Study—Dean's List,* with both documents stored in the Exploring Access folder. Open the Access database and create the required queries, then select each query individually, pull down the Tools menu, click Office Links, and click the command to Merge it with Microsoft Word. Word provides step-by-step assistance, and you should be able to complete the mail merge without difficulty. Print the first form letter for each query to show your instructor that you have completed the assignment.

Oh Canada

If you ask the average Canadian how many states there are in the United States, you are very likely to get the correct answer. If you reverse the question and ask the average American about Canadian provinces, the response is far less accurate. This assignment enables you to learn about our neighbor to the North. Open the *Chapter 3 Mini Case Study—Oh Canada* database in the Exploring Access folder. You will find a single table with four fields—the name of the province or territory, the estimated population for 2002 (in thousands), the area in square kilometers, and an indication of whether the data pertains to a province or territory.

Your assignment is to create a report that parallels the Population Density report in the United States database that was described in practice exercise 2 on page 153. Your first task will be to create a query to compute the population density, after which you can create a report based on that query. The report should be grouped by province or territory, with population and area totals for each group, the average population density for each group, as well as statistics for Canada as a whole.

The Oh Canada database also contains an About Canada form that cites the source of the statistics that appear in the database. The form contains a map of Canada that you are asked to copy to the report you create. Last, but not least, modify the About Canada form so that it contains your name and student number. Print the completed form and report for your instructor.

Compacting versus Compressing

An Access database becomes fragmented, and thus unnecessarily large, as objects (e.g., reports and forms) are modified or deleted. It is important, therefore, to periodically compact a database to reduce its size (enabling you to back it up on a floppy disk). Choose a database with multiple objects, such as the Our Students database used in this chapter. Use the Windows Explorer to record the file size of the database as it presently exists. Start Access, open the database, pull down the Tools menu, and select Database Utilities to compact the database, then record the size of the database after compacting. You can also compress a compacted database (using a standard Windows utility such as WinZip) to further reduce the requirement for disk storage. Summarize your findings in a short report to your instructor. Try compacting and compressing at least two different databases to better appreciate these techniques.

4

Proficiency:
Relational Databases, Pivot Charts, and the Switchboard

OBJECTIVES

After reading this chapter you will:

1. Import data from an Excel workbook for inclusion in an Access database
2. Use the Relationships window to create a one-to-many relationship; define referential integrity.
3. Create a report that contains a relationships diagram
4. Create and modify a multiple-table select query.
5. Create a totals query.
6. Use Microsoft Graph to create a chart for inclusion in a report.
7. Create a pivot table and associated pivot chart.
8. Create and modify a switchboard.
9. Show the object dependencies that exist within a database.
10. Compact and repair a database; back up a database.

hands-on exercises

1. IMPORTING DATA FROM EXCEL
   Input: Investment Data workbook; Investment database (Access)
   Output: Investment Data workbook (modified); Investment database (modified)

2. TOTAL QUERIES, CHARTS, AND PIVOT TABLES
   Input: Investment database (after exercise 1)
   Output: Investment database (modified)

3. THE SWITCHBOARD MANAGER
   Input: Investment database (after exercise 2)
   Output: Investment database (modified)

CASE STUDY
ATTORNEYS FOR ATHLETES

Matt Denham was always a blue-chip athlete, and it came as no surprise when he went in the second round of the most recent NFL draft. Matt was very distrustful of professional agents and asked you to negotiate his first contract, given your recent graduation from law school at the top of your class. Matt is your best friend, and he also asked you to represent three teammates who were drafted by teams in other cities.

Your reputation for negotiating huge signing bonuses spread quickly and you now represent more than 100 athletes. As your business grew, you began to hire other attorneys, so that you have offices in several cities, each of which employs multiple attorneys. The downside is that your business has grown so quickly that it is becoming more difficult to provide the quality service of which you are so proud. A consultant has recommended that you create a relational database to store the data for your offices, attorneys, and the athletes they represent. The consultant has submitted a preliminary design in the form of a simple database that includes the required tables and the associated relationships diagram. The consultant has also chosen a logo (clip art) and color scheme, and has created a descriptive form to show the visual design. ∎

Your assignment is to read the chapter and focus on the one-to-many relationships that exist within the database. Put yourself in the place of the consultant and create the initial version of the database, including the switchboard. You will need three tables to track offices, attorneys, and athletes. There is a one-to-many relationship between offices and attorneys (one office has several attorneys, but a given attorney works in only one office). There is a second one-to-many relationship between attorneys and athletes (one attorney represents many athletes, but a specific athlete is represented by only one attorney). Your switchboard should contain three menu items: to display an About Attorneys for Athletes form, to print the relationships diagram, and to exit the application. The visual design is important. Print the relationships diagram, the Switchboard form, and the Switchboard Items table for your instructor.

query 查询

Each application in Microsoft Office is independent of the others, but it is often necessary or advantageous to share data between the applications. Data may be collected in Excel, imported or linked to an Access database to take advantage of its relational capability, then exported back to Excel for data analysis, or to Microsoft Word for a mail merge. This chapter describes how to share data between applications in the context of a database for an investment firm.

The Investment database is a relational database with two tables, one for clients, and one for financial consultants. Data from both tables can be displayed in a single query that contains fields from each table, and therein lies the real power of Microsoft Access. The chapter also introduces the concept of a total query to produce summary information. The results of a total query are then presented in graphical form through Microsoft Graph. The last portion of the chapter describes the creation of a user interface (or switchboard) that lets a nontechnical person move easily from one object to another by clicking a menu item. The switchboard is created through the Switchboard Manager, one of several utilities in Microsoft Access.

The database in Figure 4.1 is designed for an investment firm that monitors its clients and their financial consultants. The firm requires the typical data for each client—name, birth date, telephone, assets under management, and so on. The firm also stores data about its employees who are the financial consultants that service the clients. Each entity (clients and consultants) requires its own table in the database in order to add, edit, and/or delete data for individual clients and consultants, independently of one another.

If, for example, you wanted to know (or change) the account type and assets for Bradley Adams, you would search the Clients table for Bradley's record, where you would find the account type (Retirement), and assets ($90,000). In similar

Bradley Adams' record

ConsultantID points to Andrea Carrion (ConsultantID of 1)

	SSN	FirstName	LastName	ConsultantID	BirthDate	Gender	Account Type	Assets
▶	100-00-0000	Eileen	Marder	2	9/12/1935	F	Standard	$14,000
	111-11-1111	Bradley	Adams	1	8/22/1961	M	Retirement	$90,000
	111-22-2333	Linda	Laquer	3	3/16/1981	F	Corporate	$25,000
	200-00-0000	Kevin	Stutz	3	5/31/1972	M	Retirement	$150,000
	222-22-2222	Nickolas	Gruber	2	11/11/1961	M	Corporate	$90,000
	300-00-0000	Cedric	Stewart	4	4/12/1974	M	Retirement	$90,000
	333-33-3333	Lori	Graber	3	7/1/1972	F	Deluxe	$120,000
	400-00-0000	Ryan	Yanez	1	9/30/1974	M	Standard	$18,000
	444-44-4444	Christopher	Milgrom	4	3/12/1953	M	Corporate	$100,000
	444-55-5666	Jessica	Benjamin	1	10/31/1973	F	Deluxe	$125,000
	500-00-0000	Erica	Milgrom	2	5/1/1972	F	Retirement	$150,000
	555-55-5555	Peter	Carson	1	3/8/1953	M	Standard	$12,000
	600-00-0000	Michelle	Zacco	2	10/24/1975	F	Deluxe	$90,000
	666-66-6666	Kimberly	Coulter	2	11/11/1974	F	Corporate	$180,000
	700-00-0000	Steven	Frazier	4	9/9/1968	M	Retirement	$150,000
	777-77-7777	Ana	Johnson	3	4/18/1948	F	Standard	$12,000
	800-00-0000	Christa	Parulis	1	7/15/1972	F	Corporate	$120,000
	888-88-8888	David	James	4	8/1/1945	M	Deluxe	$100,000
	900-00-0000	Ronnie	Jones	2	6/1/1949	F	Standard	$12,000
	999-99-9999	Wendy	Simon	1	1/31/1945	F	Retirement	$10,000
*								

(a) The Clients Table

Andrea Carrion has ConsultantID of 1

	ConsultantID	FirstName	LastName	Phone	DateHired	Status
▶	1	Andrea	Carrion	(954) 346-1980	9/1/1995	Partner
	2	Ken	Grauer	(954) 346-1955	9/1/1999	Associate
	3	Robert	Arnold	(954) 346-1958	10/18/2000	Associate
	4	Issac	Milgrom	(954) 346-1961	3/16/2002	Partner
*						

(b) The Consultants Table

FIGURE 4.1   The Investments Database

fashion, you could search the Consultants table for Andrea Carrion and learn that she was hired on September 1, 1995, and that she is a partner in the firm. You could also use the ConsultantID field in Bradley Adams' record to learn that Andrea Carrion is Bradley's financial consultant.

The investment firm imposes a ***one-to-many relationship*** between financial consultants and their clients. One consultant can have many clients, but a given client is assigned to only one consultant. This relationship is implemented in the database by including a common field, ConsultantID, in both tables. The ConsultantID is the ***primary key*** (the field or combination of fields that ensures each record is unique) in the Consultants table. It also appears as a ***foreign key*** (the primary key of another table) in the Clients table in order to relate the two tables to one another.

The data from both tables can be combined through this relationship to provide complete information about any client and the consultant who serves him/her, or about any consultant and the clients he or she services. For example, to determine the name, telephone number, and status of Bradley Adams' financial consultant, you would search the Clients table to determine the ConsultantID assigned to Bradley (consultant number 1). You would then search the Consultants table for that consultant number and retrieve the associated data.

Multiple-table Queries

You have just seen how to manually relate data from the Clients and Consultants tables to one another. As you might expect, it can also be done automatically through the creation of a multiple-table query as shown in Figure 4.2. Figure 4.2a shows the Design view, whereas Figure 4.2b displays the associated dynaset. Bradley Adams appears first in the dynaset since the query lists clients in alphabetical order by last name. Note, too, that Carrion appears as Bradley's financial consultant, which is the same conclusion we reached when we looked at the tables initially.

The one-to-many relationship between consultants and clients is shown graphically in the Query window. The tables are related through the ConsultantID

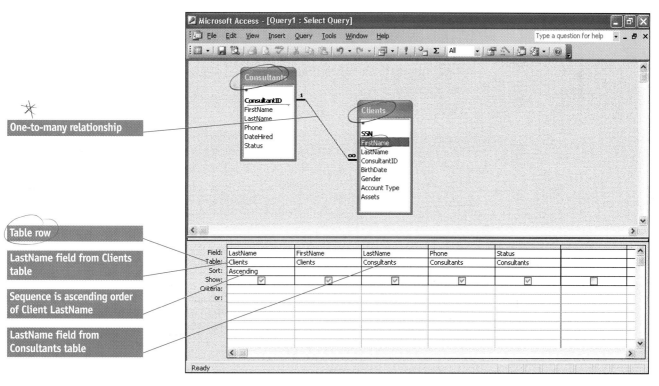

(a) Design View

FIGURE **4.2** Multiple-table Query

Sequence is alphabetical
order by Client LastName

Consultant LastName

Clients.LastName	FirstName	Consultants.LastName	Phone	Status
Adams	Bradley	Carrion	(954) 346-1980	Partner
Benjamin	Jessica	Carrion	(954) 346-1980	Partner
Carson	Peter	Carrion	(954) 346-1980	Partner
Coulter	Kimberly	Grauer	(954) 346-1955	Associate
Frazier	Steven	Milgrom	(954) 346-1961	Partner
Graber	Lori	Arnold	(954) 346-1958	Associate
Gruber	Nickolas	Grauer	(954) 346-1955	Associate
James	David	Milgrom	(954) 346-1961	Partner
Johnson	Ana	Arnold	(954) 346-1958	Associate
Jones	Ronnie	Grauer	(954) 346-1955	Associate
Laquer	Linda	Arnold	(954) 346-1958	Associate
Marder	Eileen	Grauer	(954) 346-1955	Associate
Milgrom	Erica	Grauer	(954) 346-1955	Associate
Milgrom	Christopher	Milgrom	(954) 346-1961	Partner
Parulis	Christa	Carrion	(954) 346-1980	Partner
Simon	Wendy	Carrion	(954) 346-1980	Partner
Stewart	Cedric	Milgrom	(954) 346-1961	Partner
Stutz	Kevin	Arnold	(954) 346-1958	Associate
Yanez	Ryan	Carrion	(954) 346-1980	Partner
Zacco	Michelle	Grauer	(954) 346-1955	Associate

(b) Dynaset

FIGURE 4.2   Multiple-table Query (*continued*)

field that appears in both tables. ConsultantID is the primary key of the "one" table (the Consultants table in this example), but it is also a field in the "many" table (the Clients table). This in turn links the tables to one another, making it possible to join data from the two tables in a single query.

The lower half of the Query window is similar to the queries you created in Chapter 3. The difference is that the design grid contains a ***Table row*** to indicate the table from where the field was taken. The client's last name and first name are taken from the Clients table. The consultant's last name, phone, and status are taken from the Consultants table. The records appear in alphabetical order (in ascending sequence) according to the value of the client's last name.

Maintaining the Database

You have seen how easy it is to obtain information from the investment database. The design of the investment database, with separate tables for clients and consultants, makes it easy to add, edit, or delete information about a client or consultant. Thus, to add a new client or consultant, just go to the respective table and add the record. In similar fashion, to change the data for an existing client or consultant, you again go to the appropriate table, locate the record, and make the change. The advantage of the relational database, however, is that you have to change the consultant information in only one place; for example, change the phone number of a consultant, and the change will be automatically reflected for every client associated with that consultant.

Realize, too, that the tables in the database must be consistent with one another, a concept known as ***referential integrity***. For example, you can always delete a record from the Clients table (the "many" table in this example). You cannot, however, delete a record from the Consultants table (the "one" table) when there are clients assigned to that consultant, because those clients would then be assigned to a financial consultant who did not exist. Access monitors the relationships that are in effect and prevents you from making changes that do not make sense. It will enforce referential integrity automatically.

THE IMPORT SPREADSHEET WIZARD

It is important to realize that data is data regardless of where it originates. You may prefer to work in Access, but others in the organization may use Excel or vice versa. In any event, there is a need to send data back and forth between applications. The ***Get External Data command*** imports or links data from an external source into Access. The data may come from an Excel workbook (as in our next hands-on exercise), or from a text file that was created by an application outside of Microsoft Office. The ***Export command*** does the reverse and copies an Access database object to an external destination.

The ***Import Spreadsheet Wizard*** is illustrated in Figure 4.3. The Wizard asks you a series of questions, then it imports the Excel worksheet into the Access table. You select the worksheet in Figure 4.3a, designate the Excel column headings and Access field names in Figure 4.3b, and specify the primary key in Figure 4.3c. You can then view and/or modify the resulting table as shown in Figure 4.3d.

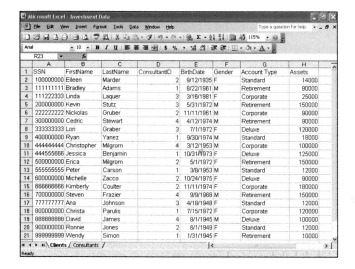

(a) The Excel Workbook

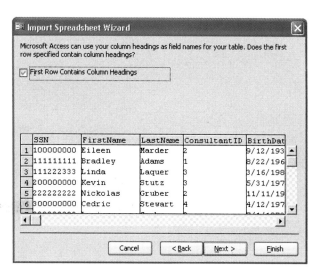

(b) Designate Column Headings (field names)

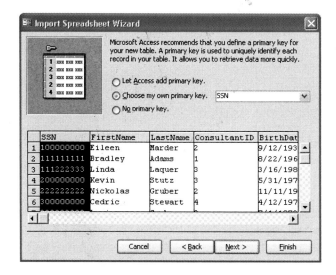

(c) Choose the Primary Key

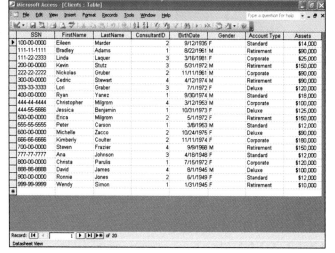

(d) The Clients Table

FIGURE 4.3   The Import Spreadsheet Wizard

1   Importing Data from Excel

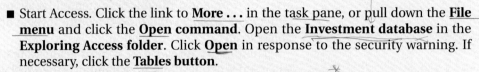

Objective   To import an Access table from an Excel workbook; to create a one-to-many relationship; to create a multiple-table query.

Step 1:   **Import the Excel Worksheet**

■ Start Access. Click the link to **More . . .** in the task pane, or pull down the **File menu** and click the **Open command**. Open the **Investment database** in the **Exploring Access folder**. Click **Open** in response to the security warning. If necessary, click the **Tables button**.

■ Pull down the **File menu**, click (or point to) the **Get External Data command**, then click **Import** to display the Import dialog box in Figure 4.4a.

■ Click the **down arrow** on the Look in list box and change to the **Exploring Access folder** (the same folder that contains the Access databases).

■ Click the **down arrow** on the Files of type list box and select **Microsoft Excel**. Select the **Investment Data workbook**. Click the **Import button**.

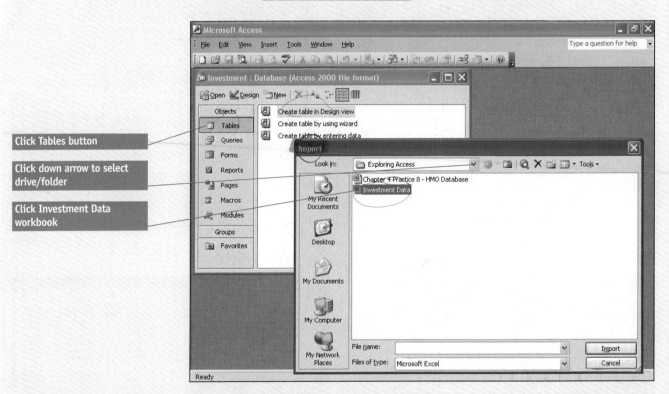

Click Tables button

Click down arrow to select drive/folder

Click Investment Data workbook

(a) Import the Excel Worksheet (step 1)

FIGURE 4.4   Hands-on Exercise 1

IMPORTING VERSUS LINKING

The Get External Data command displays a cascaded menu to import or link tables. Importing a table brings a copy of the table into the database and does not maintain a tie to the original data. Linking, on the other hand, does not bring the table into the database but only a pointer to the data source. Any changes to the data are made in the original data source and are reflected automatically in any database that is linked to that source.

Step 2: **The Import Spreadsheet Wizard**

- You should see the first step in the Import Spreadsheet Wizard as shown in Figure 4.4b. The option button to **Show Worksheets** is selected. The Clients worksheet is also selected. Click **Next**.

- Access will use the column headings in the Excel workbook as field names in the Access table, provided you check the box indicating that the first row contains column headings. Click **Next**.

- Select the option button to store the data in a new table. Click **Next**.

- You do not need information about the individual fields. Click **Next**.

- Select the option to choose your own primary key. Click the **drop-down arrow** on the list box, and select **SSN**. Click **Next**.

- Access indicates that it will import the data to a Clients table. Click the **Finish button**, then click **OK** when the wizard indicates it has finished importing the data. The Clients table appears within the Database window.

- Repeat the steps to import the **Consultants table** into the Investment database from the Investment Data workbook. Use the **ConsultantID field** as the primary key for this table.

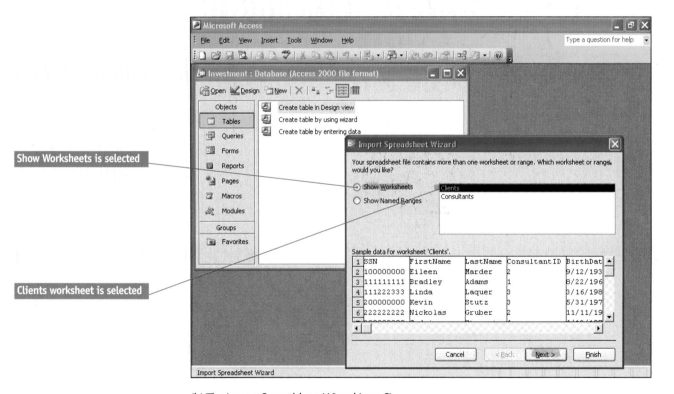

(b) The Import Spreadsheet Wizard (step 2)

FIGURE 4.4   Hands-on Exercise 1 (*continued*)

THE IMPORT TEXT WIZARD

The most common format for data originating outside of Microsoft Office is a text (or ASCII) file that stores the data without formatting of any kind. Pull down the File menu, click the Get External Data command, click Import, and specify Text Files as the file format to start the Import Text Wizard.

Step 3:   Create the Relationship

- Pull down the **Tools menu** and click the **Relationships command** to open the Relationships window in Figure 4.4c. (The tables are not yet visible.)

- Pull down the **Relationships menu** and click the **Show Table command** to display the Show Table dialog box. Click (select) the **Clients table** (within the Show Table dialog box), then click the **Add button**.

- Double click the **Consultants table** to add this table to the Relationships window. Close the Show Table dialog box. Click and drag the title bar of each table so that the positions of the tables match those in Figure 4.4c.

- Click and drag the bottom (and/or right) border of each table so that you see all of the fields in each table.

- Click and drag the **ConsultantID field** in the Consultants table field list to the **ConsultantID field** in the Clients field list. You will see the Edit Relationships dialog box.

- Check the box to **Enforce Referential Integrity**. Click the **Create button** to create the relationship.

- Click the **Save button** to save the Relationships window.

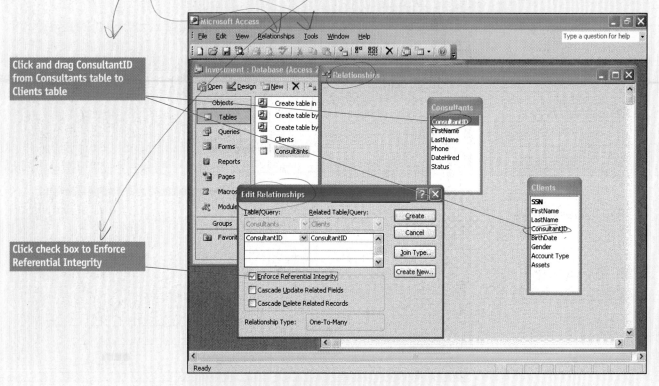

Click and drag ConsultantID from Consultants table to Clients table

Click check box to Enforce Referential Integrity

(c) Create the Relationship (step 3)

FIGURE 4.4   Hands-on Exercise 1 (*continued*)

REFERENTIAL INTEGRITY

The tables in a database must be consistent with one another, a concept known as referential integrity. Thus, Access automatically implements certain types of data validation to prevent errors of inconsistency from occurring. You cannot, for example, enter a record in the Clients table that references a Consultant who does not exist. Nor can you delete a record in the Consultants table if it has related records in the Clients table.

Step 4: Print the Relationship

- Pull down the **File menu** and click the **Print Relationships command**. You will see the Print Preview screen of a report. Maximize the window.

- Click the **View button** to change to the Design view as shown in Figure 4.4d. If necessary, click the **Toolbox button** to display the Toolbox toolbar.

- Click the **Label tool** on the Toolbox toolbar, then click and drag in the Report Header section of the report to create an unbound control.

- The insertion point is positioned automatically within the label you just created. Type **Prepared by:** followed by your name. Size the labels within the header as necessary.

- Click the **Save button** to display the Save As dialog box. Change the name of the report to **Relationships Diagram**, then click **OK**.

- Click the **View button** to change to the **Print Preview** view of the report. Click the **Print button**. Close the Print Preview window.

- Close the Report window. Close the Relationships window.

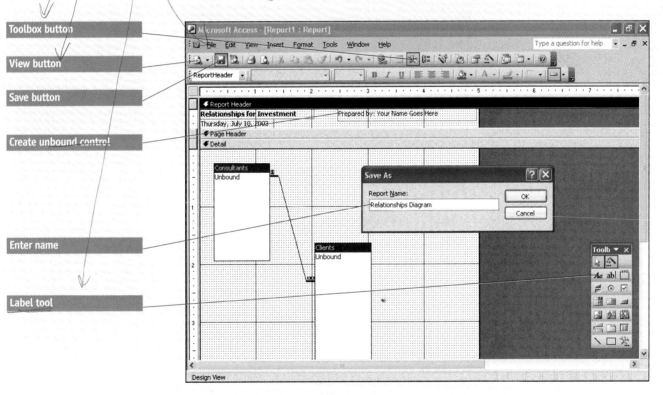

(d) Print the Relationship (step 4)

FIGURE 4.4   Hands-on Exercise 1 (*continued*)

DISPLAY THE CURRENT DATE

A report typically displays one of two dates—the date it was created, or the current date (i.e., the date on which it is printed). We prefer the latter, which is obtained through the Now() function. Click in the Report header and delete the control containing today's (fixed) date. Click the Text Box tool, click and drag where you want the date to appear, then release the mouse. Click in the text box and enter the function =Now(). Save the report. The next time you open the report, it will display the current date.

Step 5: Add Your Own Record

- Click the **Forms button** in the Database window, then double click the **Consultants form** to open the form.

- Click the **Add Record button** and enter the data for your instructor. Enter **5** as the ConsultantID, enter your **instructor's name**, and use today's date as the date of hire. Your instructor is a **partner**. Close the form.

- Double click the **Clients form** in the Database window to open the form as shown in Figure 4.4e. Click the **Add Record button**, then enter the appropriate data for yourself.
  - ❑ Click the **down arrow** on the Consultants list box, then select your instructor (Barber in our example) as your financial consultant.
  - ❑ Enter **Standard** as the Account Type.
  - ❑ Enter **$25,000** in the Assets field.

- Click the **Print Record button** to print the form.

- Click the **Close Form button**.

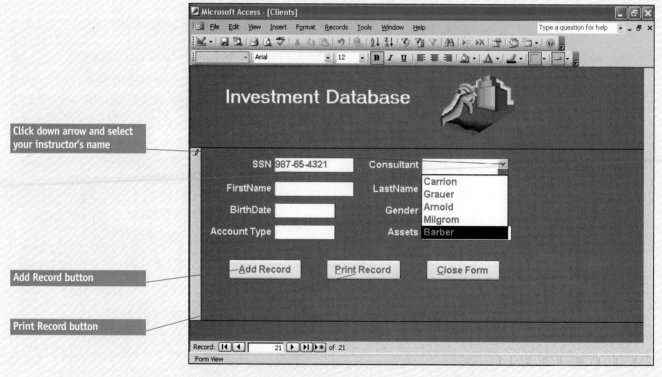

Click down arrow and select your instructor's name

Add Record button

Print Record button

(e) Add Your Own Record (step 5)

FIGURE 4.4   Hands-on Exercise 1 (*continued*)

ADD A HYPERLINK

You can enhance the appeal of your form through inclusion of a hyperlink. Open the form in Design view, then click the Insert Hyperlink button to display the Insert Hyperlink dialog box. Enter the Web address and click OK to close the dialog box and return to the Design view. Right click the hyperlink to display a shortcut menu, click the Properties command to display the Properties dialog box, then change the caption, font, and/or point size as appropriate.

Step 6: Create the Multiple-table Query

- Click the **Queries button** in the Database window. Double click the icon to **Create query in design view** to open the Design window. The Show Table dialog box appears automatically.

- Press and hold the **Ctrl key** to select the Clients and Consultants tables, then click the **Add button** to add these tables to the query. Close the Show Table dialog box.

- Click the **Maximize button** so that the Query Design window takes the entire desktop. Point to the line separating the field lists from the design grid (the mouse pointer changes to a cross), then click and drag in a downward direction. This gives you more space to display the field lists.

- Click and drag the title bars of each table to arrange the tables as shown in Figure 4.4f. Click and drag the bottom of each field list until you can see all of the fields in the table.

- You are ready to complete the query, which will contain fields from both the Clients and Consultants tables.

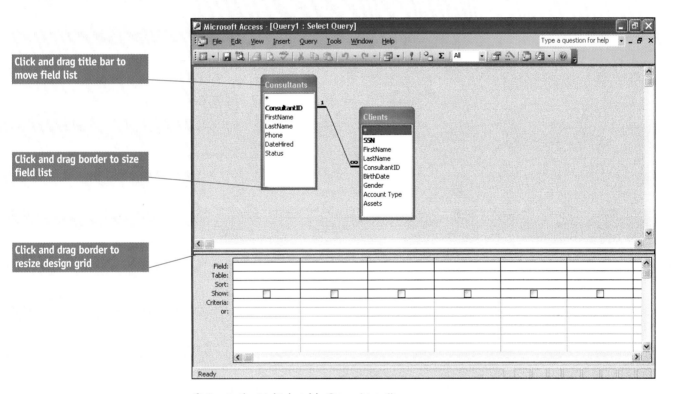

(f) Create the Multiple-table Query (step 6)

FIGURE 4.4 Hands-on Exercise 1 (*continued*)

THE JOIN LINE

Access joins the tables in a query automatically if a relationship exists between the tables within the database. Access will also join the tables (even if no relationship exists) if both tables have a field with the same name and data type, and if one of the fields is a primary key. And finally, you can create the join yourself by dragging a field from one table to the other, but this type of join applies only to the query in which it was created.

Step 7: Complete the Multiple-table Query

- The Table row should be visible within the design grid. If not, pull down the **View menu** and click **Table Names** to display the Table row in the design grid as shown in Figure 4.4g.

- Double click the **LastName** and **Status fields** from the Consultants table to add these fields to the design grid. Double click the **LastName**, **Assets**, and **Account Type fields** from the Clients table to add these fields as well.

- Click the **Sort row** under the **LastName field** from the **Consultants table**, then click the **down arrow** to open the drop-down list box. Click **Ascending**.

- Click the **Save button** on the Query Design toolbar to display the Save As dialog box. Save the query as **Assets Under Management**. Click **OK** to save the query.

- Click the **Run button** (the exclamation point) to run the query. The results are displayed on a dynaset.

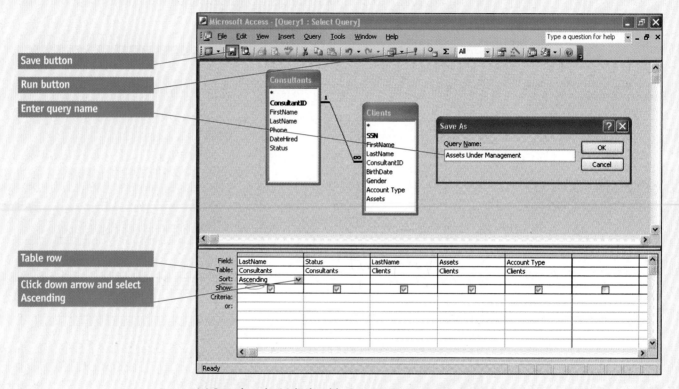

(g) Complete the Multiple-table Query (step 7)

FIGURE 4.4   Hands-on Exercise 1 (continued)

SORT ON MULTIPLE FIELDS

A query can be sorted on multiple fields (e.g., by consultant, and by client's last name within consultant), provided the fields are in the proper order within the design grid. Access sorts from left to right (the leftmost field is the most important field), so the consultant's last name must appear to the left of the client's last name. To move a field within the design grid, click the column selector above the field name to select the column, then drag the column to its new position. Click the Sort row for both fields and choose the ascending sequence.

Step 8: **Export the Query**

■ You should see the dynaset created by the query as shown in Figure 4.4h. The query lists all of the client records grouped by the last name of the financial consultant. There should be one record for your instructor.

■ Pull down the **File menu**, click (or point to) the **Export command** to display the Export Query dialog box. Click the **down arrow** in the Save as type list box to select **Microsoft Excel 97-2003**.

■ Select the **Investment Data workbook** and click the **Export All button** to save the query as a worksheet in the Investment Data workbook. Click **Yes** if asked whether to replace the file. Close the Query window.

■ Click the **Tables button** in the Database window. Select the **Clients table**, pull down the **File menu**, click the **Export command**, and change the file type to **Microsoft Excel 97-2003**. Select (click) the **Investment Data workbook**. Click **Export**. Click **Yes** if asked to replace the file.

■ Export the **Consultants table** in similar fashion.

■ Start Excel. Open the **Investment Data workbook** in the **Exploring Access folder**. The workbook should contain Clients, Consultants, and Assets under Management worksheets.

■ If the workbook contains two Client worksheets (Clients and Clients1), it is because you did not replace the original worksheet. Delete that worksheet now.

■ Format the individual worksheets as necessary, and then print the completed workbook for your instructor. Use the **Page Setup command** to show row and column headings. Include a **custom footer** with your name, the name of the worksheet, and today's date. Exit Excel.

■ Exit Access if you do not want to continue with the next exercise at this time.

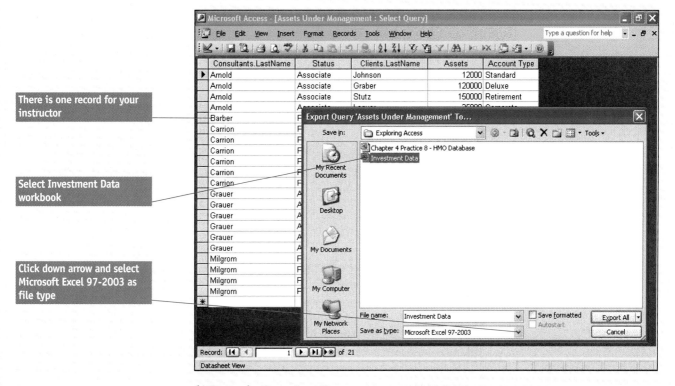

(h) Export the Query (step 8)

FIGURE 4.4 Hands-on Exercise 1 (*continued*)

Chapter 3 described several types of queries, including a select query, various action queries, and a crosstab query. Now we present a ***total query***, which performs calculations on a group of records using one of several ***aggregate (summary) functions*** available within Access. These include the Sum, Count, Avg, Max, and Min functions to determine the total, number, average, maximum, and minimum values, respectively. Figure 4.5 shows a total query to compute the total assets under management for each financial consultant.

Figure 4.5a displays the results of a select query similar to the query created in the first hands-on exercise. The records are displayed in alphabetical order according to the last name of the financial consultant. The dynaset contains one record for each client in the Clients table and enables us to verify the results of the total query in Figure 4.5c. Arnold, the first consultant listed, has four clients (Johnson, Graber, Stutz, and Laquer). The total assets that Arnold has under management are $307,000, which is obtained by adding the Assets field in the four records.

Figure 4.5b shows the Design view of the total query to calculate the total assets managed by each consultant. The query contains three fields, the LastName (from the Consultants table), followed by the LastName and Assets fields from the Clients table. The design grid also displays a ***Total row*** in which each field in the query has either a Group By or aggregate entry. The ***Group By*** entry under the consultant's last name indicates that the records in the dynaset are to be grouped (aggregated) according to the like values of the consultant's last name; that is, there will be one record in the total query for each consultant. The ***Count function*** under the client's last name indicates that the query is to count the number of records for each consultant. The ***Sum function*** under the Assets field specifies that the values in this field are to be summed for each consultant.

The dynaset in Figure 4.5c displays the result of the total query and contains *aggregate* records, as opposed to *individual* records. There are four records for Arnold in Figure 4.5a, but only one record in Figure 4.5c. This is because each record in a total query contains a calculated result for a group of records.

Microsoft Graph

Microsoft Office includes a supplementary application called ***Microsoft Graph*** that enables you to create a graph (or chart) within an Access form or report. The chart can be based on any table or query, such as the Assets Under Management query in Figure 4.5. The easiest way to create the chart is to open the report or form in Design view, pull down the Insert menu, click the Chart command, then let the ***Chart Wizard*** take over.

The Chart Wizard guides you every step of the way as can be seen in Figure 4.6. The wizard asks you to choose the table or query (Figure 4.6a), the fields within the table or query (Figure 4.6b), and the type of chart (Figure 4.6c). You then have the chance to preview or modify the chart (Figure 4.6d) and add a title (Figure 4.6e). Figure 4.6f displays the completed chart.

EMPHASIZE YOUR MESSAGE

A graph is used to deliver a message, and you want that message to be as clear as possible. One way to help put your point across is to choose a title that will lead the audience. A neutral title, such as "Assets Under Management," is nondescriptive and requires the audience to reach its own conclusion. A better title might be, "Grauer Leads All Consultants," if the objective is to emphasize an individual's performance.

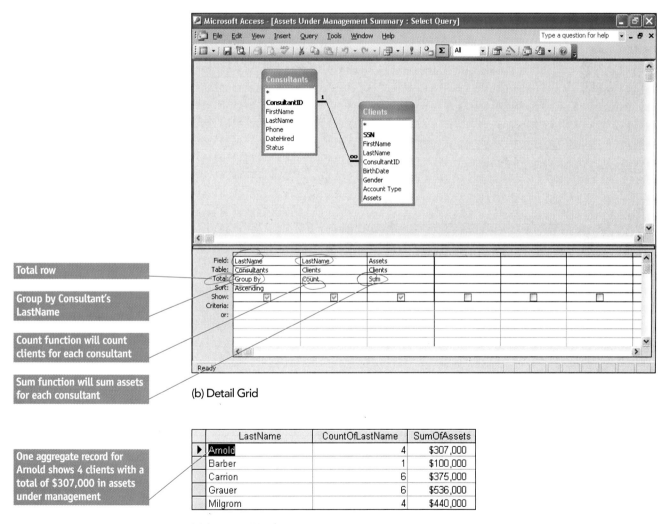

Arnold is the consultant for first four clients

Arnold's total assets under management is $307,000

Barber's total assets under management has increased to $100,000

Consultants.LastName	Status	Clients.LastName	Assets	Account Type
Arnold	Associate	Johnson	12000	Standard
Arnold	Associate	Graber	120000	Deluxe
Arnold	Associate	Stutz	150000	Retirement
Arnold	Associate	Laquer	25000	Corporate
Barber	Partner	Doe	100000	Standard
Carrion	Partner	Yanez	18000	Standard
Carrion	Partner	Benjamin	125000	Deluxe
Carrion	Partner	Carson	12000	Standard
Carrion	Partner	Parulis	120000	Corporate
Carrion	Partner	Simon	10000	Retirement
Carrion	Partner	Adams	90000	Retirement
Grauer	Associate	Jones	12000	Standard
Grauer	Associate	Marder	14000	Standard
Grauer	Associate	Gruber	90000	Corporate
Grauer	Associate	Milgrom	150000	Retirement
Grauer	Associate	Coulter	180000	Corporate
Grauer	Associate	Zacco	90000	Deluxe
Milgrom	Partner	Stewart	90000	Retirement
Milgrom	Partner	Milgrom	100000	Corporate
Milgrom	Partner	Frazier	150000	Retirement
Milgrom	Partner	James	100000	Deluxe

(a) Detail Records

Total row

Group by Consultant's LastName

Count function will count clients for each consultant

Sum function will sum assets for each consultant

(b) Detail Grid

One aggregate record for Arnold shows 4 clients with a total of $307,000 in assets under management

LastName	CountOfLastName	SumOfAssets
Arnold	4	$307,000
Barber	1	$100,000
Carrion	6	$375,000
Grauer	6	$536,000
Milgrom	4	$440,000

(c) Summary Totals

FIGURE 4.5 A Total Query

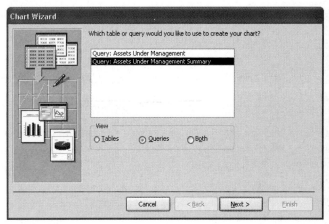

(a) Choose the Query

(b) Choose the Fields

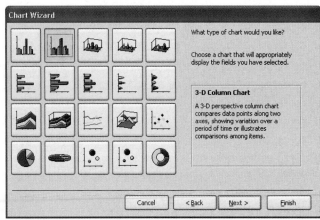

(c) Choose the Chart Type

(d) Preview the Chart

(e) Title the Chart

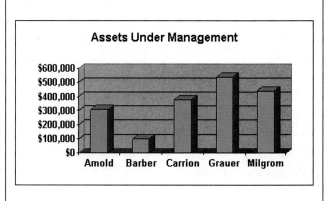

(f) The Completed Chart

FIGURE 4.6   The Chart Wizard

PIVOT TABLES AND PIVOT CHARTS

Microsoft Graph is a simple and effective way to visualize the data in a table or query. Pivot tables and the associated pivot charts provide a more powerful way of analyzing the same data as can be seen in Figure 4.7. A ***pivot table*** computes summary statistics for the records in a table (or query) according to the parameters you supply. A ***pivot chart*** provides the same information in graphical form.

The pivot table in Figure 4.7a displays the assets under management for each combination of consultant and account type within the Investment database. Arnold, for example, has $307,000 under management that is distributed over the different account types. In similar fashion, Barber and Carrion have assets under management of $100,000 and $375,000, respectively. The combined assets for all consultants are $1,758,000. The columns show the total assets for each account type as distributed over the various consultants. The combined assets for all account types also total to $1,758,000.

A pivot table is very flexible in that the fields in the row and column areas, Consultant's LastName and Account Type in this example, can be expanded or collapsed to show detail or summary statistics. We have elected to suppress the details for all consultants except Carrion to illustrate the distinction. Carrion, for example, has two retirement accounts of $10,000 and $90,000, and the individual amounts are displayed, as opposed to the total.

There is additional flexibility in that you can display (remove) data for any consultant or account type, by clicking the down arrow in the field name and checking (or clearing) the box for the specific value of the field. Note, too, the third dimension in the pivot table (the filter area) that indicates all of the records in the database. The Status field in this example (is from the Consultant's table, and it) contains one of two values, Partner or Associate, to indicate the status of the consultant. As with the row and column fields, you can click the down arrow to filter the table to display or hide the records according to the value of the Status field.

You can also change the overall structure of the pivot table to add or remove fields by dragging the field names on or off the table. You can switch the orientation (pivot the table) by dragging a field to or from the row, column, or filter area. You can change the means of calculation by switching to the Average, Minimum, or Maximum value, as opposed to the Sum function value in the present table. And finally, you can change the data in the underlying table, then refresh the pivot table to reflect the changes in the table.

Best of all, a pivot table is very easy to create. You may recall that a table (or query) has four different views: Datasheet view, Design view, Pivot Table view, and Pivot Chart view. The pivot table is created within the Pivot Table view. In essence, all you do is click and drag a field from the ***field list*** to the indicated drop area. The Consultant's LastName, Account Type, and Status fields, for example, have been dragged to the row, column, and filter areas, respectively. The Assets field is dragged to the body of the table, and the row and column totals are specified.

The Pivot Chart view in Figure 4.7b displays the graphical equivalent of the associated pivot table. The pivot chart is created automatically when you create the associated pivot table. You can pivot the chart just as you can pivot the table, and any changes made to the pivot chart are automatically reflected in the pivot table and vice versa. You can filter the data to display (hide) selected records. You could, for example, click the down arrow next to Account Type field, then clear the check box that appears next to any of the account types to suppress these values. And finally, you can change the properties of any of the chart's components to display different fonts, formatting, styles, and so on.

Pivot tables have been available for several years in Microsoft Excel, but they are still a well-kept secret in that many otherwise knowledgeable individuals do not know of their existence. Pivot tables and charts are relatively new to Microsoft Access, however, as they were first introduced in Office XP.

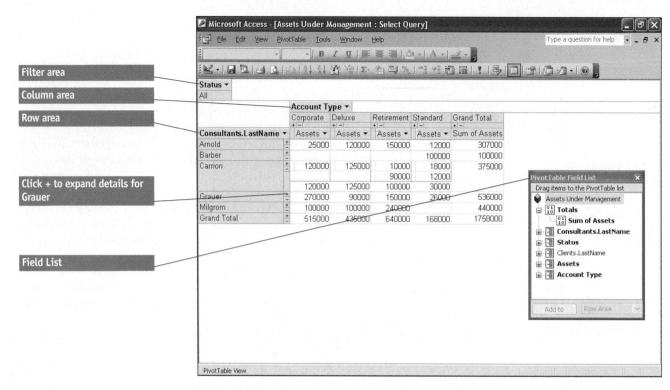

Filter area

Column area

Row area

Click + to expand details for Grauer

Field List

(a) Pivot Table

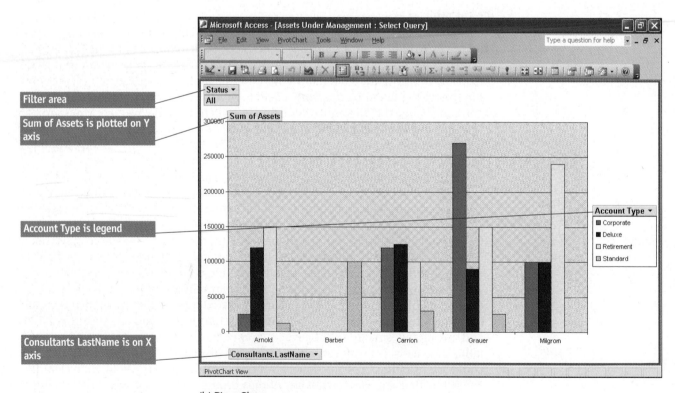

Filter area

Sum of Assets is plotted on Y axis

Account Type is legend

Consultants LastName is on X axis

(b) Pivot Chart

FIGURE 4.7 Pivot Tables and Pivot Charts

2 Total Queries, Charts, and Pivot Tables

Objective To create a total query; to use Microsoft Graph to present data from an Access object in graphical form. Use Figure 4.8 as a guide.

Step 1: **Copy the Assets Under Management Query**

- Open the **Investment database**. Click the **Queries button** in the Database window and select the **Assets Under Management query** that was created earlier.

- Click the **Copy button** on the Database toolbar (or press **Ctrl+C**) to copy the query to the clipboard. Click the **Paste button** (or press **Ctrl+V**) to display the Paste As dialog box in Figure 4.8a.

- Enter **Assets Under Management Summary** as the name of the new query. Click **OK**. There are now two queries in the database window, the original query that was created in the previous exercise, as well as a copy of that query that you will modify in this exercise.

- Select (click) the **Assets Under Management Summary query** that was just created via the Copy and Paste commands. Click the **Design button** to open the query in Design view.

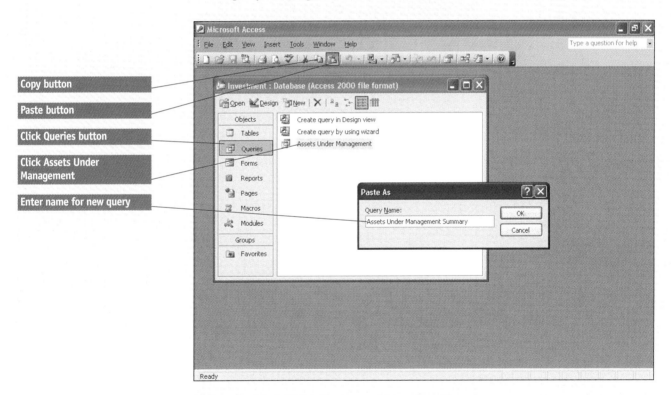

(a) Copy the Assets Under Management Query (step 1)

FIGURE 4.8 Hands-on Exercise 2

KEYBOARD SHORTCUTS—CUT, COPY, AND PASTE

Ctrl+X, Ctrl+C, and Ctrl+V are shortcuts to cut, copy, and paste, respectively, and apply to all applications in the Office suite as well as to Windows applications in general. The shortcuts are easier to remember when you realize that the operative letters X, C, and V are next to each other at the bottom left side of the keyboard.

Step 2: Create the Total Query

- You should see the Assets Under Management Summary in Design view as shown in Figure 4.8b. Maximize the window. Pull down the **View menu** and click **Totals** to display the Total row.

- Click the **Total row** under the **Client's LastName field**, click the **down arrow** to display the list of summary functions, then click the **Count function**.

- Click the **Total row** under the Assets field, click the **down arrow** to display the list of summary functions, then click the **Sum function**.

- Click the column selector for the **Consultants Status field** to select the entire column, then press the **Del key** to remove the column from the query. Delete the column containing the **Client's Account Type field** in similar fashion. Your query should now contain three fields.

- Pull down the **Query menu** and click **Run** (or click the **Run button**) to run the query. You should see a dynaset with five records, one for each financial consultant. Each record contains the total assets for one consultant.

- Save the query. Close the query.

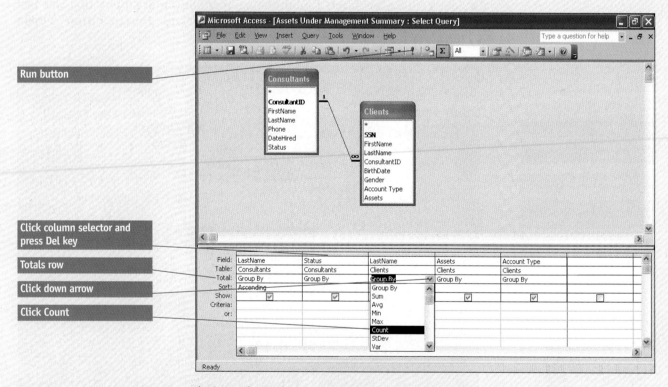

(b) Create the Total Query (step 2)

FIGURE 4.8   Hands-on Exercise 2 (*continued*)

THE UNMATCHED QUERY WIZARD

Any business wants all of its employees to be productive, and our hypothetical financial services concern is no exception. The Unmatched Query Wizard identifies records in one table (e.g., Consultants) that do not have matching records in another table (e.g., clients). In other words, it will tell you which consultants (if any) do not have any clients. Click the Queries button in the Database window, click the New button, select the Find Unmatched Query Wizard, and click OK. Answer the prompts to create the query and see the results.

Step 3: **Start the Chart Wizard**

- Click the **Reports button** in the Database window. Double click the **Assets Under Management report** to run the report. Click the **View button** to switch to Design view.

- You should see the Assets Under Management report in Design view as shown in Figure 4.8c. Click and drag the **Report Header** down in the report to increase the size of the Report Header.

- Click the control that is to contain the name of the person who prepared the report and enter your name. Arrange and format the controls in the Report Header as shown.

- Pull down the **Insert menu** and click the **Chart command**. The mouse pointer changes to a tiny crosshair. Click and drag in the **Report Header** to draw the outline of the chart as shown in Figure 4.8c.

- The Chart Wizard starts automatically and asks for the table or query on which to base the chart. Click the **Queries button**, click the **Assets Under Management Summary query**, and click **Next**.

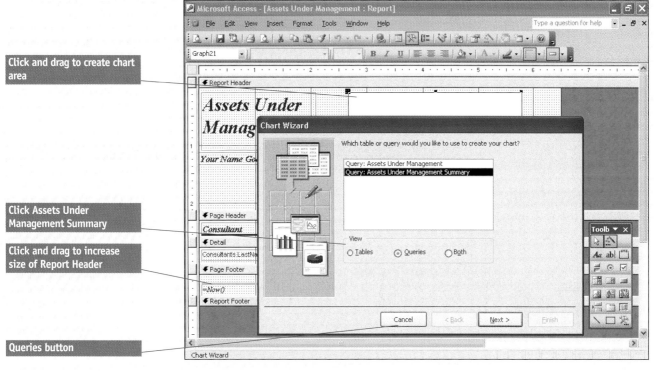

(c) Start the Chart Wizard (step 3)

FIGURE 4.8 Hands-on Exercise 2 (*continued*)

ANATOMY OF A REPORT

All reports are divided into sections that print at designated times. The Report Header and Report Footer are each printed once at the beginning and end of the report. The Page Header appears under the Report Header on the first page and at the top of every page thereafter. The Page Footer appears at the bottom of every page in the report, including the last page, where it appears after the Report Footer. The Detail section is printed once for each record in the underlying query or table.

Step 4:   **Complete the Chart Wizard**

- Answer the questions posed by the Chart Wizard to complete the chart.

- Double click the **LastName** and **SumOfAssets fields** to move these fields from the list of Available fields to the list containing the fields for the chart. Click **Next** to continue.

- Select the **3-D Column Chart** as the chart type. Click **Next**.

- The Chart Wizard lays out the chart for you, with the SumOfAssets field on the Y axis and the LastName field on the X axis. Click **Next**.

- The chart should not change from record to record because we are plotting the total for each consultant. Thus, click the **down arrow** in both the Report Fields list and the Chart Fields list and select No Field. Click **Next**.

- Assets Under Management Summary is entered automatically as the title for the chart. Click the option button that indicates you do not want to display a legend. Click **Finish**.

- The completed chart appears in the report as shown in Figure 4.8d. Do not be concerned that the values along the Y axis do not match the Asset totals or that the labels on the X axis do not correspond to the names of the financial consultants.

- Click the **Save button** to save the report. Click anywhere in the **Report Header** to deselect the chart. Click the **View button** to view the chart within the report. The appearance of the chart more closely resembles the finished product, but the chart still needs work.

- Click the **View button** to return to the Design view.

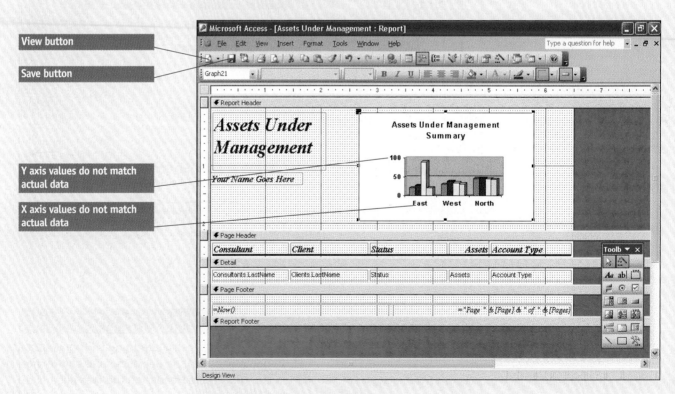

(d) Complete the Chart Wizard (step 4)

FIGURE 4.8   Hands-on Exercise 2 (*continued*)

Step 5:   Increase the Plot Area

- Click anywhere in the chart to display the sizing handles, then (if necessary) drag the sizing handle on the right border to increase the width of the chart.

- You might also want to drag the Report Header down (to increase the size of the header), then click and drag the bottom border of the chart to make it deeper. The chart area should be large enough so that you will be able to see the names of all the financial consultants along the X axis.

- Click off the chart to deselect it, then double click within the chart to display the hashed border as shown in Figure 4.8e.

- Close the chart datasheet if it appears. Click (select) the title of the chart and press the **Del key**.

- Right click the **Y axis**, click **Format Axis**, click the **Number tab**, and set to **Currency format** with **zero** decimals. Click **OK**.

- Click off the chart to deselect the chart, then click the **View button**. Continue to move back and forth between the Design view and the finished report, until you can see all of the consultants' names along the X axis.

- Close the report. Click **Yes** if asked whether to save the changes to the report.

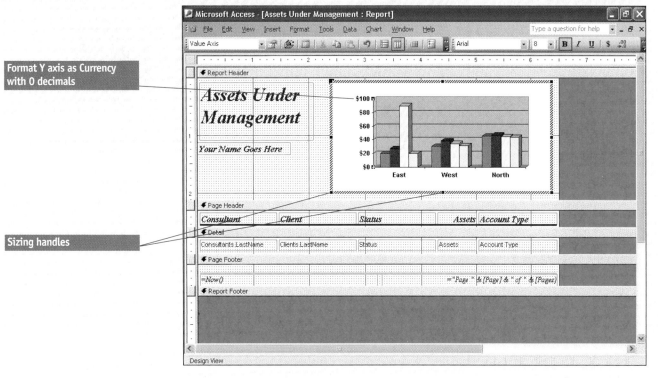

(e) Increase the Plot Area (step 5)

FIGURE 4.8   Hands-on Exercise 2 (*continued*)

TO CLICK OR NOT TO CLICK

Click anywhere on the chart to select the chart and display the sizing handles; this allows you to move and/or size the chart within the report. Click off the chart to deselect it, then double click the chart to start the Microsoft Graph in order to modify the chart itself.

Step 6: The Completed Report

- Click the **Forms button**, open the **Clients form**, locate your record, and change your assets to **$100,000**. Click the ▶ **button** to record your changes and move to the next record. Close the Clients form.

- Click the **Queries button**, then double click the **Assets Under Management Summary query** to rerun the query. The increased value of your account should be reflected in the Assets Under Management of your instructor. Close the query.

- Click the **Reports button**, and double click the **Assets Under Management report** to open the report as shown in Figure 4.7f.

- The detailed information for your account (Doe in this example) appears within the detailed records in the body of the report. The value of your account ($100,000) is reflected in the total for your instructor.

- Click the **Setup button** and change all margins to **one-half an inch**. Click the **Print button** to print the report for your instructor. Close the Report window.

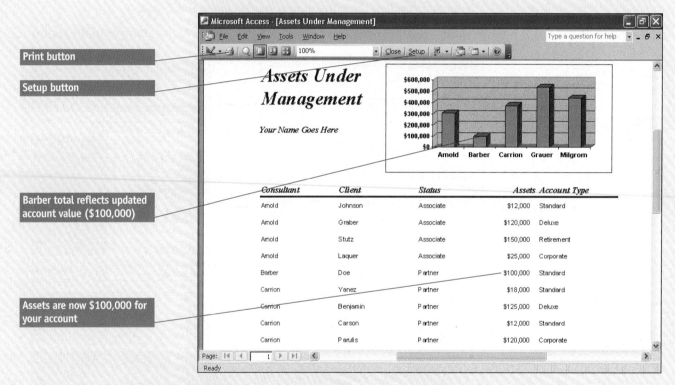

(f) The Completed Report (step 6)

FIGURE 4.8 Hands-on Exercise 2 *(continued)*

OPEN THE SUBDATASHEET

Take advantage of the one-to-many relationship that exists between consultants and clients to add and/or delete records in the Clients table while viewing the information for the associated consultant. Go to the Database window, open the Consultants table in Datasheet view, then click the plus sign next to the consultant. You now have access to all of the client records for that consultant and can add, edit, or delete a record as necessary. Click the minus sign to close the client list.

Step 7: **Create the Pivot Table**

- Open the **Assets Under Management query**. Pull down the **View menu** and select the **PivotTable View** to display an empty pivot table. If necessary, pull down the **View menu** a second time and click the **Field List command** (or simply click the **Field List button** on the Pivot Table toolbar) to display the field list.

- Click and drag the **Consultants.LastName field** to the row area as shown in Figure 4.8g. Click and drag the **Account Type field** to the column area and the **Status field** to the filter area.

- Click and drag the **Assets field** to the Totals or Detail Fields area as shown in Figure 4.8g. You should see the total assets for each consultant, account type, and the database as a whole. Click the **Save button**. Close the field list.

- Right click on the **25,000** Corporate Assets for Arnold. Click **AutoCalc**; click **Sum**. You will see the sum of each client's assets in the Grand Total column.

- Click the **minus sign** next to each consultant's name to show just the totals for each consultant in each Account Type category.

- Pull down the **File menu**, click the **Print command**, and click **OK** (or click the **Print button** on the PivotTable toolbar) to print the pivot table.

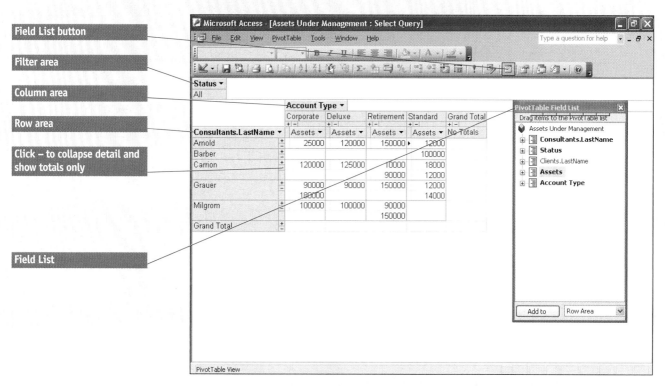

(g) Create the Pivot Table (step 7)

FIGURE 4.8 Hands-on Exercise 2 (*continued*)

CHANGE THE ORDER

Click within any row or column, then click the Ascending or Descending button on the PivotChart toolbar to display the entries in the selected sequence. Click in the Consultants.LastName column, for example, and click the Ascending button to display the rows alphabetically. Click a single cell in the Grand Total column, then click the Descending button to display the consultant with the highest assets first.

Step 8: The Pivot Chart

- Pull down the **View menu** and select the **PivotChart view** to display the pivot chart in Figure 4.8h. The chart corresponds to the pivot table you just created. Close the Field list.

- Pull down the **PivotChart menu** and click the **Show Legend command** (or click the **Show Legend button** on the PivotChart toolbar) to display the legend. The names of the different account types appear as a legend.

- Pull down the **PivotChart menu** and click the **By Row/By Column command** to reverse the rows and columns. The Account Types now appear as the category names, and the names of the consultants appear in the legend.

- The label "Axis Title" does not enhance either the X or Y axis. Click the label on either axis, then press the **Delete key**. Delete the other label in similar fashion.

- Pull down the **File menu**, click the **Page Setup command**, click the **Page tab**, change to **Landscape printing**, and click **OK**. Click the **Print button** on the PivotTable toolbar to print the pivot table.

- Close the query. Click **Yes** when asked whether to save the changes. Exit Access if you do not want to continue with the next exercise at this time.

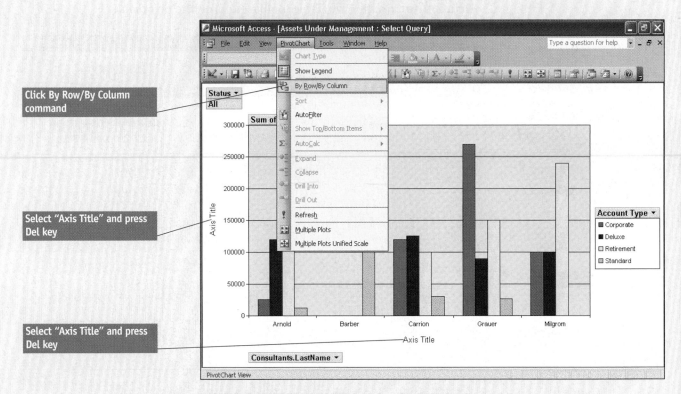

(h) The Pivot Chart (step 8)

FIGURE 4.8 Hands-on Exercise 2 *(continued)*

IMPOSE OR CLEAR A FILTER

Click the down arrow next to any field name to display all of the values for that field, then check or clear the boxes next to the field values. Click the down arrow next to the Account Type field, for example, then clear the box for the Corporate account type. Click OK and the associated column disappears from the table. There is no Undo command, but you can restore the column by reversing the process. And remember, any changes to the pivot chart are automatically reflected in the associated pivot table.

THE USER INTERFACE

The Investment database has grown in sophistication throughout the chapter. It contains two tables, for clients and consultants. There is a one-to-many relationship between consultants and clients, and referential integrity is enforced. There is a form to enter data into each table. There are also queries and reports based on these tables. You are proficient in Access and are familiar with its Database window to the extent that you can select different objects to accomplish the work you have to do. But what if the system is to be used by a nontechnical user who might not know how to open the various forms and reports within the system?

It is important, therefore, to create a user interface that ties the objects together so that the database is easy to use. The interface displays a menu (or series of menus) enabling a nontechnical person to open the various objects within the database, and to move easily from one object to another. This type of interface is called a ***switchboard***, and it is illustrated in Figure 4.9. The switchboard itself is stored as a form within the database, but it is subtly different from the forms you have developed in previous chapters. Look closely and note that the record selector and navigation buttons have been suppressed because the switchboard is not used for data entry, but rather as a menu for the user.

The switchboard is intuitive and easy to use. Click About Investments, the first button on the switchboard in Figure 4.9a, and the system displays the informational screen we like to include in all of our applications. Click any other button, and you display the indicated form or report. Close the form or report, and you will be returned to the switchboard, where you can select another item.

You should try to develop a switchboard that will appeal to your users. Speak in depth to the people who will use your application to determine what they expect from the system. Identify the tasks they consider critical, and be sure you have an easily accessible menu option for those tasks.

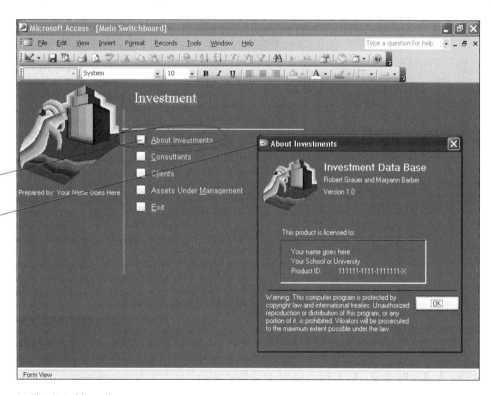

Click button to open About Investments form

About Investments form

(a) The Switchboard

FIGURE 4.9 The Switchboard

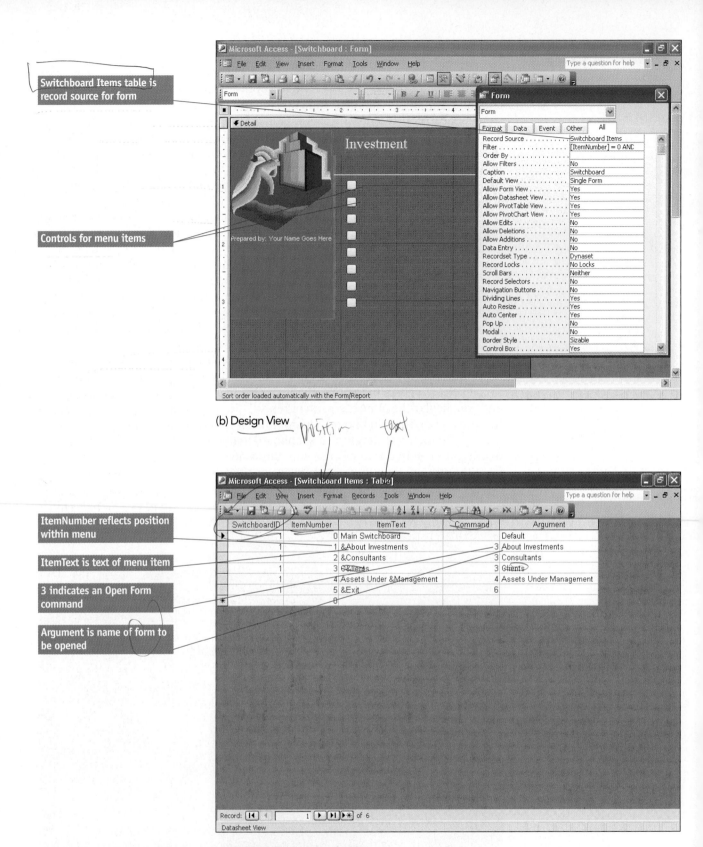

Switchboard Items table is record source for form

Controls for menu items

(b) Design View

ItemNumber reflects position within menu

ItemText is text of menu item

3 indicates an Open Form command

Argument is name of form to be opened

(c) The Switchboard Items Table

FIGURE 4.9 The Switchboard (*continued*)

The Switchboard Manager

The switchboard is quite powerful, but it is also very easy to create. All of the work is done by the ***Switchboard Manager,*** an Access utility that prompts you for information about each menu. You supply the text of the item, as it is to appear on the switchboard (e.g., Clients), together with the underlying command (e.g., Open Clients Form). Access does the rest. It creates the switchboard form and an associated ***Switchboard Items table*** that is the basis for the switchboard. Figure 4.9b displays the Design view of the switchboard in Figure 4.9a.

At first, the two views do not appear to correspond to one another, in that text appears next to each button in the Form view, but it is absent in the Design view. This, however, is the nature of a switchboard, because the text for each button is taken from the Switchboard Items table in Figure 4.9c, which is the record source for the form, as can be inferred from the Form property sheet shown in Figure 4.9b. In other words, each record in the Switchboard Items table has a corresponding menu item in the switchboard form.

The Switchboard Items table is created automatically and need never be modified explicitly. It helps, however, to have an appreciation for each field in the table. The SwitchboardID field identifies the number of the switchboard, which becomes important in applications with more than one switchboard. Access limits each switchboard to eight items, but you can create as many switchboards as you like, each with a different value for the SwitchboardID. Every database has a main switchboard by default, which can in turn display other switchboards as necessary.

The ItemNumber and ItemText fields identify the position and text of the item, respectively, as it appears on the switchboard form. (The & that appears within the ItemText field will appear as an underlined letter on the switchboard to enable a keyboard shortcut; for example, &Consultants is displayed as Consultants and recognizes the Alt+C keyboard shortcut in lieu of clicking the button.) The Command and Argument fields determine the action that will be taken when the corresponding button is clicked. Command number 3, for example, opens a form.

Other Access Utilities

The ***Convert Database command*** changes the file format of an Access 2003 database to the format used by earlier versions. Think, for a moment, why such a command is necessary. Access 2003 is the current release of Microsoft Access, and thus it is able to read files that were created in all previous versions. The converse is not true, however. Access 2000, for example, cannot read an Access 2003 database because the latter uses a file format that was unknown when Access 2000 was developed. The Convert Database command solves the problem by translating an Access 2003 database to the earlier format. (Access 2003 also enables you to create and modify databases in the Access 2000 format, without going through the conversion process.)

The ***Compact and Repair Database command*** serves two functions, as its name suggests. The compacting process eliminates the fragmentation and wasted disk space that occur during development as you add, edit, and delete the various objects in a database. Compacting can be done when the database is open or closed. Compacting a database when it's open saves the database under the same name. Compacting a database when it is closed is safer, however, since the compacted database is stored as a new file (enabling you to return to the original file should anything go wrong). The Repair function takes place automatically if Access is unable to read a database when the database is opened initially.

The ***Back Up Database command*** compacts the open database, and then it saves the compacted database under a different name that contains the date the backup was created. Thus, if you were to back up a database named "Investment", the backup copy would be named "Investment_2003-07-16", given that the backup was created on July 16, 2003.

3 The Switchboard Manager

Objective   To create a switchboard and user interface; to compact a database. Use Figure 4.10 as a guide in the exercise.

Step 1: **Start the Switchboard Manager**

- Open the **Investment database**. Minimize the Database window to give yourself more room in which to work.
- Pull down the **Tools menu**, click the **Options command**, click the **Forms/Report tab** to display the associated dialog box, then check the box to **Use Windows Themed Controls on Forms**.
- Pull down the **Tools menu**, click the **Database Utilities command**, and choose **Switchboard Manager**.
- Click **Yes** if you see a message indicating that there is no valid switchboard and asking if you want to create one. You should see the Switchboard Manager dialog box as shown in Figure 4.10a.
- Click the **Edit command button** to edit the Main Switchboard, which displays the Edit Switchboard Page dialog box. Click the **New command button** to add an item to this page, which in turn displays the Edit Switchboard item dialog box. Add the first switchboard item as follows.
    - ❏ Click in the **Text list box** and type **&About Investments**, which is the name of the command, as it will appear in the switchboard.
    - ❏ Click the **drop-down arrow** on the Command list box and choose the command to Open the Form in either the Add or Edit mode.
    - ❏ Click the **down arrow** in the Form list box and choose **About Investments**.
- Click **OK** to create the switchboard item. The Edit Switchboard Item dialog box closes, and the item appears in the Main Switchboard page.

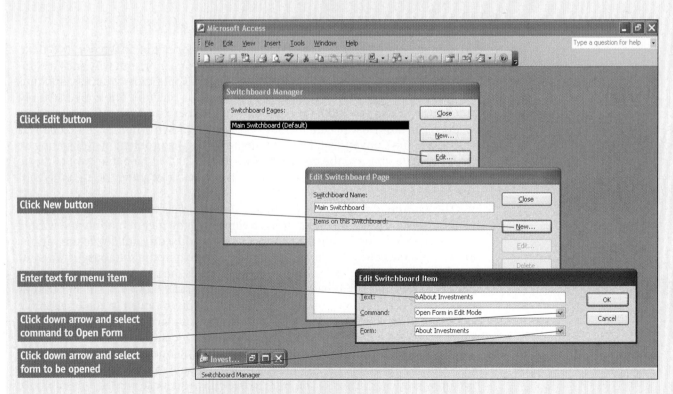

(a) Start the Switchboard Manager (step 1)

FIGURE 4.10   Hands-on Exercise 3

Step 2: **Complete the Switchboard**

■ Click the **New command button** in the Edit Switchboard Page dialog box to add a second item to the switchboard.

■ Click in the **Text list box** and type **&Consultants**. Click the **drop-down arrow** on the Command list box and choose **Open Form in Edit Mode**. Click the **drop-down arrow** in the Form list box and choose **Consultants**. Click **OK**.

■ The &Consultants command appears as an item on the switchboard (The switchboard will display Consultants to indicate a keyboard shortcut—see boxed tip.)

■ Add the remaining items to the switchboard as shown in Figure 4.10b. The menu items are as follows:
  ❑ **C&lients**—Opens the Clients form in Edit mode.
  ❑ **Assets Under &Management**—Opens the Assets report.
  ❑ **&Exit**—Exits the application (closes the database but remains in Access).

■ Click the **Close button** to close the Edit Switchboard Page dialog box after you have added the last item. Close the Switchboard Manager dialog box.

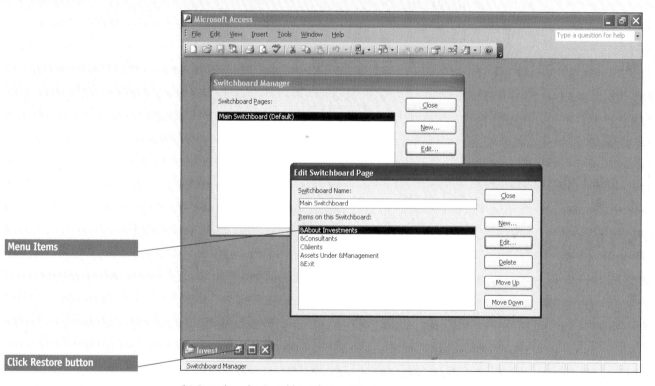

Menu Items

Click Restore button

(b) Complete the Switchboard (step 2)

FIGURE 4.10 Hands-on Exercise 3 (*continued*)

CREATE A KEYBOARD SHORTCUT

The & has special significance when used within the name of an Access object because it creates a keyboard shortcut to that object. Enter "&About Investments", for example, and the letter A (the letter immediately after the ampersand) will be underlined and appear as "About Investments" on the switchboard. From there, you can execute the item by clicking its button, or you can use the Alt+A keyboard shortcut (where "A" is the underlined letter in the menu option).

Step 3: **Test the Switchboard**

- Click the **Restore button** in the Database window to view the objects in the database, then click the **Forms button**. The Switchboard Manager has created the Switchboard form automatically.

- Double click the **Switchboard form** to open the Main Switchboard. Do not be concerned about the design of the switchboard at this time, as your immediate objective is to make sure that the buttons work.

- Click the **About Investments button** (or use the **Alt+A** shortcut) to display the About Investments form as shown in Figure 4.10c. Click the **OK button** to close the form.

- Click the **Consultants button** (or use the **Alt+C** keyboard shortcut) to open the Consultants form. Click the **Close Form button** on the form to close this form and return to the switchboard.

- Test the remaining items on the switchboard (except the Exit button). You can click the button and/or use the keyboard shortcut as you see fit.

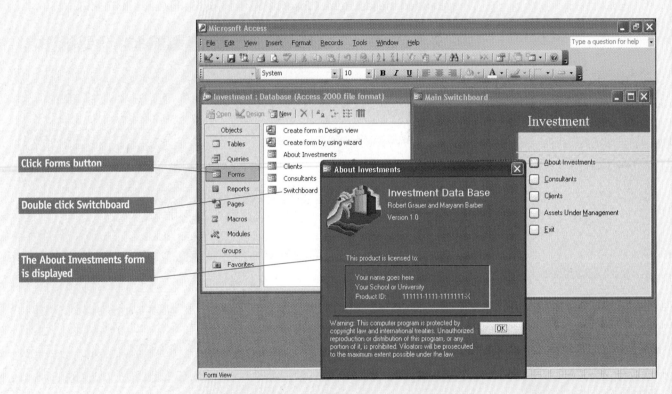

(c) Test the Switchboard (step 3)

FIGURE 4.10 Hands-on Exercise 3 (*continued*)

THE SWITCHBOARD ITEMS TABLE

You can modify an existing switchboard in one of two ways—by using the Switchboard Manager or by making changes directly in the underlying table of switchboard items. Press the F11 key to display the Database window, click the Tables button, then open the Switchboard Items table where you can make changes to the various entries on the switchboard. We encourage you to experiment, but start by changing one entry at a time. The ItemText field is a good place to begin.

Step 4:   **Insert the Clip Art**

- Change to Design view. Maximize the window so that you have more room to work. Click in the left side of the switchboard. Pull down the **Insert menu** and click the **Picture command** to display the Insert Picture dialog box as shown in Figure 4.10d.

- Select the **Exploring Access folder**. Click the **Views button** repeatedly until you see the **Thumbnails View**. Select (click) a picture. Click **OK**.

- Move and/or size the image as necessary. Do not be concerned if you do not see the entire image as you change its size and position.

- Right click the clip art after it has been sized to display a shortcut menu, then click **Properties** to display the Properties dialog box. Select (click) the **Size Mode property**, click the **down arrow**, and select **Stretch** from the associated list. Close the dialog box.

- Click to the right of the picture in the Detail (gray) area of the form. Click the **drop-down arrow** on the **Fill/Back Color button** on the Formatting toolbar to display a color palette. Select the same shade as the rest of the form (the fifth square from the left in the second row).

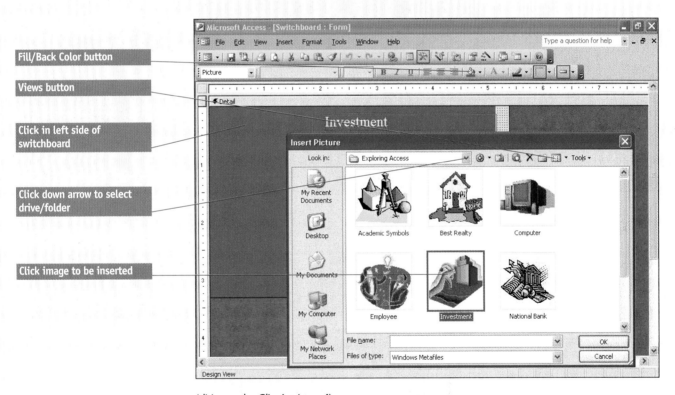

(d) Insert the Clip Art (step 4)

FIGURE 4.10   Hands-on Exercise 3 (*continued*)

SEARCHING FOR CLIP ART

The Insert Picture command functions differently in Access than in the other Office applications since it does not display the Clip Art task pane. You can still search for clip art explicitly, however, by starting the Clip Organizer as a separate application. Click the Start button, click the All Programs button, click Microsoft Office, click Microsoft Office Tools, then start the Microsoft Clip Organizer. Select a clip art image from within the Clip Organizer, and click the Copy button. Use the Windows taskbar to return to Access, open the form in Design view, and click the Paste button.

Step 5: Complete the Design

- If necessary, click the **Toolbox tool** to display the toolbox. Click the **Label tool**, then click and drag to create a text box under the picture.

- Enter your name in an appropriate font, point size, and color. Move and/or size the label containing your name as appropriate.

- Press and hold the **Shift button** as you click each text box in succession. Be sure that you select all eight, even if you do not have eight menu choices.

- Click the **drop-down arrow** on the Font/Fore color button and change the font to white as shown in Figure 4.10e. Change the font and point size to **Arial** and **10 pt**, respectively.

- Click the **Save button** to save the changes, then switch to the Form view to see the modified switchboard. Return to the Design view as necessary and make final adjustments to the switchboard. Save the form.

- Click the **View button** to see the switchboard.

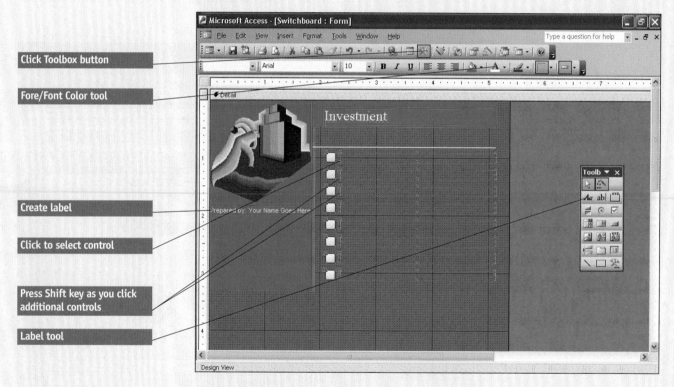

(e) Complete the Design (step 5)

FIGURE 4.10 Hands-on Exercise 3 (*continued*)

THE STARTUP PROPERTY

The ideal way to open a database is to present the user with the main switchboard, without the user having to take any special action. Pull down the Tools menu, click Startup to display the Startup dialog box, click the drop-down arrow in the Display Form/Page list box, and select the Switchboard as the form to open. Add a personal touch to the database by clicking in the Application Title text box and entering your name. Click OK to accept the settings and close the Startup dialog box. The next time the database is opened, the switchboard will be displayed automatically.

Step 6: **The Completed Switchboard and Object Dependencies**

- You should see the completed switchboard in Figure 4.10f. Click the **Maximize button** so that the switchboard takes the entire screen.
- Press **Alt+L** (when the switchboard is active) to open the Clients form. Locate your record. Change the Assets to $2,000,000 (wishful thinking). Close the Clients form and return to the switchboard.
- Press **Alt+M** to open the Assets Under Management report. The chart should reflect the increased value of your account. Close the report.
- Pull down the **View menu** and click the **Object Dependencies command** to open the task pane in Figure 4.10f. Click the option button that says **Objects that I depend on**.
- If necessary, click the **plus sign** that appears next to Tables within the task pane. You should see the Switchboard Items table indicating that the switchboard is dependent on an underlying table.
- Click the **Close button** at the extreme right of the menu bar to close the switchboard but leave the database open.

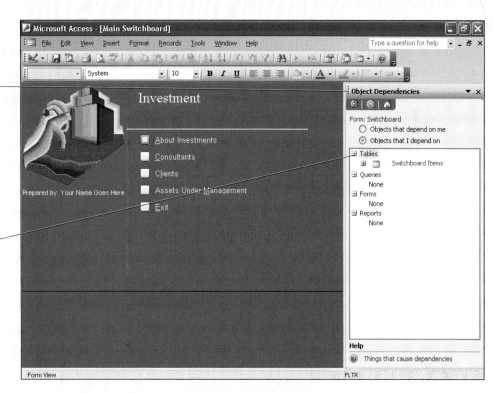

Object Dependencies task pane

Switchboard form is dependent on Switchboard Items table

(f) The Completed Switchboard and Object Dependencies (step 6)

FIGURE 4.10   Hands-on Exercise 3 (*continued*)

OBJECT DEPENDENCIES

The objects in an Access database depend on one another; for example, a report is based on an underlying query, which in turn is based on a table. Over time, the report may become obsolete, so you delete the report and the underlying query, but if the same query were the basis of another report, the latter object would no longer function. The ability to view object dependencies can prevent this type of error from occurring. Select the object in the Database window, pull down the View menu, and click Object Dependencies to open the task pane and view the objects that depend on the selected object.

Step 7: **Compact and Back Up the Database**

- Pull down the **Tools menu**, click (or point to) the **Database Utilities command**, and then click the **Compact and Repair Database command**.

- The system pauses as it compacts the database, closes it, then reopens it, which in turn displays the Security Warning dialog box. Click the **Open button** to open the database. You should see the Database window for the Investment database.

- Pull down the **Tools menu**, click the **Database Utilities command**, and then click the **Back Up Database command** to display the Save Backup As dialog box as shown in Figure 4.10g.

- Access supplies a default file name consisting of the original name of the database followed by the date on which the backup was made (July 7, 2003 in our example). Click the **Save button**.

- The system pauses as it backs up the Investment database, closes the backup copy, then reopens the original Access database, which in turn displays the Security Warning dialog box.

- Click **Cancel** since we are finished working. Close Access. Congratulations on a job well done.

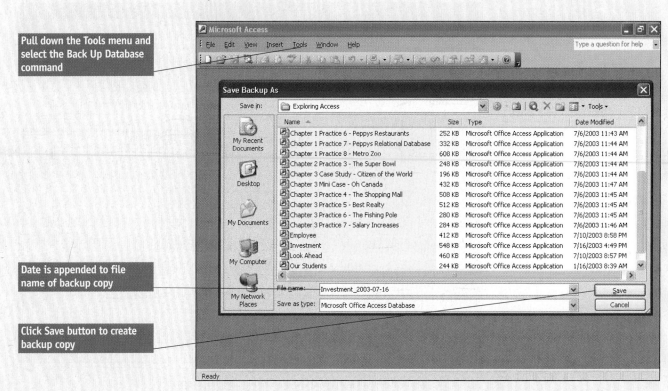

(g) Compact and Back Up the Database

FIGURE 4.10 Hands-on Exercise 3 (*continued*)

A FALSE SENSE OF SECURITY

The backup copy you just created helps to protect you against the accidental deletion or corruption of the Investment database. It does not, however, protect you against damage to your hard drive (if both copies are on the same drive). Nor does it protect you against the loss of your system due to theft or natural disaster. It is important, therefore, that you store the backup copy (or copies) offsite, away from your computer. Note, too, that any backup copy is static and that frequent backup is necessary to retain the most recent copy of your database.

SUMMARY

A relational database contains multiple tables. Each table stores data about a specific entity in the physical system, such as clients and consultants in the Investment database. The tables are related to one another through a one-to-many relationship; for example, one consultant can have many clients, as in the database from this chapter. The relationship is created in the Relationships window by dragging the join field from the one table to the related table. Referential integrity ensures that all of the data in the two tables are consistent.

A select query can contain fields from multiple tables. The relationship between those tables is shown graphically in the Query Design view. The Tables row displays the name of the table that contains each field in the query.

The Get External Data command starts a wizard that will import (or link) data from an external source—such as an Excel workbook—into an Access database. The Export command does the reverse and copies an Access object to an external destination.

A total query performs calculations on a group of records using one of several summary (aggregate) functions. Execution of the query displays a summary record for each group, and individual records do not appear. The results of a total query can be input to Microsoft Graph to display the information graphically in a form or report.

A pivot table is a very flexible way to display summary statistics for the records in a table (or query) according to the parameters you supply. A pivot chart provides the same information as the corresponding pivot table in graphical form. Any changes to the pivot table are automatically reflected in the associated pivot chart and vice versa.

A switchboard is a user interface that enables a nontechnical person to open the objects in an Access database by selecting commands from a menu. The switchboard is created through the Switchboard Manager, a tool that prompts you for the information about each menu item. The switchboard itself is stored as a form within the database that reads data from an underlying table of switchboard items.

The Convert Database command changes the file format of an Access database to the format used by earlier versions of the program. The Compact and Repair Database command serves two functions, as its name suggests. The compacting process eliminates the fragmentation and wasted disk space that occur during development as you add, edit, and delete the various objects in a database. The Repair function takes place automatically if Access is unable to read a database when the database is opened initially. The Back Up Database command compacts the open database, and then it saves the compacted database under a different name that contains the date the backup was created.

The objects in an Access database depend on one another; for example, a report is based on an underlying query, which in turn is based on a table. Over time, the report may become obsolete, and hence it is deleted along with the underlying query; but if the same query were the basis of another report, the latter object would no longer function. The ability to examine object dependencies can prevent this type of error from occurring.

KEY TERMS

MULTIPLE CHOICE

1. A database has a one-to-many relationship between physicians and patients (one physician can have many patients). Which of the following is true?

   (a) The PhysicianID will appear in the Patients table
   (b) The PatientID will appear in the Physicians table
   (c) Both (a) and (b)
   (d) Neither (a) nor (b)

2. You are creating a database for an intramural league that has a one-to-many relationship between teams and players. Which of the following describes the correct database design?

   (a) Each record in the Teams table should contain the PlayerID field
   (b) Each record in the Players table should contain the TeamID field
   (c) Both (a) and (b)
   (d) Neither (a) nor (b)

3. Which of the following will create a problem of referential integrity in the Investments database that was developed in the chapter?

   (a) The deletion of a consultant record with a corresponding client record
   (b) The deletion of a consultant record that does not have any client records
   (c) The deletion of a client record who is assigned to a consultant
   (d) All of the above

4. Which of the following is true about a select query?

   (a) It may reference fields from more than one table
   (b) It may have one or more criteria rows
   (c) It may sort on one or more fields
   (d) All of the above

5. Which of the following is a true statement about Access tables?

   (a) An Access query can be exported to an Excel workbook
   (b) An Excel worksheet can be imported as an Access table
   (c) Both (a) and (b)
   (d) Neither (a) nor (b)

6. The Get External Data command will:

   (a) Import a worksheet from an Excel workbook as a new Access table
   (b) Import a text file as a new Access table
   (c) Both (a) and (b)
   (d) Neither (a) nor (b)

7. An Excel worksheet has been imported into an Access database as a new table, after which the data has been modified. Which of the following is *false*?

   (a) The Excel worksheet will be updated to reflect the modified table
   (b) A query run after the table has been modified will reflect the new data
   (c) A report run after the table has been modified will reflect the new data
   (d) All of the above

8. Which of the following is true about the rows in the Query Design grid?

   (a) The Total row can contain different functions for different fields
   (b) The Table row can reflect different tables
   (c) The Sort row can include entries for multiple fields
   (d) All of the above

9. Which of the following is available as an aggregate function within a query?

   (a) Sum and Avg
   (b) Min and Max
   (c) Both (a) and (b)
   (d) Neither (a) nor (b)

10. Which of the following is true about clicking and double clicking a chart within a report?

    (a) Clicking the chart selects the chart, enabling you to change the size of the chart, click and drag it to a new position, or delete it altogether
    (b) Double clicking the chart opens the underlying application (Microsoft Graph), enabling you to change the appearance of the chart
    (c) Both (a) and (b)
    (d) Neither (a) nor (b)

... continued

multiple choice

11. Which of the following is created by the Switchboard Manager?

   (a) A switchboard form

   (b) A Switchboard Items table

   (c) Both (a) and (b)

   (d) Neither (a) nor (b)

12. How do you insert clip art into a switchboard?

   (a) Start the Switchboard Manager, then use the Insert Clip Art command

   (b) Open the switchboard form in Design view, then add the clip art using the same techniques as for any other form

   (c) Both (a) and (b)

   (d) Neither (a) nor (b)

13. Which of the following is true about compacting a database?

   (a) Compacting a database when the database is open saves the compacted database under the original file name

   (b) Compacting a closed database saves the compacted database under a different file name

   (c) Both (a) and (b)

   (d) Neither (a) nor (b)

14. Which of the following best describes how to create a pivot chart?

   (a) Use the Get External Data command to import an Excel worksheet into an Access database

   (b) Use Microsoft Graph to create a multicolumn chart, then convert that chart to a pivot chart

   (c) Use the Import Spreadsheet Wizard command to convert a worksheet to a pivot chart

   (d) None of the above

15. The database of a commercial bank has a one-to-many relationship between Customers and Loans; that is, one customer can have many loans, but a specific loan is associated with only one customer. Which table(s) should contain the LoanID?

   (a) Only the Loans table

   (b) Only the Customers table

   (c) Both the Loans table and the Customers table

   (d) None of the above; the LoanID is not relevant to the database

16. The database of a commercial bank has a one-to-many relationship between Customers and Loans; that is, one customer can have many loans, but a specific loan is associated with only one customer. Which table(s) should contain the CustomerID?

   (a) Only the Loans table

   (b) Only the Customers table

   (c) Both the Loans table and the Customers table

   (d) None of the above; the CustomerID is not relevant to the database

17. Which of the following was suggested as essential to a backup strategy?

   (a) Backing up data files at the end of every session

   (b) Storing the backup file(s) at another location

   (c) Both (a) and (b)

   (d) Neither (a) nor (b)

18. Which of the following is an advantage of a pivot table?

   (a) You can add or remove fields by dragging the field names on or off the table.

   (b) You can switch the orientation by dragging a field to or from the row, column, or filter area.

   (c) You can change the means of calculation by changing the average value to sum, minimum, or maximum value.

   (d) All of the above

ANSWERS

1. a	**7.** a	**13.** c
2. b	**8.** d	**14.** d
3. a	**9.** c	**15.** a
4. d	**10.** c	**16.** c
5. c	**11.** c	**17.** c
6. c	**12.** b	**18.** d

PRACTICE WITH ACCESS

1. **The Oscars:** The switchboard in Figure 4.11 contains seven commands, three of which reference reports that were created in an end-of-chapter exercise in Chapter 3. You can do this exercise even if you did not create the reports, since the other objects are already in the database. You do, however, have to create the About the Oscars form, which is best accomplished by importing (and modifying) the similar form from the Investment database.

   a. Open the *Chapter 1 Practice 1* database in the Exploring Access folder. Click the Forms button in the Database window, pull down the File menu, click the Get External Data command, click Import, and then import the About Investments form from the Investment database. Return to the Database window. Right click the newly imported form, and change the name of the form to About the Oscars, then open that form in Design view. Change the clip art, labels, and colors as necessary. And finally, right click the form selector button, click Properties, select the Caption property and change the text to reflect the Oscars.

   b. Use the Switchboard Manager to create the switchboard in Figure 4.11. The Award Winners form, which is used to enter Oscar data, is already in the database (open the form in Edit mode). The report to list the major winners by year is also in the database, but the availability of the additional reports depends on whether you completed the end-of-chapter exercise in Chapter 3. Format the switchboard so that its appearance is consistent with Figure 4.11.

   c. Test each button on the switchboard to be sure that the commands work properly. Click the button to enter Oscar data, and then view the last record in the table to see the most recent awards. If necessary, click the link on the form to go to the Oscars Web site to obtain the additional awards (if any) since the publication of our book. Enter that data into the database.

   d. Click the appropriate button to view, and then print each report in the database.

   e. Pull down the Tools menu, and click the Startup command. Select the switchboard as the form to display when the database is opened. Click OK to close the Startup dialog box. Pull down the Tools menu, click Database Utilities, and then click the Compact and Repair Database command. The database should compact itself and reopen with the switchboard displayed automatically.

   f. Print the Switchboard form and Switchboard Items table for your instructor.

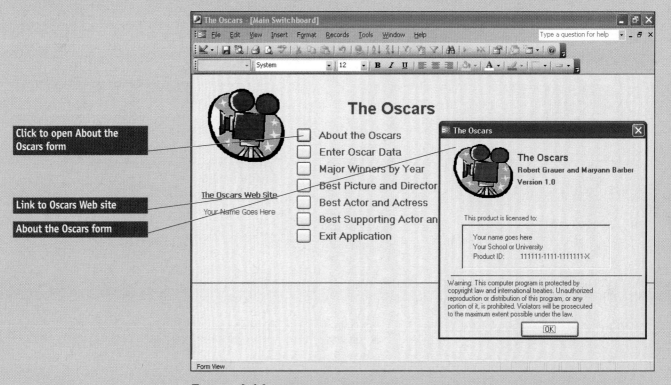

FIGURE 4.11   The Oscars (exercise 1)

2. **Employee Health Plans:** Figure 4.12 displays the relationships diagram of a database that tracks employees, the cities in which they work, and the health plans to which they subscribe. The database contains the typical data for every employee (name, birth date, salary, and so on) and for every office location (address, telephone, and so on). The database also stores data about the available health plans such as the name and description of the plan, the monthly contribution, the deductible each employee is required to pay, and the percent of expenses that an employee will be reimbursed. Your task is to create the tables (you do not have to enter any data), implement the relationships, and create a simple switchboard. Note the following:

a. Each employee is assigned to one city, but a given city has multiple employees. In similar fashion, each employee chooses one health plan, but a given health plan has multiple employees. An employee cannot be hired without being assigned to a city. New employees have 30 days, however, to decide on a health plan.

b. The report in Figure 4.12 is created from the Relationships window after the relationships have been specified. Pull down the Tools menu and click Relationships to open the Relationships window, then pull down the File menu and click the Print Relationships command to display the Print Preview screen of a report that displays the contents of the Relationships window. Change to the Design view to modify the report to include your name and an appropriate clip art image.

c. Create a simple About the Employee Health Plans form similar to the other forms in this chapter.

d. Create a switchboard with three menu options—a button to display the About Employee Health Plans form, a button to print the relationships diagram, and a button to exit the application. The switchboard should contain the same clip art as the relationships diagram. Use the Startup property to display the switchboard automatically when the database is opened.

e. Test the switchboard thoroughly to be sure it works correctly. Use the Startup property in the Tools menu to display the switchboard automatically when the database is opened initially. Print the relationships diagram, the Switchboard form, and the Switchboard Items table for your instructor.

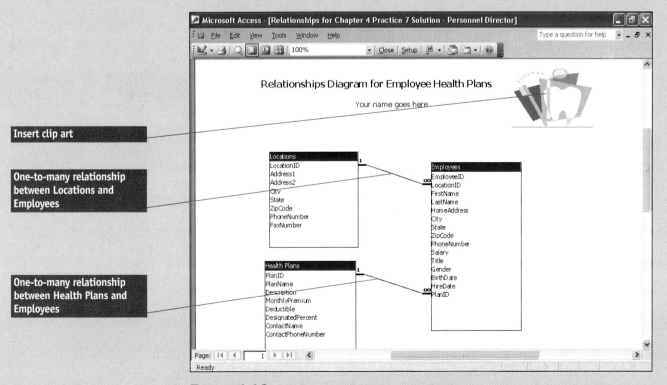

FIGURE 4.12 Employee Health Plans (exercise 2)

3. **The Metro Zoo:** The switchboard in Figure 4.13 is based on the Metro Zoo database that was introduced in Chapter 1. You do not have to match our design exactly, but you are required to duplicate the functionality. All of the objects (i.e., the forms and reports) have been created for you and are found in the database. Proceed as follows:

a. Open the *Chapter 1 Practice 8* database and complete that exercise if you have not already done so. Pull down the Tools menu, click the Relationships command, and create the one-to-many relationships that exist in the system. Enforce referential integrity for every relationship.

b. Start the Switchboard Manager, which will display the Switchboard Manager dialog box. Click New to create a new switchboard (in addition to the main switchboard that is created by default). Enter Report Menu as the name of the new switchboard page, then click OK.

c. You will return to the Switchboard Manager dialog box. Select the Main Switchboard, click Edit, and build the items for the main switchboard as shown in Figure 4.13. Be sure to open all of the forms in the Edit mode. After you have built the main switchboard, click Close on the Edit Switchboard Page dialog box to return to the Switchboard Manager dialog box.

d. Select the Report Menu switchboard, and click Edit. Build the items for the Report Menu, which consist of a separate command for each report plus a command to return to main menu. (The latter is a Go To Switchboard command that opens the Main switchboard.) Close the switchboard page. Close the Switchboard Manager.

e. Open the Switchboard form in Design view to format the switchboard as shown in Figure 4.13. You do not have to match our design exactly.

f. Test both switchboards to be sure that they work correctly. Verify that the data entry operations for the Trainer and Animal tables have been implemented correctly as described in Chapter 1. Use the report menu to print each report in the database.

g. Which report is based on a query rather than a table? How many tables are referenced in that query? Go to the Database window and print the dynaset for the underlying query for the report in question. Print the Switchboard form and Switchboard Items table and then submit all items to your instructor.

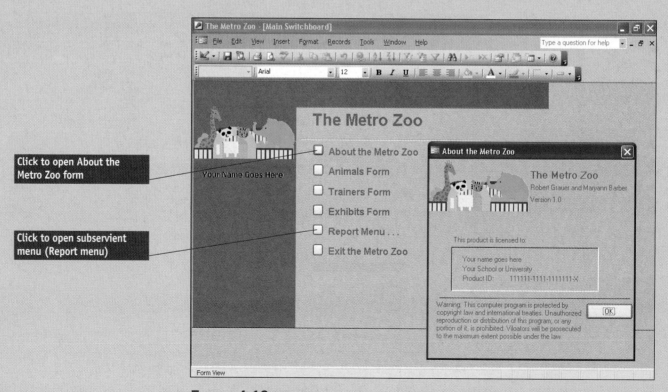

FIGURE 4.13 The Metro Zoo (exercise 3)

4. **The Shopping Mall (secondary switchboard):** Figure 4.14 displays a switchboard for the Shopping Mall database that has been developed in previous chapters, most recently in Chapter 3. Your present assignment is to create the switchboard in Figure 4.14, which includes an option to display a report menu. The latter is a second (subsidiary) switchboard that includes commands to print all of the reports that were created in Chapter 3, as well as an option to return to the Main Menu. Proceed as follows:

   a. Start the Switchboard Manager. At the Switchboard Manager dialog box, click New to create a new switchboard. In the Create New dialog box, enter a name for the new switchboard, such as Report Menu, then click OK.

   b. You will return to the Switchboard Manager dialog box. Select the Main Switchboard, click Edit, and build the items for the Main Switchboard (open the "About the Mall" form, open the Coral Pines Shopping Mall form to enter/edit data, go to the Report Menu switchboard, and Exit). After you have built the main switchboard, click Close on the Edit Switchboard Page dialog box to return to the Switchboard Manager.

   c. Select the Report Menu switchboard, and click Edit. Build the items for the Report Menu (one each to open the individual reports and one to return to the Main Menu—which is actually a Go To Switchboard command that opens the Main Switchboard).

   d. Open the Switchboard form in Design view to format the switchboard in an attractive fashion. You do not have to match our design exactly, but your switchboard should enhance the default design.

   e. Use the Startup property in the Tools menu to display the switchboard automatically when the database is opened initially. Pull down the Tools menu, click the Database Utilities command, then click the command to Compact and Repair the Database. Access will close, and then reopen, the database; the switchboard should be displayed automatically.

   f. Be sure you test both switchboards completely to be sure that they work correctly. Print the Switchboard form and the Switchboard Items table for your instructor.

   g. Take a minute to reflect on what you have accomplished over the last several chapters. You created the database and designed a table and associated form in Chapter 2, you created various reports in Chapter 3, and you put everything together via the switchboard in this exercise. Well done!

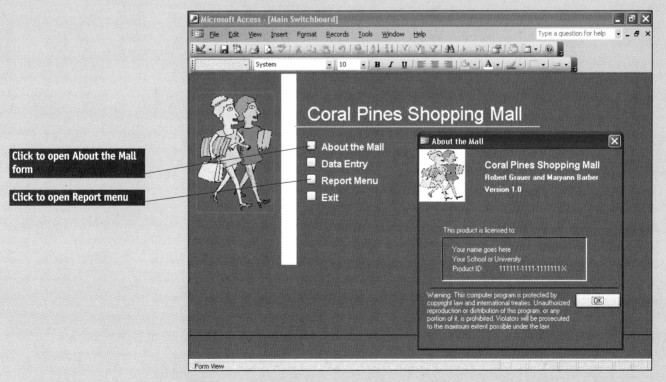

FIGURE 4.14 The Shopping Mall (exercise 4)

5. **Best Realty (secondary switchboard):** Figure 4.15 displays a switchboard for the *Best Realty* database that has been developed in previous chapters, most recently in Chapter 3. Your present assignment is to create the switchboard shown in Figure 4.15, which includes an option to display a report menu. The latter is a second (subsidiary) switchboard that includes commands to print all of the reports that were created in Chapter 3, as well as an option to return to the Main Menu. The technique for creating the subsidiary menu was described in the previous problem.

a. Create the switchboards as indicated in Figure 4.15. You do not have to copy our design exactly, but you are to incorporate all of the indicated functionality. Format the switchboard in an attractive way and include clip art. The report menu is to provide access to all of the reports that were created in Chapter 3.

b. Go to the main menu, and open the form to modify the property data. Use the form to indicate that property P0008 has sold for $140,000. Use today's date as the date the property was sold.

c. Go to the Report menu, and open the report that shows the properties that have been sold. This report should include the property from part (b). Print this report for your instructor.

d. Use the Startup property in the Tools menu to display the switchboard automatically when the database is opened initially. Pull down the Tools menu, click the Database Utilities command, then click the command to Compact and Repair the Database. Access will close, and then reopen, the database; the switchboard should be displayed automatically.

e. Be sure that you test both switchboards completely to be sure that they work correctly. Print the switchboard form and table of Switchboard Items. Use landscape printing if necessary to be sure that each item fits on one page. Add a cover sheet and submit everything to your instructor.

f. Take a minute to reflect on what you have accomplished over the last several chapters. You created the database and designed a table and associated form in Chapter 2, you created various reports in Chapter 3, and you put everything together via the switchboard in this exercise. Well done!

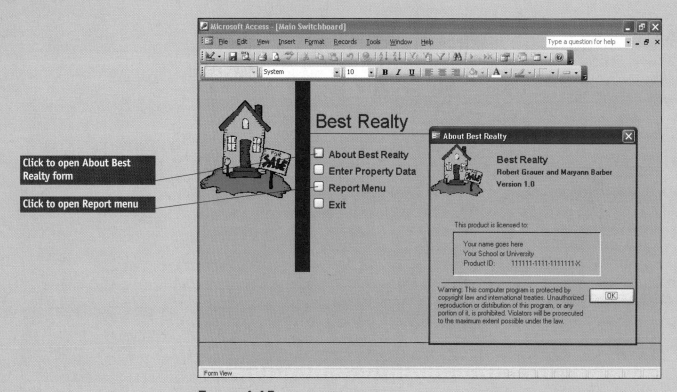

FIGURE 4.15 Best Realty (exercise 5)

6. **The Fishing Pole:** Figure 4.16 displays a switchboard for the Fishing Pole database that has been developed in previous chapters. Your assignment is to create a comparable switchboard that includes an option to display a report menu. The latter is a second (subsidiary) switchboard that includes commands to print all of the reports in the database, as well as an option to return to the Main Menu. Open the *Chapter 3 Practice 6* database in the Exploring Access folder and proceed as follows:

a. Start the Switchboard Manager, which will display the Switchboard Manager dialog box. Click New to create a new switchboard (in addition to the main switchboard that is created by default). Enter Report Menu as the name of the new switchboard page, then click OK.

b. You will return to the Switchboard Manager dialog box. Select the Main Switchboard, click Edit, and build the items for the main switchboard (open the About the Fishing Pole form, which is included in the database, open the Customers form in edit mode, open the Report Menu switchboard, and exit the application). After you have built the main switchboard, close the Switchboard Page dialog box to return to the Switchboard Manager dialog box.

c. Select the Report Menu switchboard, and click Edit. Build the items for the Report Menu, which consist of a separate command for each report in the database, plus a command to return to main menu. (The latter is a Go To Switchboard command that opens the Main switchboard.) Close the switchboard page. Close the Switchboard Manager.

d. Open the Switchboard form in Design view to format the switchboard as shown in Figure 4.16. You do not have to match our design exactly, but your switchboard should enhance the default design.

e. Use the Startup property in the Tools menu to display the switchboard automatically when the database is opened initially. Pull down the Tools menu, click the Database Utilities command, then click the command to Compact and Repair the Database. Access will close, and then reopen; the database and the switchboard should be displayed automatically. Test both switchboards completely.

f. Print the Switchboard form and Switchboard Items table for your instructor.

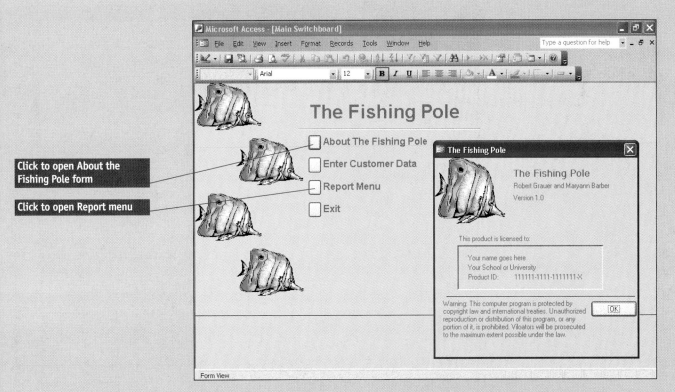

FIGURE 4.16   The Fishing Pole (exercise 6)

7. **The Database Wizard:** The switchboard in Figure 4.17 is for a contact management database that maintains information about the individuals contacted and the associated telephone calls. There is nothing remarkable in the switchboard per se, except that it and the underlying database (the tables, forms, queries, and reports) were created in a matter of minutes using one of several Database Wizards that are built into Microsoft Access. Proceed as follows:

a. Start Access. Pull down the File menu and select the New command to open the task pane. Click the link to Other templates on My Computer to display the Templates dialog box. Click the Databases tab, then double click the Contact Management database to start the Database Wizard. You should see the File New Database dialog box in which you specify the name of the database (use Contact Management) and the folder where to store the database (use the Exploring Access folder). Click Create.

b. You will see several screens that prompt you for information about the database that you want to create. The first screen tells you that the database stores contact and call information. Click Next.

c. The next screen displays the tables in the database. You have to accept all of the tables, but you have the option of adding or removing fields within each table. Accept all fields for all of the tables. Click Next.

d. The third and fourth screens let you choose the style for your forms and reports, respectively. These choices parallel those for the Form and Report Wizards. Select any style and click Next at each screen.

e. The next two screens ask you for the title of your database (as it is to appear in the switchboard) and also give you the option of including a picture on the forms and reports. Check the option to start the database after it is built, and click the Finish button to display a switchboard similar to Figure 4.17.

f. Explore the functionality of the database that was just created. Write a paragraph or two to your instructor describing whether the database is useful and what additional information you would like to see included. Are you able to modify the database to include the additional features you suggested?

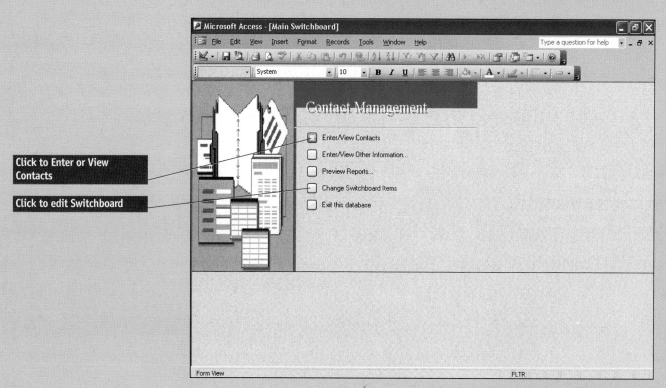

FIGURE 4.17 The Database Wizard (exercise 7)

practice exercises

8. **The HMO Database:** This comprehensive exercise asks you to create an Access database from the Excel workbook in Figure 4.18. There is a one-to-many relationship between physicians and patients; that is, one physician can have many patients, but a specific patient sees only one physician. Proceed as follows:

a. Start Access and create a new database. Use the Get External Data command to import the worksheets from the *Chapter 4 Practice 8* Excel workbook into the new Access database. Specify that Social Security Number and PhysicianID are the primary keys in the Patients and Physicians tables, respectively.

b. Use the Relationships window to create a one-to-many relationship between Physicians and Patients. Check the box to enforce referential integrity. Create a report that displays the relationships diagram.

c. Create a query that lists all patients in alphabetical order by last name. The query should include the patient's first and last name, birth date, and gender, as well as the last name of the patient's physician and the physician's phone number. Create a report based on this query, grouping patients by physician. Format the report and add appropriate clip art.

d. Create two simple forms for data entry, one for patients, and one for physicians. The patients form should include a list box that enables you to select a physician by name, as opposed to entering the physician's ID.

e. Create an "About the HMO" form similar to the examples in the other exercises. You can create this form from scratch in the Design view, and/or you can import a similar form from another database, then modify the form for the HMO database.

f. Create a simple (one-level) switchboard that provides access to six commands: About the HMO, the Patient's form, the Physician's form, the relationships diagram, the report to list patients by physician, and a command to exit the database. Format the switchboard to include your name and an appropriate clip art image.

g. Test the switchboard completely. Use the Physician's form to enter a record for your instructor, then use the Patient's form to enter data for yourself, with your instructor as your physician. Print both of these forms, print both reports, and finally, print the Switchboard form and the Switchboard Items table.

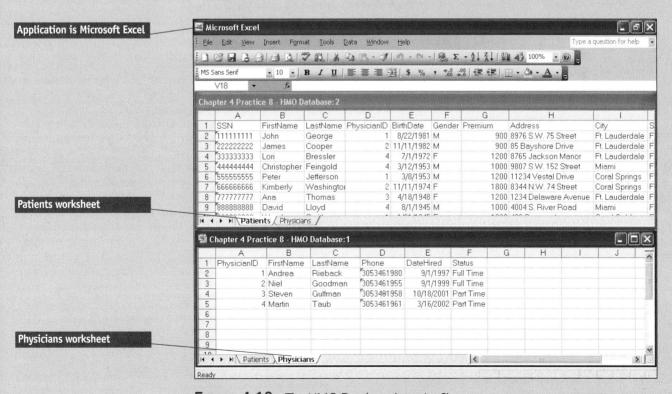

FIGURE 4.18 The HMO Database (exercise 8)

Recreational Sports League

Design a database for a recreational sports league to maintain data on the league's teams, players, coaches, and sponsors. There can be any number of teams in the league. Each team has multiple players, but a specific player is associated with only one team. A team may have multiple coaches, but a given coach is associated with only one team. The league also depends on local businesses to sponsor various teams to offset the cost of uniforms and referees. One business can sponsor many teams, but a team cannot have more than one sponsor.

Design a database with four tables, for teams, players, coaches, and sponsors. You do not have to enter data into any of the tables, but you do need to design the tables in order to create a relationships diagram. Print the report containing the relationships diagram for your instructor as proof that you completed this exercise.

The Franchise

The management of a national restaurant chain is automating its procedure for monitoring its restaurants, restaurant-owners (franchisees), and the contracts that govern the two. Each restaurant has one owner (franchisee), but a given individual can own multiple restaurants.

The payment from the franchisee to the company varies according to the contract in effect for the particular restaurant. The company offers a choice of contracts, which vary according to the length of the contract, the franchise fee, and the percentage of the restaurant's sales paid to the company for marketing and royalty fees. Each restaurant has one contract, but a given contract may pertain to many restaurants.

The company needs a database capable of retrieving all data for a given restaurant, such as its annual sales, location, phone number, owner, and type of contract in effect. It would also like to know all restaurants owned by one person as well as all restaurants governed by a specific contract type.

Design a database with the necessary tables. You do not have to enter data into any of the tables, but you do need to design the tables in order to create a relationships diagram. Print the report containing the relationships diagram for your instructor as proof that you completed this exercise.

The Loan Officer

You are working in the IT department of a commercial bank and have been asked to design a database for customer loans. The bank needs to track its customers, the loans for each customer, the loan officer who approved the individual loan, and the payments received for each loan. One customer can have multiple loans, but a specific loan is associated with only one customer. A loan officer (who is an employee of the bank) must approve each loan before it is made.

One critical report is the list of all loans for each loan officer. Another important report is the list of all payments for each loan, which contains the amount of the payment and the date the payment was received. You do not have to enter data into any of the tables, but you do need to create the tables in order to create a relationships diagram and associated report. Be sure to set the required property properly for the various fields in different tables. You should not, for example, be able to create a new record in the Loans table unless that loan has been assigned to a customer and was approved by a loan officer. Print the report containing the relationships diagram for your instructor as proof that you completed this exercise.

Getting Started with Microsoft® Windows® XP

CASE STUDY
UNFORESEEN CIRCUMSTANCES

Steve and his wife Shelly have poured their life savings into the dream of owning their own business, a "nanny" service agency. They have spent the last two years building their business and have created a sophisticated database with numerous entries for both families and nannies. The database is the key to their operation. Now that it is up and running, Steve and Shelly are finally at a point where they could hire someone to manage the operation on a part-time basis so that they could take some time off together.

Unfortunately, their process for selecting a person they could trust with their business was not as thorough as it should have been. Nancy, their new employee, assured them that all was well, and the couple left for an extended weekend. The place was in shambles on their return. Nancy could not handle the responsibility, and when Steve gave her two weeks' notice, neither he nor his wife thought that the unimaginable would happen. On her last day in the office Nancy "lost" all of the names in the database—the data was completely gone!

Nancy claimed that a "virus" knocked out the database, but after spending nearly $1,500 with a computer consultant, Steve was told that it had been cleverly deleted from the hard drive and could not be recovered. Of course, the consultant asked Steve and Shelly about their backup strategy, which they sheepishly admitted did not exist. They had never experienced any problems in the past, and simply assumed that their data was safe. Fortunately, they do have hard copy of the data in the form of various reports that were printed throughout the time they were in business. They have no choice but to manually reenter the data. ■

Your assignment is to read the chapter, paying special attention to the information on file management. Think about how Steve and Shelly could have avoided the disaster if a backup strategy had been in place, then summarize your thoughts in a brief note to your instructor. Describe the elements of a basic backup strategy. Give several other examples of unforeseen circumstances that can cause data to be lost.

Windows® XP is the newest and most powerful version of the Windows operating system. It has a slightly different look than earlier versions, but it maintains the conventions of its various predecessors. You have seen the Windows interface many times, but do you really understand it? Can you move and copy files with confidence? Do you know how to back up the Excel spreadsheets, Access databases, and other documents that you work so hard to create? If not, now is the time to learn.

We begin with an introduction to the desktop, the graphical user interface that lets you work in intuitive fashion by pointing at icons and clicking the mouse. We identify the basic components of a window and describe how to execute commands and supply information through different elements in a dialog box. We stress the importance of disk and file management, but begin with basic definitions of a file and a folder. We also introduce Windows Explorer and show you how to move or copy a file from one folder to another. We discuss other basic operations, such as renaming and deleting a file. We also describe how to recover a deleted file (if necessary) from the Recycle Bin.

Windows XP is available in different versions. Windows *XP Home Edition* is intended for entertainment and home use. It includes a media player, new support for digital photography, and an instant messenger. Windows *XP Professional Edition* has all of the features of the Home Edition plus additional security to encrypt files and protect data. It includes support for high-performance multiprocessor systems. It also lets you connect to your computer from a remote station.

The login screen in Figure 1 is displayed when the computer is turned on initially and/or when you are switching from one user account to another. Several individuals can share the same computer. Each user, however, retains his or her individual desktop settings, individual lists of favorite and recently visited Web sites, as well as other customized Windows settings. Multiple users can be logged on simultaneously, each with his or her programs in memory, through a feature known as *fast user switching*.

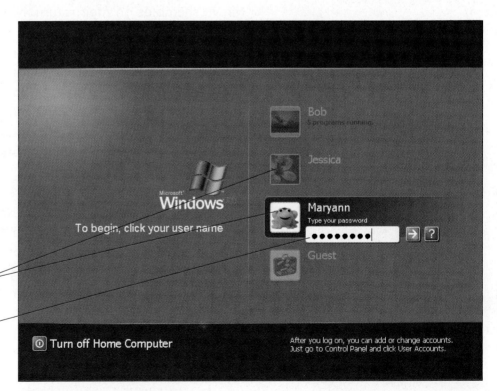

Multiple users can be logged on

Accounts can be password-protected

FIGURE 1 Windows XP Login

Windows XP, as well as all previous versions of Windows, creates a working environment for your computer that parallels the working environment at home or in an office. You work at a desk. Windows operations take place on the *desktop*. There are physical objects on a desk such as folders, a dictionary, a calculator, or a phone. The computer equivalents of those objects appear as icons (pictorial symbols) on the desktop. Each object on a real desk has attributes (properties) such as size, weight, and color. In similar fashion, Windows assigns properties to every object on its desktop. And just as you can move the objects on a real desk, you can rearrange the objects on the Windows desktop.

Windows XP has a new interface, but you can retain the look and feel of earlier versions as shown in Figure 2. The desktop in Figure 2a uses the default *Windows XP theme* (the wallpaper has been suppressed), whereas Figure 2b displays the "same" desktop using the *Windows Classic theme*. The icons on either desktop are used to access specific programs or other functions.

The *Start button*, as its name suggests, is where you begin; it works identically on both desktops. Click the Start button to see a menu of programs and other functions. The Windows XP *Start menu* in Figure 2a is divided into two columns. The column on the left displays the most recently used programs for easy access, whereas the column on the right contains a standard set of entries. It also shows the name of the individual who is logged into the computer. The *Classic Start menu* in Figure 2b contains only a single column. (Note the indication of the Windows XP Professional operating system that appears at the left of the menu.)

Do not be concerned if your desktop is different from ours. Your real desk is arranged differently from those of your friends, just as your Windows desktop will also be different. Moreover, you are likely to work on different systems—at school, at work, or at home; what is important is that you recognize the common functionality that is present on all desktops.

Look now at Figure 2c, which displays an entirely different desktop, one with four open windows that is similar to a desk in the middle of a working day. Each window in Figure 2c displays a program or a folder that is currently in use. The ability to run several programs at the same time is known as *multitasking*, and it is a major benefit of the Windows environment. Multitasking enables you to run a word processor in one window, create a spreadsheet in a second window, surf the Internet in a third window, play a game in a fourth window, and so on. You can work in a program as long as you want, then change to a different program by clicking its window.

The *taskbar* at the bottom of the desktop contains a button for each open window, and it enables you to switch back and forth between the open windows by clicking the appropriate button. A *notification area* appears at the right end of the taskbar. It displays the time and other shortcuts. It may also provide information on the status of such ongoing activities as a printer or Internet connection.

The desktop in Figure 2d is identical to the desktop in Figure 2c except that it is displayed in the Windows Classic theme. The open windows are the same, as are the contents of the taskbar and notification area. The choice between the XP theme or Windows Classic (or other) theme is one of personal preference.

Moving and Sizing a Window

A window can be sized or moved on the desktop through appropriate actions with the mouse. To *size a window*, point to any border (the mouse pointer changes to a double arrow), then drag the border in the direction you want to go—inward to shrink the window or outward to enlarge it. You can also drag a corner (instead of a border) to change both dimensions at the same time. To *move a window* while retaining its current size, click and drag the title bar to a new position on the desktop.

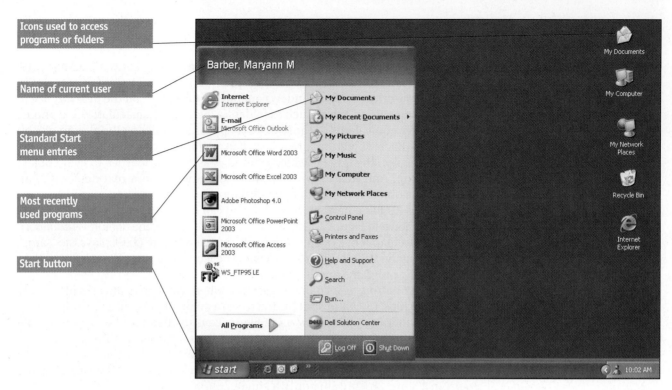

Icons used to access programs or folders

Name of current user

Standard Start menu entries

Most recently used programs

Start button

(a) Windows XP Theme and Start Menu

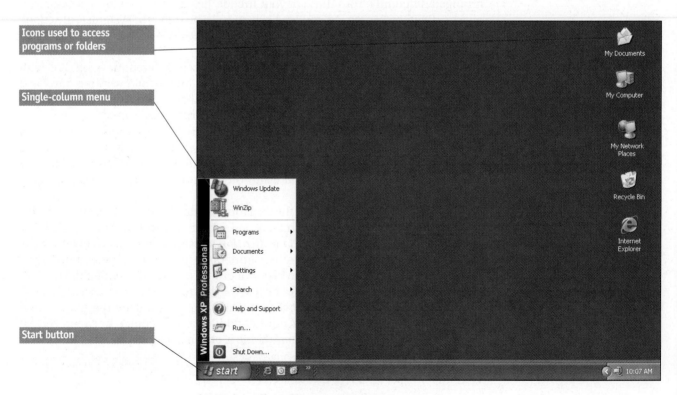

Icons used to access programs or folders

Single-column menu

Start button

(b) Windows Classic Theme and Start Menu

FIGURE 2   The Desktop and Start Menu

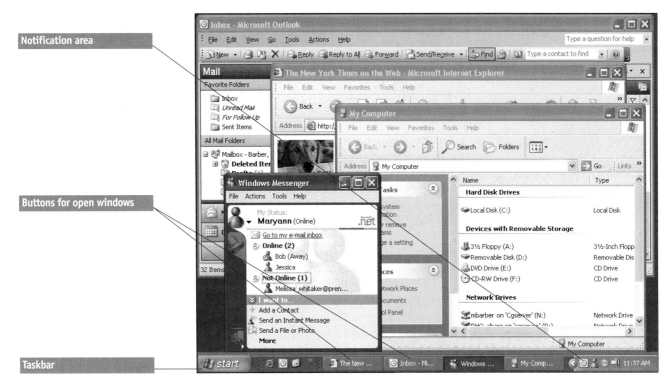

(c) Windows XP Theme

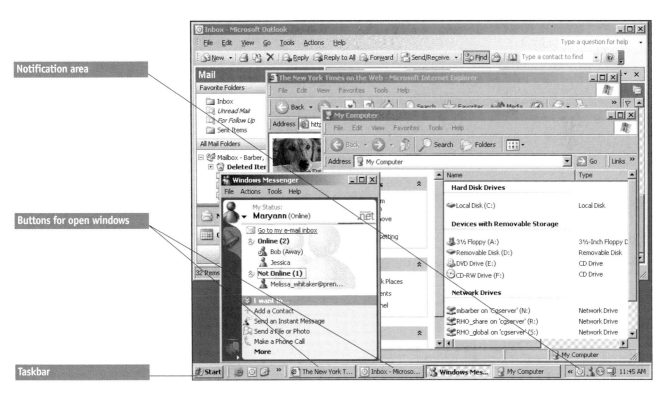

(d) Windows Classic Theme

FIGURE 2   The Desktop and Start Menu (*continued*)

ANATOMY OF A WINDOW

All Windows applications share a common user interface and possess a consistent command structure. This means that every Windows application works essentially the same way, which provides a sense of familiarity from one application to the next. In other words, once you learn the basic concepts and techniques in one application, you can apply that knowledge to every other application.

The *My Computer folder* in Figure 3 is used to illustrate basic technology. This folder is present on every system, and its contents depend on the hardware of the specific computer. Our system, for example, has one local disk, a floppy drive, a removable disk (an Iomega Zip® drive), a DVD drive, and a CD-RW (recordable) drive. Our intent at this time, however, is to focus on the elements that are common to every window. A *task pane* (also called a task panel) is displayed at the left of the window to provide easy access to various commands that you might want to access from this folder.

The *title bar* appears at the top of every window and displays the name of the folder or application. The icon at the extreme left of the title bar identifies the window and also provides access to a control menu with operations relevant to the window, such as moving it or sizing it. Three buttons appear at the right of the title bar. The *Minimize button* shrinks the window to a button on the taskbar, but leaves the window in memory. The *Maximize button* enlarges the window so that it takes up the entire desktop. The *Restore button* (not shown in Figure 3) appears instead of the Maximize button after a window has been maximized, and restores the window to its previous size. The *Close button* closes the window and removes it from memory and the desktop.

The *menu bar* appears immediately below the title bar and provides access to pull-down menus. One or more *toolbars* appear below the menu bar and let you execute a command by clicking a button, as opposed to pulling down a menu. The *status bar* at the bottom of the window displays information about the window as a whole or about a selected object within a window.

A vertical (or horizontal) *scroll bar* appears at the right (or bottom) border of a window when its contents are not completely visible and provides access to the unseen areas. The vertical scroll bar at the right of the task panel in Figure 3 implies that there are additional tasks available that are not currently visible. A horizontal scroll bar does not appear since all of the objects in the My Computer folder are visible at one time.

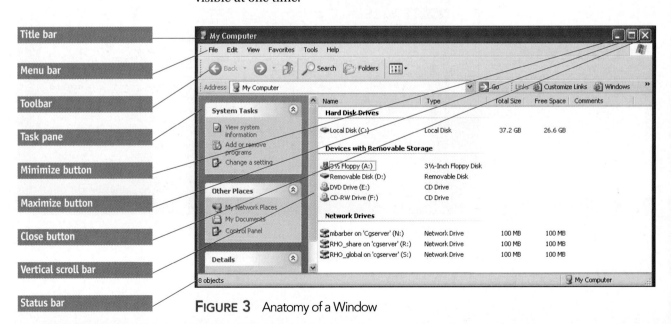

FIGURE 3   Anatomy of a Window

Pull-down Menus

The menu bar provides access to ***pull-down menus*** that enable you to execute commands within an application (program). A pull-down menu is accessed by clicking the menu name or by pressing the Alt key plus the underlined letter in the menu name; for example, press Alt+V to pull down the View menu. (You may have to press the Alt key to see the underlines.) Figure 4 displays three pull-down menus that are associated with the My Computer folder.

Commands within a menu are executed by clicking the command or by typing the underlined letter. Alternatively, you can bypass the menu entirely if you know the equivalent shortcuts shown to the right of the command in the menu (e.g., Ctrl+X, Ctrl+C, or Ctrl+V to cut, copy, or paste as shown within the Edit menu). A dimmed command (e.g., the Paste command in the Edit menu) means the command is not currently executable, and that some additional action has to be taken for the command to become available.

An ellipsis (. . .) following a command indicates that additional information is required to execute the command; for example, selection of the Format command in the File menu requires the user to specify additional information about the formatting process. This information is entered into a dialog box (discussed in the next section), which appears immediately after the command has been selected.

A check next to a command indicates a toggle switch, whereby the command is either on or off. There is a check next to the Status Bar command in the View menu of Figure 4, which means the command is in effect (and thus the status bar will be displayed). Click the Status Bar command and the check disappears, which suppresses the display of the status bar. Click the command a second time and the check reappears, as does the status bar in the associated window.

A bullet next to an item, such as Icons in the View menu, indicates a selection from a set of mutually exclusive choices. Click a different option within the group—such as Thumbnails—and the bullet will move from the previous selection (Icons) to the new selection (Thumbnails).

An arrowhead after a command (e.g., the Arrange Icons by command in the View menu) indicates that a submenu (also known as a cascaded menu) will be displayed with additional menu options.

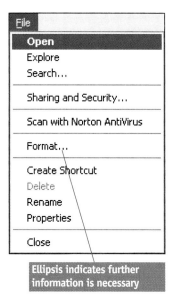

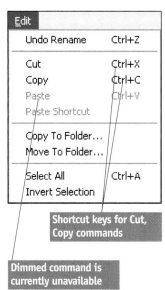

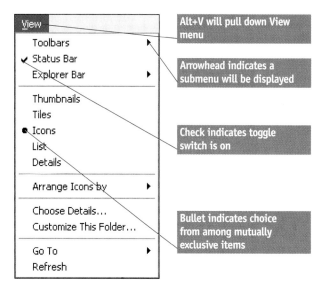

FIGURE 4   Pull-down Menus

Dialog Boxes

A *dialog box* appears when additional information is necessary to execute a command. Click the Print command in Internet Explorer, for example, and you are presented with the Print dialog box in Figure 5, requesting information about precisely what to print and how. The information is entered into the dialog box in different ways, depending on the type of information that is required. The tabs at the top of the dialog box provide access to different sets of options. The General tab is selected in Figure 5.

Option (radio) buttons indicate mutually exclusive choices, one of which *must* be chosen, such as the page range. In this example you can print all pages, the selection (if it is available), the current page (if there are multiple pages), or a specific set of pages (such as pages 1–4), but you can choose *one and only one* option. Any time you select (click) an option, the previous option is automatically deselected.

A *text box* enters specific information such as the pages that will be printed in conjunction with selecting the radio button for pages. A *spin button* is another way to enter specific information such as the number of copies. Click the up or down arrow to increase or decrease the number of pages, respectively. You can also enter the information explicitly by typing it into a spin box, just as you would a text box.

Check boxes are used instead of option buttons if the choices are not mutually exclusive or if an option is not required. The Collate check box is checked, whereas the Print to file box is not checked. Individual options are selected and cleared by clicking the appropriate check box, which toggles the box on and off. A *list box* (not shown in Figure 5) displays some or all of the available choices, any one of which is selected by clicking the desired item.

The *Help button* (a question mark at the right end of the title bar) provides help for any item in the dialog box. Click the button, then click the item in the dialog box for which you want additional information. The Close button (the X at the extreme right of the title bar) closes the dialog box without executing the command.

All dialog boxes also contain one or more *command buttons*, the function of which is generally apparent from the button's name. The Print button in Figure 5, for example, initiates the printing process. The Cancel button does just the opposite and ignores (cancels) any changes made to the settings, then closes the dialog box without further action.

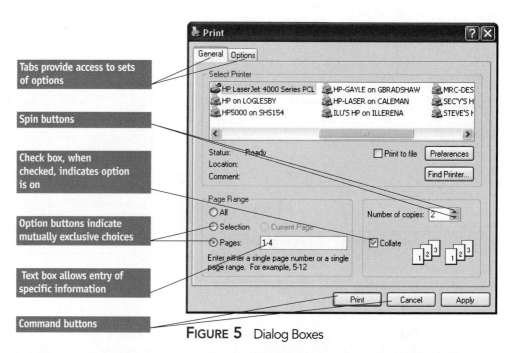

FIGURE 5 Dialog Boxes

HELP AND SUPPORT CENTER

The *Help and Support Center* combines such traditional features as a search function and an index of help topics. It also lets you request remote help from other Windows XP users, and/or you can access the Microsoft Knowledge base on the Microsoft Web site. Click the Index button, type the keyword you are searching for, then double click the subtopic to display the associated information in the right pane. The mouse is essential to Windows, and you are undoubtedly familiar with its basic operations such as pointing, clicking, and double clicking. Look closely, however, at the list of subtopics in Figure 6 and you might be surprised at the amount of available information. Suffice it to say, therefore, that you will find the answer to almost every conceivable question if only you will take the trouble to look.

The toolbar at the top of the window contains several buttons that are also found in *Internet Explorer 6.0*, the Web browser that is built into Windows XP. The Back and Forward buttons enable you to navigate through the various pages that were viewed in the current session. The Favorites button displays a list of previously saved (favorite) help topics from previous sessions. The History button shows all pages that were visited in this session.

The Support button provides access to remote sources for assistance. Click the Support button, then click the link to ask a friend to help, which in turn displays a Remote Assistance screen. You will be asked to sign in to the Messenger service (Windows Messenger is discussed in more detail in a later section). Your friend has to be running Windows XP for this feature to work, but once you are connected, he or she will be able to view your computer screen. You can then chat in real time about the problem and proposed solution. And, if you give permission, your friend can use his or her mouse and keyboard to work on your computer. Be careful! It is one thing to let your friend see your screen. It is quite a leap of faith, however, to give him or her control of your machine.

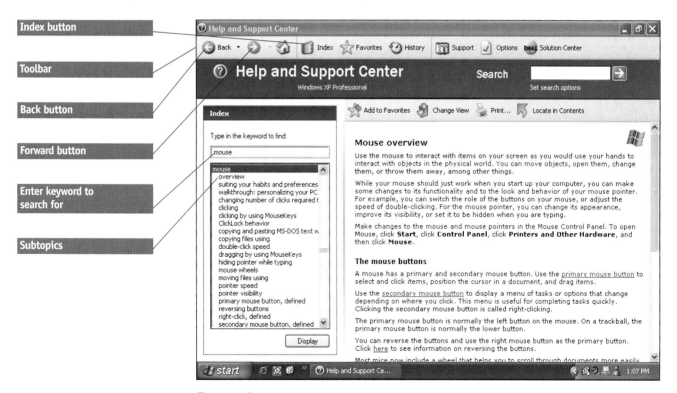

FIGURE 6 Help and Support Center

1   Welcome to Windows XP

Objective   To log on to Windows XP and customize the desktop; to open the My Computer folder; to move and size a window; to format a floppy disk and access the Help and Support Center. Use Figure 7 as a guide.

Step 1:   **Log On to Windows XP**

- Turn on the computer and all of the peripheral devices. The floppy drive should be empty prior to starting your machine.

- Windows XP will load automatically, and you should see a login screen similar to Figure 7a. (It does not matter which version of Windows XP you are using.) The number and names of the potential users and their associated icons will be different on your system.

- Click the icon for the user account you want to access. You may be prompted for a password, depending on the security options in effect.

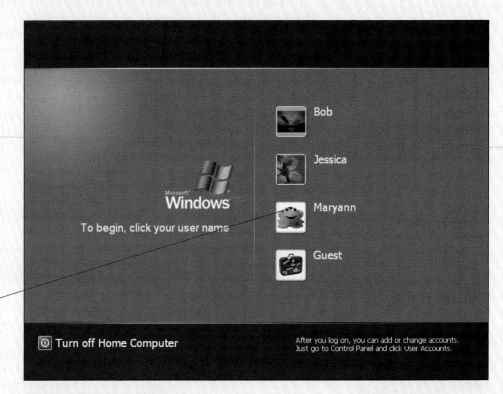

Click icon for user account to be accessed

(a) Log On to Windows XP (step 1)

FIGURE 7   Hands-on Exercise 1

USER ACCOUNTS

The available user names are created automatically during the installation of Windows XP, but you can add or delete users at any time. Click the Start button, click Control Panel, switch to the Category view, and select User Accounts. Choose the desired task, such as creating a new account or changing an existing account, then supply the necessary information. Do not expect, however, to be able to modify user accounts in a school setting.

Step 2: Choose the Theme and Start Menu

- Check with your instructor to see if you are able to modify the desktop and other settings at your school or university. If your network administrator has disabled these commands, skip this step and go to step 3.

- Point to a blank area on the desktop, click the **right mouse button** to display a context-sensitive menu, then click the **Properties command** to open the Display Properties dialog box. Click the **Themes tab** and select the **Windows XP theme** if it is not already selected. Click **OK**.

- We prefer to work without any wallpaper (background picture) on the desktop. **Right click** the desktop, click **Properties**, then click the **Desktop tab** in the Display Properties dialog box. Click **None** as shown in Figure 7b, then click **OK**. The background disappears.

- The Start menu is modified independently of the theme. **Right click** a blank area of the taskbar, click the **Properties command** to display the Taskbar and Start Menu Properties dialog box, then click the **Start Menu tab**.

- Click the **Start Menu option button**. Click **OK**.

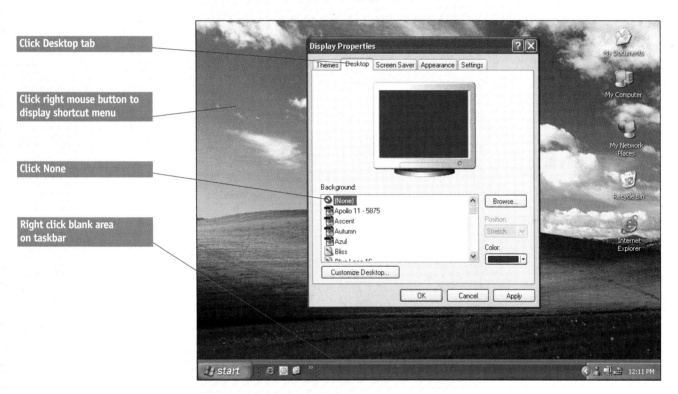

Click Desktop tab

Click right mouse button to display shortcut menu

Click None

Right click blank area on taskbar

(b) Choose the Theme and Start Menu (step 2)

FIGURE 7   Hands-on Exercise 1 *(continued)*

IMPLEMENT A SCREEN SAVER

A screen saver is a delightful way to personalize your computer and a good way to practice with basic commands in Windows XP. Right click a blank area of the desktop, click the Properties command to open the Display Properties dialog box, then click the Screen Saver tab. Click the down arrow in the Screen Saver list box, choose the desired screen saver, then set the option to wait an appropriate amount of time before the screen saver appears. Click OK to accept the settings and close the dialog box.

Step 3: **Open the My Computer Folder**

- Click the **Start button** to display a two-column Start menu that is characteristic of Windows XP. Click **My Computer** to open the My Computer folder. The contents of your window and/or its size and position on the desktop will be different from ours.

- Pull down the **View menu** as shown in Figure 7c to make or verify the following selections. (You have to pull down the View menu each time you make an additional change.)
  - ❑ The **Status Bar command** should be checked. The Status Bar command functions as a toggle switch. Click the command and the status bar is displayed; click the command a second time and the status bar disappears.
  - ❑ Click the **Tiles command** to change to this view. Selecting the Tiles view automatically deselects the previous view.

- Pull down the **View menu**, then click (or point to) the **Toolbars command** to display a cascaded menu. If necessary, check the commands for the **Standard Buttons** and **Address Bar**, and clear the other commands.

- Click the **Folders button** on the Standard Buttons toolbar to toggle the task panel on or off. End with the task panel displayed as shown in Figure 7c.

(c) Open the My Computer Folder (step 3)

FIGURE 7 Hands-on Exercise 1 (*continued*)

DESIGNATING THE DEVICES ON A SYSTEM

The first (usually only) floppy drive is always designated as drive A. (A second floppy drive, if it were present, would be drive B.) The first hard (local) disk on a system is always drive C, whether or not there are one or two floppy drives. Additional local drives, if any, such as a zip (removable storage) drive, a network drive, a CD and/or a DVD, are labeled from D on.

Step 4: Move and Size a Window

- Move and size the My Computer window on your desktop to match the display in Figure 7d.
  - ❏ To change the width or height of the window, click and drag a border (the mouse pointer changes to a double arrow) in the direction you want to go; drag the border inward to shrink the window or outward to enlarge it.
  - ❏ To change the width and height at the same time, click and drag a corner rather than a border.
  - ❏ To change the position of the window, click and drag the title bar.

- Click the **Minimize button** to shrink the My Computer window to a button on the taskbar. My Computer is still active in memory although its window is no longer visible. Click the **My Computer button** on the taskbar to reopen the window.

- Click the **Maximize button** so that the My Computer window expands to fill the entire screen. Click the **Restore button** (which replaces the Maximize button and is not shown in Figure 7d) to return the window to its previous size.

- Practice these operations until you can move and size a window with confidence.

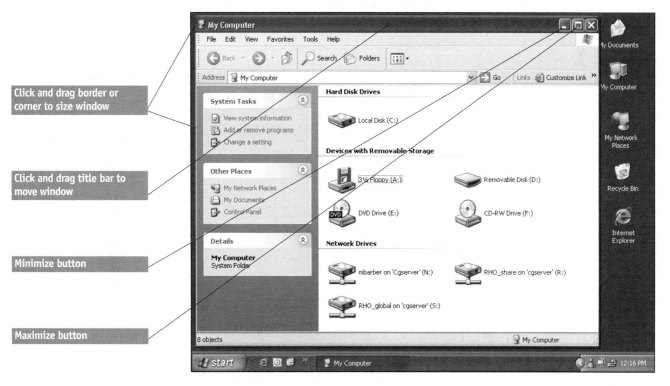

(d) Move and Size a Window (step 4)

FIGURE 7 Hands-on Exercise 1 (*continued*)

MINIMIZING VERSUS CLOSING AN APPLICATION

Minimizing a folder or an application leaves the object open in memory and available at the click of the appropriate button on the taskbar. Closing it, however, removes the object from memory, which also causes it to disappear from the taskbar. The advantage of minimizing an application or folder is that you can return to it immediately with the click of the mouse. The disadvantage is that too many open applications will eventually degrade the performance of a system.

Step 5: **Capture a Screen**

■ Prove to your instructor that you have sized the window correctly by capturing the desktop that currently appears on your monitor. Press the **Print Screen key** to copy the current screen display to the **clipboard**, an area of memory that is available to every application.

■ Nothing appears to have happened, but the screen has in fact been copied to the clipboard and can be pasted into a Word document. Click the **Start button**, click the **All Programs command**, then start **Microsoft Word** and begin a new document.

■ Enter the title of your document (I Did My Homework) followed by your name as shown in Figure 7e. Press the **Enter key** two or three times to leave blank lines after your name.

■ Pull down the **Edit menu** and click the **Paste command** (or click the **Paste button** on the Standard toolbar) to copy the contents of the clipboard into the Word document.

■ Print this document for your instructor. There is no need to save this document. Exit Word.

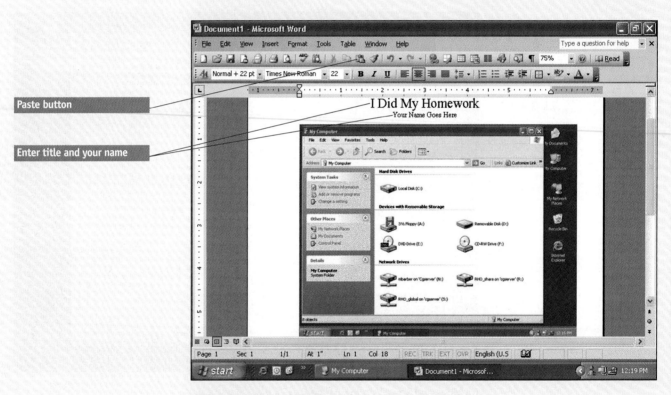

(e) Capture a Screen (step 5)

FIGURE 7 Hands-on Exercise 1 (*continued*)

THE FORMAT PICTURE COMMAND

Use the Format Picture command to facilitate moving and/or sizing an object within a Word document. Right click the picture to display a context-sensitive menu, then click the Format Picture command to display the associated dialog box. Click the Layout tab, choose any layout other than Inline with text, and click OK. You can now click and drag the picture to position it elsewhere within the document.

Step 6: Format a Floppy Disk

- Place a floppy disk into drive A. Select (click) **drive A** in the My Computer window, then pull down the **File menu** and click the **Format command** to display the Format dialog box in Figure 7f.
  - ❏ Set the **Capacity** to match the floppy disk you purchased (1.44MB for a high-density disk and 720KB for a double-density disk. The easiest way to determine the type of disk is to look for the label HD or DD, respectively.).
  - ❏ Click the **Volume label text box** if it's empty, or click and drag over the existing label if there is an entry. Enter a new label (containing up to 11 characters), such as **Bob's Disk**.
  - ❏ You can check the **Quick Format box** if the disk has been previously formatted, as a convenient way to erase the contents of the disk.

- Click the **Start button,** then click **OK**—after you have read the warning message—to begin the formatting operation. The formatting process erases anything that is on the disk, so be sure that you do not need anything on the disk.

- Click **OK** after the formatting is complete. Close the dialog box, then save the formatted disk for the next exercise. Close the My Computer window.

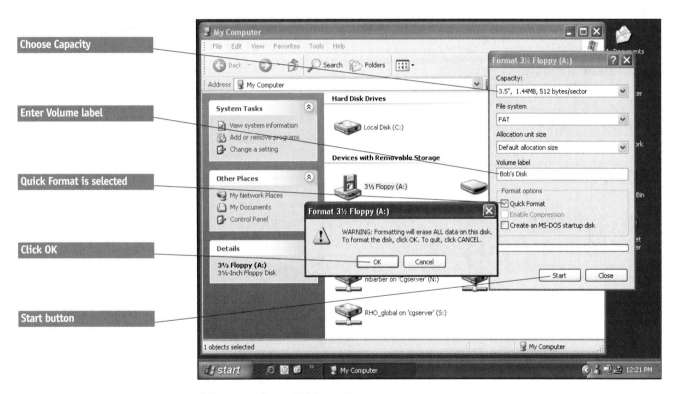

Choose Capacity

Enter Volume label

Quick Format is selected

Click OK

Start button

(f) Format a Floppy Disk (step 6)

FIGURE 7   Hands-on Exercise 1 (*continued*)

THE DEMISE OF THE FLOPPY DISK

You may be surprised to discover that your system no longer has a floppy disk drive, but it is only the latest victim in the march of technology. Long-playing records have come and gone. So too have 8-track tapes and the laser disk. The 3½-inch floppy disk has had a long and successful run, but it, too, is slated for obsolescence with Dell's recent announcement that it will no longer include a floppy drive as a standard component in desktop systems. Still, the floppy disk will "live forever" in the Save button that has the floppy disk as its icon.

Step 7: **The Help and Support Center**

■ Click the **Start button**, then click the **Help and Support command** to open the Help and Support Center. Click the **Index button** to open the index pane. The insertion point moves automatically to the text box where you enter the search topic.

■ Type **help**, which automatically moves you to the available topics within the index. Double click **central location for Help** to display the information in the right pane as shown in Figure 7g.

■ Toggle the display of the subtopics on and off by clicking the plus and minus sign, respectively. Click the **plus sign** next to Remote Assistance, for example, and the topic opens. Click the **minus sign** next to Tours and articles, and the topic closes.

■ Right click anywhere within the right pane to display the context-sensitive menu shown in Figure 7g. Click the **Print command** to print this information for your instructor.

■ Close the Help and Support window.

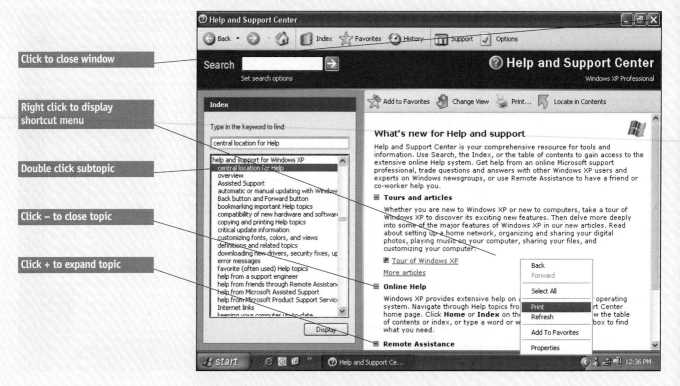

(g) The Help and Support Center (step 7)

FIGURE 7 Hands-on Exercise 1 (*continued*)

THE FAVORITES BUTTON

Do you find yourself continually searching for the same information? If so, you can make life a little easier by adding the page to a list of favorite help topics. Start the Help and Support Center, use the Index button to display the desired information in the right pane, and then click the Add to Favorites button to add the topic to your list of favorites. You can return to the topic at any time by clicking the Favorites button at the top of the Help and Support window, then double clicking the bookmark.

Step 8: Log (or Turn) Off the Computer

- It is very important that you log off properly, as opposed to just turning off the power. This enables Windows to close all of its system files and to save any changes that were made during the session.

- Click the **Start button** to display the Start menu in Figure 7h, then click the **Log Off button** at the bottom of the menu. You will see a dialog box asking whether you want to log off or switch users.
    - ❏ Switching users leaves your session active. All of your applications remain open, but control of the computer is given to another user. You can subsequently log back on (after the new user logs off) and take up exactly where you left off.
    - ❏ Logging off ends your session, but leaves the computer running at full power. This is the typical option you would select in a laboratory setting at school.

- To turn the computer off, you have to log off as just described, then select the **Turn Computer Off command** from the login screen. Welcome to Windows XP!

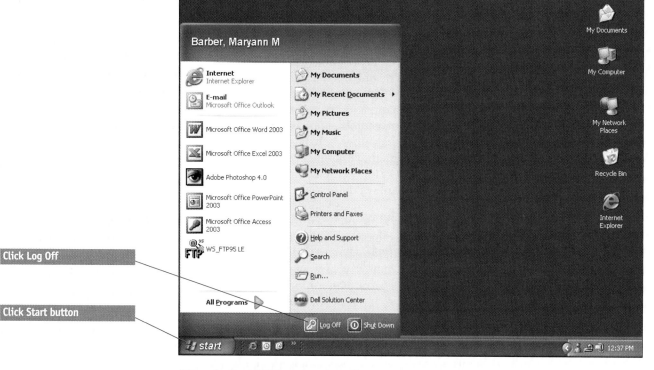

(h) Log (or Turn) Off Computer (step 8)

FIGURE 7   Hands-on Exercise 1 (*continued*)

THE TASK MANAGER

The Start button is the normal way to exit Windows. Occasionally, however, an application may "hang"—in which case you want to close the problem application but continue with your session. Press Ctrl+Alt+Del to display the Windows Task Manager dialog box, then click the Applications tab. Select the problem application (it will most likely say "not responding"), and click the End Task button. This capability is often disabled in a school setting.

FILES AND FOLDERS

A *file* is a set of instructions or data that has been given a name and stored on disk. There are two basic types of files, *program files* and *data files*. Microsoft Word and Microsoft Excel are examples of program files. The documents and workbooks that are created by these programs are data files. A program file is executable because it contains instructions that tell the computer what to do. A data file is not executable and can be used only in conjunction with a specific program. In other words, you execute program files to create and/or edit the associated data files.

Every file has a *filename* that identifies it to the operating system. The filename can contain up to 255 characters and may include spaces and other punctuation. (Filenames cannot contain the following characters: \, /, :, *, ?, ", <, >, and |.) We find it easier, however, to restrict the characters in a filename to letters, numbers, and spaces, as opposed to having to remember the special characters that are not permitted.

Files are kept in *folders* to better organize the thousands of files on a typical system. A Windows folder is similar to an ordinary manila folder that holds one or more documents. To continue the analogy, an office worker stores his or her documents in manila folders within a filing cabinet. Windows stores its files in electronic folders that are located on a disk, CD-ROM, or other device.

Many folders are created automatically by Windows XP, such as the My Computer or My Documents folders that are present on every system. Other folders are created whenever new software is installed. Additional folders are created by the user to hold the documents he or she creates. You might, for example, create a folder for your word processing documents and a second folder for your spreadsheets. You could also create a folder to hold all of your work for a specific class, which in turn might contain a combination of word processing documents and spreadsheets. The choice is entirely up to you, and you can use any system that makes sense to you. A folder can contain program files, data files, or even other folders.

Figure 8 displays the contents of a hypothetical folder with nine documents. Figure 8a displays the folder in *Tiles view*. Figure 8b displays the same folder in *Details view*, which also shows the date the file was created or last modified. Both views display a file icon next to each file to indicate the *file type* or application that was used to create the file. *Introduction to E-mail*, for example, is a PowerPoint presentation. *Basic Financial Functions* is an Excel workbook.

The two figures have more similarities than differences, such as the name of the folder (*Homework*), which appears in the title bar next to the icon of an open folder. The Minimize, Restore, and Close buttons are found at the right of the title bar. A menu bar with six pull-down menus appears below the title bar. The Standard Buttons toolbar is below the menu, and the Address bar (indicating the drive and folder) appears below the toolbar. Both folders also contain a task pane that provides easy access to common tasks for the folder or selected object.

Look closely and you will see that the task panes are significantly different. This is because there are no documents selected in Figure 8a, whereas the *Milestones in Communications* document is selected (highlighted) in Figure 8b. Thus, the File and Folder Tasks area in Figure 8a pertains to folders in general, whereas the available tasks in Figure 8b are pertinent to the selected document. The Details areas in the two task panes are also consistent with the selected objects and display information about the Homework folder and selected document, respectively. A status bar appears at the bottom of both windows and displays the contents of the selected object.

The last difference between the task panes reflects the user's preference to open or close the Other Places area. Click the upward chevron in Figure 8a to suppress the display and gain space in the task pane, or click the downward chevron in Figure 8b to display the specific links to other places. The task pane is new to Windows XP and did not appear in previous versions of Windows.

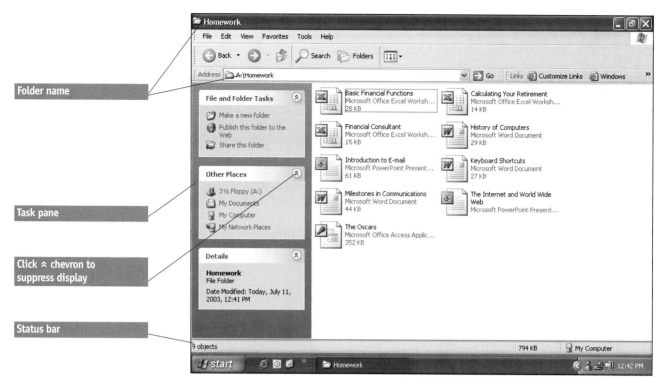

Folder name

Task pane

Click ⊗ chevron to
suppress display

Status bar

(a) Tiles View

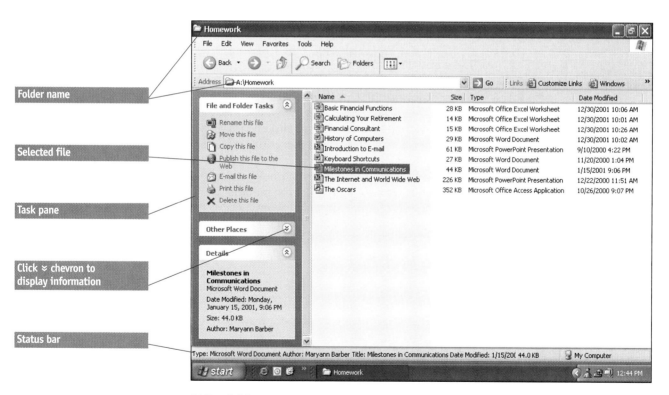

Folder name

Selected file

Task pane

Click ⊗ chevron to
display information

Status bar

(b) Details View

FIGURE 8   Files and Folders

THE EXPLORING OFFICE PRACTICE FILES

There is only one way to master disk and file management and that is to practice at the computer. To do so requires that you have a series of files with which to work. We have created these files for you, and we use the files in the next two hands-on exercises. Your instructor will make the practice files available to you in different ways:

■ The files can be downloaded from our Web site at www.prenhall.com/grauer. Software and other files that are downloaded from the Internet are typically compressed (made smaller) to reduce the amount of time it takes to transmit the file. In essence, you will download a single *compressed file* and then uncompress the file into multiple files onto a local drive as described in the next hands-on exercise.

■ The files may be on a network drive at your school or university, in which case you can copy the files from the network drive to a floppy disk.

■ There may be an actual "data disk" in the computer lab. Go to the lab with a floppy disk, then use the Copy Disk command (on the File menu of My Computer when drive A is selected) to duplicate the data disk and create a copy for yourself.

It doesn't matter how you obtain the practice files, only that you are able to do so. Indeed, you may want to try different techniques to gain additional practice with Windows XP. Note, too, that Windows XP provides a *firewall* to protect your computer from unauthorized access while it is connected to the Internet. (See exercise 2 at the end of the chapter.)

CONNECTING TO THE INTERNET

The easiest way to obtain the practice files is to download the files from the Web, which requires an Internet connection. There are two basic ways to connect to the Internet—from a local area network (LAN) or by dialing in. It's much easier if you connect from a LAN (typically at school or work) since the installation and setup have been done for you, and all you have to do is follow the instructions provided by your professor. If you connect from home, you will need a modem, a cable modem, or a DSL modem, and an Internet Service Provider (or ISP).

A *modem* is the hardware interface between your computer and the telephone system. In essence, you instruct the modem, via the appropriate software, to connect to your ISP, which in turn lets you access the Internet. A cable modem provides high-speed access (20 to 30 times that of an ordinary modem) through the same type of cable as used for cable TV. A DSL modem also provides high-speed access through a special type of phone line that lets you connect to the Internet while simultaneously carrying on a conversation.

An *Internet Service Provider* is a company or organization that maintains a computer with permanent access to the Internet. America Online (AOL) is the largest ISP with more than 30 million subscribers, and it provides a proprietary interface as well as Internet access. The Microsoft Network (MSN) is a direct competitor to AOL. Alternatively, you can choose from a host of other vendors who provide Internet access without the proprietary interface of AOL or MSN.

Regardless of which vendor you choose as an ISP, be sure you understand the fee structure. The monthly fee may entitle you to a set number of hours per month (after which you pay an additional fee), or it may give you unlimited access. The terms vary widely, and you should shop around for the best possible deal. Price is not the only consideration, however. Reliability of service is also important. Be sure that the equipment of your provider is adequate so that you can obtain access whenever you want.

2 Download the Practice Files

Objective To download a file from the Web and practice basic file commands. The exercise requires a formatted floppy disk and access to the Internet. Use Figure 9 as a guide.

Step 1: Start Internet Explorer

■ Click the **Start button**, click the **All Programs command**, and then click **Internet Explorer** to start the program. If necessary, click the **Maximize button** so that Internet Explorer takes the entire desktop.

■ Click anywhere within the **Address bar**, which automatically selects the current address (so that whatever you type replaces the current address). Enter **www.prenhall.com/grauer** (the http:// is assumed). Press **Enter**.

■ You should see the Exploring Office Series home page as shown in Figure 9a. Click the book for **Office 2003**, which takes you to the Office 2003 home page.

■ Click the **Student Downloads tab** (at the top of the window) to go to the Student Download page.

(a) Start Internet Explorer (step 1)

FIGURE 9 Hands-on Exercise 2

A NEW INTERNET EXPLORER

The installation of Windows XP automatically installs a new version of Internet Explorer. Pull down the Help menu and click the About Internet Explorer command to display the current release (version 6.0). Click OK to close the About Internet Explorer window.

Step 2: **Download the Practice Files**

- You should see the Student Download page in Figure 9b. Place the formatted floppy disk from the first exercise in drive A. Be sure there are no files on this disk.

- Scroll down the page until you see the link to the student data disk for **Windows XP**. Click the link to download the practice files.

- You will see the File Download dialog box, asking what you want to do. Click the **Save button** to display the Save As dialog box. Click the **drop-down arrow** on the Save in list box, and select (click) **drive A**.

- Click **Save** to download the file. The File Download window may reappear and show you the status of the downloading operation as it takes place.

- If necessary, click **Close** when you see the dialog box indicating that the download is complete. Minimize Internet Explorer.

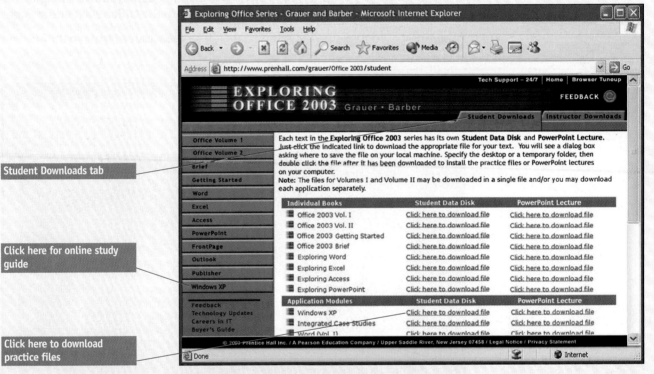

(b) Download the Practice Files (step 2)

FIGURE 9   Hands-on Exercise 2 (*continued*)

EXPLORE OUR WEB SITE

The Exploring Office Series Web site offers an online study guide (multiple-choice, true/false, and matching questions) for each individual textbook to help you review the material in each chapter. You can take practice quizzes by yourself and/or e-mail the results to your instructor. These online study guides are available via the tabs in the left navigation bar. You can return to the Student Download page at any time by clicking the tab toward the top of the window and/or you can click the link to Home to return to the home page for the Office 2003 Series. And finally, you can click the Feedback button at the top of the screen to send a message directly to Bob Grauer.

Step 3: Install the Practice Files

■ Click the **Start button**, then click the **My Computer command** on the menu to open the My Computer folder. If necessary, click the Maximize button so that the My Computer window takes up the entire desktop. Change to the **Details view**.

■ Click the icon for **drive A** to select it. The description of drive A appears at the left of the window. Double click the icon for **drive A** to open this drive. The contents of the My Computer window are replaced by the contents of drive A as shown in Figure 9c.

■ Double click the **XPData file** to install the practice files, which displays the dialog box in Figure 9c. When you have finished reading, click **OK** to continue the installation and display the WinZip Self-Extractor dialog box.

■ Check that the Unzip To Folder text box specifies **A:** to extract the files to the floppy disk. Click the **Unzip button** to extract (uncompress) the practice files and copy them onto the designated drive.

■ Click **OK** after you see the message indicating that the files have been unzipped successfully. Close the WinZip dialog box.

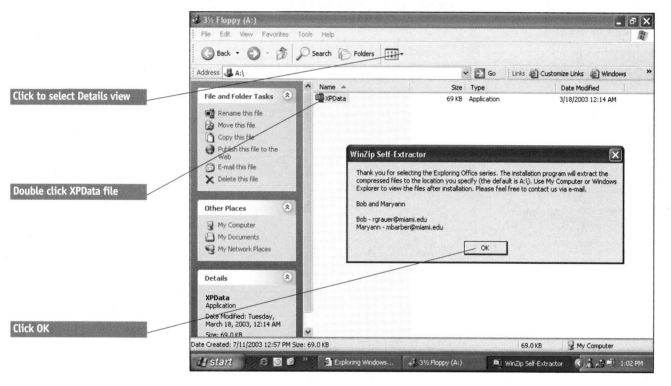

(c) Install the Practice Files (step 3)

FIGURE 9 Hands-on Exercise 2 (*continued*)

DOWNLOADING A FILE

Software and other files are typically compressed (made smaller) to reduce the amount of storage space the files require on disk and/or the time it takes to download the files. In essence, you download a compressed file (which may contain multiple individual files), then you uncompress (expand) the file on your local drive to access the individual files. After the file has been expanded, it is no longer needed and can be deleted.

Step 4: **Delete the Compressed File**

- The practice files have been extracted to drive A and should appear in the Drive A window. If you do not see the files, pull down the **View menu** and click the **Refresh command**.

- If necessary, pull down the **View menu** and click **Details** to change to the Details view in Figure 9e. You should see a total of eight files in the drive A window. Seven of these are the practice files on the data disk. The eighth file is the original file that you downloaded earlier. This file is no longer necessary, since it has been already been expanded.

- Select (click) the **XPData file**. Click the **Delete this file command** in the task pane (or simply press the **Del key**). Pause for a moment to be sure you want to delete this file, then click **Yes** when asked to confirm the deletion as shown in Figure 9d.

- The XPData file is permanently deleted from drive A. (Items deleted from a floppy disk or network drive are not sent to the Recycle bin, and cannot be recovered.)

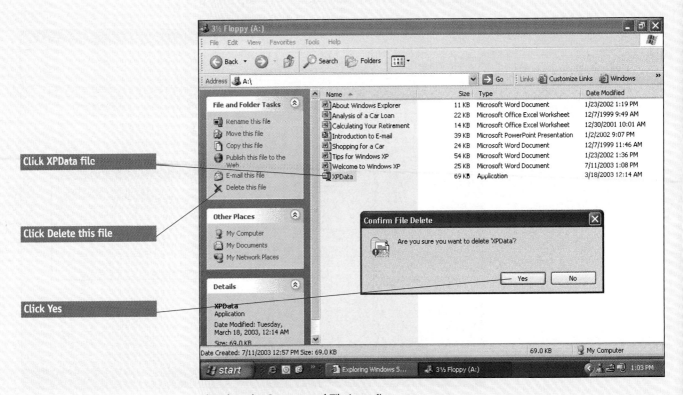

(d) Delete the Compressed File (step 4)

FIGURE 9   Hands-on Exercise 2 (*continued*)

SORT BY NAME, DATE, FILE TYPE, OR SIZE

The files in a folder can be displayed in ascending or descending sequence, by name, date modified, file type, or size, by clicking the appropriate column heading. Click Size, for example, to display files in the order of their size. Click the column heading a second time to reverse the sequence; that is, to switch from ascending to descending, and vice versa. Click a different column heading to display the files in a different sequence.

Step 5: **Modify a Document**

■ Double click the **Welcome to Windows XP** document from within My Computer to open the document as shown in Figure 9e. (The document will open in the WordPad accessory if Microsoft Word is not installed on your machine.)

■ Maximize the window for Microsoft Word. Read the document, and then press **Ctrl+End** to move to the end of the document. Do not be concerned if your screen does not match ours exactly.

■ Add the sentence shown in Figure 9e, press the **Enter key** twice, then type your name. Click the **Save button** on the Standard toolbar to save the document.

■ Pull down the **File menu**, click the **Print command**, and click **OK** (or click the **Print button** on the Standard toolbar) to print the document and prove to your instructor that you did the exercise.

■ Pull down the **File menu** and click **Exit** to close Microsoft Word. You should be back in the My Computer folder.

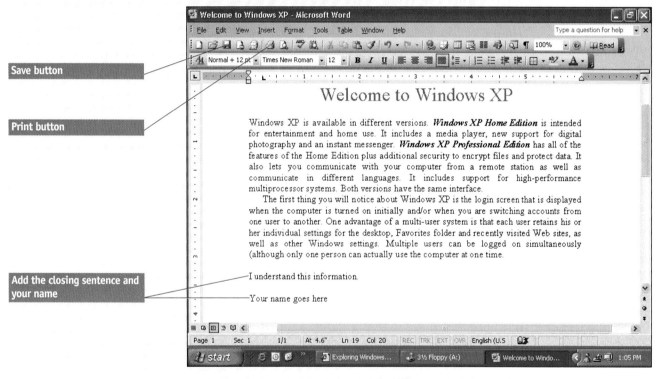

(e) Modify a Document (step 5)

FIGURE 9   Hands-on Exercise 2 (*continued*)

THE DOCUMENT, NOT THE APPLICATION

The Windows operating system is document oriented, which means that you are able to think in terms of the document rather than the application that created it. You can still open a document in traditional fashion, by starting the application that created the document, then using the File Open command in that program to retrieve the document. It's often easier, however, to open the document from within a folder by double clicking its icon. Windows will start the associated application and then open the document for you.

Step 6: Create a New Folder

- Look closely at the date and time that are displayed next to the Welcome to Windows XP document in Figure 9f. It should show today's date and the current time (give or take a minute) because that is when the document was last modified. Your date will be different from ours.

- Look closely and see that Figure 9f also contains an eighth document, called "Backup of Welcome to Windows XP." This is a backup copy of the original document that will be created automatically by Microsoft Word if the appropriate options are in effect. (See the boxed tip below.)

- Click **a blank area** in the right pane to deselect the Welcome to Windows XP document. The commands in the File and Folder Tasks area change to basic folder operations.

- Click the command to **Make a New folder**, which creates a new folder with the default name "New Folder". Enter **New Car** as the new name. You will move files into this folder in step 7.

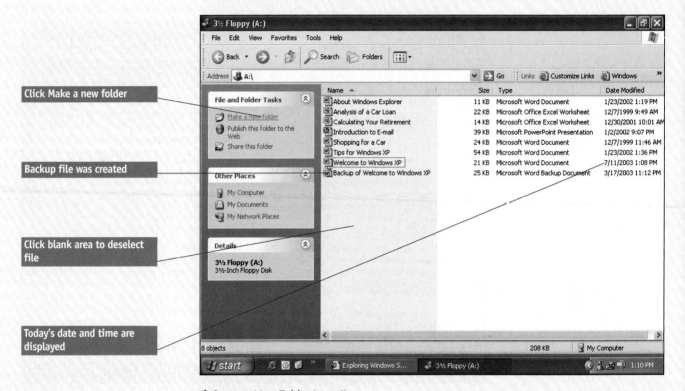

(f) Create a New Folder (step 6)

FIGURE 9 Hands-on Exercise 2 (*continued*)

USE WORD TO CREATE A BACKUP COPY

Microsoft Word enables you to automatically keep the previous version of a document as a backup copy. The next time you are in Microsoft Word, pull down the Tools menu, click the Options command, click the Save tab, then check the box to Always create backup copy. Every time you save a file from this point on, the previously saved version is renamed "Backup of document," and the document in memory is saved as the current version. The disk will contain the two most recent versions of the document, enabling you to retrieve the previous version if necessary.

Step 7:   Move the Files

- There are different ways to move a file from one folder to another. The most basic technique is to
  - ❏ Select (click) the **Analysis of a Car Loan** workbook to highlight the file, then click the **Move this file command** in the task pane.
  - ❏ You will see the Move Items dialog box in Figure 9g. Click the plus sign (if it appears) next to the 3½ floppy disk to expand the disk and view its folders. Click the **New Car folder**, then click the **Move button**.
  - ❏ The selected file is moved to the New Car folder and the dialog box closes. The Analysis of a Car Loan document no longer appears in the right pane of Figure 9g because it has been moved to a new folder.

- If the source and destination folders are both on the same drive, as in this example, you can simply click and drag the file to its new destination. Thus, click and drag the **Shopping for a Car** Word document to the New Car folder. Release the mouse when the file is directly over the folder to complete the move.

- Double click the **New Car folder** to view the contents of this folder, which should contain both documents. The Address bar now says A:\New Car.

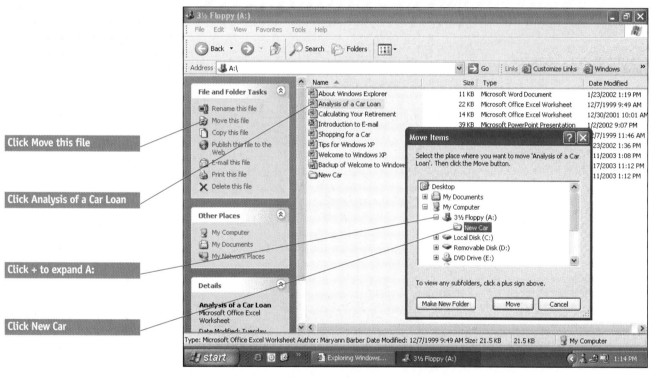

(g) Move the Files (step 7)

FIGURE 9   Hands-on Exercise 2 (*continued*)

THE PLUS AND MINUS SIGNS

Any drive, be it local or on the network, may be expanded or collapsed to display or hide its folders. A minus sign indicates that the drive has been expanded and that its folders are visible. A plus sign indicates the reverse; that is, the device is collapsed and its folders are not visible. Click either sign to toggle to the other. Clicking a plus sign, for example, expands the drive, then displays a minus sign next to the drive to indicate that the folders are visible. Clicking a minus sign has the reverse effect.

Step 8: A Look Ahead

- Click the **Folders button** to display a hierarchical view of the devices on your computer as shown in Figure 9h. This is the same screen that is displayed through Windows Explorer, a program that we will study after the exercise.

- The Folders button functions as a toggle switch; click the button a second time and the task pane (also called task panel) returns. Click the **Folders button** to return to the hierarchical view.

- The New Car folder is selected (highlighted) in the left pane because this is the folder you were working in at the previous step. The contents of this folder are displayed in the right pane.

- Click the icon for the **3½ floppy drive** to display the contents of drive A. The right pane displays the files on drive A as well as the New Car folder.

- Close the My Computer folder. Close Internet Explorer. Log off if you do not want to continue with the next exercise at this time.

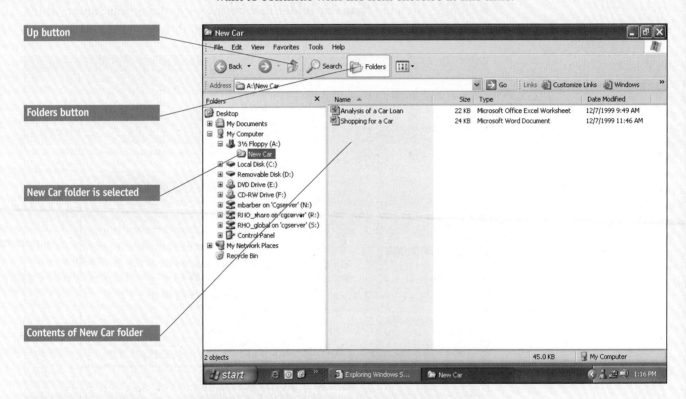

(h) A Look Ahead (step 8)

FIGURE 9   Hands-on Exercise 2 (*continued*)

NAVIGATING THE HIERARCHY

Click the Up button on the Standard Buttons toolbar to move up one level in the hierarchy in the left pane and display the associated contents in the right pane. Click the Up button when you are viewing the New Car folder, for example, and you are returned to drive A. Click the Up button a second time and you will see the contents of My Computer. Note, too, how the contents of the Address bar change each time you view a different folder in the right pane.

Windows Explorer is a program that displays a hierarchical (tree) structure of the devices on your system. Consider, for example, Figure 10a, which displays the contents of a hypothetical Homework folder as it exists on our computer. The hierarchy is displayed in the left pane, and the contents of the selected object (the Homework folder) are shown in the right pane. The advantage of viewing the folder in this way (as opposed to displaying the task pane) is that you see the location of the folder on the system; that is; the Homework folder is physically stored on drive A.

Let's explore the hierarchy in the left pane. There is a minus sign next to the icon for drive A to indicate that this drive has been expanded and thus you can see its folders. Drive C, however, has a plus sign to indicate that the drive is collapsed and that its contents are not visible. Look closely and you see that both drive A and drive C are indented under My Computer, which in turn is indented under the desktop. In other words, the desktop is at the top of the hierarchy and it contains the My Computer folder, which in turn contains drive A and drive C. The desktop also contains a My Documents folder, but the plus sign next to the My Documents folder indicates the folder is collapsed. My Computer, on the other hand, has a minus sign and you can see its contents, which consist of the drives on your system as well as other special folders (Control Panel and Shared Documents).

Look carefully at the icon next to the Homework folder in the left pane of the figure. The icon is an open folder, and it indicates that the (Homework) folder is the active folder. The folder's name is also shaded, and it appears in the title bar. Only one folder can be active at one time, and its contents are displayed in the right pane. The Milestones in Communications document is highlighted (selected) in the right pane, which means that subsequent commands will affect this document, as opposed to the entire folder. If you wanted to work with a different document in the Homework folder, you would select that document. To see the contents of a different folder, such as Financial Documents, you would select (click) the icon for that folder in the left pane (which automatically closes the Homework folder). The contents of the Financial Documents folder would then appear in the right pane.

You can create folders at any time just like the Homework and Financial Documents folders that we created on drive A. You can also create folders within folders; for example, a correspondence folder may contain two folders of its own, one for business correspondence and one for personal letters.

Personal Folders

Windows automatically creates a set of personal folders for every user. These include the ***My Documents folder*** and the ***My Pictures folder*** and ***My Music folder*** within the My Documents folder. The My Documents folder is collapsed in Figure 10a, but it is expanded in Figure 10b, and thus its contents are visible. The My Music folder is active, and its contents are visible in the right pane.

Every user has a unique set of personal folders, and thus Windows has to differentiate between the multiple "My Documents" folders that may exist. It does so by creating additional folders to hold the documents and settings for each user. Look closely at the Address bar in Figure 10b. Each back slash indicates a new folder, and you can read the complete path from right to left. Thus, the My Music folder that we are viewing is contained in My Documents folder within Maryann's folder, which in turn is stored in a Documents and Settings folder on drive C.

Fortunately, however, Windows does the housekeeping for you. All you have to do is locate the desired folder—for example, My Music or My Pictures—in the left pane, and Windows does the rest. ***Personal folders*** are just what the name implies—"personal," meaning that only one person has access to their content. Windows also provides a ***Shared Documents folder*** for files that Maryann may want to share with others.

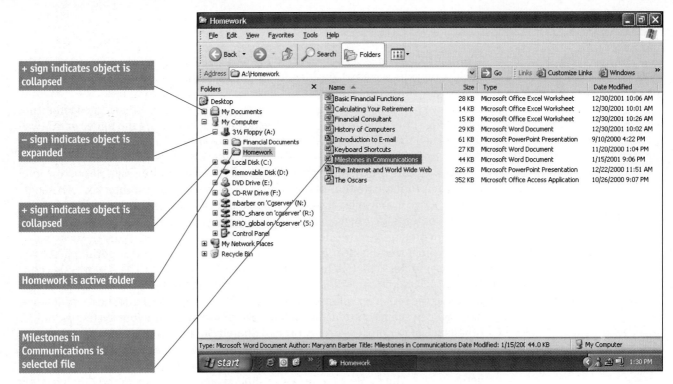

+ sign indicates object is collapsed

– sign indicates object is expanded

+ sign indicates object is collapsed

Homework is active folder

Milestones in Communications is selected file

(a) Homework Folder

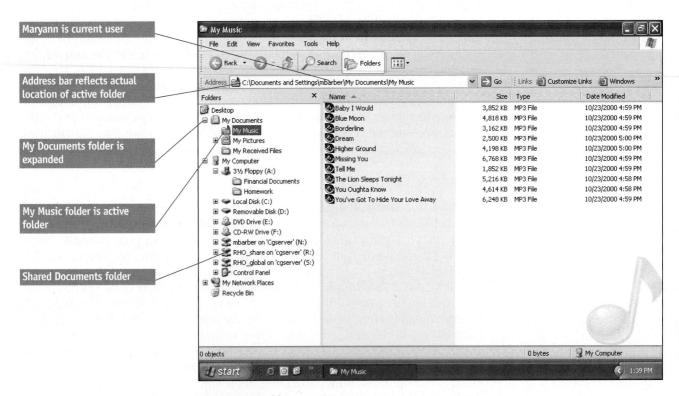

Maryann is current user

Address bar reflects actual location of active folder

My Documents folder is expanded

My Music folder is active folder

Shared Documents folder

(b) My Music Folder

FIGURE 10   Windows Explorer

Moving and Copying a File

The essence of file management is to **move** and **copy a file** or folder from one location to another. This can be done in different ways. The easiest is to click and drag the file icon from the source drive or folder to the destination drive or folder, within Windows Explorer. There is one subtlety, however, in that the result of dragging a file (i.e., whether the file is moved or copied) depends on whether the source and destination are on the same or different drives. Dragging a file from one folder to another folder on the same drive moves the file. Dragging a file to a folder on a different drive copies the file. The same rules apply to dragging a folder, where the folder and every file in it are moved or copied, as per the rules for an individual file.

This process is not as arbitrary as it may seem. Windows assumes that if you drag an object (a file or folder) to a different drive (e.g., from drive C to drive A), you want the object to appear in both places. Hence, the default action when you click and drag an object to a different drive is to copy the object. You can, however, override the default and move the object by pressing and holding the Shift key as you drag.

Windows also assumes that you do not want two copies of an object on the same drive, as that would result in wasted disk space. Thus, the default action when you click and drag an object to a different folder on the same drive is to move the object. You can override the default and copy the object by pressing and holding the Ctrl key as you drag. It's not as complicated as it sounds, and you get a chance to practice in the hands-on exercise, which follows shortly.

Deleting a File

The **Delete command** deletes (erases) a file from a disk. The command can be executed in different ways, most easily by selecting a file, then pressing the Del key. It's also comforting to know that you can usually recover a deleted file, because the file is not (initially) removed from the disk, but moved instead to the Recycle Bin, from where it can be restored to its original location. Unfortunately, files deleted from a floppy disk are not put into the Recycle Bin and hence cannot be recovered.

The **Recycle Bin** is a special folder that contains all files that were previously deleted from any hard disk on your system. Think of the Recycle Bin as similar to the wastebasket in your room. You throw out (delete) a report by tossing it into a wastebasket. The report is gone (deleted) from your desk, but you can still get it back by taking it out of the wastebasket as long as the basket wasn't emptied. The Recycle Bin works the same way. Files are not deleted from the hard disk per se, but moved instead to the Recycle Bin from where they can be restored to their original location. (The protection afforded by the Recycle Bin does not extend to files deleted from a floppy disk.)

Backup

It's not a question of *if* it will happen, but *when*—hard disks die, files are lost, or viruses may infect a system. It has happened to us and it will happen to you, but you can prepare for the inevitable by creating adequate backup *before* the problem occurs. The essence of a **backup strategy** is to decide which files to back up, how often to do the backup, and where to keep the backup.

Our strategy is very simple—back up what you can't afford to lose, do so on a daily basis, and store the backup away from your computer. You need not copy every file, every day. Instead, copy just the files that changed during the current session. Realize, too, that it is much more important to back up your data files than your program files. You can always reinstall the application from the original disks or CD, or if necessary, go to the vendor for another copy of an application. You, however, are the only one who has a copy of the term paper that is due tomorrow. Once you decide on a strategy, follow it, and follow it faithfully!

3   Windows Explorer

Objective   Use Windows Explorer to move, copy, and delete a file; recover a deleted file from the Recycle Bin. Use Figure 11 as a guide.

Step 1:   **Create a New Folder**

■ Place the floppy disk from the previous exercise into drive A. Click the **Start Button**, click the **All Programs command**, click **Accessories**, then click **Windows Explorer**. Click the **Maximize button**.

■ Expand or collapse the various devices on your system so that My Computer is expanded, but all of the devices are collapsed.

■ Click (select) **drive A** in the left pane to display the contents of the floppy disk. You should see the New Car folder that was created in the previous exercise.

■ Point to a blank area anywhere in the **right pane**, click the **right mouse button**, click the **New command**, then click **Folder** as the type of object to create.

■ The icon for a new folder will appear with the name of the folder (New Folder) highlighted. Type **Windows Information** to change the name. Press **Enter**.

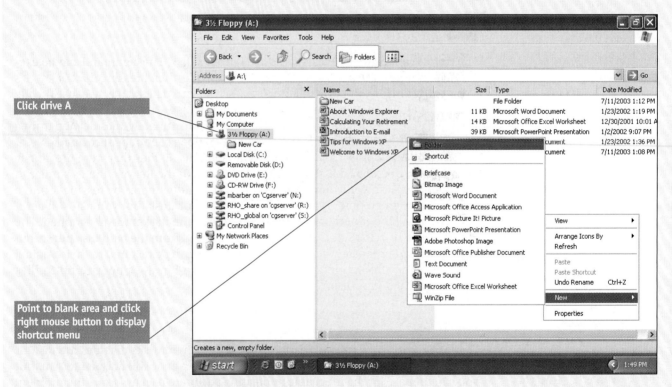

(a) Create a New Folder (step 1)

FIGURE 11   Hands-on Exercise 3 (*continued*)

THE RENAME COMMAND

Right click the file or a folder whose name you want to change to display a context-sensitive menu, and then click the Rename command. The name of the folder will be highlighted with the insertion point at the end of the name. Enter (or edit) the new (existing) name and press Enter.

Step 2: Move the Files

- If necessary, change to the **Details view** and click the **plus sign** next to drive A to expand the drive as shown in Figure 11b. Note the following:
  - ❏ The left pane shows that drive A is selected. The right pane displays the contents of drive A (the selected object in the left pane). The folders are shown first and appear in alphabetical order. If not, press the **F5 (Refresh) key** to refresh the screen.
  - ❏ There is a minus sign next to the icon for drive A in the left pane, indicating that it has been expanded and that its folders are visible. Thus, the folder names also appear under drive A in the left pane.

- Click and drag the **About Windows Explorer** document in the right pane to the **Windows Information folder** in the left pane, to move the file into that folder.

- Click and drag the **Tips for Windows XP** and the **Welcome to Windows XP** documents to move these documents to the **Windows Information folder**.

- Click the **Windows Information folder** in the left pane to select the folder and display its contents in the right pane. You should see the three files that were just moved.

- Click the **Up button** to return to drive A.

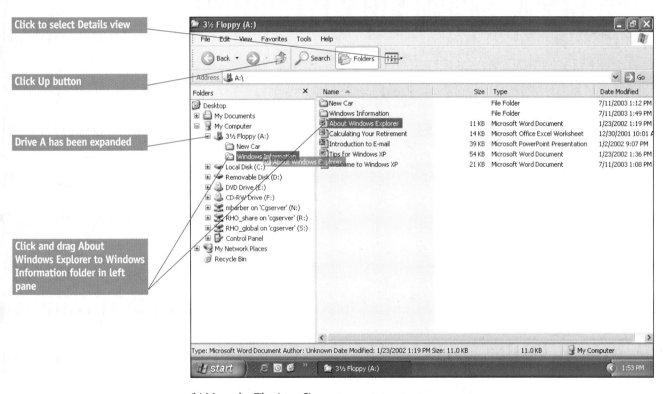

(b) Move the Files (step 2)

FIGURE 11   Hands-on Exercise 3 (continued)

SELECT MULTIPLE FILES

Selecting (clicking) one file automatically deselects the previously selected file. You can, however, select multiple files by clicking the first file, then pressing and holding the Ctrl key as you click each additional file. Use the Shift key to select multiple files that are adjacent to one another by clicking the icon of the first file, then pressing and holding the Shift key as you click the icon of the last file.

Step 3: Copy a Folder

- Point to the **Windows Information folder** in the right pane, then **right click and drag** this folder to the **My Documents folder** (on drive C) in the left pane. Release the mouse to display a context-sensitive menu.

- Click the **Copy Here command** as shown in Figure 11c.
  - ❏ You may see a Copy files message box as the individual files within the Windows Information folder are copied to the My Documents folder.
  - ❏ If you see the Confirm Folder Replace dialog box, it means that you (or another student) already copied these files to the My Documents folder. Click the **Yes to All button** so that your files replace the previous versions in the My Documents folder.

- Click the **My Documents folder** in the left pane. Pull down the **View menu** and click the **Refresh command** (or press the **F5 key**) so that the hierarchy shows the newly copied folder. (Please remember to delete the Windows Information folder from drive C at the end of the exercise.)

Right click and drag the Windows Information folder to the My Documents folder

Click Copy Here from shortcut menu

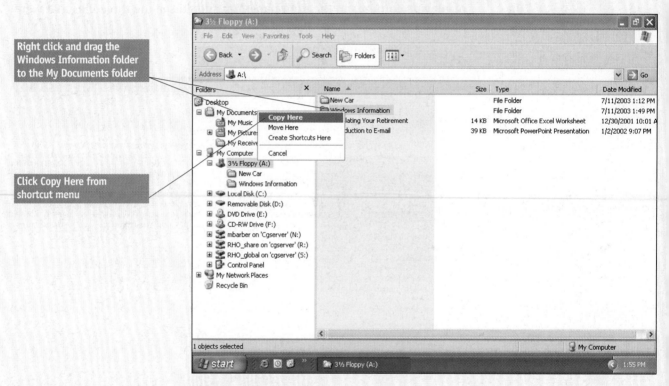

(c) Copy a Folder (step 3)

FIGURE 11 Hands-on Exercise 3 (*continued*)

RIGHT CLICK AND DRAG

The result of dragging a file with the left mouse button depends on whether the source and destination folders are on the same or different drives. Dragging a file to a folder on a different drive copies the file, whereas dragging the file to a folder on the same drive moves the file. If you find this hard to remember, and most people do, click and drag with the right mouse button to display a context-sensitive menu asking whether you want to copy or move the file. This simple tip can save you from making a careless (and potentially serious) error. Use it!

Step 4: Modify a Document

- Click the **Windows Information folder** within the My Documents folder to make it the active folder and to display its contents in the right pane. Change to the **Details view**.

- Double click the **About Windows Explorer** document to start Word and open the document. Do not be concerned if the size and/or position of the Microsoft Word window are different from ours. Read the document.

- If necessary, click inside the document window, then press **Ctrl+End** to move to the end of the document. Add the text shown in Figure 11d.

- Pull down the **File menu** and click **Save** to save the modified file (or click the **Save button** on the Standard toolbar). Pull down the **File menu** and click **Exit** to exit from Microsoft Word.

- Pull down the **View menu** and click the **Refresh command** (or press the **F5 key**) to update the contents of the right pane. The date and time associated with the About Windows Explorer document (on drive C) have been changed to indicate that the file has been modified.

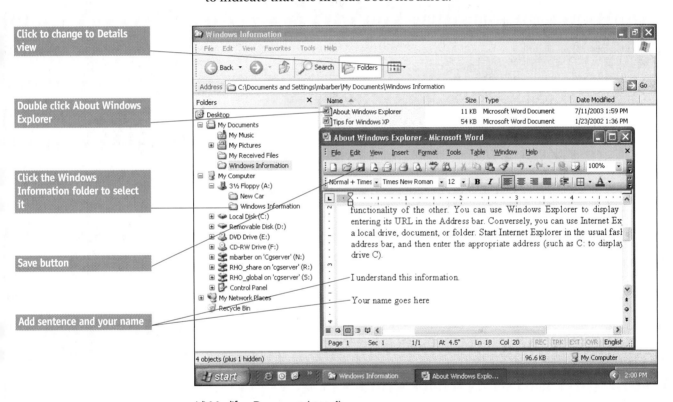

(d) Modify a Document (step 4)

FIGURE 11   Hands-on Exercise 3 (*continued*)

KEYBOARD SHORTCUTS

Most people begin with the mouse, but add keyboard shortcuts as they become more proficient. Ctrl+B, Ctrl+I, and Ctrl+U are shortcuts to boldface, italicize, and underline, respectively. Ctrl+X (the X is supposed to remind you of a pair of scissors), Ctrl+C, and Ctrl+V correspond to Cut, Copy, and Paste, respectively. Ctrl+Home and Ctrl+End move to the beginning or end of a document. These shortcuts are not unique to Microsoft Word, but are recognized in virtually every Windows application.

Step 5: **Copy (Back up) a File**

- Verify that the **Windows Information folder** (on drive C) is the active folder, as denoted by the open folder icon. Click and drag the icon for the **About Windows Explorer** document from the right pane to the **Windows Information folder** on **drive A** in the left pane.

- You will see the message in Figure 11e, indicating that the folder (on drive A) already contains a file called About Windows Explorer and asking whether you want to replace the existing file.

- Click **Yes** because you want to replace the previous version of the file on drive A with the updated version from the My Documents folder.

- You have just backed up a file by copying the About Windows Explorer document from a folder on drive C to the disk in drive A. In other words, you can use the floppy disk to restore the file to drive C should anything happen to it.

- Keep the floppy disk in a safe place, away from the computer.

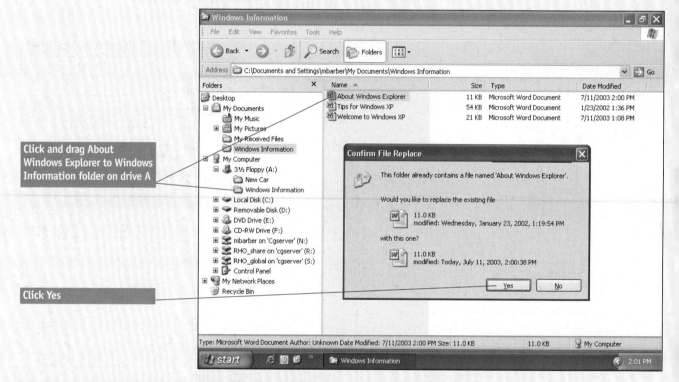

(e) Copy (Back up) a File (step 5)

FIGURE 11 Hands-on Exercise 3 (*continued*)

THE MY DOCUMENTS FOLDER

The My Documents folder is created by default with the installation of Windows XP. There is no requirement that you store your documents in this folder, but it is convenient, especially for beginners who may lack the confidence to create their own folders. The My Documents folder is also helpful in a laboratory environment where the network administrator may prevent you from modifying the desktop and/or from creating your own folders on drive C, in which case you will have to use the My Documents folder.

Step 6: **Delete a Folder**

■ Select (click) **Windows Information folder** within the My Documents folder in the left pane. Pull down the **File menu** and click **Delete** (or press the **Del key**).

■ You will see the dialog box in Figure 11f, asking whether you are sure you want to delete the folder and send its contents to the Recycle Bin, which enables you to restore the folder at a later date.

■ Click **Yes** to delete the folder. The folder disappears from drive C. Note that you have deleted the folder and its contents.

■ Now pretend that you do not want to delete the folder. Pull down the **Edit menu**. Click **Undo Delete**.

■ The deletion is cancelled and the Windows Information folder reappears in the left pane. If you do not see the folder, pull down the **View menu** and click the **Refresh command** (or press the **F5 key**).

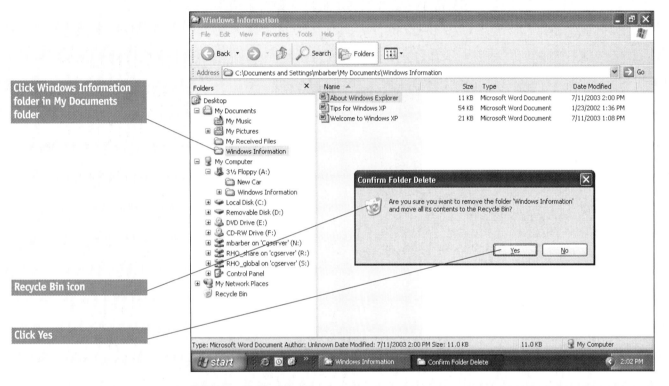

(f) Delete a Folder (step 6)

FIGURE 11   Hands-on Exercise 3 (*continued*)

CUSTOMIZE WINDOWS EXPLORER

Increase or decrease the size of the left pane within Windows Explorer by dragging the vertical line separating the left and right panes in the appropriate direction. You can also drag the right border of the various column headings (Name, Size, Type, and Modified) in the right pane to increase or decrease the width of the column and see more or less information in that column. And best of all, you can click any column heading to display the contents of the selected folder in sequence by that column. Click the heading a second time and the sequence changes from ascending to descending and vice versa.

Step 7: The Recycle Bin

- If necessary, select the **Windows Information folder** within the My Documents folder in the left pane. Select (click) the **About Windows Explorer** file in the right pane. Press the **Del key**, then click **Yes** when asked to delete the file.

- Click the **down arrow** in the vertical scroll bar in the left pane until you can click the icon for the **Recycle Bin**.

- The Recycle Bin contains all files that have been previously deleted from the local (hard) disks, and hence you will see a different number of files than those displayed in Figure 11g.

- Change to the **Details view**. Pull down the **View menu**, click (or point to) **Arrange Icons by**, then click **Date Deleted** to display the files in this sequence. Execute this command a second time (if necessary) so that the most recently deleted file appears at the top of the window.

- Right click the **About Windows Explorer** file to display the context-sensitive menu in Figure 11g, then click the **Restore command**.

- The file disappears from the Recycle bin because it has been returned to the Windows Information folder. You can open the Windows Information folder within the My Documents folder to confirm that the file has been restored.

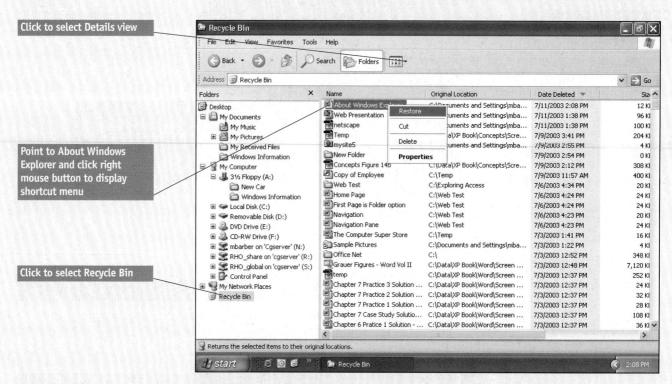

(g) The Recycle Bin (step 7)

FIGURE 11 Hands-on Exercise 3 (*continued*)

TWO WAYS TO RECOVER A FILE

The Undo command is present in Windows Explorer. Thus, you do not need to resort to the Recycle Bin to recover a deleted file provided you execute the Undo command immediately (within a few commands) after the Delete command was issued. Some operations cannot be undone (in which case the Undo command will be dimmed), but Undo is always worth a try.

Step 8: **The Group By Command**

- Select (click) the **Windows Information folder** on drive A. You should see the contents of this folder (three Word documents) in the right pane.

- Pull down the **View menu**, (click or) point to the **Arrange Icons by command**, then click the **Show in Groups command** from the cascaded menu.

- You see the same three files as previously, but they are displayed in groups according to the first letter in the filename. Click the **Date Modified** column, and the files are grouped according to the date they were last modified.

- The Show in Groups command functions as a toggle switch. Execute the command and the files are displayed in groups; execute the command a second time and the groups disappear.

- Select (click) the icon for **drive A** in the left pane to display the contents of drive A. You should see two folders and two files. Pull down the **View menu**, (click or) point to the **Arrange Icons by command**, and then click the **Show in Groups command** from the cascaded menu.

- Change to the **Details view**. Click the **Type column** to group the objects by folder and file type.

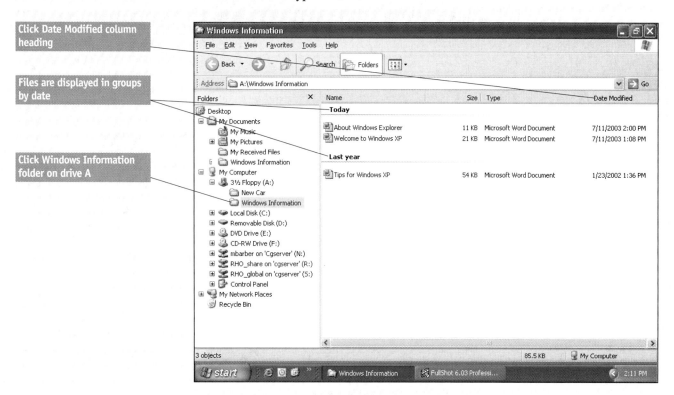

(h) The Group By Command (step 8)

FIGURE 11 Hands-on Exercise 3 (*continued*)

KEEP THE VIEW

Once you set the desired view in a folder, you may want to display every other folder according to those parameters. Pull down the Tools menu, click the Folder Options command, and click the View tab. Click the button to Apply to All folders, then click Yes when prompted to confirm. Click OK to close the Folder Options dialog box. The next time you open another folder, it will appear in the same view as the current folder.

Step 9: Complete the Exercise

- Prove to your instructor that you have completed the exercise correctly by capturing the screen on your monitor. Press the **Print Screen key**. Nothing appears to have happened, but the screen has been copied to the clipboard.

- Click the **Start button**, click the **All Programs command**, then start Microsoft Word and begin a new document. Enter the title of your document, followed by your name as shown in Figure 11i. Press the **Enter key** two or three times.

- Pull down the **Edit menu** and click the **Paste command** (or click the **Paste button** on the Standard toolbar) to copy the contents of the clipboard into the Word document.

- Print this document for your instructor. There is no need to save this document. Exit Word.

- Delete the **Windows Information folder** from the My Documents folder as a courtesy to the next student. Close Windows Explorer.

- Log off if you do not want to continue the next exercise at this time. (Click the **Start button**, click **Log Off**, then click **Log Off** a second time to end your session.)

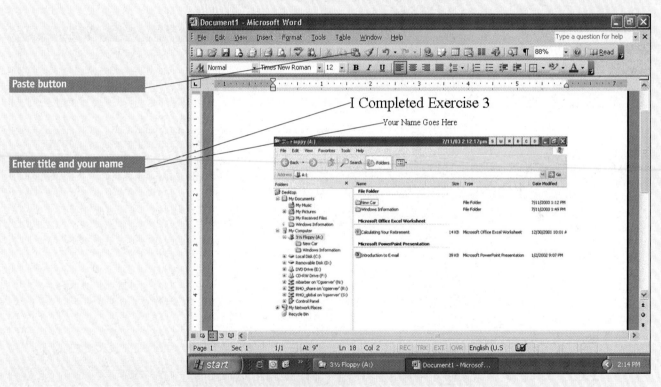

Paste button

Enter title and your name

(i) Complete the Exercise (step 9)

FIGURE 11 Hands-on Exercise 3 (*continued*)

SWITCHING USERS VERSUS LOGGING OFF

Windows XP gives you the choice of switching users or logging off. Switching users leaves all of your applications open, but it relinquishes control of the computer to another user. This lets you subsequently log back on (after the new user logs off) and take up exactly where you were. Logging off, on the other hand, closes all of your applications and ends the session, but it leaves the computer running at full power and available for someone else to log on.

You have learned the basic concepts of disk and file management, but there is so much more. Windows XP has something for everyone. It is easy and intuitive for the novice, but it also contains sophisticated tools for the more knowledgeable user. This section describes three powerful features to increase your productivity. Some or all of these features may be disabled in a school environment, but the information will stand you in good stead on your own computer.

The Control Panel

The *Control Panel* affects every aspect of your system. It determines the appearance of your desktop, and it controls the performance of your hardware. You can, for example, change the way your mouse behaves by switching the function of the left and right mouse buttons and/or by replacing the standard mouse pointers with animated icons that move across the screen. You will not have access to the Control Panel in a lab environment, but you will need it at home whenever you install new hardware or software. You should be careful about making changes, and you should understand the nature of the new settings before you accept any of the changes.

The Control Panel in Windows XP organizes its tools by category as shown in Figure 12. Point to any category and you see a Screen Tip that describes the specific tasks within that category. The Appearance and Themes category, for example, lets you select a screen saver or customize the Start menu and taskbar. You can also switch to the Classic view that displays every tool in a single screen, which is consistent with all previous versions of Windows.

The task pane provides access to the *Windows Update* function, which connects you to a Web site where you can download new device drivers and other updates to Windows XP. You can also configure your system to install these updates automatically as they become available. Some updates, especially those having to do with Internet security, are absolutely critical.

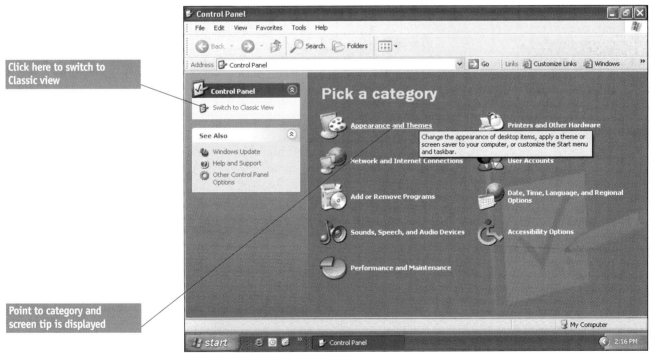

Click here to switch to Classic view

Point to category and screen tip is displayed

FIGURE 12   The Control Panel

Shortcuts

A *shortcut* is a link to any object on your computer, such as a program, file, folder, disk drive, or Web page. Shortcuts can appear anywhere, but are most often placed on the desktop or on the Start menu. The desktop in Figure 13 contains a variety of shortcuts, each of which contains a jump arrow to indicate a shortcut icon. Double click the shortcut to Election of Officers, for example, and you start Word and open this document. In similar fashion, you can double click the shortcut for a Web page (Exploring Windows Series), folder, or disk drive (drive A) to open the object and display its contents.

Creating a shortcut is a two-step process. First, you use Windows Explorer to locate the object such as a file, folder, or disk drive. Then you select the object, use the right mouse button to drag the object to the desktop, and then click the Create Shortcut command from the context-sensitive menu. A shortcut icon will appear on the desktop with the phrase "shortcut to" as part of the name. You can create as many shortcuts as you like, and you can place them anywhere on the desktop or in individual folders. You can also right click a shortcut icon after it has been created to change its name. Deleting the icon deletes the shortcut and not the object.

Windows XP also provides a set of predefined shortcuts through a series of desktop icons that are shown at the left border of the desktop in Figure 13. Double click the My Computer icon, for example, and you open the My Computer folder. These desktop icons were displayed by default in earlier versions of Windows, but not in Windows XP. They were added through the Control Panel as you will see in our next exercise.

Additional shortcuts are found in the *Quick Launch toolbar* that appears to the right of the Start button. Click any icon and you open the indicated program. And finally, Windows XP will automatically add to the Start menu shortcuts to your most frequently used programs. Desktop shortcuts are a powerful technique that will increase your productivity by taking you directly to a specified document or other object.

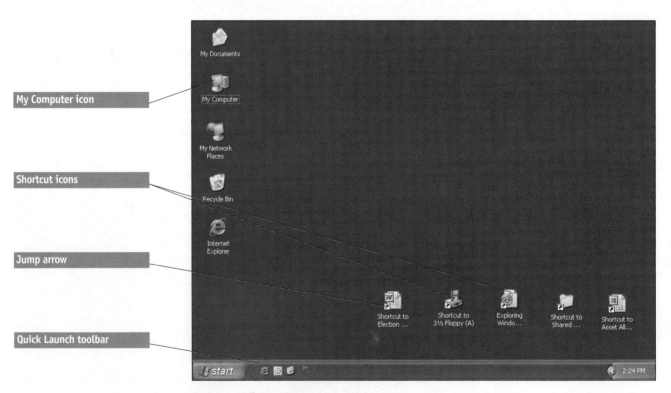

FIGURE 13 Desktop with Shortcuts

The Search Companion

Sooner or later you will create a file, and then forget where (in which folder) you saved it. Or you may create a document and forget its name, but remember a key word or phrase in the document. Or you may want to locate all files of a certain file type—for example, all of the sound files on your system. The **Search Companion** can help you to solve each of these problems and is illustrated in Figure 14.

The Search Companion is accessed from within any folder by clicking the Search button on the Standard Buttons toolbar to open the search pane at the left of the folder. You are presented with an initial search menu (not shown in Figure 14) that asks what you want to search for. You can search your local machine for media files (pictures, music, or video), documents (such as spreadsheets or Word documents), or any file or folder. You can also search the Help and Support Center or the Internet.

Once you choose the type of information, you are presented with a secondary search pane as shown in Figure 14. You can search according to a variety of criteria, each of which will help to narrow the search. In this example we are looking for any document on drive C that has "Windows" as part of its filename and further, contains the name "Maryann" somewhere within the document. The search is case sensitive. This example illustrates two important capabilities, namely that you can search on the document name (or part of its name) and/or its content.

Additional criteria can be entered by expanding the chevrons for date and size. You can, for example, restrict your search to all documents that were modified within the last week, the past month, or the last year. You can also restrict your search to documents of a certain size. Click the Search button after all of the criteria have been specified to initiate the search. The results of the search (the documents that satisfy the search criteria) are displayed in the right pane. You can refine the search if it is unsuccessful and/or you can open any document in which you are interested. The Search Companion also has an indexing service to make subsequent searches faster.

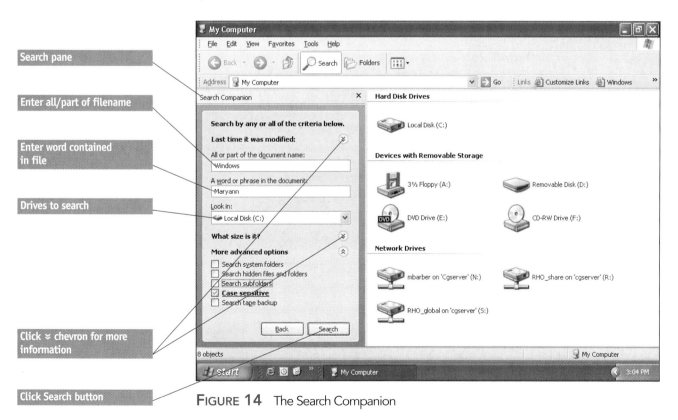

FIGURE 14 The Search Companion

4 Increasing Productivity

Objective   To create and use shortcuts; to locate documents using the Search Companion; to customize your system using the Control Panel; to obtain a passport account. The exercise requires an Internet connection. Use Figure 15 as a guide.

Step 1:   **Display the Desktop Icons**

- Log on to Windows XP. Point to a blank area on the desktop, click the **right mouse button** to display a context-sensitive menu, then click the **Properties command** to open the Display Properties dialog box in Figure 15a.

- Click the **Desktop tab** and then click the **Customize Desktop button** to display the Desktop Items dialog box.

- Check the boxes to display all four desktop icons. Click **OK** to accept these settings and close the dialog box, then click **OK** a second time to close the Display Properties dialog box.

- The desktop icons should appear on the left side of your desktop. Double click any icon to execute the indicated program or open the associated folder.

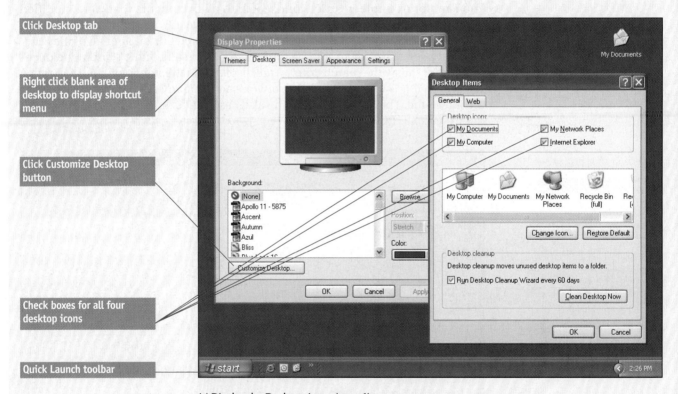

Click Desktop tab

Right click blank area of desktop to display shortcut menu

Click Customize Desktop button

Check boxes for all four desktop icons

Quick Launch toolbar

(a) Display the Desktop Icons (step 1)

FIGURE 15   Hands-on Exercise 4

THE QUICK LAUNCH TOOLBAR

The Quick Launch toolbar is a customizable toolbar that executes a program or displays the desktop with a single click. Right click a blank area of the taskbar, point to (or click) the Toolbars command, then check the Quick Launch toolbar to toggle its display on or off.

Step 2: Create a Web Shortcut

- Start Internet Explorer. You can double click the newly created icon at the left of the desktop, or you can single click its icon in the Quick Launch toolbar. Click the **Restore button** so that Internet Explorer is not maximized, that is, so that you can see a portion of the desktop.

- Click in the Address bar and enter the address **www.microsoft.com/ windowsxp** to display the home page of Windows XP. Now that you see the page, you can create a shortcut to that page.

- Click the **Internet Explorer icon** in the Address bar to select the entire address, point to the Internet Explorer icon, then click and drag the icon to the desktop (you will see a jump arrow as you drag the text). Release the mouse to create the shortcut in Figure 15b.

- Prove to yourself that the shortcut works. Close Internet Explorer, and then double click the shortcut you created. Internet Explorer will open, and you should see the desired Web page. Close (or minimize) Internet Explorer since you do not need it for the remainder of the exercise.

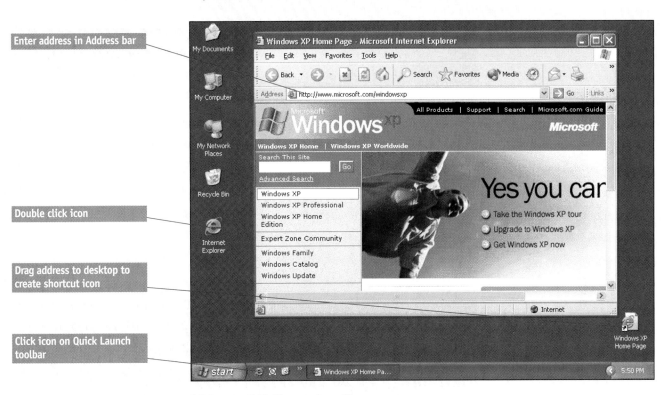

(b) Create a Web Shortcut (step 2)

FIGURE 15 Hands-on Exercise 4 (*continued*)

WORKING WITH SHORTCUTS

You can work with a shortcut icon just as you can with any other icon. To move a shortcut, drag its icon to a different location on the desktop. To rename a shortcut, right click its icon, click the Rename command, type the new name, then press the enter key. To delete a shortcut, right click its icon, click the Delete command, and click Yes in response to the confirming prompt. Deleting a shortcut deletes just the shortcut and not the object to which the shortcut refers.

Step 3: Create Additional Shortcuts

- Double click the **My Computer icon** to open this folder. Place the floppy disk from hands-on exercise 3 into the floppy drive. Double click the icon for **drive A** to display the contents of the floppy disk as shown in Figure 15c.

- The contents of the Address bar have changed to A:\ to indicate the contents of the floppy disk. You should see two folders and two files.

- Move and size the window so that you see a portion of the desktop. Right click and drag the icon for the **Windows Information folder** to the desktop, then release the mouse. Click the **Create Shortcuts Here command** to create the shortcut.

- Look for the jump arrow to be sure you have created a shortcut (as opposed to moving or copying the folder). If you made a mistake, right click a blank area of the desktop, then click the **Undo command** to reverse the unintended move or copy operation.

- Right click and drag the icon for the **PowerPoint presentation** to the desktop, release the mouse, and then click the **Create Shortcuts Here command**.

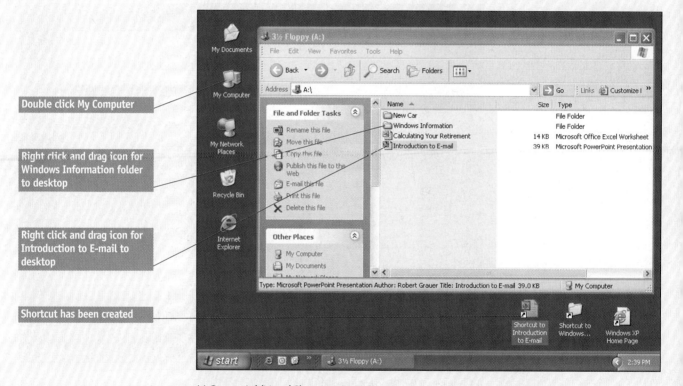

(c) Create Additional Shortcuts (step 3)

FIGURE 15   Hands-on Exercise 4 (*continued*)

THE ARRANGE ICONS COMMAND

The most basic way to arrange the icons on your desktop is to click and drag an icon from one place to another. It may be convenient, however, to have Windows arrange the icons for you. Right click a blank area of the desktop, click (or point to) the Arrange Icons by command, then click Auto Arrange. All existing shortcuts, as well as any new shortcuts, will be automatically aligned along the left edge of the desktop. Execute the Auto Arrange command a second time to cancel the command, and enable yourself to manually arrange the icons.

Step 4: Search for a Document

- Maximize the My Computer window. Click the **Search button** on the Standard Buttons toolbar to display the Search pane. The button functions as a toggle switch. Click the button and the Search pane appears. Click the button a second time and the task pane replaces the Search Companion.

- The initial screen (not shown in Figure 15d) in the Search Companion asks what you are searching for. Click **Documents (word processing, spreadsheet, etc.)**.

- You may be prompted to enter when the document was last modified. Click the option button that says **Don't Remember**, then click **Use advanced search options**. You should see the screen in Figure 15d.

- Enter the indicated search criteria. You do not know the document name and thus you leave this text box blank. The other criteria indicate that you are looking for any document that contains "interest rate" that is located on drive A, or in any subfolder on drive A.

- Click the **Search button** to initiate the search. You will see a Search dialog box to indicate the progress of the search, after which you will see the relevant documents.

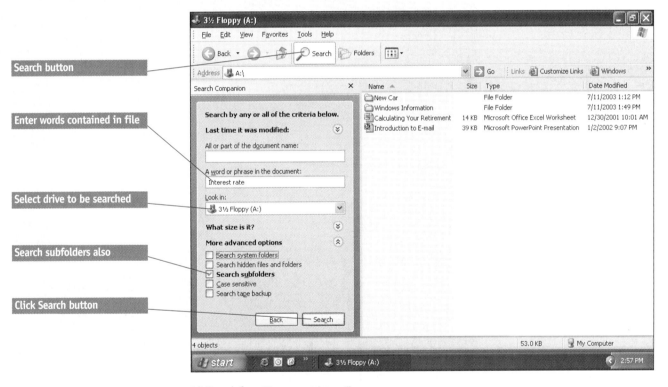

(d) Search for a Document (step 4)

FIGURE 15   Hands-on Exercise 4 (*continued*)

YOU DON'T NEED THE COMPLETE FILENAME

You can enter only a portion of the filename, and the Search Companion will still find the file(s). If, for example, you're searching for the file "Marketing Homework," you can enter the first several letters such as "Marketing" and Windows will return all files whose name begins with the letters you've entered—for example, "Marketing Homework" and "Marketing Term Paper."

Step 5: Search Results

- The search should return two files that satisfy the search criteria as shown in Figure 15e. Click the **Views button** and select **Tiles view** if you want to match our figure. If you do not see the same files, it is for one of two reasons:
  - ❏ You did not specify the correct search criteria. Click the **Back button** and reenter the search parameters as described in step 4. Repeat the search.
  - ❏ Your floppy disk is different from ours. Be sure to use the floppy disk as it existed at the end of the previous hands-on exercise.

- Click the **Restore button** so that you again see a portion of the desktop. Right click and drag the **Calculating Your Retirement** workbook to the desktop to create a shortcut on the desktop.

- Close the Search Results window, close the My Documents window, then double click the newly created shortcut to open the workbook.

- Retirement is a long way off, but you may want to experiment with our worksheet. It is never too early to start saving.

- Exit Excel when you are finished.

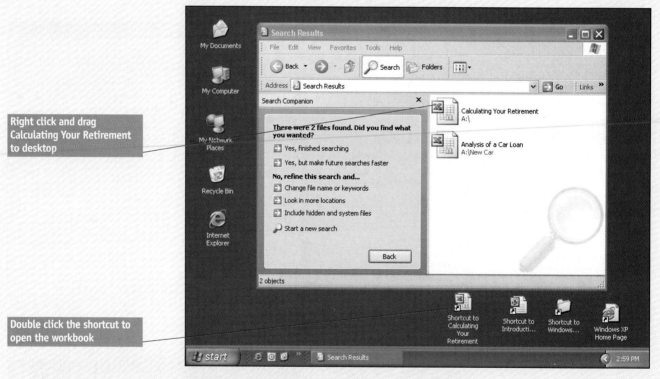

(e) Search Results (step 5)

FIGURE 15   Hands-on Exercise 4 (continued)

SHORTCUT WIZARD

Shortcuts can be created in many ways, including the use of a wizard. Right click a blank area of the desktop, click (or point) to the New command, then choose Shortcut to start the wizard. Enter the Web address in the indicated text box (or click the Browse button to locate a local file). Click Next, then enter the name for the shortcut as it is to appear on the desktop. Click the Finish button to exit the wizard. The new shortcut should appear on the desktop.

Step 6: **Open the Control Panel Folder**

- Click the **Start button**, then click **Control Panel** to open the Control Panel folder. Click the command to **Switch to Classic View** that appears in the task pane to display the individual icons as shown in Figure 15f. Maximize the window.

- Double click the **Taskbar and Start Menu icon** to display the associated dialog box. Click the **Taskbar tab**, then check the box to **Auto-hide the taskbar.** Your other settings should match those in Figure 15f. Click **OK** to accept the settings and close the dialog box.

- The taskbar (temporarily) disappears from your desktop. Now point to the bottom edge of the desktop, and the taskbar reappears. The advantage of hiding the taskbar in this way is that you have the maximum amount of room in which to work; that is, you see the taskbar only when you want to.

- Double click the **Fonts folder** to open this folder and display the fonts that are installed on your computer. Change to the **Details view**.

- Double click the icon of any font other than the standard fonts (Arial, Times New Roman, and Courier New) to open a new window that displays the font. Click the **Print button**. Close the Font window.

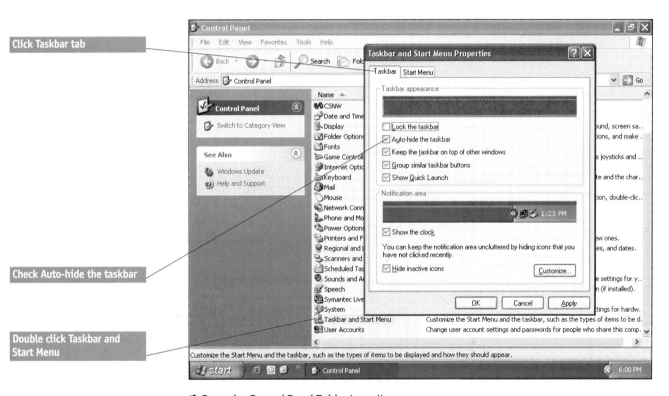

(f) Open the Control Panel Folder (step 6)

FIGURE 15   Hands-on Exercise 4 (*continued*)

MODIFY THE START MENU

Click and drag a shortcut icon to the Start button to place the shortcut on the Start menu. It does not appear that anything has happened, but the shortcut will appear at the top of the Start menu. Click the Start button to display the Start menu, then press the Esc key to exit the menu without executing a command. You can delete any item from the menu by right clicking the item and clicking the Unpin from the Start menu command.

Step 7: **Obtain a .NET Passport**

- Click the **Back button** to return to the Control Panel, then double click the **User Accounts icon** in the Control Panel folder. Maximize the User Accounts window so that it takes the entire desktop.

- Click the icon corresponding to the account that is currently logged to display a screen similar to Figure 15g. Click the command to **Set up my account to use a .NET passport**. You will see the first step in the Passport Wizard.

- Click the link to **View the privacy statement**. This starts Internet Explorer and goes to the .NET Passport site on the Web. Print the privacy agreement. It runs nine pages, but it contains a lot of useful information.

- Close Internet Explorer after you have printed the agreement. You are back in the Passport Wizard. Click **Next** to continue.

- Follow the instructions on the next several screens. You will be asked to enter your e-mail address and to supply a password. Click **Finish** when you have reached the last screen.

- You will receive an e-mail message after you have registered successfully. You will need your passport in our next exercise when we explore Windows Messenger and the associated instant messaging service.

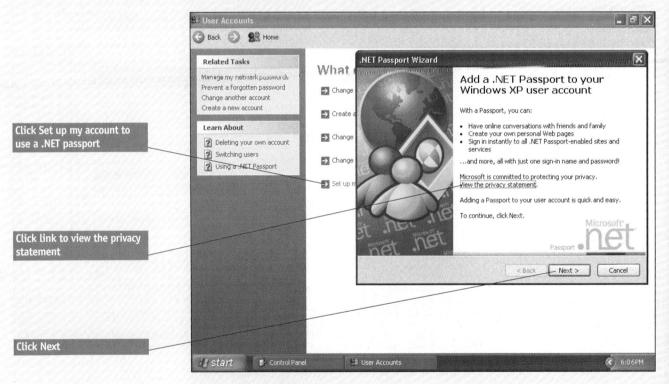

(g) Obtain a .NET Passport (step 7)

FIGURE 15 Hands-on Exercise 4 (*continued*)

UPDATING YOUR PASSPORT

You can modify the information in your passport profile at any time. Open the Control Panel, click User Accounts, select your account, then click the command to Change Your .NET passport. You can change your password, change the question that will remind you about your password should you forget it, and/or change the information that you authorize the passport service to share with others.

Step 8: **Windows Update**

- Close the User Accounts window to return to the Control Panel folder. Click the link to **Windows Update** to display a screen similar to Figure 15h.

- Click the command to **Scan for updates**. (This command is not visible in our figure.) This command will take several seconds as Windows determines which (if any) updates it recommends. Our system indicates that there are no critical updates but that additional updates are available.

- Click the link(s) to review the available updates. You do not have to install the vast majority of available updates. It is essential, however, that you install any updates deemed critical. One critical update appeared shortly after the release of Windows XP and closed a hole in the operating system that enabled hackers to break into some XP machines.

- Click the link to **View installation history** to see which updates were previously installed. Print this page for your instructor.

- Close the Update window. Log off the computer if you do not want to continue with the next exercise at this time.

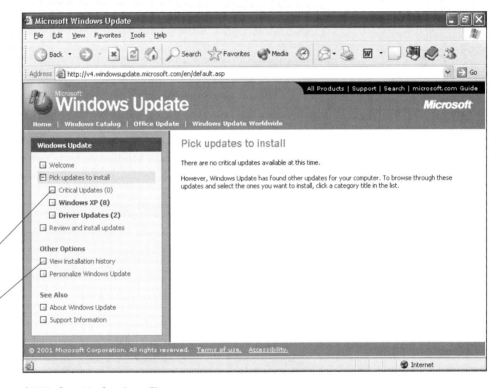

(h) Windows Update (step 8)

FIGURE 15 Hands-on Exercise 4 (*continued*)

THE SHOW DESKTOP BUTTON

The Show Desktop button or command minimizes every open window and returns you immediately to the desktop. You can get to this command in different ways, most easily by clicking the Show Desktop icon on the Quick Launch toolbar. The button functions as a toggle switch. Click it once and all windows are minimized. Click it a second time and the open windows are restored to their position on the desktop.

FUN WITH WINDOWS XP

The "XP" in Windows XP is for the experience that Microsoft promises individuals who adopt its operating system. Windows XP makes it easy to enjoy music and video, work with **digital photographs**, and chat with your friends. This section describes these capabilities and then moves to a hands-on exercise in which you practice at the computer. All of the features are available on your own machine, but some may be disabled in a laboratory setting. It's not that your professor does not want you to have fun, but listening to music or engaging in instant messaging with your friends is not practical in a school environment. Nevertheless, the hands-on exercise that follows enables you to practice your skills in disk and file management as you work with multiple files and folders.

Windows Media Player

The **Windows Media Player** combines the functions of a radio, a CD, or DVD player, and an information database into a single program. It lets you listen to radio stations anywhere in the world, play a CD, or watch a DVD movie (provided you have the necessary hardware). You can copy selections from a CD to your computer, organize your music by artist and album, and then create a customized **playlist** to play the music in a specified order. The playlist may include as many songs from as many albums as you like and is limited only by the size of your storage device. The Media Player will also search the Web for audio or video files and play clips from a favorite movie.

The buttons at the left of the Media Player enable you to switch from one function to the next. The Radio Tuner button is active in Figure 16, and the BBC station is selected. Think of that—you are able to listen to radio stations from around the world with the click of a button. The Media Guide button connects you to the home page of the Windows Media Web site, where you can search the Web for media files and/or play movie clips from your favorite movies.

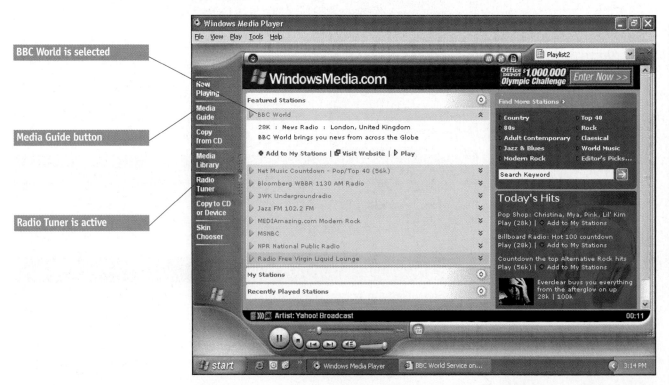

BBC World is selected

Media Guide button

Radio Tuner is active

FIGURE 16 Windows Media Player

Digital Photography

Windows XP helps you to organize your pictures and share them with others. The best place to store photographs is in the My Pictures folder or in a subfolder within this folder as shown in Figure 17. The complete path to the folder appears in the Address bar and is best read from right to left. Thus, you are looking at pictures in the Romance Folder, which is in the My Pictures folder, which in turn is stored in a My Documents folder. Remember that each user has his or her unique My Documents folder, so the path must be further qualified. Hence, you are looking at the My Documents folder, within a folder for Jessica (one of several users), within the Documents and Settings folder on drive C. The latter folder maintains the settings for all of the users that are registered on this system.

The pictures in Figure 17 are shown in the ***Thumbnails view***, which displays a miniature image of each picture in the right pane. (Other views are also available and are accessed from the View menu or Views button.) The Picture Tasks area in the upper right lists the functions that are unique to photographs. You can view the pictures as a slide show, which is the equivalent of a PowerPoint presentation without having to create the presentation. You can print any picture, use it as the background on your desktop, or copy multiple pictures to a CD, provided you have the necessary hardware. You can also order prints online. You choose the company; select print sizes and quantities, supply the billing and shipping information, and your photographs are sent to you.

One photo is selected (BenWendy) in Figure 17, and the associated details are shown in the Details area of the task pane. The picture is stored as a JPG file, a common format for photographs. It was created on January 21, 2002.

The File and Folder Tasks area is collapsed in our figure, but you can expand the area to gain access to the normal file operations (move, copy, and delete). You can also e-mail the photograph from this panel. Remember, too, that you can click the Folders button on the Standard Buttons toolbar to switch to the hierarchical view of your system, which is better suited to disk and file management.

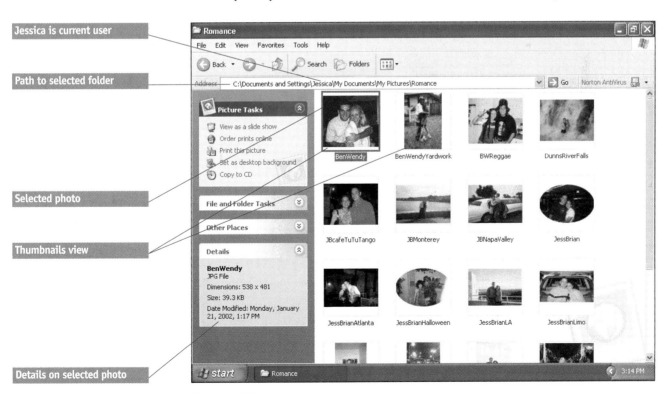

FIGURE 17 Working with Pictures

Windows Messenger

Windows Messenger is an instant messaging system in which you chat with friends and colleagues over the Internet. (It is based on the same technology as the "buddies list" that was made popular by America Online.) You need an Internet connection, a list of contacts, and a **Microsoft passport** that is based on your e-mail address. The passport is a free Microsoft service that enables you to access any passport-enabled Internet site with a single user name and associated password. (Step 7 in the previous hands-on exercise described how to obtain a passport.)

You can initiate a conversation at any time by monitoring the contacts list to see who is online and starting a chat session. Up to four people can participate in the same conversation. It is easy, fun, and addictive. You know the instant someone signs on, and you can begin chatting immediately. The bad news, however, is that it is all too easy to chat incessantly when you have real work to do. Hence you may want to change your status to indicate that you are busy and unable to participate in a conversation.

Figure 18 displays a conversation between Maryann and Bob. The session began when Maryann viewed her contact list, noticed that Bob was online, and started a conversation. Each person enters his or her message at the bottom of the conversation window, and then clicks the Send button. Additional messages can be sent without waiting for a response. Emoticons can be added to any message for effect. Note, too, the references to the file transfer that appear within the conversation, which are the result of Maryann clicking the command to send a file or photo, then attaching the desired file.

Windows Messenger is more than just a vehicle for chatting. If you have speakers and a microphone, you can place phone calls from your computer without paying a long distance charge. The most intriguing feature, however, is the ability to ask for remote assistance, whereby you can invite one of your contacts to view your desktop as you are working in order to ask for help. It is as if your friend were in the room looking over your shoulder. He or she will see everything that you do and can respond immediately with suggestions.

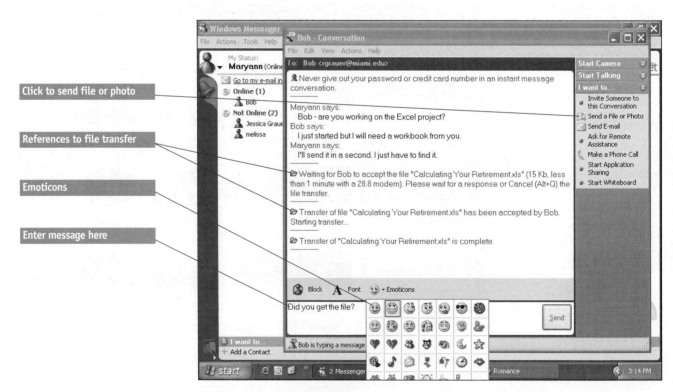

FIGURE 18   Windows Messenger

5 Fun with Windows XP

Objective To use Windows Media Player, work with photographs, and experiment with Windows Messenger. Check with your professor regarding the availability of the resources required for this exercise. Use Figure 19.

Step 1: **Open the Shared Music Folder**

■ Start Windows Explorer. Click the **Folders button** to display the tree structure. You need to locate some music to demonstrate the Media Player.

■ The typical XP installation includes some files within the Shared Documents folder. Expand the My Computer folder to show the **Shared Documents folder**, expand the **Shared Music folder**, and then open the **Sample Music folder** as shown in Figure 19a.

■ Point to any file (it does not matter if you have a different selection of music) to display the ScreenTip describing the music. Double click the file to start the Media Player and play the selected music.

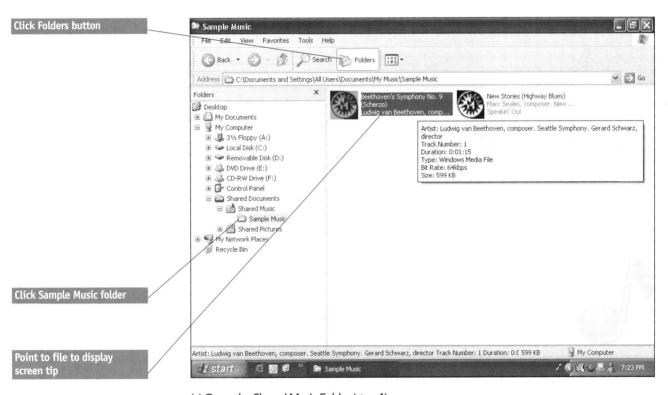

(a) Open the Shared Music Folder (step 1)

FIGURE 19 Hands-on Exercise 5

SHARED FOLDERS VERSUS PERSONAL FOLDERS

Windows XP automatically creates a unique My Documents folder for every user, which in turn contains a unique My Pictures folder and My Music folder within the My Documents folder. These folders are private and cannot be accessed by other users. Windows also provides a Shared Documents folder that is accessible to every user on a system.

Step 2: Listen to the Music

- You should hear the music when the Windows Media Player opens in its own window as shown in Figure 19b. The controls at the bottom of the window are similar to those on any CD player.
  - ❏ You can click the **Pause button**, then click the **Play button** to restart the music at that point.
  - ❏ You can click the **Stop button** to stop playing altogether.
  - ❏ You can also drag the slider to begin playing at a different place.

- You can also adjust the volume as shown in Figure 19b. Double click the **Volume Control icon** in the notification area at the right of the taskbar to display the Volume Control dialog box. Close this window.

- Click the **Radio Tuner button** at the side of the Media Player window. The system pauses as it tunes into the available radio stations.

- Select a radio station (e.g., **BBC World**) when you see the list of available stations, then click the **Play button** after you choose a station.

- You will see a message at the bottom of the window indicating that your computer is connecting to the media, after which you will hear the radio station.

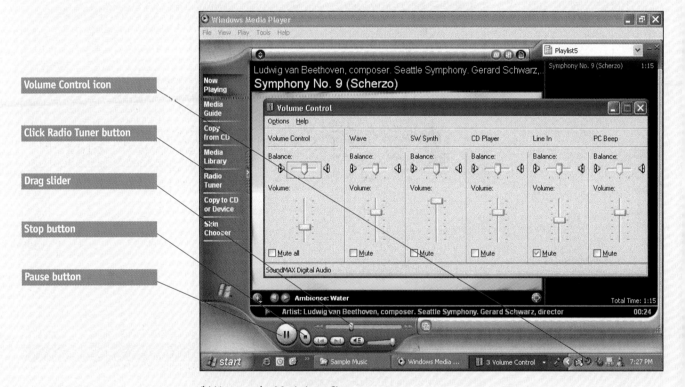

(b) Listen to the Music (step 2)

FIGURE 19   Hands-on Exercise 5 (continued)

OTHER MEDIA PLAYERS

If you double click a music (MP3) file, and a program other than Windows Media starts to play, it is because your system has another media player as its default program. You can still use the Windows Media Player, but you will have to start the program explicitly from the Start menu. Once the Media Player is open, pull down the File menu and click the Open command, then select the music file you want to play.

Step 3: **Create a Playlist**

■ Click the **Media Library button** at the side of the Media player to display the media files that are currently on your computer.
  ❑ The left pane displays a tree structure of your media library. Thus, you click the plus or minus sign to collapse or expand the indicated folder.
  ❑ The right pane displays the contents of the selected object (the My Music playlist) in Figure 19c.

■ Do not be concerned if your media library is different from ours. Click the **New playlist button**, enter **My Music** as the name of the new list, and click **OK**.

■ Click the newly created playlist in the left pane to display its contents in the left pane. The playlist is currently empty.

■ Start **Windows Explorer**. Open the **My Music Folder** within the My Documents folder. If necessary, click the **Restore button** to move and size Windows Explorer so that you can copy documents to the Media library.

■ Click and drag one or more selections from the My Music folder to the right pane of the Media library to create the playlist. Close Windows Explorer.

■ Click the **down arrow** in the list box at the upper right of the Media Gallery and select the My Music playlist to play the songs you have selected.

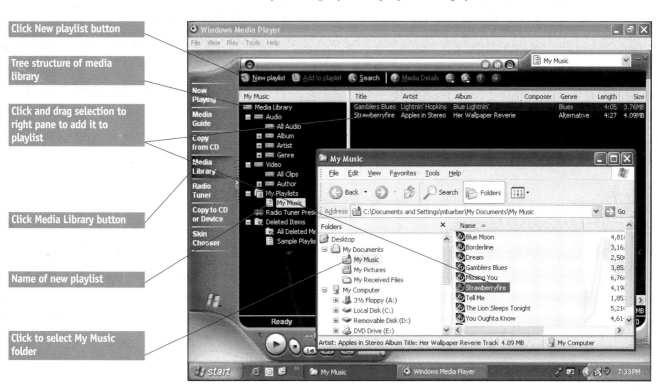

(c) Create a Playlist (step 3)

FIGURE 19 Hands-on Exercise 5 (*continued*)

THE MEDIA GUIDE

Click the Media Guide button at the left of the Media Player to display the home page of the Windows Media Site. You can also get there by starting Internet Explorer and entering windowsmedia.com in the Address bar. Either way, you will be connected to the Internet and can search the Web for media files and/or play clips from your favorite movie.

Step 4: **Create a Pictures Folder**

- You can use your own pictures, or if you don't have any, you can use the sample pictures provided with Windows XP. Start (or maximize) Windows Explorer. Open the **My Pictures folder** within the **My Documents folder**.

- Do not be concerned if the content of your folder is different from ours. Our folder already contains various subfolders with different types of pictures in each folder.

- Click the **Views button** and change to the **Thumbnails view**. This view is especially useful when viewing folders that contain photographs because (up to four) images are displayed on the folder icon.

- Right click anywhere in the right pane to display a context-sensitive menu as shown in Figure 19d. Click **New**, and then click **Folder** as the type of object to create.

- The icon for a new folder will appear with the name of the folder (New Folder) highlighted. Enter a more appropriate name (we chose **Romance** because our pictures are those of a happy couple), and press **Enter**.

- Copy your pictures from another folder, a CD, or floppy disk to the newly created folder.

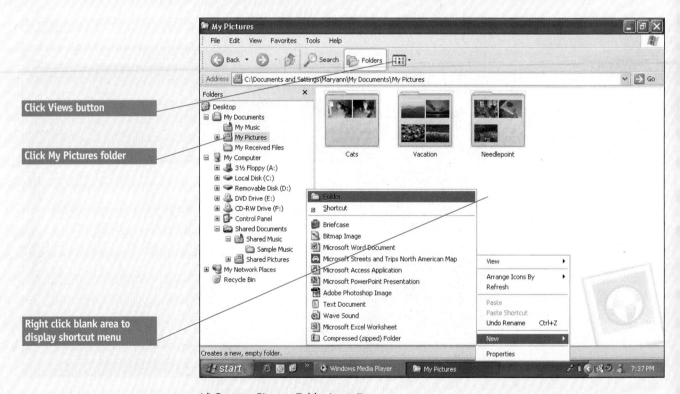

Click Views button

Click My Pictures folder

Right click blank area to display shortcut menu

(d) Create a Pictures Folder (step 4)

FIGURE 19 Hands-on Exercise 5 (*continued*)

DESIGN GALLERY LIVE

The Microsoft Design Gallery is an excellent source of photographs and other media. Start Internet Explorer and go to the Design Gallery at dgl.microsoft.com. Enter the desired topic in the Search for text box, indicate that you want to search everywhere, and specify that the results should be photos. Download one or more of the photos that are returned by the search and use those pictures to complete this exercise.

Step 5: Display Your Pictures

■ Double click the newly created folder to display its contents. Click the **Folders button** to display the Windows Explorer task pane, as opposed to the hierarchy structure. Click the **Views button** and change to the **Filmstrip view** as shown in Figure 19e.

■ Click the **Next Image** or (**Previous Image**) **button** to move from one picture to the next within the folder. If necessary, click the buttons to rotate pictures clockwise or counterclockwise so that the pictures are displayed properly within the window.

■ Click the command to **View as a slide show**, then display your pictures one at a time on your monitor. This is a very easy way to enjoy your photographs. Press the **Esc key** to stop.

■ Choose any picture, then click the command to **Print this picture** that appears in the left pane. Submit this picture to your instructor.

■ Choose a different picture and then click the command to **Set as desktop background**. Minimize Windows Explorer.

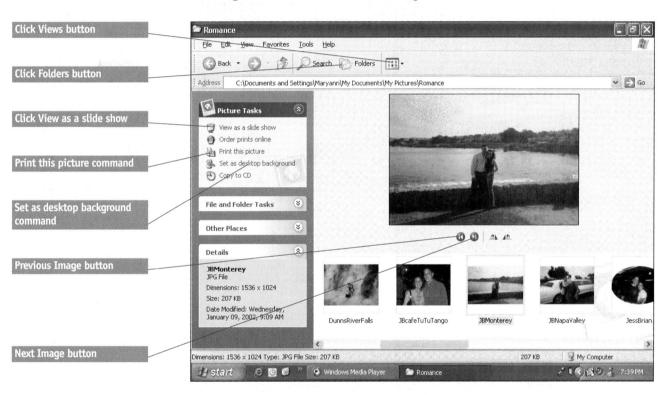

(e) Display Your Pictures (step 5)

FIGURE 19   Hands-on Exercise 5 (*continued*)

CHANGE THE VIEW

Click the down arrow next to the Views button on the Standard toolbar to change the way files are displayed within a folder. The Details view provides the most information and includes the filename, file type, file size, and the date that the file was created or last modified. (Additional attributes are also possible.) Other views are more visual. The Thumbnails view displays a miniature image of the file and is best used with clip art, photographs, or presentations. The Filmstrip view is used with photographs only.

Step 6: Customize the Desktop

- Your desktop should once again be visible, depending on which (if any) applications are open. If you do not see the desktop, right click a blank area of the taskbar, then click the **Show Desktop command**.

- You should see the picture you selected earlier as the background for your desktop. The picture is attractive (you chose it), but it may be distracting.

- To remove the picture, **right click** the background of the desktop and click the **Properties command** to display the Display Properties dialog box in Figure 19f.

- Click the **Desktop tab**, then click **None** in the Background list box. Click **OK** to accept this setting and close the dialog box. The picture disappears.

- Regardless of whether you keep the background, you can use your pictures as a screen saver. Redisplay the Display Properties dialog box. Click the **Screen Saver tab** in the Display Properties box, then choose **My Picture Slideshow** from the screen saver list box.

- Wait a few seconds and the picture within the dialog box will change, just as it will on your desktop. Click **OK** to accept the screen saver and close the Display Properties dialog box.

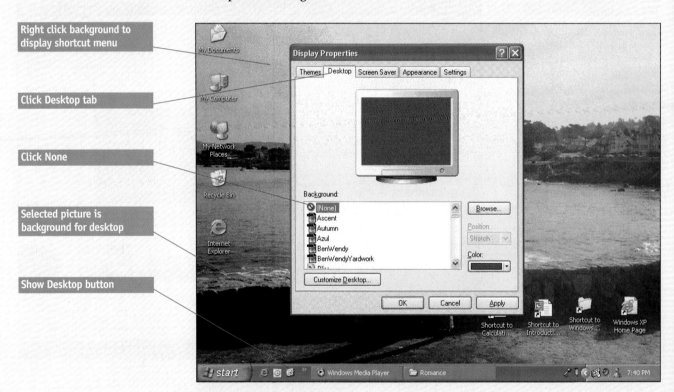

(f) Customize the Desktop (step 6)

FIGURE 19   Hands-on Exercise 5 (continued)

CHANGE THE RESOLUTION

The resolution of a monitor refers to the number of pixels (picture elements or dots) that are displayed at one time. The higher the resolution, the more pixels are displayed, and hence you see more of a document at one time. You can change the resolution at any time. Right click the desktop, click the Properties command to show the Display Properties dialog box, then click the Settings tab. Drag the slider bar to the new resolution, then click OK.

Step 7: Start Windows Messenger

- You need a passport to use Windows Messenger. Double click the **Windows Messenger icon** in the notification area of the taskbar to sign in.

- Maximize the Messenger window. You will see a list of your existing contacts with an indication of whether they are online.

- Add one or more contacts. Pull down the **Tools menu**, click the command to **Add a Contact**, then follow the onscreen instructions. (The contact does not have to have Windows XP to use instant messaging.)

- Double click any contact that is online to initiate a conversation and open a conversation window as shown in Figure 19g.

- Type a message at the bottom of the conversation window, then click the **Send button** to send the message. The text of your message will appear immediately on your contact's screen. Your friend's messages will appear on your screen.

- Continue the conversation by entering additional text. You can press the **Enter key** (instead of clicking the **Send button**) to send the message. You can also use **Shift + enter** to create a line break in your text.

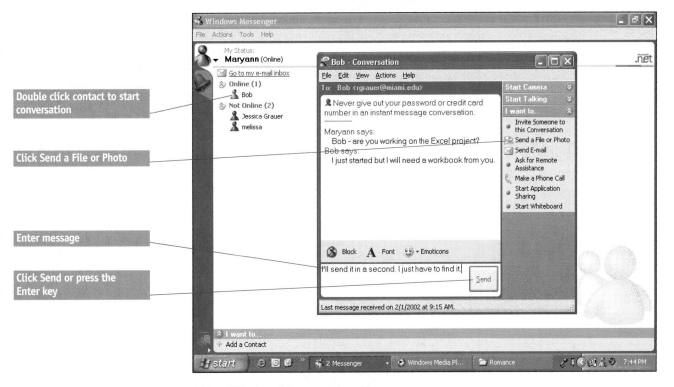

(g) Start Windows Messenger (step 7)

FIGURE 19   Hands-on Exercise 5 (*continued*)

CHANGE YOUR STATUS

Anyone on your contact list knows immediately when you log on; thus, the larger your contact list, the more likely you are to be engaged in idle chitchat when you have real work to do. You can avoid unwanted conversations without being rude by changing your status. Click the down arrow next to your name in the Messenger window and choose a different icon. You can appear offline or simply indicate that you are busy. Either way you will be more likely to get your work done.

Step 8: Attach a File

■ Click the command to **Send a File or Photo**, which displays the Send a File dialog box in Figure 19h. It does not matter which file you choose, since the purpose of this step is to demonstrate the file transfer capability.

■ A series of three file transfer messages will appear on your screen. Windows Messenger waits for your friend to accept the file transfer, then it indicates the transfer has begun, and finally, that the transfer was successful.

■ Click the command to **Invite someone to this conversation** if you have another contact online. You will see a second dialog box in which you select the contact.

■ There are now three people in the conversation. (Up to four people can participate in one conversation.) Your friends' responses will appear on your screen as soon as they are entered.

■ Send your goodbye to end the conversation, then close the conversation window to end the chat session. You are still online and can participate in future conversations.

■ Close Windows Messenger. You will be notified if anyone wants to contact you.

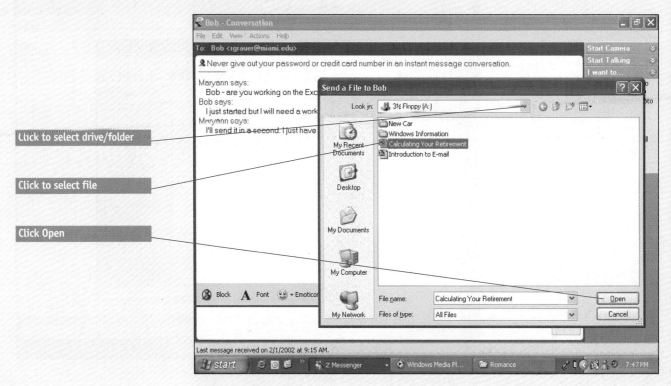

(h) Attach a File (step 8)

FIGURE 19   Hands-on Exercise 5 (*continued*)

E-MAIL VERSUS INSTANT MESSAGING

E-mail and instant messaging are both Internet communication services, but there are significant differences. E-mail does not require both participants to be online at the same time. E-mail messages are also permanent and do not disappear when you exit your e-mail program. Instant messaging, however, requires both participants to be online. Its conversations are not permanent and disappear when you end the session.

Step 9: Ask for Assistance

■ Your contacts do not require Windows XP to converse with you using Windows Messenger. Windows XP is required, however, to use the remote assistance feature.

■ Click the **Start button**, then click the **Help and Support command** to display the home page of the Help and Support Center. Click the **Support button**, then click the command to **Ask a friend to help**.

■ A Remote Assistance screen will open in the right pane. Click the command to **Invite someone to help**, which will display your contact list as shown in Figure 19i. You can choose any contact who is online, or you can enter the e-mail address of someone else.

■ You will see a dialog box indicating that an invitation has been sent. Once your friend accepts the invitation, he or she will be able to see your screen. A chat window will open up in which you can discuss the problem you are having. Close the session when you are finished.

■ Pull down the **File menu** and click the command to **Sign out**. The Windows Messenger icon in the notification will indicate that you have signed out.

Click Ask a friend to help

Dialog box indicates invitation to help has been sent

(i) Ask for Assistance (step 9)

FIGURE 19 Hands-on Exercise 5 *(continued)*

SUPPORT ONLINE

Microsoft provides extensive online support in a variety of formats. Start at the Windows XP home page (www.microsoft.com/windowsxp), then click the Support button to see what is available. You will be able to search the Microsoft Knowledge Base for detailed information on virtually any subject. You can also post questions and participate in threaded discussions in various newsgroups. Support is available for every Microsoft product.

SUMMARY

Windows XP is the newest and most powerful version of the Windows operating system. It has a slightly different look than earlier versions, but it maintains the conventions of its predecessors. All Windows operations take place on the desktop. Every window contains the same basic elements, which include a title bar, a Minimize button, a Maximize or Restore button, and a Close button. All windows may be moved and sized. The taskbar contains a button for each open program and enables you to switch back and forth between those programs by clicking the appropriate button. You can obtain information about every aspect of Windows through the Help and Support Center.

A file is a set of data or set of instructions that has been given a name and stored on disk. There are two basic types of files, program files and data files. A program file is an executable file, whereas a data file can be used only in conjunction with a specific program. Every file has a filename and a file type.

Files are stored in folders to better organize the hundreds (or thousands) of files on a disk. A folder may contain program files, data files, and/or other folders. Windows automatically creates a set of personal folders for every user. These include the My Documents folder and the My Pictures folder and My Music folder within the My Documents folder. Windows also provides a Shared Documents folder that can be accessed by every user. The My Computer folder is accessible by all users and displays the devices on a system.

Windows Explorer facilitates every aspect of disk and file management. It presents a hierarchical view of your system that displays all devices and, optionally, the folders on each device. Any device may be expanded or collapsed to display or hide its folders.

Windows XP contains several tools to help you enjoy your system. The Windows Media Player combines the functions of a radio, CD player, DVD player, and an information database into a single program. Windows Messenger is an instant messaging system in which you chat with friends and colleagues over the Internet.

The Control Panel affects every aspect of your system. It determines the appearance of your desktop and it controls the performance of your hardware. A shortcut is a link to any object on your computer, such as a program, file, folder, disk drive, or Web page. The Search Companion enables you to search for a file according to several different criteria.

KEY TERMS

MULTIPLE CHOICE

1. Which of the following is true regarding a dialog box?

   (a) Option buttons indicate mutually exclusive choices

   (b) Check boxes imply that multiple options may be selected

   (c) Both (a) and (b)

   (d) Neither (a) nor (b)

2. Which of the following is the first step in sizing a window?

   (a) Point to the title bar

   (b) Pull down the View menu to display the toolbar

   (c) Point to any corner or border

   (d) Pull down the View menu and change to large icons

3. Which of the following is the first step in moving a window?

   (a) Point to the title bar

   (b) Pull down the View menu to display the toolbar

   (c) Point to any corner or border

   (d) Pull down the View menu and change to large icons

4. Which button appears immediately after a window has been maximized?

   (a) The Close button

   (b) The Minimize button

   (c) The Maximize button

   (d) The Restore button

5. What happens to a window that has been minimized?

   (a) The window is still visible but it no longer has a Minimize button

   (b) The window shrinks to a button on the taskbar

   (c) The window is closed and the application is removed from memory

   (d) The window is still open but the application has been removed from memory

6. What is the significance of a faded (dimmed) command in a pull-down menu?

   (a) The command is not currently accessible

   (b) A dialog box appears if the command is selected

   (c) A Help window appears if the command is selected

   (d) There are no equivalent keystrokes for the particular command

7. The Recycle Bin enables you to restore a file that was deleted from

   (a) Drive A

   (b) Drive C

   (c) Both (a) and (b)

   (d) Neither (a) nor (b)

8. Which of the following was suggested as essential to a backup strategy?

   (a) Back up all program files at the end of every session

   (b) Store backup files at another location

   (c) Both (a) and (b)

   (d) Neither (a) nor (b)

9. A shortcut may be created for

   (a) An application or a document

   (b) A folder or a drive

   (c) Both (a) and (b)

   (d) Neither (a) nor (b)

10. What happens if you click the Folders button (on the Standard Buttons toolbar in the My Computer folder) twice in a row?

    (a) The left pane displays a task pane with commands for the selected object

    (b) The left pane displays a hierarchical view of the devices on your system

    (c) The left pane displays either a task pane or the hierarchical view depending on what was displayed prior to clicking the button initially

    (d) The left pane displays both the task pane and a hierarchical view

... continued

multiple choice

11. The Search Companion can

    (a) Locate all files containing a specified phrase
    (b) Restrict its search to a specified set of folders
    (c) Both (a) and (b)
    (d) Neither (a) nor (b)

12. Which views display miniature images of photographs within a folder?

    (a) Tiles view and Icons view
    (b) Thumbnails view and Filmstrip view
    (c) Details view and List view
    (d) All views display a miniature image

13. Which of the following statements is true?

    (a) A plus sign next to a folder indicates that its contents are hidden
    (b) A minus sign next to a folder indicates that its contents are hidden
    (c) A plus sign appears next to any folder that has been expanded
    (d) A minus sign appears next to any folder that has been collapsed

14. Ben and Jessica are both registered users on a Windows XP computer. Which of the following is a *false statement* regarding their personal folders?

    (a) Ben and Jessica each have a My Documents folder
    (b) Ben and Jessica each have a My Pictures folder that is stored within their respective My Documents folders
    (c) Ben can access files in Jessica's My Documents folder
    (d) Jessica cannot access files in Ben's My Documents folder

15. When is a file permanently deleted?

    (a) When you delete the file from Windows Explorer
    (b) When you empty the Recycle Bin
    (c) When you turn the computer off
    (d) All of the above

16. What happens if you (left) click and drag a file to another folder on the same drive?

    (a) The file is copied
    (b) The file is moved
    (c) The file is deleted
    (d) A shortcut menu is displayed

17. How do you shut down the computer?

    (a) Click the Start button, then click the Turn Off Computer command
    (b) Right click the Start button, then click the Turn Off Computer command
    (c) Click the End button, then click the Turn Off Computer command
    (d) Right click the End button, then click the Turn Off Computer command

18. Which of the following can be accomplished with Windows Messenger?

    (a) You can chat with up to three other people in the conversation window
    (b) You can place telephone calls (if you have a microphone and speaker) without paying long-distance charges
    (c) You can ask for remote assistance, which enables your contact to view your screen as you are working
    (d) All of the above

ANSWERS

1.	c	7.	b	13.	a
2.	c	8.	b	14.	c
3.	a	9.	c	15.	b
4.	d	10.	c	16.	b
5.	b	11.	c	17.	a
6.	a	12.	b	18.	d

PRACTICE WITH WINDOWS XP

1. **Two Different Views:** The document in Figure 20 is an effective way to show your instructor that you understand the My Computer folder, the various views available, the task pane, and the hierarchy structure. It also demonstrates that you can capture a screen for inclusion in a Word document. Proceed as follows:

   a. Open the My Computer folder, click the Views button, and switch to the Tiles view. Click the Folders button to display the task pane. Size the window as necessary so that you will be able to fit two folders onto a one-page document as shown in Figure 20.

   b. Press and hold the Alt key as you press the Print Screen key to copy the My Computer window to the Windows clipboard. (The Print Screen key captures the entire screen. Using the Alt key, however, copies just the current window.) Click the Start menu, click Programs, and then click Microsoft Word to start the program. Maximize the window.

   c. Enter the title of the document, press Enter, and type your name. Press the Enter key twice in a row to leave a blank line.

   d. Pull down the Edit menu. Click the Paste command to copy the contents of the clipboard to the document. Press the Enter key to add a figure caption, then press the Enter key two additional times.

   e. Click the taskbar to return to the My Computer folder. Change to the Details view. Click the Folders button to display the hierarchy structure, as opposed to the task pane. Expand My Computer in the left pane, but collapse all of the individual devices. Press Alt+Print Screen to capture the My Computer folder in this configuration.

   f. Click the taskbar to return to your Word document. Press Ctrl+V to paste the contents of the clipboard into your document. Enter an appropriate caption below the figure. Save the completed document and print it for your instructor.

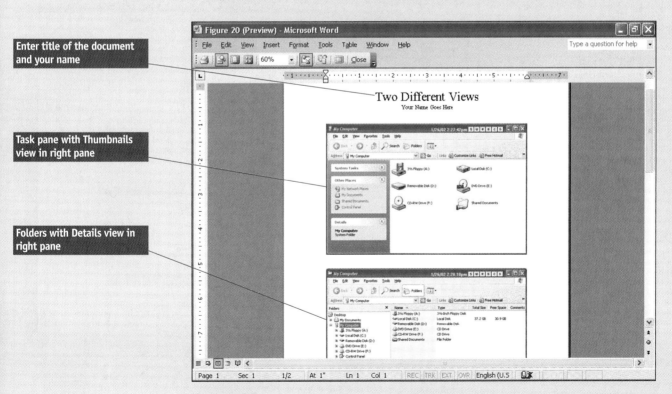

Enter title of the document and your name

Task pane with Thumbnails view in right pane

Folders with Details view in right pane

FIGURE 20   Two Different Views (exercise 1)

2. **Network Connections:** The document in Figure 21 displays the network connections on our system as well as the status of one of those connections. Your assignment is to create the equivalent document for your computer. Proceed as follows:

a. Open the Control Panel, switch to the Classic view, then double click the Network Connections icon to display the Network Connections folder. (You can also get to this folder from My Computer, by clicking the link to My Network Places, and then clicking Network Connections from within the Network Tasks area.)

b. Maximize the Network Connections folder so that it takes the entire desktop. Change to the Tiles view. Click the Folders button to display the task pane. Select (click) a connection, then click the link to View status of the connection, to display the associated dialog box.

c. Press the Print Screen key to print this screen. Start Microsoft Word and open a new document. Press the Enter key several times, then click the Paste button to copy the contents of the clipboard into your document.

d. Press Ctrl+Home to return to the beginning of the Word document, where you can enter the title of the document and your name. Compose a paragraph similar to the one in our figure that describes the network connections on your computer. Print this document for your instructor.

e. Experiment with the first two network tasks that are displayed in the task pane. How difficult is it to set up a new connection? How do you set a firewall to protect your system from unauthorized access when connected to the Internet? How do you establish a home or small office network?

f. Use the Help and Support Center to obtain additional information. Print one or two Help screens for your instructor.

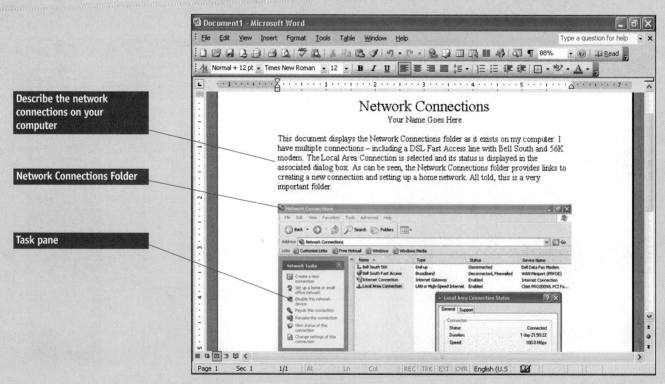

FIGURE 21   Network Connections (exercise 2)

3. **Create Your Own Folders:** Folders are the key to the Windows storage system. Folders can be created at any time and in any way that makes sense to you. The My Courses folder in Figure 22, for example, contains five folders, one folder for each class you are taking. In similar fashion, the Correspondence folder in this figure contains two additional folders according to the type of correspondence. Proceed as follows:

a.   Place the floppy disk from hands-on exercise 3 into drive A. Start Windows Explorer. Click the Folders button to display the hierarchy structure in the left pane. Change to the Details view.

b.   Create a Correspondence folder on drive A. Create a Business folder and a Personal folder within the Correspondence folder.

c.   Create a My Courses folder on drive A. Create a separate folder for each course you are taking within the My Courses folder. The names of your folders will be different from ours.

d.   Pull down the View menu, click the Arrange Icons by command, and click the command to Show in Groups. Click the Date Modified column header to group the files and folders by date. The dates you see will be different from the dates in our figure.

e.   The Show in Groups command functions as a toggle switch. Execute the command, and the files are displayed in groups; execute the command a second time, and the groups disappear. (You can change the grouping by clicking the desired column heading.)

f.   Use the technique described in problems 1 and 2 to capture the screen in Figure 22 and incorporate it into a document. Add a short paragraph that describes the folders you have created, then submit the document to your instructor.

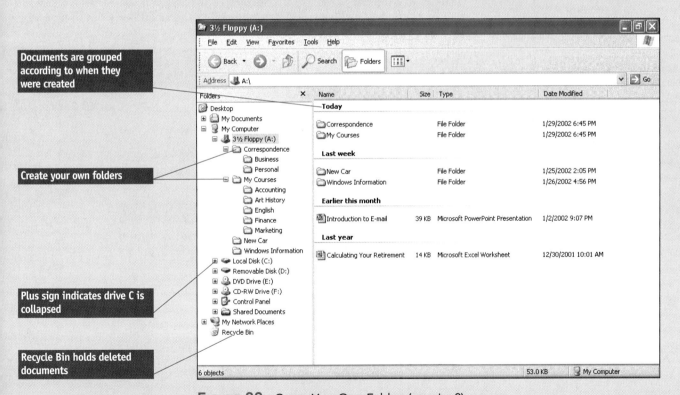

FIGURE 22   Create Your Own Folders (exercise 3)

4. **What's New in Windows XP:** Anyone, whether an experienced user or a computer novice, can benefit from a quick overview of new features in Windows XP. Click the Start button, click Help and Support, and then click the link to What's New in Windows XP. Click the second link in the task pane (taking a tour or tutorial), select the Windows XP tour, and choose the desired format. We chose the animated tour with animation, music, and voice narration.

a. Relax and enjoy the show as shown in Figure 23. The task bar at the bottom of the figure contains three buttons to restart the show, exit, or toggle the music on and off. Exit the tutorial when you are finished. You are back in the Help and Support window, where you can take a tour of the Windows Media Player. Try it. Click the Close button at the upper right of any screen or press Escape to exit the tour. Write a short note to your instructor with comments about either tour.

b. Return to the Help and Support Center and find the topic, "What's New in Home Networking." Print two or three subtopics that describe how to create a home network. Does the task seem less intimidating after you have read the information?

c. Locate one or more topics on new features in digital media such as burning a CD or Windows Movie Maker. Print this information for your instructor.

d. Return once again to the Help and Support Center to explore some of the other resources that describe new features in Windows XP. Locate the link to Windows News Groups, and then visit one of these newsgroups online. Locate a topic of interest and print several messages within a threaded discussion. Do you think newsgroups will be useful to you in the future?

e. You can also download a PowerPoint presentation by the authors that describes new features in Windows XP. Go to www.prenhall.com/grauer, click the text for Office XP, then click the link to What's New in Windows XP, from where you can download the presentation.

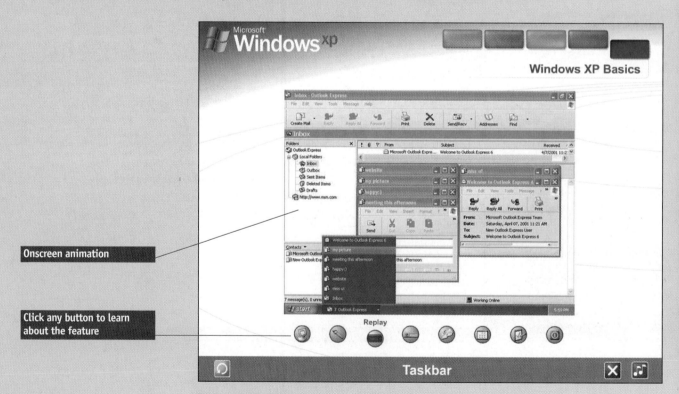

FIGURE 23 What's New in Windows XP (exercise 4)

5. **Keyboard Shortcuts:** Almost every command in Windows can be executed in different ways, using either the mouse or the keyboard. Most people start with the mouse and add keyboard shortcuts as they become more proficient. There is no right or wrong technique, just different techniques, and the one you choose depends entirely on personal preference. If, for example, your hands are already on the keyboard, it is faster to use the keyboard equivalent if you know it.

There is absolutely no need to memorize these shortcuts, nor should you even try. A few, however, have special appeal and everyone has favorites. You are probably familiar with general Windows shortcuts such as Ctrl+X, Ctrl+C, and Ctrl+V to cut, copy, and paste, respectively. (The X is supposed to remind you of a pair of scissors.) Ctrl+Z is less well known and corresponds to the Undo command. You can find additional shortcuts through the Help command.

a. Use the Help and Support Center to display the information in Figure 24, which shows the available shortcuts within a dialog box. Two of these, Tab and Shift+Tab, move forward and backward, respectively, from one option to the next within the dialog box. The next time you are in a physician's office or a dentist's office, watch the assistant as he or she labors over the keyboard to enter information. That person will typically type information into a text box, then switch to the mouse to select the next entry, return to the keyboard, and so on. Tell that person about Tab and Shift+Tab; he or she will be forever grateful.

b. The Help and Support Center organizes the shortcuts by category. Select the Natural keyboard category (not visible in Figure 24), then note what you can do with the ⊞ key. Press the ⊞ key at any time, and you display the Start menu. Press ⊞+M and you minimize all open windows. There are several other, equally good shortcuts in this category.

c. Select your five favorite shortcuts in any category, and submit them to your instructor. Compare your selections to those of your classmates. Do you prefer the mouse or your newly discovered shortcuts?

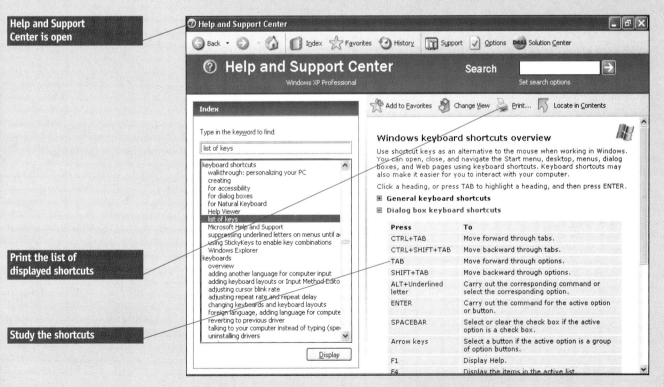

FIGURE 24   Keyboard Shortcuts (exercise 5)

MINI CASES

Planning for Disaster

Do you have a backup strategy? Do you even know what a backup strategy is? You had better learn, because sooner or later you will wish you had one. You will erase a file, be unable to read from a floppy disk, or worse yet, suffer a hardware failure in which you are unable to access the hard drive. The problem always seems to occur the night before an assignment is due. The ultimate disaster is the disappearance of your computer, by theft or natural disaster. Describe, in 250 words or less, the backup strategy you plan to implement in conjunction with your work in this class.

Tips for Windows XP

Print the *Tips for Windows XP* document that was downloaded as one of the practice files in the hands-on exercises. This document contains many of the boxed tips that appeared throughout the chapter. Read the document as a review and select five of your favorite tips. Create a new document for your instructor consisting of the five tips you selected. Add a cover page titled, "My Favorite Tips." Include your name, your professor's name, and a reference to the Grauer/Barber text from where the tips were taken.

File Compression

You've learned your lesson and have come to appreciate the importance of backing up all of your data files. The problem is that you work with large documents that exceed the 1.44MB capacity of a floppy disk. Accordingly, you might want to consider the acquisition of a file compression program to facilitate copying large documents to a floppy disk in order to transport your documents to and from school, home, or work. You can download an evaluation copy of the popular WinZip program at www.winzip.com. Investigate the subject of file compression and submit a summary of your findings to your instructor.

The Threat of Virus Infection

A computer virus is an actively infectious program that attaches itself to other programs and alters the way a computer works. Some viruses do nothing more than display an annoying message at an inopportune time. Most, however, are more harmful, and in the worst case, erase all files on the disk. Use your favorite search engine to research the subject of computer viruses to answer the following questions. When is a computer subject to infection by a virus? What precautions does your school or university take against the threat of virus infection in its computer lab? What precautions, if any, do you take at home? Can you feel confident that your machine will not be infected if you faithfully use a state-of-the-art anti-virus program that was purchased in June 2002?

Your First Consultant's Job

Go to a real installation such as a doctor's or attorney's office, the company where you work, or the computer lab at school. Determine the backup procedures that are in effect, then write a one-page report indicating whether the policy is adequate and, if necessary, offering suggestions for improvement. Your report should be addressed to the individual in charge of the business, and it should cover all aspects of the backup strategy; that is, which files are backed up and how often, and what software is used for the backup operation. Use appropriate emphasis (for example, bold italics) to identify any potential problems. This is a professional document (it is your first consultant's job), and its appearance should be perfect in every way.

Index